Grandpa's US Colonial History to 1800

Terrence Hagen

abbott press®
A DIVISION OF WRITER'S DIGEST

GRANDPA'S US COLONIAL HISTORY TO 1800

Abbott Press books may be ordered through booksellers or by contacting:

Abbott Press
1663 Liberty Drive
Bloomington, IN 47403
www.abbottpress.com
Phone: 1-866-697-5310

ISBN: 978-1-4582-0773-9 (sc)
ISBN: 978-1-4582-0772-2 (hc)
ISBN: 978-1-4582-0771-5 (e)

Printed in the United States of America

Library of Congress Control Number: 2013900317

Abbott Press rev. date: 03/28/13

Table of Contents

Introduction

While growing up and receiving what I believe was an excellent education, I began to realize that my knowledge of American History seemed to "jump" from Christopher Columbus to Jamestown and Plymouth Rock with no attention paid to the intervening 115 years, and then another "jump" to the 1770's and the Boston Massacre, Tea Party, and subsequent battles at Lexington and Concord, another unexplained period of roughly 150 years.

My overall goal in this book is to fill in some of those "blank spaces" in our colonial history to provide a fuller understanding of the events which led to our Independence, Constitution, and the formation of our own unique government.

I realized that one cannot truly understand the American colonial experience without understanding those world events which led to the initial explorations and discovery of new lands. That background information should include some knowledge of the English Monarchy and its battles with its' Parliament and how those events impacted the colonists. America didn't just happen and we will discuss those events which set in motion the eventual discovery and development of America. I hope to explain those events, their origins and significance, so the reader will understand that there is more to history than just dates and places and that events are interconnected, almost in a cause and effect relationship.

There is no intent in this effort to discuss the military aspects of the Revolutionary War other than to identify a few of the major battles in terms of their significance to the larger political, social, and economic issues. The military aspects of the Revolutionary War have been extensively and effectively covered by many others.

Another point to make is that I chose the year 1800 as the terminal point in the book because the election of Thomas Jefferson in 1800 marked not only the end of the Federalist era but the beginning of the impact of political parties on American political life.

As we observe countries around the world attempting to break free of oppressive governments and replace them with an American-styled representative form of self-government, Americans don't understand why those countries can't make that change more quickly. For example, consider our frustration with the slow development of the Iraqi government, or the absence of an effective government in Afghanistan, etc, as if that changeover should be made within a few short years. We need to be reminded that our independence occurred only after 150+ years of self-government with a strong assist from England before we became formally independent and developed our own constitution and government and functioned on our own.

So, I hope my Grandchildren will learn from this book that American colonial history was shaped by events around the world and that many people, from diverse backgrounds and beliefs, mixed their ideas and values together to produce the country from which we now derive so many benefits and liberties.

I should also point out that I am not a professional author or former teacher, and have absolutely no understanding of "author-protocol". I have used a few quotes which will be footnoted but, in general, I will not include many footnotes because I have written this book from a conglomeration of sources and the final thoughts are my own.

I hope that doesn't violate any protocols or rules of the trade. If so, I apologize and didn't intend to "steal" anything from any other writers. My primary source of information was a book I used in college, "The Colonial Experience" by David Hawke. I would heartily recommend it to anyone wanting a more detailed and professional account of this period in American History.

Dedication

This book is dedicated to our Grandchildren, Kathleen Margaret Halloran, who attends Downers Grove North High School and Sean Timothy Halloran who attends St. Mary's of Gostyn Grade School in Downers Grove, Illinois.

The idea for the book came from them while on vacation in New England. While visiting some historic sites they suggested that I write a book about American History since I was always explaining the significance of the sites we visited. Although flattered, I laughed it off believing it would be presumptuous of me to believe that I could write a book about American History which hasn't already been written.

The idea, however, stuck in my mind. One day at Mass, the Priest began his Homily with the phrase, "through different eyes" and reminded us all of the need to try to see things through other perspectives. In addition to getting his point I began thinking about my embryonic idea to write a book through the eyes of a senior citizen who had the benefit of being taught by some wonderful teachers and raised by parents who supplemented my education with travel to many of the historical places where our nations' heritage was developed.

As the idea bounced around in my mind I began to realize there were also other reasons for this project. For example, I have observed that it doesn't seem like much attention is paid in the schools today to the teaching of our national heritage. Combined with that observation was another observation that "political correctness" was causing a dilution of what is being taught about our Founding Fathers. Some information I was taught is now either eliminated all-together or de-emphasized in favor of other theories designed to make us "feel good" about our national heritage, rather than following the facts.

I began to believe that the sum total of these events was the very real possibility that our Grandchildren might not learn and appreciate the same American History that my wife and I were taught in the 1940's and 1950's. However, I should admit there must always be respect for new information which can help us better interpret events in our past but we can never lose sight of the need to understand history in the perspective of the times in which it happened, in other words, we can't apply a 21st century moral standard to 17th century actions..

I identified one more reason for attempting to write this book. **Citizenship.** I believe there is a connection between understanding and respecting your country's heritage and the responsibility to enhance those traditions by casting informed votes for our elected officials. Many of our Founders warned their fellow citizens that it was their responsibility to be informed in order to best continue the work done by those who came before them.

So, I decided to write this book as a resource for our Grandchildren as they continue through elementary school, high school, and college. They will continue to grow in their understanding of their American heritage and we wanted this book to accompany them on that journey so that when they are adults they will have developed a love and respect for their country, based on the knowledge of what it took on the part of so many millions of people to produce the liberties and other benefits which they enjoy. Hopefully, that experience will motivate them to help preserve that heritage by becoming knowledgeable and active citizens and voters and in the process pass along to their children and grandchildren that same heritage.

I was blessed with an outstanding home library to serve as the primary sources for this endeavor. Thanks to those wonderful elementary and high school teachers plus my parents for buying my earliest American History books. It was those experiences which motivated me to major in American History at the downtown campus of De Paul University where I was introduced to another outstanding teacher, Professor Ralph J. Maillard, who continued to bring the American experience alive to me. As a result, that outstanding collection of books on my bookshelf were just sitting there waiting for me to put them to use.

At the end of the Constitutional Convention in 1787, Ben Franklin was asked, "Well, Doctor, what have we got, a Republic or a Monarchy?" He answered, "A Republic, if you can keep it". He may have had many concerns in mind when he made that statement but we know from other statements of the Founders that they believed self-government required the "*informed consent*" of the governed, the key word being "informed". This Grandfather just wants to do his part in helping our Grandchildren become "informed" so they can grow into effective citizens.

A Special Thank You

A very special thanks to my wife, Bonnie, for her conversion of some of my Excel materials into Microsoft Word so this endeavor could be printed and published.

Not only was that a very time-consuming effort on her part but she also provided me with the time, freedom, and peaceful moments to research, organize my thoughts, and put together this book from multiple sources.

I also owe thanks to my other family members who participated in this effort, such as our daughter, Colleen Halloran, her husband, Brian, and both grandchildren, Kathleen and Sean, who contributed many ideas which are included in this effort, such as:

- Revue questions and answers

- A Glossary of terms

- Chapter summaries

My gratitude to all of them for not only providing the ideas, but for pushing me to finish when it seemed overwhelming.

I also want to thank Kathleen and Sean for picking out some books from the Public Library as sources of pictures, maps, and other attachments, and Brian for his hours of Technical assistance in scanning, saving, and attaching those selected documents to this book, especially when he was so busy with so many other tasks.

I should also thank Karen Claffy of the Watters Secretarial Services in Downers Grove, Illinois, for her extensive formatting and editing efforts.

Prologue

Although I have been a student of American History since Elementary School and majored in it in college, I learned many new facts about America which I either didn't previously know or even think about their significance. Some of those major "revelations" for me were:

1. America could be called "America the Accident" because no explorer set out to discover "America". The earliest explorers were pursuing an all-water route to the riches of Asia, either for their own personal wealth and glory or, later, on behalf of their Governments in their efforts to enrich their national treasuries. We will see that many explorers first identified "America" as some sort of land mass which Columbus, for example, thought was the East Indies or the coast of Asia. Others thought America was a large island which they just had to navigate around. Bottom-line, America was eventually discovered accidentally while pursuing other goals.

2. Columbus did not discover "America". He never set foot on the American mainland. His multiple voyages to the Caribbean region put him in the vicinity but never on the mainland.

3. America did not discover the concept of "self or representative government". We can go back to the English Magna Carta of 1215 for the first known example of a Monarch being required to allow some form of representation. Many English political traditions derived from that document and were eventually passed along to English citizens , many of whom eventually immigrated to America. America might have perfected those principles but we didn't discover the concept.

4. We were all taught that the Pilgrims and many of the earliest immigrants came to the New World to escape religious persecution, among other reasons. What is ironic is that the Puritans, who just wished to be left alone to freely practice their religion, became among the least tolerant of other people's religions and faith. Because of their opposition to the abuses of the Roman Catholic religion, many of the Protestants emigrating from Europe brought with them their dislike and bias against Catholicism. We will see, in reading the histories of the 13 original colonies, a number of examples of intolerance against Catholics.

   For example, a 1700 Massachusetts Law mandated that all Roman Catholic Priests were to leave the colony within 3 months under the threat of life imprisonment or execution. Maryland, in 1704, passed "An Act to Prevent the Growth of Popery within this Province" which basically closed down all Roman Catholic Churches and schools.[1]

5. American independence didn't really begin on 7/4/1776. From the earliest settlement at Jamestown in 1607, the settlers lived under some form of representative government, as we will see. In the 169 years from Jamestown to the Declaration of Independence there were many examples of colonial efforts to achieve some measure of Representative Government. *One historian said it best when he declared that America did not fight the Revolutionary War to become free, they fought it to retain the freedoms they had already achieved.*

---

1   For further information see; "Let None Dare Call It Liberty: The Catholic Church in Colonial America" Marian T. Horvat, Ph.D. www. Traditioninaction.org

Bibliography

PRIMARY SOURCES:

THE OXFORD HISTORY OF THE AMERICAN PEOPLE by S.E. MORRISON,
    1965 OXFORD UNIVERSITY PRESS, NEW YORK

THE COLONIAL EXPERIENCE by D. HAWKE,
    1966 THE BOBBS-MERRILL COMPANY, INC., INDIANAPOLIS, NEW
    YORK, KANSAS CITY

THE ENCYCLOPEDIA OF AMERICAN HISTORY by R.B. MORRIS,
    1961 HARPER & ROW PUBLISHERS, NEW YORK NY & EVANSTON IL

AMERICAN HISTORY BEFORE 1877 by R.A. BILLINGTON,
    1966 LITTLEFIELD, ADAMS & CO., TOTOWA NJ

EMPIRES AT WAR by W.M. FOWLER JR.,
    2005 WALKER & CO, NEW YORK

REVIEW TEXT IN AMERICAN HISTORY by I.L GORDON,
    1973 AMSCO SCHOOL PUBLICATIONS, NEW YORK

AMERICAN HISTORY TO 1877...VOLUME I by N. KLOSE,
    1965 BARRON'S EDUCATIONAL SERIES, INC, WOODBURY, NEW
    YORK

THE FEDERALIST ERA (1789-1801) by J.C. MILLER,
    1960 HARPER & ROW PUBLISHERS, NEW YORK

THE BLUE BOOK OF AMERICAN HISTORY by W. WEINTRAUB,
    1960 REGENTS PUBLISHING COMPANY, INC., NEW YORK

OTHER SOURCES:

POLITICAL IDEAS OF THE AMERICAN REVOLUTION by R.G. ADAMS,
    1958 BARNES & NOBLE INC., NEW YORK

THE COLONIAL BACKGROUND OF THE AMERICAN REVOLUTION by C.M.
    ANDREWS,
    1965 YALE UNIVERSITY PRESS, NEW HAVEN & LONDON

THE DIPLOMACY OF THE AMERICAN REVOLUTION by S.F. BEMIS,,
    1957 INDIANA UNIVERSITY PRESS, BLOOMINGTON IN

THE YOUNG PATRIOTS by C. CERAMI,
2005 SOURCEBOOKS, INC., NAPERVILLE IL

THE ORIGINS OF THE AMERICAN PARTY SYSTEM by J. CHARLES,
1956 HARPER & ROW PUBLISHERS, NEW YORK NY & EVANSTON IL

THE LEGEND OF THE FOUNDING FATHERS by W.F. CRAVEN,
1956 CORNELL UNIVERSITY PRESS, ITHACA, NEW YORK

THE AMERICAN CREATION by J.J. ELLIS,
2007 VINTAGE BOOKS, DIVISION OF RANDOM HOUSE, NEW YORK
& TORONTO

FORT TICONDEROGA, KEY TO A CONTINENT by E.P. HAMILTON,
1964 LITTLE, BROWN, & CO., BOSTON MA

AMERICAN HISTORY ATLAS by C.S. HAMMOND,
1965 C. S. HAMMOND & CO., MAPLEWOOD, NEW JERSEY

PATRIOTS....THE MEN WHO STARTED THE AMERICAN REVOLUTION by
A.J. LANGGUTH,
1988 SIMON & SCHUSTER INC., NEW YORK, LONDON, TORONTO,
SYDNEY, TOKYO

PARTIES & POLITICS IN AMERICA by C. ROSSITER,
1960 CORNELL UNIVERSITY PRESS, ITHACA, NEW YORK

THE AMERICAN GOVERNMENT by W.S. SAYRE,
1960 BARNES & NOBLE INC., NEW YORK

AMERICAN HISTORY AT A GLANCE by M. SMELSER,
1961 BARNES & NOBLE INC., NEW YORK

THE FEDERAL CONVENTION & THE FORMATION OF THE UNION by W.U.
SOLBERG,
1958 THE BOBBS-MERRILL COMPANY INC., INDIANAPOLIS, NEW
YORK, KANSAS CITY

CAUSES & CONSEQUENCES OF THE AMERICAN REVOLUTION by E.
WRIGHT,
1966 QUADRANGLE BOOKS, CHICAGO

"LET NONE DARE CALL IT LIBERTY: THE CATHOLIC CHURCH IN
COLONIAL AMERICA
MARIAN T. HORVAT, PH.D., WEBSITE "TRADITIONINACTION.ORG"

"CRUCIBLE OF WAR", FRED ANDERSON, VINTAGE BOOKS, NEW YORK,
2001.

Chapter 1

The Background for Exploration & Discovery

In this chapter we will learn that the discovery of the Americas (North and South) didn't "just happen". It was the result of years of the growth and expansion of European civilization. During the Middle Ages Europe was extending its' political power and commerce to all parts of the world as the knowledge of science and geography expanded. The eventual discovery of the Americas was the most significant step in the overall expansion of European culture. This activity set the stage for discovery and if Christopher Columbus had not discovered the Americas, someone else would have eventually done so.

We will study each of the major world events which led to the age of exploration and discovery, such as:

- **The Crusades from 1095-1291**

- **The Renaissance from the 14th Century through the 17th Century**

- **The rise of absolute Monarchs and their Nation States**

- **The expansion of World-wide Commerce and Mercantilism**

- **A Growing Geographic Curiosity**

A. THE CRUSADES

In the year 1095, Christians, led by Pope Urban II, sought to control the Holy Land and Palestine from the Moslem Turks in what became known as the "First Crusade". Over the next 200 years, Western Europe launched six more Crusades with the unintended consequences of those Crusades creating an interaction with the more advanced Moslem and Byzantine Civilizations.

Despite some initial successes, the Crusades failed to establish a permanent Christian presence in Palestine. Another unintended consequence was the expansion of world trade by creating a market, in Europe, for those eastern civilization products, such as, spices, sugar, silk, rugs, paper, glassware, and precious stones. This profitable trade became the monopoly of:

- Asian middle-men who brought eastern goods by overland caravan to eastern Mediterranean ports, especially Alexandria and Constantinople.

- Italian merchants from city-states such as Genoa and Venice who shipped their products from the eastern Mediterranean region to Western Europe.

Because of the many middle-men, each adding to the cost of the goods, eastern goods remained high-priced luxuries. Meanwhile, the Italian city-states grew prosperous. But, it became difficult and expensive for Europe to obtain Asiatic goods. Merchants began looking for better and more economic ways to obtain them but had to overcome the following obstacles:

- 1. The goods were expensive after being transported over long and difficult routes.

- 2. The shortage of gold in Europe and the absence of demand in the east for European goods made it difficult for Europe to pay for Asiatic imports or exchange goods for them.

In spite of the obstacles, Europeans were eager for the commodities of Asia.

B.   THE RENAISSANCE

By definition, "renaissance" means "rebirth or revival". The Renaissance was a period of growing intellectual interest by western Europeans in the worldly aspects of civilization. Scholars of this period emphasized reason, questioned authority, and pursued free inquiry. They focused their interest in the Byzantine and Moslem civilizations as well as the ancient Greek and Roman civilizations.

The center of the Renaissance was in the Italian city-sates because:

1.   Italy had been a center of the Greek-Roman cultures.

2.   Italians were in close contact with the advanced Byzantine and Moslems worlds.

3.   There were many wealthy Italian merchants with considerable interest in and exposure to literature, science, and the arts.

During the middle-ages, western Europeans traveled little and such travel was mainly over land by foot or horse or along the Atlantic and/or Mediterranean coasts in small ships. The geographic knowledge of western Europeans was limited to Europe, Northern Africa, and Western Asia. When the Renaissance focused attention on scientific matters, Europeans wanted to know more about the world's size, shape, and cultures.

In order to reach distant lands by water, they drew precise maps, built faster and safer ships, and achieved greater accuracy in using the compass to determine direction and in using the astrolabe to determine latitude. By the 15th century, educated Europeans accepted the belief, held by ancient Greeks, that the world was not flat but round.

C.   THE RISE OF ABSOLUTE MONARCHS & NATION STATES

During the middle-ages, most Kings exercised minimal power, ruling only their immediate royal domains and had little control over their Feudal Lords who held most of the land. Near the end of the middle-ages the Kings began to extend their authority over the Lords and eventually became absolute Monarchs. Royal power was strengthened by:

1. The Crusades and other wars which killed many Feudal Lords.

2. The rising merchant or middle class which supported the King to insure the protection of their property and trade.

3. The growing spirit of nationalism in which the King was considered the symbol of national unity.

Since the Kings protected domestic and foreign commerce, the merchants lent money and willingly paid taxes to them and thereby enabled the Monarchs to gain power at the expense of the nobility. As these nation-states became strong, their Kings tried to gain advantages for their own nations over the others in a contest to dominate territory and trade.

In western Europe, Monarchs sought to unite peoples of a common nationality and developed unified national states, such as England, France, Portugal and Spain, all created by the end of the 15th century.

The most significant result of the growing national states and their need for increased commercial trade was the encouragement of voyages of discovery because:

1. Nation-states possessed sufficient wealth to finance such voyages.

2. The absolute Monarchs desired colonial empires to increase their national wealth, power and prestige.

3. The middle-class wanted increased trade and the benefits it provided.

4. Portugal and Spain sought to diminish the monopoly of the Italian city-states by seeking an all-water route to Asia and took the lead in sponsoring such discovery voyages.

D.   EXPANSION OF WORLD-WIDE COMMERCE & MERCANTILISM

World commerce was built on new methods of financing, such as the use of borrowed capital, with interest, the use of money as vehicle of exchange, and the creation of banks. The world began to see significant growth in the volume and variety of goods traded. These long- developing changes were soon followed by a shift in the eventual commercial supremacy of Western Europe over Italy. The expansion of commerce was an essential element in the background of discovery.

The term, "mercantilism" referred to an economic philosophy underlying early European colonial policy. It referred to the objective of a nation increasing its wealth through a favorable "balance of trade" which meant that a nation should sell more than it purchased, thus creating a surplus in its treasury.

As the name suggests, merchants were key to the successful implementation of this theory and policy. Merchants would sell products to foreign nations and also purchase items to be sold within their own country. The goal was to gain wealth at the expense of other nations and the ideal was to become economically self-sufficient by minimizing imports, which cost money, and maximizing exports which would add revenues to the national treasury.

E.   GEOGRAPHIC CURIOSITY

The net result of these economic, political, and social forces during this period of time was to increase a general level of interest in other parts of the world. Marco Polo and other members of his family of merchants visited the Imperial Court of China and then wrote of his 17 years in China which helped arouse an interest in Asia. His book, "The Travels of Marco Polo", was printed in 1477 and had a strong influence on would-be explorers. One of the key points made by Polo was that the eastern border of Asia was edged not by great marshes, as had been thought, but by an ocean, which meant that Asia could be reached by sea-going ships. Missionaries also traveled in the East which added to the general interest in other parts of the world.

F. SUMMARY

By the time Columbus began his multiple explorations, a new and different world was emerging in the minds of Europeans. By 1492, values that had long characterized the life of Europe had been replaced with new ideas, knowledge, and values.

That shift in values did not end the past, it just expanded it. Much of the medieval world successfully traveled the ocean and some of them survived the trips well enough to play important roles in the eventual discovery of the America's. Outwardly, life in the 1300's Europe had changed very little in more than a thousand years and to the medieval mind that was the way it should be.

The universe, for medieval people, was regulated from top to bottom and organized in a firm, hierarchical order. All things had their place and anyone who promoted change or sought to disturb that order risked the wrath of God. All institutions of the age, i.e. feudalism, the manorial system, the towns and Church, were designed to maintain the stability that characterized the medieval world.

One historian said, "The settlement of America had its origins in the unsettlement of Europe". For example, inventions aided commerce and that commerce further broadened the horizons of the medieval people.

G. KEY DATES

1000   Leif Erickson, a Viking seaman, explores the east coast of North America and sights Newfoundland, establishing a short-lived settlement there.

1095   The Crusades begin, end 1291

1215   The Magna Carta is adopted in England, guaranteeing liberties to the English people, and proclaiming basic rights and procedures which later become the foundation of modern democracy

1254   Marco polo born, dies 1324

1295   Model Parliament of England

1298   Marco Polo writes of great Asian wealth

1300   Money shortage creates a depression in Europe

H.   KEY EVENTS

1. Magna Carta   1215

    King John of England was forced to sign a document
    which limited the authority of the King with restrictions
    on taxation and administration of justice. It established the
    right to a trial by one's peers and taxation only with the
    consent of the taxed.

    It also included a provision that the Church was to be
    free from Royal interference especially in the election of
    Bishops.

    *Its influence on American political thought and documents
    can be seen in Article 21 of the Declaration of Rights in
    the Maryland Constitution of 1776 and other subsequent
    documents.*

2. Model Parliament 1295

    The Parliament of King Edward I of England's reign
    consisted of members of the clergy and aristocracy as well
    as representatives from the various counties and boroughs.
    Each county had 2 knights and 2 burgesses elected from each
    borough, and each city provided 2 citizens. The composition
    became the *model for future Parliaments.*

3. Marco Polo   1254-1324

    He was the most famous westerner to travel the "silk road"
    (Asia). His journey through Asia lasted 24 years, reaching
    further than any of his predecessors, beyond Mongolia to
    China. He became friends with Kublia Khan (1214-1294)
    and traveled all of China. He eventually returned to write of

his experiences. He grew up in Venice, Italy, although it is not known for certain where he was born. At that time, Venice was the center for commerce in the Mediterranean region. He received the normal education of young gentlemen of his time, learning about the classical authors, the Bible, and the basic theology of the Latin Church. He was able to adequately speak French along with his native Italian.

He was 6 years old when his father and uncle made their first trip east to Cathay/China. He was 15 when they returned to Venice. In 1271 he left with them on a return trip to Cathay via Armenia, Persia, Afghanistan, and crossing the Pamir Mountains, the "highest place in the world" as they described it, and then along the Silk Road to China, crossing the great Gobi Desert.

He became an expert on the history of the Mongol Empire and the great Khan. In May, 1275, the Polo's arrived at the original capital of Khan at Shang-tu, the Khan's summer residence, and then traveled to Beijing/Cambaluc, ("City of the Khan") his winter palace. By then they had traveled 3.5 years and 5600 miles.

Marco became a favorite of the Khan and served in many high political posts within the Khan administration. As such, he traveled extensively in China and was amazed at the enormous power and wealth of China, dwarfing the economies of Europe.

Khan appointed Marco Polo as an official of the Privy Council in 1277 and, for 3 years, he was a tax inspector in the city of Yanzhou northeast of Nanking. The Polo's stayed in Khan's administration for 17 years and acquired great wealth in jewels and gold. The sea journey home took 2 years during which 600 passengers and crew died. The Polo's eventually returned to Venice in the winter of 1295.

His book, "The Travels of Marco Polo", became one of the most popular books in medieval Europe although many doubted the tales. It was the first western record of porcelain, coal, gunpowder, printing, paper, money, and silk, and was written sometime around 1298. By many, it was considered as the most important account of the world outside of Europe available at the time. His tales were eventually confirmed by travelers of the 18th and 19th centuries. Some of his information was incorporated into some important maps of the later Middle Ages, such as the Catalan World Map of 1375, and in the next century it was read with great interest by Henry the Navigator of Portugal, and by Columbus. After returning home to Venice he married and had 3 daughters and eventually died in 1324 at age 70.

Terrence Hagen

I.   REVIEW QUESTIONS

(Multiple Choice)

1. The growth of the commerce and wealth of the cities of Italy resulted from:
    a. the failure of Spain to open an all-water route to the Far East
    b. the contacts made during the Crusades
    c. Columbus's discovery of an all-water route to the Far East
    d. Turkish conquests in the region of the Far East.

2. The rise of the nation-states of the late Middle-Ages is due mostly to:
    a. the Church
    b. the Nobility
    c. the Serfs
    d. the Middle Class

3. The opening of an all-water route to Asia:
    a. came after Columbus' first voyage
    b. prevented Dutch exploitation of the Far East
    c. ended the Italian monopoly of trade with Asia
    d. gave the English an immediate monopoly in Asia

(True or False)

4. The Crusades caused a great increase in trade between Europe and Asia because Asia wished to enjoy the luxuries of Europe's more advanced civilization.
    a. TRUE
    b. FALSE

10

5. Imports from Asia were expensive mainly because they were transported by land.
    a. TRUE
    b. FALSE

6. The term "Commercial Revolution" refers partly to the introduction of modern business methods, including the use of money.
    a. TRUE
    b. FALSE

J. CHAPTER GLOSSARY

1. **Commerce**   The buying and selling of goods

2. **Byzantine**   Ancient city of Byzantium as part of the Eastern portion of the Holy Roman Empire.

3. **Astrolabe**   An ancient astronomical tool for solving problems relating to time and the position of the sun and stars in the sky. Typical uses included finding the time during the day or night, and finding the time of a celestial sunrise or sunset. The typical astrolabe was not a navigational instrument although an instrument named the "Mariner Astrolabe" was used in the Renaissance. The astrolabe was the most popular astronomical instrument used until about 1650 when it was replaced by more specialized and accurate instruments.

4. **Middle Ages** Deals with the years 1066-1485 which was a very difficult period in English history and often deals with the time between the end of the Holy Roman Empire and the Renaissance. The early Middle Ages are referred to as the "Dark Ages" and the Middle Ages are referred to as the "Medieval Era". Life in the middle ages was dominated by the "feudal system". Christianity, religion, and the Church played a key role in the life of the middle ages. Pilgrimages to Jerusalem were made during this time. In 1516, Jerusalem was captured by the Ottoman Turks.

   Famous people in the middle ages were:
   Marco Polo, famous explorer
   Kublai Khan, Mongol leader and Emperor of China in
       the Middle-Ages
   Johann Gutenberg, famous inventor
   Frederick Barbarossa, King of Germany and Crusader
   Joan of Arc, led France to victory during the Hundred
       Years War
   Peter the Hermit, religious crusader
   Robert the Bruce, famous King of Scotland

William Wallace, Braveheart hero of Scotland
Thomas Becket, Saint and Archbishop of Cantebury

5. **Feudalism**   It was the basis by which the upper nobility class maintained control over the lower classes. The government consisted of Kings, Lords, and peasants.

6. **Nationalism** Loyalty or devotion to a nation, a sense of national awareness placing one nation above all others and placing one nation and its culture above other nations.

7. **Hierarchial**   Arrangement of items or objects in some sort of order.

CHAPTER ONE SUMMARY

MULTIPLE WORLD EVENTS LEAD TO AGE OF EXPLORATION AND DISCOVERY:

A. **CRUSADES**
    1. 1095-1291
    2. Exposure to other Cultures
    3. Creates European Market for Asian Products

B. **RENAISSANCE**
    1. Definition ...."Rebirth, Revival"
    2. Growing Intellectual Curiosity
    3. Interest in Byzantine and Moslem Civilizations

C. **RISE OF ABSOLUTE MONARCHS RESULT FROM:**
    1. Crusades & Other Wars Kill Many Feudal Lords
    2. Rising Merchant Class Support Kings for Protection
    3. Growing Spirit of Nationalism considers King as Symbol of National Unity

D. **EXPANSION OF WORLD-WIDE COMMERCE**
    1. New Methods of Financing Increases Trade
    2. Mercantilism....."Favorable Balance of Trade"
    3. Leads to Eventual Supremacy of Western European Trade

E. **GEOGRAPHIC CURIOSITY**
    1. Economic, Political, and Social World Events Lead to a Growing Interest in the Larger World
    2. Influence of the Travels of Marco Polo

Chapter 2

European Explorations & Discoveries

A.   Motives

The primary motivation of the major European nations for exploration and discovery were:

1.   To seek an all-water route to Asia to trade for their goods and create markets for their European goods. Some explorers thought there was a "northwest passage" to Asia which caused many explorers to pursue water routes near today's northeastern Canada.

2.   To secure new raw materials in support of its' commercial objectives.

3.   To create a national competition to prevent losing trade opportunities to their rival nations.

4.   To expand their nation-states by creating colonies for the expansion of their national wealth.

All of the European countries believed in the mercantilist doctrines that colonies served to enrich the Mother country. If regulated along mercantilist lines, colonies would assure raw materials and markets for their country's products, trade for their merchants, and revenues for their national treasuries.

We learned the definition of "mercantilism" in the previous chapter. In this and subsequent chapters we will see how this policy also had political and nationalistic uses for a country.

Among the earliest, documented, explorations were those of the Vivaldi Brothers of Genoa, Italy. In 1291, they led an expedition along the West African coast in search of Asia by an all-water route. They never returned and the records suggest that Moslem merchants reported them shipwrecked and enslaved on the African coast.

B.   Overview of the Explorations

The earliest known explorations of the "New World' were made by the Norsemen about the year 1000 A.D. following a series of island stepping-stones such as the Shetland and Faroe Islands, Iceland, Greenland, and Baffin Land. Historians claim that the Norsemen expelled some Irish settlers from Iceland in 850 AD. There is some documentary evidence of the Norsemen having settled Greenland which was discovered and colonized from Iceland by Eric the Red about 985 AD with two settlements on the west coast. These Norse settlements lasted for several centuries with evidence of 16 Churches and many homes having been built. Eric's son, knick-named, "Leif the Lucky", settled in today's Labrador while searching for "Vinland the Good" which was previously identified by another Norseman but never again located. Historians today believe it was the northern part of Newfoundland.

If Europe had been ready for exploration and expansion in the 11th Century, the Norse discoveries might have led to settlement, but Europe was not ready at that time. No one even suspected that Greenland and Vinland were keys to a New World. Greenland appears on several early maps both before and after 1500 as an extension of Europe or Asia curving west over Iceland. The Norse occupation of this area left no evidence of their presence in North America.

Generally, the Portuguese were the first of the major European nations to embark on nationally sponsored explorations, generally during the years of 1420-1503. Spain followed, primarily because of their national rivalry with Portugal, generally during the years of 1492-1598. The English made the bulk of their explorations during the years 1497-1610. The French made their explorations during the years of 1523-1681 and then the Dutch from 1609-1626 primarily in the present-day New York City, Hudson river Valley, and Long Island and Connecticut river valley.

(Attachment 2a summarizes the years of European exploration. Attachment 2b represents a chronological summary of European explorations and Attachment 2c represents the same information but sorted by the Sponsoring Country/Government.).

C.   PORTUGAL

In the early 15th Century, Portugal did more to enlarge the boundaries of the known world and improve methods of navigation than all of the other nations combined. They were the best suited for this role because they faced the Atlantic Ocean which provided a long seacoast and a large sea-going population. Because they didn't face the Mediterranean Sea they were not able to take advantage of the lucrative Mediterranean and mid-eastern trade.

1.   PRINCE HENRY THE NAVIGATOR   (1394-1460)
Portugal's leading sailor, Infante Don Henrique, known as, "Prince Henry the Navigator", was not as interested in discovering an ocean route to Asia as in locating the source of Moslem gold and the ivory trade. He returned from a Crusade against the Moslems in 1418 and created an informal "University of the Sea" where he welcomed anyone who could help unravel the mystery of the unknown. He sent out ships from 1420-1460 where they discovered and conquered the Canary, Madeira, and Azore Islands. These activities led to improvements in ship design, making them faster and more durable. One of these improvements was known as the "Caravel", a ship which became the favorite of explorers throughout the 15th and 16th centuries. A later version were the "Nina and Pinta" used by Columbus in his first voyage. The Portuguese sailors also improved the navigation and map-making methods and procedures. They

improved on the works of Ptolemy, the Alexandrian geographer who believed the earth was round and distance on it could be measured in degrees, and, by taking "fixes" on known celestial bodies one could precisely determine their location north or south of the equator (latitude) and east or west of an arbitrary line (longitude). They learned to use the Quadrant which was more easily handled at sea than the awkward Astrolabe used by Ptolemy to make celestial observations. By the end of the 15th Century, with the skills, knowledge, and tools available, it was possible for an experienced sailor to determine direction and latitude with some precision.

Exploration lagged for nearly a decade but then, motivated by the Crown's suggestions, Portuguese sailors finally succeeded in rounding the dreaded "Cape Bojardor" (1472) on the west coast of the Sahara where previous ships had been lost (1433) due to unexpected and severe wind-changes. Until 1472, Portuguese sailors were reluctant to attempt to sail beyond that point.

Further explorations were put on hold while Spain and Portugal were in conflict over the Spanish throne. The resulting "Treaty of Alcacovas' (1479) gave Portugal the right to all African lands discovered and to all known islands in the Atlantic Ocean except the Canary Islands. The treaty eventually benefited Spain and Columbus because the closing of Africa to Spain motivated them to investigate the possibility of an all-water route to India.

2. BARTHOLOMEW DIAZ   (1457-1500)

In 1487, Diaz was the first of many Portuguese sailors to seek the all-water route to Asia. After departing from Lisbon he was blown out to sea by a major storm but after sailing for a few months his crew sighted land on 2/5/1488 which he thought was India, but it was still the coast of Africa. After another 400 miles his crew forced him to return home where he discovered the "Tempestuous Cape" as he named it, or, "The Cape of Good Hope" as Portugal King John preferred.

3. OTHER PORTUGUESE EXPLORERS

In 1498, Vasco da Gama sailed to India, actually landing at Calcutta in May, 1499, to establish a profitable trade between Portugal and the Far East, the first to achieve the goal of so many past and future explorers.

Other Portuguese explorers discovered the coast of Brazil (Cabral), Argentina (Vespucci) and parts of present-day Newfoundland, Greenland, and Labrador (Gaspar Corte-Real, Joao Fernandes 1500-1502).

4. TREATY OF TORDESILLAS (6/7/1494) (Ratified by Spain 7/2/1494 and Portugal 9/5/1494)

This treaty was intended to resolve a dispute created following the return of a Christopher Columbus voyage in 1493. In 1481, a Papal decree, "Aeterni Regis", granted all land south of the Canary Islands to Portugal. But, on 6/21/1493, the Spanish-born Pope Alexander Vl decreed a "line of Demarcation" that all lands west and south of a line 100 leagues west and south of any of the islands of the Azores or Cape Verde Islands should belong to Spain although territory under Christian rule as of Christmas 1492 would remain untouched. The Papal Decree ("Bull") did not mention Portugal or its lands, so Portugal couldn't claim newly discovered lands even if they were east of the line.

Another Papal "Bull" of 9/25/1493 gave lands belonging to India to Spain even if they were east of the line. Portugal King John ll opposed this arrangement because it denied many lands, including India, to Portugal. He then opened negotiations with King Ferdinand and Queen Isabella of Spain to move the line to the west and allow him to claim newly discovered lands east of the line. The resulting Treaty of Tordesillas, 6/7/1494, re-established the line further west, more favorable to Spain.

The Treaty basically invalidated the "Bulls" of Pope Alexander VI and was eventually approved by Pope Julius ll on 1/24/1506. Even though the Treaty was negotiated without consulting the Pope, some historians have called the resulting line the "Papal Line of Demarcation". Spain did not object since they were not aware of the existence of South America and the "eastward bulge" of Brazil, so Brazil would eventually belong to Portugal.

Very little of the newly divided area had actually been seen by Europeans as it was only divided by Treaty. Spain gained lands including most of the America's. The eastern-most part of Brazil was granted to Portugal when the explorer Pedro Alvares Cabral landed there while en-route to India. This is why, today, Portuguese is the official language spoken in Brazil. The Treaty was viewed as meaningless between 1580-1640 while the Spanish King was also the King of Portugal. It turned out that Portugal did not attempt to colonize America but focused its efforts on Brazil and other parts of Central and South America.

The role of the Pope in negotiating the Treaty provoked hostility throughout Europe, which combined with other irritants, eventually helped trigger the Protestant Reformation of the 16th century in which most of the northern European nations severed ties with the Church of Rome.

D.　SPAIN

1.　CHRISTOPHER COLUMBUS

There were many Spanish explorers but Columbus was among the first. He was aware of the voyage of Bartholomew Diaz of Portugal in 1487-1488. He had sailed for Portugal for a number of years and had been promoting a plan for a direct ocean route to Asia. His plan was to sail west along the 28 degree latitude to Japan. He thought the Ocean was narrow and no one was aware of another continent (America) in between Europe and Asia while sailing west. By the 1480's he was obsessed with the desire to reach the east by sailing west.

Columbus first tried to interest King John II of Portugal in his project. The King was still aware of the problems associated with Portuguese efforts to explore down the coast of Africa. He listened but eventually rejected his plan. In 1485, Columbus made another request, this time to Spain. A wealthy merchant agreed to finance the voyage but Queen Isabella refused to permit a private venture without future benefit to the Crown. She was also dealing with domestic problems and warfare with the Moslems which required her full-time attention. However, the Queen agreed to appoint a commission to study the idea. While the commission was considering his plan, Columbus again approached King John II of Portugal who was now more receptive since he had not heard from Diaz and his Asian trip. While the King was still considering the Columbus plan, Diaz returned to announce that he had rounded the tip of Africa, causing the King to reject the Columbus plan. Columbus then approached King Henry VII of England and King Charles VII of France who both also rejected his plan. In 1490, the Queen's commission finally rejected the plan on grounds that the Ocean was too large for a non-stop voyage to Asia. Finally, at the end of 1491 another commission recommended approval and signed a contract authorizing him to discover and acquire certain lands and take for himself 10% of all the precious metals he would discover.

The First Columbus Voyage of 8/3/1492

He left on-board the Santa Maria with the Nina, Pinta, and a crew of 90 and carried a letter of introduction from the King & Queen of Spain to the "Grand Khan", the supposed title of the Emperor of China.

He proposed establishing trading posts on islands near the Asian coast. They had traveled 2400 miles without sighting land. They had actually passed present-day Puerto Rico without realizing it. On the 31st day a mutiny was threatened but it was prevented by the sighting of land on 10/21/1492 in the Bahamas which Columbus named "San Salvador" (Holy Saviour). Since he believed this was an outpost of the West Indies he named the inhabitants "Indians".

He explored the West Indies for more than two months searching for gold and spices and discovered Haiti, which he named Hispaniola, and also Cuba, which he thought was Asia. He also discovered significant amounts of what he thought was gold which caused him to believe that he had arrived in Asia. He lost the ship Santa Maria and left behind its crew to establish a trading post named "Navidad". He started his return home 1/16/1493 and returned there 3/15/1493 convinced that he had discovered the all-water route to Asia.

He sent ahead an overly-optimistic report to generate interest in a subsequent voyage. All of Europe, except King John II of Portugal, believed he had reached Asia and, although he was doubtful, the King did not want to lose any advantage to Spain so he claimed the lands found by Columbus for Portugal under the terms of the "Treaty of Alcacovas" arguing that the islands lay close enough to the Azore islands to be considered part of that group.

As stated earlier, the "Treaty of Alcacovas" of 9/4/1479, settled the issues of control of certain Atlantic Ocean islands essentially giving Portugal the freedom to explore the African coast. It is considered as a landmark in the history of colonialism which confirmed the principle that European powers were entitled to divide the rest of the world into "spheres of influence" and colonize within those spheres without the consent of those living in the areas.

The Second Columbus Voyage of 11/1493 to 1496

He departed with a fleet of 17 ships and 1200 settlers to colonize Hispaniola. They discovered the "Lesser Antilles" islands and St. Croix, the largest of the Virgin Islands and the first future U.S. territory he touched. He also discovered another island which one of his crew, Ponce de Leon, named "Puerto Rico". In 1494, he discovered Jamaica on his return to Cuba which he still thought of as Asia. When he arrived at Hispaniola he learned that the Indians had killed the crew he left behind. He had intended for everyone to live there but when they learned there was no gold to be found, they refused to work the land and sought their own trade with the natives.

To keep the colony going he divided the native's land among the settlers and set up a system of forced labor for private profit. He raided the smaller, nearby islands for more laborers. Indians who refused to work were either killed or sold as slaves. Negro slaves were imported from Africa to work the sugar and cotton plantations and sift the earth for gold.

He left his brother, Bartholomew, in charge of the colony, named "Isabella", while he returned to Spain. Back in Spain he learned that some of the early enthusiasm for his claims had diminished even though the Crown was aware that Portugal was getting ready to send Vasco da Gama on another trip to Asia and England was preparing John Cabot to explore Cipangu (Japan). Competition required Spain to continue the Columbus effort.

<u>The Third Columbus Voyage (1498-1500)</u>

Fearful of Portuguese competition, King Ferdinand and Queen Isabella ordered Columbus to take a more southerly route to Asia than his previous voyages. He left with a fleet of 6 ships and 350 settlers. He visited Trinidad and noticed some fresh water mixing with the ocean and assumed it meant a large river draining from a large body of land which he believed to be the mainland of Asia. Actually it was the Gulf of Paria, off the coast of Venezuela. He believed this must be a land mass trailing off from a mainland and, if so, there must be a passage through it, especially since Marco Polo had sailed all the way home from China.

He returned to Hispaniola to find that his brothers had abandoned Isabella for higher ground, now known as Santo Domingo, capital of the Dominican Republic. He found dissension among the settlers requiring an investigator to be sent from Spain who arrived and decided to solve all of the problems by sending Columbus and his brothers home in chains.

The Crown took six weeks to release Columbus but denied him his promised 10% of the precious metals. They also began to grant lands which was part of his authority. At the same time,

Da Gama returned home to announce that he had located Asia and returned with great wealth in 1499. Also, Cabral, sailing for Portugal, returned with news that he had accidentally discovered Brazil, which Portugal claimed.

The Fourth Columbus Voyage (1502-1504)

During the final search for the ocean route to Asia, he spent a full year in Jamaica while also reaching Martinique, Cuba, Honduras, the Gulf of Darien off the coast of Columbia, and spent the winter of 1502-1503 near the northern entrance of the present-day Panama Canal where he tried to establish a trading post but was driven off by the local Indians. He then returned to Jamaica where he was marooned for a year before being rescued.

He finally returned to Spain to find minimal interest in his reports in spite of his insistence that he had reached Asia. After some disputes with the King over his financial contract, King Ferdinand offered him a compromise for his claims against the Crown, which he refused and died penniless in 1506.

Significance of the Columbus Explorations

Although Columbus never achieved his goal of locating the all-water route to Asia, his travels provided valuable information for others to utilize. His colony at Hispaniola eventually became profitable and exported close to a million dollars worth of gold in 1512. Cattle raising and sugar planting also began.

In truth, America could be called "America the Accident" because it was accidentally discovered by other great seamen who were looking for something else and most of the exploration for the next 50 years was done in the hope of getting through or around it to Asia. However, he has been given credit for discovering a country upon which he never set foot.

2. OTHER SPANISH EXPLORERS

Amerigo Vesppucci explored the same general area as Columbus from 1497-1500 and confirmed it as the New World containing great wealth. Spain now realized it needed to fully commit to exploration. Vespucci was credited by an educator named Waldseemuller at a French college as the discoverer of the New World and it should be named after him, "America", he claimed. The idea spread and by 1530 it was widely recognized in Europe although some historians dispute it to this day. Vespucci also reached Venezuela in 1499 and returned to Spain with pearls.

Sebastian de Ocampo in 1508 circumnavigated Cuba and proved that it could not be the mainland of Asia.

Ponce de Leon in 1513 conquered the eastern half of Haiti and explored Puerto Rico, the Bahamas, and eastern shore of Florida seeking the "Fountain of Youth".

Vasco Nunez de Balboa in 1513 discovered the Isthmus of Panama, thus discovering the Pacific Ocean and claiming it for Spain.

Juan Diaz de Solis in 1515 discovered Rio de Janeiro, Brazil.

Ferdinand Magellan circumnavigated the globe (1519) and died in the Philippines. He had previously explored the small islands near Indonesia which were considered the source of great spices. His voyage revealed to Europe the width of the Pacific Ocean and where the real "Indies" were situated relative to the New World.

Hernando Cortez captured the Aztec Chief Montezuma and claimed the wealth of Mexico for Spain.

Alvarez Pineda_explored the Gulf of Mexico from Florida to Vera Cruz, Mexico.

In 1521, Francisco de Gordillo explored the Atlantic coast from Florida to present-day South Carolina.

Estevan Gomez in 1524 explored the Atlantic coast from Florida to the Grand Banks of Newfoundland searching for the passage leading to the "Kingdom of him whom we call the Grand Khan".

In 1528, Panfilo de Navaez landed near Tampa Bay with 600 troops and marched to Tallahassee. He then sailed to Mexico where his ship was sunk and he was lost on the way. One of his crew, Cabeza de Vaca survived and reached Mexico City in 1536.

Francisco Pizarro conquered the Inca's in Peru from 1532-1535.

Hernando De Soto in 1539 explored Florida to the Mississippi river valley and parts of the southwest. He died in 1542 near the Mississippi river.

Francisco Coronado in 1540 explored Arizona and New Mexico seeking the "Cities of Gold".

Juan Cabrillo in 1542 explored the California coast to the north.

Juan de Onate in 1598 explored from Kansas to the Gulf of California and eventually founded Santa Fe, New Mexico, in 1609.

3. SUMMARY OF SPANISH EFFORTS

Spain made its imprint first in the south although subsequent explorations moved into the mainland, to the Mississippi river valley, throughout the southeast, the plains, and the southwest. Many years later their efforts took them to the Pacific coast as far as the Oregon and California border. Within little more than a generation Spain had discovered, conquered, and colonized the most extensive empire in European history.

The challenge now was to devise ways to develop and control her expanding wealth. Half of the territory of the continental United States once belonged to Spain. The oldest surviving building in America is the Spanish Fort at St. Augustine, Florida, built in 1565. In the southwest, the Indians speak Spanish, the architecture is Spanish, and the Roman Catholic Church is predominant.

Spain established such a strong presence in those parts of the New World wherever she wished that she forced other countries to settle elsewhere. She lost little that she really wanted. When intruders came they settled where Spain allowed them to settle. Because the land north of St. Augustine seemed worthless; they gave it to those who followed. By 1600, before the English made their first settlement, Spanish colonists in the New World numbered about 200,000.

But, from the European point of view, the New World was a disappointment. It blocked the western route to Asia, its' precious metals were exhausted, the spices brought home by Columbus were not real, and the climate was unhealthy. Spain would have been happy to forget about America and withdraw but for the competitive fear that some other country, such as Portugal, might eventually benefit from the New World.

E.   ENGLAND

English explorations generally occurred during the years 1497–1610, beginning with the John Cabot voyage seeking a Northwest Passage to Asia and continuing to the colonization period. England was about five years behind Spain in its explorations. Eventually, England established a policy of exploration and colonization based on:

- The country was over-populated with many poor people and beggars sleeping in the streets.

- What better solution than to give the poor and unemployed an opportunity for a new life overseas?

- England needed markets for her woolens and North America seemed ideal with its' cold climate. Not only settlers but Indians might be persuaded to swap furs and skins for coats and blankets.

- England needed precious metals and there were rumors of silver and gold in the New World.

- England had been paying the Mediterranean countries for olive oil, currants, and wine. Why not try to produce these in new English colonies? She was dependent on the Baltic countries for ship timber and tar. Surely, the Royal Navy would welcome a new source of supplies from the New World.

- Like other European nations, England needed to locate a shorter, more direct, route to Asia. Maybe the "Northwest Passage" might be located somewhere in the New World.

- England felt the duty to spread Protestant Christianity and prevent Roman Catholic Spain from converting the native population of the New World. Such a place might also serve as a Protestant refuge.

These were the basic motives of English exploration and colonization policy for a century and a half. From the first it was understood that any English settlement must have English law and liberties. So, the first Charter of the Virginia Company in 1606 declared that the colonists and their descendants would enjoy all of the rights and liberties as if they had been born and raised in England.

1. JOHN CABOT   (1450-1499)

    In 1497, Cabot explored the shores of Newfoundland, Nova Scotia, and Labrador, giving England its first claim to the New World although no settlement was attempted. His claim included all of North America east of the Rocky Mountains and north of Florida. He was the first European since the Vikings to explore the East Coast of the New World and the first to search for the Northwest Passage. He was born in Genoa, Italy, in 1450 and his name was actually Giovanni Caboto.

    In 1476, he lived in Venice, Italy, the main trading center for the entire Mediterranean region. He worked there as a merchant and navigator. Horrible experiences with Arab traders probably influenced his decision to find a sea route to Asia which would allow merchants to trade directly with Asian traders instead of the Arab traders.

    By 1483, he had moved to Bristol, England. He believed that Asia could be reached by sailing west. In 1493, when word of Columbus' reports of his successful journey to the New World arrived, he convinced King Henry VII that England did not have to stand by while the Spanish gained an advantage in the New World. The Pope had given Spain control of all the new lands in the New World, per the Treaty of Tordesillas of 6/7/1494, which the King opposed.

King Henry VII agreed to finance an exploration of the New World primarily because Cabot convinced him that he could reach the Asian mainland by following a more northerly route than did Columbus, plus it was shorter. The idea that a northern route to Asia existed began the search for the Northwest Passage to the Indies.

He sailed from Bristol, England, on his ship, "Matthew", on 5/2/1497, with a crew of 18 and landed somewhere on the east coast (6/24/1497) thinking he had landed on the east coast of Asia although historians don't know if it was Maine or Newfoundland. Where-ever he landed, he claimed it in the name of King Henry VII and became the first European explorer to discover the mainland of North America. He sailed further north only to find ice-crusted waters. His original goal was to establish a trading post off the coast of Asia to engage in the spice trade.

He returned to England on 8/6/1497 and was given a hero's welcome for supposedly reaching the "land of the spices". He was made an Admiral and ordered to take five ships to return and discover Japan. Some historians believe that, in 1498, he returned from that expedition but died in 1499 in England while others believe that he never returned and was never heard from again.

Soon after Cabot's final voyage, in 1501, an Azore farmer ("lavrador") named Joao Fernandes joined some Englishmen and Portuguese in making a northwesterly voyage from England. They made landfall somewhere on the northeast coast of the New World and named it "Tierra del Lavrador", or present-day Labrador.

In 1509, after a failed attempt by Cabot's son, Sebastian, to locate the Northwest Passage, it was many years before England decided to launch further explorations. This was due to many domestic and overseas problems distracting the Crown.

2. FACTORS INFLUENCING ENGLAND'S
    EXPLORATION POLICY

    a. <u>Protestant Reformation</u> (1517-1648 & the Treaty of Westphalia ending the European Religious Wars)

    When King Henry VII divorced his wife, Catherine of Spain in 1533, and wished to remarry against the wishes of the Pope, he broke with Catholicism in 1534 and began his

    Anglican Church of England. Although the Protestant Reformation began in Europe in the 16th century, the action of King Henry VII in breaking with the Catholic Church allied England with the European Reformation movement which brought England into further conflict with Catholic Spain, which was already an exploration rival.

    The Reformation was led by Martin Luther, John Calvin, and other early Protestants. The efforts of "reformers" who protested the doctrines, rituals, and abuses of the Catholic Church led to the creation of new Protestant Churches. The Catholics responded with a "Counter-Reformation", led by the Jesuits, which reclaimed large parts of Europe. In general, northern Europe, except Ireland and some parts of England, turned Protestant while southern Europe plus Poland remained Roman Catholic.

    The largest of the new denominations were the Anglicans (England), Lutherans (Germany and Scandinavia), and the Reformed Churches in parts of Germany, Switzerland, Netherlands, and Scotland.

    Reformers in the Church of England alternated for centuries between sympathies for Catholic tradition and Protestantism, creating a compromise between tradition and reform.

    The Reformation led to a series of religious wars which culminated in the "30 years war" which damaged much of Germany and killed between 25-40% of its population. From 1618-1648, the Catholic "House of Habsburg" and its allies fought against the various Princes of Germany, supported at times by Denmark, Sweden, and France.

b. The Treaty of Westphalia (1648)

Ended the "30 Years War". The terms of the Treaty were:

All parties would recognize the Peace of Augsburg" of 1555 by which each prince would have the right to determine the religion of his own "state", such as Catholicism, Lutheranism, or Calvinism.

Christians living in principalities where their denomination was not the established Church were guaranteed the right to practice their faith in public during allotted hours and in private.

Pope Innocent X denounced and disagreed with the Treaty of Westphalia and the religious conflicts continued.

The Habsburg's, who ruled Spain, Austria, the Spanish Netherlands, and much of Germany and Italy, were strong supporters of Catholicism. Some historians believe that the era of the Reformation came to a close when Catholic France allied itself with the Protestant states against the Habsburg dynasty. For the first time since the days of Luther, political and national convictions outweighed religious convictions in Europe.

c. Puritanism

The early Puritan movement was Reformed or Calvinist and was a movement for reform within the Church of England. They believed the Reformation didn't go far enough in reforming the traditions of the Catholic Church. The later Puritan movement was referred to as "dissenters & non-conformists" and eventually led to the formation of other reformed denominations.

The most famous and well-known emigration to America was the migration of the Puritan "separatists" from the Anglican Church of England who first fled to Holland and then to America to establish the English colonies of New England.

These Puritan Separatists were also known as "Pilgrims". After establishing a colony at Plymouth, Massachusetts, which would eventually become a part of the colony of Massachusetts, the Puritan Pilgrims received a charter from the King of England which legalized their colony, allowing them to trade with the merchants of England in accordance with the principles of mercantilism.

This apparently successful colonization marked the beginning of the Protestant presence in America and became an oasis of spiritual and economic freedom to which persecuted Protestants and other minorities fled to for peace, freedom, and opportunity.

The Pilgrims of New England disapproved of Christmas and the celebration was outlawed in Boston from 1659 until revoked by Governor Sir Edmund Andros in 1681. The original intent of the New England colonists was to establish spiritual Puritanism, which had been denied to them in England, engage in peaceful commerce with England and the native Indians, and Christianize the peoples of the America's.

d. <u>England's Growing Awareness of the World</u>

It wasn't until an English translation of Spanish explorations written by Richard Eden in 1555 called "Decades of the New World" that people in England began to realize that a bigger world existed than just England.

The English government lacked the military strength to challenge Spain in spite of the growing interest in explorations but the government allowed interest in areas where the Spanish had no presence. Consistent with that policy, the Newfoundland fisheries offered a safe way to quietly increase English wealth and influence.

Fishing led to furs and by the 1540's, England had developed a profitable fur-trade which resurrected the idea of the all-water route to the riches of Asia as long as it didn't create conflict with the Spanish or Portuguese, so the obvious place to focus their attention was in northeast North America.

In 1553, a group of London merchants sent Hugh Willoughby and Richard Chancellor to search for a passage beyond the Gulf of Archangel in the Barents Sea. Willoughby died but Chancellor survived and eventually formed the Muscovy Company which was used to open trade with Russia. In subsequent years other agents of the Muscovy Company traveled throughout the mid-east and reported the availability of riches. In 1579,

William Harbone reached Constantinople and received approval from the Sultan for English merchants to trade in the mid-east. In 1581, Queen Elizabeth I granted a charter to the Levant Company and through the rest of her reign luxuries of the east entered England thanks to her efforts.

e. Reign of Queen Elizabeth I (Born September 1533–Died 1603) (Ruled 1558-1603)

Born as Elizabeth Tudor to King Henry VIII and Anne Boleyn as the second daughter, she inherited the Throne upon the death of her older half-sister, Mary I, in November, 1558. England was facing many domestic and international problems at the time. Mary I was Catholic, like her parents, and had devoted much of her reign undoing Protestant reforms of her half-brother King Edward VI. Elizabeth inherited a Catholic nation since the Church had been reconciled with Rome and she then began to restore the Protestant national Church. She began by passing the "Act of Supremacy of 1559" which made her the "Supreme Govenor of the Church of England" which caused another break with Rome. She made other reforms which caused Catholic unrest which grew so strong in 1568, led by Mary Queen of Scots, a popular Catholic, that eventually Elizabeth I had her executed on 2/8/1587 for plotting the assassination of Queen Elizabeth I. The execution actually occurred without her approval as she had constantly delayed it for humanitarian reasons.

The Catholic persecution of European Protestants forced Elizabeth I into a war she was trying to avoid to protect French Huguenots/Calvinists who had settled in France, after a 1572 massacre of 3000 Huguenots. The world situation was made worse when she refused an offer of marriage from King Phillip II of Spain who then sent his Armada to raid England. The Spanish Armada was defeated by the English Navy in August, 1558, but the war with Spain lasted until 1604. The Armada attack was the first of five attempts by Spain to conquer England. After King Philip II died in September, 1598, his son succeeded him. Eventually, the Spanish fought the English in Ireland and lost in 1603.

The defeat of the Armada in 1588 had two major results:

- Began the process of weakening Spain as a national power

- Helped Queen Elizabeth I secure Protestantism as the English state religion

Her reign was successful, literature grew with the works of Shakespeare and Marlowe, English influence in the world grew through the efforts of Sir Francis Drake and Sir Walter Raleigh, and other elements of English society flourished.

She was not fond of Parliament and only called it into session when absolutely necessary. The country was largely governed by the Privy Council who, in association with the Queen, proposed major legislation. She was known as "Queen Bess", the last of the Tudor family, who died at age 70 without ever marrying and producing an heir. Therefore, in the absence of a designated successor, the Crown passed to the Scottish King James VI who became King James I of England and Scotland. Even though Elizabeth I was considered a successful ruler, she left a nation at war with religious persecutions along with economic problems and heavy taxes.

3. OTHER ENGLISH EXPLORATIONS

    Sir Humphrey Gilbert was one of those English adventurers who sought to explore lands not already of interest to Spain. His stated goal was to seek the Northwest Passage to Asia which, at this time, became very popular. He wrote, in 1566, "Discourse of a Discovery for a New Passage to Catia" which was not published until the 1570's which popularized the theory of a northwest passage to India. He argued that the New World was just an island and around its' northern tip lay a clear path to Asia. He also suggested that the search for a passage could be assisted by the development of outposts permitting ships on the long voyage to Asia to pause for maintenance and supplies.

Sir Martin Frobisher set out in 1576 to test Gilbert's theory and returned with an "Asian Eskimo" and what he thought was gold to prove that he had located Asia. King Philip II of Spain doubted his claims but "Gold Fever" now motivated further attempts to discover an all-water route to Asia.

In 1578, Gilbert persuaded Queen Elizabeth I to grant a charter which would allow him six years to build a colony in the New World. Some explorers continued to seek the northwest passage for another 20+ years and soon the Crown began to change its' emphasis from exploration to active colonization.

In 1607 and again in 1608, Henry Hudson was sent by the Muscovy Company to locate a shorter, more direct water route to Asia. When he returned home from his failed second voyage the company, now almost bankrupt, let him go. After making another voyage on behalf of the Dutch West India Company seeking the Northwest Passage in 1609, he signed on with England to try again in 1611, but vanished in the effort.

F.   FRANCE

French explorations occurred primarily during the years 1523-1681 with the primary focus on the northeast coast of North America. In the late 17th century they became interested in the Mississippi river valley. They were primarily motivated by the "Treaty of Tordesillas" of 1494 when Pope Alexander VI divided the New World into Spanish and Portuguese spheres of interest.

France and England both believed the Pope had no right to make a declaration and countries should be free to explore and colonize whenever they wished. They were also motivated by a competitive desire against their European rivals.

Some of the most significant French explorers were:

1. GIOVANNI VERAZZANO

    He was an Italian sailing for France to seek the Northwest Passage through the New World to Asia. He explored the east and northeast coast of the New World in 1524 by sailing into the present-day New York harbor and explored the area around Narragansett Bay in present-day Rhode Island and then continued north to the coast of Maine. He thought he had discovered the "South Sea" (Pacific Ocean) but historians believe he may have sailed into either Chesapeake Bay, Delaware Bay, or Pamlico Sound, North Carolina. He may have also explored the coast of Newfoundland, Nova Scotia, and today's Hudson River far enough to determine that it was not a "Strait" or the northwest passage to Asia.

A map drawn by his brother "pinched" America in the center and for centuries thereafter every explorer who ventured into the wilderness hoped to come upon this "isthmus" which would carry them to the "Sea of Verazzano", or the South Sea/Pacific Ocean, to Asia. At this time he may not have known that Balboa had already discovered the Isthmus of Panama and the real Pacific Ocean in 1513.

2. JACQUES CARTIER (Accompanied Verazzano on his voyage to the New World)

    King Francis I of France was too involved in European conflicts to send Verazzano back for a second attempt. A decade passed before the King authorized further exploration by Jacques Cartier, this time, in 1534 who sailed past Labrador into the St. Lawrence river far enough to believe he had found the northwest passage to Asia. The King authorized another voyage on 5/19/1535 with three ships and 110 crew to explore the St. Lawrence River beyond present day Quebec to an Indian village known as "Hochelaga" near present-day Montreal. On 10/2/1535 he viewed "Mont Real" from the heights above the river where he could see the river growing larger in the distance. He could not proceed further because of rapids which he believed were all that prevented him from sailing to Asia. He named the site "LaChine" which was the French word for China so the town eventually became known as "Lachine, Quebec'. The Indians told Cartier that the river progressed further inland a distance of "3 moons" and doubted it was the Northwest Passage to Asia. They also spoke of cities of gold just beyond the horizon, just as Columbus had been told.

After spending a few days in Hochelaga, Cartier returned to Stadacona near present-day Quebec City on 10/11/1535 which was the capital of the native Indians, where he decided to spend the winter. They built a Fort stocked with firewood and salted down game and fish. From mid-November 1535 to mid-April 1536 his fleet was frozen at the junction of the St. Lawrence and St. Charles Rivers. During the winter most of his party and many native Indians became sick from scurvy but because of a remedy suggested by the Indians, 85 of the original 110 explorers survived the winter.

Cartier returned to France in May, 1536, and took Chief Donnacona to France so he might personally tell the King of a country further north called the "Kingdom of Saquenay" which was full of gold, rubies, and other treasures. He returned to his home in France on 7/15/1536.

When King Francis I heard these tales from his explorers and the native Chief, he decided on a full-scale expedition to present-day Canada. Spain protested on the basis of the Treaty of Tordesillas but King Francis I replied that "the Pope's have spiritual jurisdiction but it does not lie with them to distribute lands among Kings". The Spanish thought about sending an expedition against the French but finally decided to leave them alone to dissipate their wealth and energy on a doubtful venture.

Cartier left France on 5/23/1541 with five ships and a different goal, to find the "Kingdom of Saquenay" and its riches and establish a permanent settlement along the St. Lawrence River. At this time Francisco Coronado of Spain was also searching the American southwest, New Mexico and Arizona for the cities of gold. Cartier decided to move his settlement closer to present-day Quebec City where they built a fortified settlement for protection. It was named "Charlesbourg-Royal". The crew collected what they thought were diamonds and gold. Two ships were sent home on 9/12/1541 with the materials for closer inspection which revealed they were only quartz crystals.

Cartier meanwhile explored the local area in longboats seeking the "Kingdom of Saquenay" but was stopped again by rapids and bad weather so he returned to his settlement and found most of the original settlers had been killed by the Indians.

Cartier decided he had insufficient manpower to either protect the settlement or continue seeking the "Kingdom", so he decided to leave for France in early June 1542 and arrived home in October convinced that he had come home with gold and other wealth, which was untrue. The site of Charlesbourg-Royal was abandoned in 1543 because of disease, foul weather, and hostile Indians so no permanent French settlements were made in Canada before 1608 when Samuel de Champalain founded Quebec City.

The "Cartier Legacy" gave him credit for opening the greatest waterway in North America, the St. Lawrence River, and created positive relations with the local Indians. He is also given credit for documenting the name "Canada" for the territory along the shores of the St. Lawrence River and he referred to the inhabitants as Canadiens". His chief contribution to the discovery of Canada is that of the first European to penetrate the continent along the eastern region of the St. Lawrence River. His explorations consolidated France's claims of the territory which came to be known as "New France". His third voyage produced the first documented European attempt at settling North America since Lucas Vazquez de Ayllon in 1526-1527. His final contribution was to acknowledge that the New World was a separate land-mass from Europe and/or Asia.

3. SAMUEL DE CHAMPLAIN

In one of his eleven trips he explored the coast of "Norumbega" (New England) as far south as the south side of Cape Cod looking for a better site for a settlement. He found none because the further south he sailed the less the Indians had to trade.

In 1608, he established trading posts in present-day Quebec and Montreal. The St. Lawrence River drained the greatest source of beaver fur on the continent but whether the French, Dutch, or English obtained the bulk of it depended on their Indian relations. Champlain soon discovered that the St. Lawrence River valley was the center of "power politics" between the "5 Nations of the Iroquois", the Hurons, Montagnais, and other tribes of the region. He supported the other tribes against the Iroquois and helped the Montagnais win a fight with the Mohawks near present-day Lake Champlain. He explored the Ottawa River by canoe and reached Lake Huron where he wintered with the Huron Indians and won their allegiance. This placed the Hurons in a good position to become the middlemen for the fur trade between the French at Montreal and the Indians who trapped beaver in the Great Lakes region.

The Iroquois attacked the Hurons in 1624 to prevent their successful trade with the French. Initially, only traders or employees of trading companies and missionaries were allowed in the area, for their own safety. It was not until 1628 that planting or plowing began.

The French control of Canada was still not solid when, in 1629, an English Privateer captured Quebec, and a Scottish Lord, Sir William Alexander, occupied the abandoned trading post at Port Royal. England's King Charles I returned both Quebec and Port Royal to France in return for part of the Dowry of the Queen which was considered as good a bargain for France as the Louisiana Purchase for the America.

By 1633, Champlain was located at Quebec as Governor of a new company, "The Hundred Associates of New France". He died in 1635.

His "legacy" was profound and was considered the most versatile of colonial founders in North America. He was a sailor, soldier, scholar, and a man of action and explorer. Sailors admired him for his exploration of the rugged coast of New England without serious injury. His written accounts of his explorations were supplemented with drawings and maps which were not surpassed for accuracy for 50 years. His only negative was the turning of the Iroquois into enemies of France because of his support for the Huron and Algonquin tribes in 1609. The Iroquois became allies of the Dutch and English and aided them for years.

4. FATHER MARQUETTE & LOUIS JOLIET
In May 1673, Father Marquette, a Jesuit missionary, and Louis Joliet, a fur trader, and a party of five men departed from Green Bay, Wisconsin and followed the Wisconsin River to the Mississippi river. Along the way they observed the Ohio and Missouri rivers which they believed were the route to present-day California. They also observed many Indians with English weapons. They later met Indians who told them the Mississippi river emptied into the Gulf of Mexico and the Indians in the area were ferocious. In mid-July 1673, though still 700 miles from the mouth of the Mississippi river, they turned back and arrived in Green Bay in September after covering 2,500 miles in four months.

The King's desire to follow-up on their explorations were frustrated for nearly a decade due to a series of wars in Europe, which occupied his attention and resources. However, meanwhile the Marquette-Joliet explorations caught the attention of Rene-Robert Cavelier, Sieur de La Salle.

5. RENE-ROBERT CAVELIER, SIEUR DE LA SALLE
He sailed for Canada in 1666 to make his fortune and become a fur trader, learned many Indian languages and learned more about the American interior than almost any other living person in America. He set out to change the fur business by controlling it from a central location and selected Fort Frontenac near Lake Ontario from which he intended to stop the Iroquois influence in the western country and to also prevent the movement of furs south to the English. He operated the fort until 1677 when he returned to France to gain Royal support for a larger dream. He now saw that the fur trade represented only a small portion of the overall wealth potential of North America.

Jean Baptiste Colbert, who served as the Controller-General of Finance for France under King Louis XIV and was a close advisor to the King, saw the wisdom of the La Salle plan and persuaded the King to support it. Colbert was a believer in the enrichment of a country through commerce, much like the English policy of Mercantilism. The La Salle plan fit right into the larger policy of Colbert and King Louis XIV so the King granted La Salle a charter to erect a series of Forts along the Mississippi river valley to protect French interests.

La Salle was exploring the area southwest of the Mississippi river valley in Texas when he was killed by his own men in 1687. Eventually, the French explored and settled the Gulf of Mexico towns of Biloxi, Mobile, and New Orleans from 1699-1718.

6. OTHER FRENCH EXPLORATIONS AND THE FORMATION OF FRENCH COMMERCIAL POLICY

The French utilized the vast inland waterways to explore and settle North America. Champlain used the St. Lawrence River, Marquette & Joliet used the Mississippi river and Lake Michigan, and La Salle used the Mississippi river for his explorations.

French government support for further New World explorations diminished when Cartier's "gold" was found to be false, to be known as "fools gold". France was also involved in other European conflicts which distracted their efforts for a period of time. Although there were no further explorations of discovery until Champlain in 1608, there were some attempts at colonization to serve as outposts to attack and weaken their enemies.

Gaspard de Coligny, a French Huguenot (Protestant) with great political influence, persuaded the King to create outposts in the New World from which to attack treasure ships and also create a refuge for oppressed Huguenots. This plan was started in 1555 with a settlement of Huguenots on an island off the coast of Brazil in 1562. Jean Ribault, another Huguenot, placed a garrison at Port Royal, South Carolina.

When Ribault returned to France for more men and supplies the garrison fought among itself and killed its leader and returned home. Two years later Coligny promoted another attempt led by Rene de Laudonniere who placed a garrison at Fort Carolina, further south on the St. John's River in Florida. It was perfectly located to tap the treasure of the Spanish as it moved up the Florida coast. In 1565, Ribault returned with reinforcements at the same time as a Spanish expedition led by Pedro Menendez de Aviles arrived with an army from Spain to stop the French. King Phillip of Spain gave Menendez authority to establish outposts all along the North American coast.

Menendez landed 50 miles south of the French and laid the foundation for St. Augustine, Florida, and then marched overland to take Fort Carolina by force, killing 142 French settlers. Ribault attempted to retake Fort Carolina but failed and was killed with other Huguenots. This massacre alarmed the French which was presently at peace with Spain so they decided to ignore the attack since it was a Huguenot enterprise and not sponsored by the government. It was many years later that France renewed its interest in exploration of the New World.

7. EARLY SETTLEMENT OF NEW FRANCE

The early French efforts were mostly codfish-related as French fishermen visited the Grand Banks of Newfoundland as early as 1504. These efforts led to trade with the Indians who had valuable fur to barter for axes and other iron tools. Gentlemen of that era required fur for trimming coats and to make the felt of which the very popular wide-brimmed hats were made. The fishermen learned to bring with them a supply of cloth, axes, iron kettles, and other goods the Indians wanted and every fishing station became a trading post.

This led to fur-trading expeditions moving into the Gulf of St. Lawrence and a chain of trading posts, Port Royal, Quebec, Montreal, and Trois Rivieres, all of which eventually became towns or cities in Canada. In 1504, a company attempted to establish a colony on a river which now divides Maine from New Brunswick and was first established on Dochet Island, now St. Croix, for protection against the Indians. After one cold winter it was transferred to Port Royal in present-day Nova Scotia. Led by a Parisian lawyer, Lescarbot, Port Royal prospered as a settlement and concluded a Treaty with the Micmac Indians plus planted some crops and vegetables and then experienced a successful winter.

In 1590, Henry of Navarre, Henry IV, won the "Battle of Ivry", and ended the European Wars of Religion. It was time to colonize Canada, ahead of the English. A monopoly of Canadian fur trade was granted to individuals or small companies on condition that they settle a certain number of colonists per year at their own expense. The immediate results of this policy were not impressive. The companies seldom complied with the terms. Other fur traders pressured the King to cancel the monopoly and open the trade to them. However, one of these companies was responsible for bringing Samuel de Champlain to Canada who is rightly regarded as the "Father of New France.

G.   HOLLAND

1.   DUTCH EXPLORATIONS

Dutch explorations of the New World occurred during the years of 1609-1626. As the other European nations were seeking the Northwest Passage, so were the Dutch. In 1609, the Dutch West India Company sent Henry Hudson, an Englishman, to explore the North American coast from Virginia to Newfoundland. Along the way he also explored New York harbor and the Hudson River where, in 1610, he began a fur trade with the Indians. In 1624, they founded the settlement of New Amsterdam (New York) and the colony of New Netherlands while also establishing a trading post at Albany, called "Fort Orange". Since Holland was a prosperous country, not too many Dutch were interested in immigrating to the New World. As inducements, the Dutch

West India Company offered "patroonships" which were a huge tract of land to anyone who would transport fifty tenants to the colony.

2. HENRY HUDSON (Englishman sailing for Holland)

Henry Hudson had made two unsuccessful voyages on behalf of the Muscovy Company (England) and was then hired by the Dutch West India Company in 1609 to once again attempt to locate the Northwest Passage. He left in his ship, the "Half Moon", and stopped at Newfoundland to catch many codfish, visited Delaware Bay which he eventually realized was not the route to Asia, and then moved further north to the Hudson River as far north as Albany (Fort Orange) where he realized the great fur trade potential and made friends with the Mohawk Indians. In 1611, he tried again, sailing for the English for the second time but failed and vanished in the attempt.

3. OTHER DUTCH EXPLORATIONS

The Dutch government became involved in European conflicts at this time and did not seriously pursue the claims produced by Hudson although the following explorations continued:

    a.   Adriaen Block in 1613 explored Long Island Sound and the Connecticut River, gave his name to Block Island, explored Cape Cod, and traveled along the Massacusetts Coast past the site of Boston.

    b.   Also in 1613, Cornelius May explored the southern shore of Long Island, Delaware Bay, and the Delaware river as far as the mouth of the Schuylkill river.

    c.   In 1614, the merchants who had financed these explorations organized the New Netherlands Company and obtained from the "States General" (like a Parliament) a monopoly on the fur trade of the region between the 40th and 45th latitude. They determined that the heart of the fur trade was near present-day Albany where they established a trading post. They maintained good relations with the Iroquois Indians who came to trade.

d. Later in 1614, they erected a small trading post on an island near the mouth of the Hudson River.

e. In 1618 the charter of the New Netherland Company was not renewed but their last official act was to sign a formal Treaty with the Iroquois Indians which insured their continued hostility toward the French. Historians believe that this friendship between the Iroquois and the Dutch prevented the French from having a presence in the Mohawk and Hudson River valleys.

f. In 1621, another charter was issued authorizing the formation of the Dutch West India Company" which was given monopolistic control over New Netherland.

g. They did not intend to colonize, at first, but in 1624 they sent thirty families, mostly Protestant Walloons fleeing from persecution in Belgium, led by Cornelius May. Most settled around Fort Orange (present-day Albany) while others settled on the Delaware River across from the mouth of the Schuylkill river where they built a new Fort Nassau (the original having been built near Fort Orange). A few others settled on Manhattan Island and Staten Island. When May returned to Holland in 1625, he left William Verhulst in charge.

h. The Company organized the New Netherland government on the basis of the authority contained in its charter; it placed control in a Board of Directors located in Holland, representing the shareholders. The Board chose a Director General to govern the colony with full executive and judicial authority. He was assisted by a local council which was also selected by the Board. The government became an Autocracy under the Director General.

i. Peter Minuit was the first Director General. He landed on Manhattan Island in May, 1625, with additional settlers. For the equivalent of $24.00 of "trinkets" he made an agreement with the Manhattan Indians to allow the Dutch to settle among them. Historians claim that it was discovered later that the Indians didn't even "own" the land.

So, in 1626, he established the village of "Nieuw Amsterdam" (New York) which consisted of a small fort and a few homes. Many of the settlers from the other locations were moved back to New York to build up this colony.

Other than a few trading posts and settlements in New York, the Hudson river valley north to Albany, and extending into Long Island and Connecticut, the Dutch eventually focused their attention outside of North America, primarily in the West Indies.

This was the extent of the Dutch exploration and settlement activity in the New World during the early 17th century. Their settlement and colonies became more important later in the 17th and 18th centuries as the expanding colonies of England and France began to infringe on Dutch interests in the area.

H.   KEY DATES & SIGNIFICANT EVENTS

1000	Earliest known exploration of the New World by the Norsemen. Some evidence of brief settlement in Greenland.
1291	Earliest documented exploration by the Vivaldi brothers in Genoa, Italy. They explored the West African coast in search of Asia. They never returned.
1479	Treaty of Alcacovas
1487-1488	Bartholomew Diaz (Portugal) reached the southern tip of Africa looking for an all-water route to Asia.
1494	Treaty of Tordesillas
1497	John Cabot exploration along North American coast gave England a claim to American soil.
1498	Cabot makes his second voyage for the English and disappears.
1498	Vasco da Gama (Portugal) sails for India via Cape of Good Hope. Returns with a cargo of spices.
1499	Italian navigator Amerigo Vespucci sights the coast of South America during a voyage of discovery for Spain.
1500	Cabral (Portugal) seeking Asia is blown off course and eventually discovers Brazil.
1507	The name "America" is first used in a geography book referring to the New World, Americus Vespucci given credit for the discovery.
1513	Ponce de Leon of Spain lands in Florida.
1513	Balboa (Spain) seeking gold and another sea, crosses the Isthmus of Panama and discovers the Pacific Ocean
1517	Martin Luther begins the Protestant Reformation in Europe ending domination of Catholic Church in Europe. Results in the growth of numerous Protestant religious sects.
1518	Hernando Cortes conquers the Aztec empire.

1519-1522	Ferdinand Magellan is the first person to sail around the world
1524	Giovanni Verazzano sails for France and lands in the area near the Carolina's. He sails north and discovers Hudson River, continues north to Narragansett Bay and Nova Scotia.
1531	Francisco Pizarro conquers the Inca's of Peru
1533	Jacques Cartier (France) seeks the Northwest Passage to Asia but discovers the St. Lawrence River.
1534	Separation of the English Church from Rome led to English leadership of Protestant nations in the Religious wars.
1535	Jacques Cartier discovers Montreal
1541	Hernando De Soto of Spain discovers the Mississippi River.
1558	Elizabeth I (1558-1603) became Queen of England
1565	The first permanent European colony in North America is founded at St. Augustine, Florida, by Spain.
1577	Drake began a voyage of circumnavigation of the globe, completed in 1580.
1588	English defeat of the Spanish Armada
1598	Sir Francis Drake dies off the coast of Panama
1600	Spanish colonists in the New World are 200,000.
1603	James I (1603-1625) ascended to the English throne and ends war with Spain.
1603	Champlain (France) discovers Northeast North America and Quebec.
1606	The first Charter of the Virginia Company requires that any settlers and their descendants would enjoy the same rights as if they had been born and resided in England.
1608	Champlain establishes the first permanent French settlement at Quebec.

1609	Henry Hudson sails along the New Jersey shore and claims the region for the Netherlands
1614	Captain John Smith explored present-day New Hampshire
1626	Peter Minuit, Dutch Governor, buys Manhattan from the Indians for $24 equivalent.

I.   REVIEW QUESTIONS

(Multiple Choice)

1. An important motive of English and other voyages of exploration in the 16th century was:
    a.   the need for more geographic information
    b.   the search for better agricultural lands
    c.   scientific curiosity
    d.   desire for a direct water-route westward from Europe to Asia

2. Early attempts by the English to colonize in America failed because:
    a.   of war with Spain and a lack of experience
    b.   early colonies were destroyed by Spain
    c.   most colonizing expeditions were lost at sea
    d.   recruits for the colonies could not be found

3. The two most important motives of English colonization of America were:
    a.   the love of adventure and religious rivalry with Spain
    b.   the need to establish religious freedom and military bases against Spain
    c.   the desire for religious freedom and economic opportunity
    d.   the love of adventure and need to achieve a favorable balance of trade.

4. English colonization differed from that of other colonizing nations in America because:
    a.   the English colonists enjoyed a greater degree of neglect and freedom from Mother country interference
    b.   more attention was given to developing fishing and lumbering enterprises
    c.   more aid was given by the Mother country
    d.   salutary regulation and helpful paternalism provided sound foundations

5. The Papal Line of Demarcation:
    a. allowed Portugal to claim Brazil
    b. gave the Philippines to Spain
    c. permitted France to claim Canada
    d. recognized Italian domination of trade with Asia

6. Which of these explorers founded Quebec?
    a. Verazzano
    b. Champlain
    c. La Salle
    d. Cartier

7. The relationship of the Iroquois Indians to the French proved significant because the Iroquois:
    a. kept the French from colonizing South Carolina
    b. helped the French against the New Englanders
    c. Allied themselves with the English and checked French expansion south of Montreal
    b. were the most energetic for gathering Indians

8. Which of the following colonizing nations occupied the largest area in North America during the colonial period?
    a. English
    b. French
    c. Dutch
    d. Swedes

9. What was the chronological sequence of European exploration and discovery? (Which countries were first to last in their explorations?)
    a. Spain, Portugal, France, Holland, England
    b. France, Spain, England, Portugal, Holland
    c. Portugal, Spain, England, France, Holland
    d. England, Portugal, Spain, France, Holland
    e. Holland, England France, Spain, Portugal

10. Who discovered the "Cape of Good Hope"?
    a. Bartholomew Diez
    b. Prince Henry the Navigator
    c. Vasco da Gama
    d. Ferdinand Magellan

(TRUE OR FALSE)

11. After Elizabeth became Queen, the rivalry over religion and empire began in earnest between England and Spain
    a. TRUE
    b. FALSE

12. In his voyages to America Columbus never realized he had discovered new lands not part of Asia
    a. TRUE
    b. FALSE

13. In drawing the Papal Line of Demarcation, the Pope was seeking to prevent a quarrel between Spain and Portugal
    a. TRUE
    b. FALSE

14. The Dutch settled in America to gain control of land for speculative purposes
    a. TRUE
    b. FALSE

15. The Treaty of Alcacovas was considered as one of the first international documents formally outlining the principle that European powers are entitled to divide the rest of the world into "spheres of interest" and colonize those spheres without the consent of those living in the areas.
    a. TRUE
    b. FALSE

J.   GLOSSARY

1. **Quadrant**   An early instrument for measuring the altitude of celestial bodies consisting of a 90 degree graduated arc with a movable radius for measuring angles.

2. **Calvinism**   The religious doctrine of John Calvin, emphasizing the omnipotence of God and the salvation of the elite by God's grace alone.

3. **Era of Reformation**   Generally viewed as the years of 1517–1648 as a movement in Western Europe aimed at reforming some of the doctrines and practices of the Roman Catholic Church which resulted in the establishment of Protestant Churches.

CHAPTER 2 SUMMARY

WORLD EXPLORATION & DISCOVERY

A. **Primary Motivation of thee Major European Nations**
   1. Seek all-water route to Asia for new goods and markets
   2. Secure new raw materials
   3. Create national competition for trade opportunities
   4. Expand their nation states by creating colonies

B. **National Explorations Dates**
1. Portugal	1420	1503
2. Spain	1492	1598
3. England	1497	1610
4. France	1523	1681
5. Holland	1609	1626

C. **Portugal**
   1. Prince Henry the Navigator
   2. Bartholomew Diaz
   3. Vasco da Gama
   4. Cabral, Corte Real, Fernandes, Vespucci
   5. Significance of the "Treaty of Tordesillas" 6/7/1494

D. **Spain**
   1. Christopher Columbus four voyages
   2. Amerigo Vespucci
   3. Ponce De Leon

4. Vasco Nunez De Balboa

5. Ferdinand Magellan

6. Hernando Cortez

7. Francisco Pizarro

8. Hernando De Soto

9. Francisco Coronado

10. Juan Cabrillo

E.   **England**

1. John Cabot

2. Sir Humphrey Gilbert

3. Henry Hudson

4. Protestant Reformation

5. European Religious Wars & Treaty of Westhalia 1648

6. Puritanism

7. Reign of Queen Elizabeth I

8. Relations with Spain

F.   **France**

1. Giovanni Verrazzano

2. Jacques Cartier

3. Samuel De Champlain

4. Father Marquette and Louis Joliet

5. Rene-Robert Cavelier, Sieur De La Salle

6. Early Settlement of "New France"

G.   **Holland**

1. Henry Hudson

2. Adrien Block

3. Cornelius May

4. Purchase of New Amsterdam

2a

YEARS OF EUROPEAN EXPLORATION

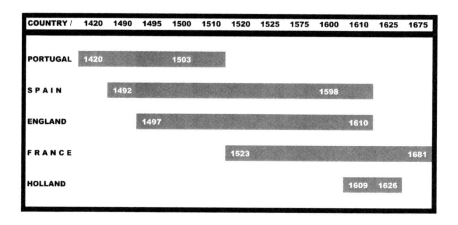

2b

EUROPEAN EXPLORATIONS
(SORT BY DATE)

EXPLORER	SPONSOR COUNTRY	DATES		EXPLORATION PURPOSE
VIVALDI BROS.	GENOA	1291	X	SEEK PASSAGE TO INDIA. FOLLOWS WEST AFRICAN COAST LOST AT SEA
PRINCE HENRY THE NAVIGATOR	PORTUGAL	1420	1460	DISCOVER ALL 8 ISLANDS OF THE AZORES ISLAND GROUPS
C. COLUMBUS	PORTUGAL	1484	X	REQUESTS KING OF PORTUGAL TO SEEK CIPANJU (JAPAN). REJECTED.
BARTHOLOMEW DIAZ	PORTUGAL	1487	1488	SEEKS INDIA. DISCOVERS CAPE OF GOOD HOPE. FORCED BY CREW TO RETURN HOME.
C. COLUMBUS	SPAIN	1492	1493	SEEKS ROUTE TO ASIA. REACHES BAHAMA'S, CUBA, HAITI.
C. COLUMBUS	SPAIN	1493	1496	2ND TRIP EXPLORE CANARY ISLANDS, PUERTO RICO, SANTO DOMINGO, JAMAICA
AMERIGO VESPUCCI	SPAIN	1497	1498	EXPLORES SOUTH AMERICAN COAST NEAR BRAZIL
JOHN CABOT	ENGLAND	1497	X	EXPLORES NORTH AMERICAN COAST, GIVES ENGLAND CLAIM TO NO. AMER.
VASCO DA GAMA	PORTUGAL	1498	1499	SEEKS INDIA VIA CAPE OF GOOD HOPE. RETURNS HOME WITH SPICES.
JOHN CABOT	ENGLAND	1498	DIED	2ND TRIP SEEKS CIPANJU VIA NEWFOUNDLAND, DELAWARE BAY, CHESAPEAKE BAY
C. COLUMBUS	SPAIN	1498	1500	3RD TRIP TO TRINIDAD, COAST OF ARGENTINA
AMERIGO VESPUCCI	SPAIN	1499	1500	2ND TRIP, EXPLORES VENEZUELA, RETURNS WITH PEARLS

PEDRO ALVAREZ CABRAL	PORTUGAL	1500	X	SEEKS INDIA BUT DISCOVERS COAST OF BRAZIL
GASPAR CORTE-REAL	PORTUGAL	1500	1501	EXPLORES LABRADOR AND NEWFOUNDLAND. LOST AT SEA.
C. COLUMBUS	SPAIN	1502	1504	4TH TRIP VISITS MARTINIQUE, CANARY ISLANDS, HISPANIOLA, HONDURAN COAST & PANAMA
AMERIGO VESPUCCI	PORTUGAL	1503	X	VISITS BRAZIL. NEW WORLD NAMED "AMERICA" FOR HIM
SEBASTIAN DE OCAMPO	SPAIN	1508	X	CIRCUMNAVIGATE CUBA. PROVES IT NOT CONNECTED TO ASIA MAINLAND
SEBASTIAN CABOT	ENGLAND	1509	X	CLAIMS TO REACH HUDSON BAY
JUAN PONCE DE LEON	SPAIN	1513	X	AWARDED PUERTO RICO IF CONQUER. SEEKS "FOUNTAIN OF YOUTH". EXPLORES BOTH FLORIDA COASTS.
VASCO NUNEZ DE BALBOA	SPAIN	1513	X	DISCOVERS ISTHMUS OF PANAMA. CLAIMS PACIFIC OCEAN FOR SPAIN. THOUGHT IT WAS INDIAN OCEAN.
ALVAREZ PINEDA	SPAIN	1519	X	EXPLORES GULF OF MEXICO FROM FLORIDA TO VERA CRUZ, MEXICO.
FERDINAND MAGELLAN	SPAIN	1519	1521	CIRCUMNAVIGATE GLOBE. DIES IN THE PHILLIPINES 1521.
HERNANDO CORTEZ	SPAIN	1519	1521	CAPTURES AZTECS OF MEXICO & CHIEF MONTEZUMA. SENDS TREASURES TO SPAIN
FRANCISCO DE GORDILLO	SPAIN	1521	X	EXPLORE ATLANTIC COAST FROM FLORIDA TO SOUTH CAROLINA
GIOVANNI VEERAZZANO	FRANCE	1524	X	SEEK NORTHWEST PASSAGE. REACH NORTH CAROLINA COAST, NEW YORK HARBOR, NARRAGANSETT BAY, AND NOVA SCOTIA
PANFILO DE NARVAEZ	SPAIN	1527	1528	LANDS NEAR TAMPA, FLORIDA. SEND TROOPS TO TALLAHASSEE. SAILS FOR MEXICO, SHIP SUNK. 2 CREW MEMBERS SURVIVE AND REACH MEX.

CABEZA DE VACA	SPAIN	1528	1536	SURVIVES NARVAEZ EXPEDITION. REACH MEXICO CITY 1536.
FRANCISCO PIZARRO	SPAIN	1531	1535	BEGINS CONQUEST OF PERU & INCA INDIANS
JACQUES CARTIER	FRANCE	1534	X	SEEKS NEWFOUNDLAND, DISCOVERS GASPE BAY, PRINCE EDWARD ISLAND
HERNANDO DE SOTO	SPAIN	1539	1542	EXPLORE FLORIDA, MISSISSIPPI RIVER VALLEY, ARKANSAS, OKLA.
FRANCISCO CORONADO	SPAIN	1540	1542	SEEKS MYTHICAL "7 CITIES OF GOLD" EXPLORES SOUTHWEST AMERICA, FOLLOWS ROUTE TO BE KNOWN AS "THE SANTA FE TRAIL" ON RETURN TO MEXICO. CLAIM LAND FOR SPAIN.
JACQUES CARTIER	FRANCE	1541	1542	SEEKS KINGDOM OF "SAQUENAY" FOR TREASURE. REACHES QUEBEC.
JUAN CABRILLO	SPAIN	1542	1543	EXPLORE CALIFORNIA COAST
BARTOLO FERRELO	SPAIN	1543	X	SUCCEEDS CABILLO, EXPLORES TO CALIFORNIA/OREGON BORDER
P. MENENDEZ	SPAIN	1565	X	EXPLORE/SETTLE ST. AUGUSTINE, FL.
MARTIN FROBISHER	ENGLAND	1576	X	SEEK NORTHWEST PASSAGE. VISITS GREENLAND, BAFFIN BAY. BELIEVES AREA IS NORTHWEST PASSAGE.
MARTIN FROBISHER	ENGLAND	1577	X	SAILS FOR MINING OPERATIONS IN BAFFIN BAY. RETURNS WITH ORE.
SIR FRANCIS DRAKE	ENGLAND	1577	1580	SEEKS NORTHWEST PASSAGE, CIRCUMNAVIGATES GLOBE, REACHES SAN FRANCISCO BAY
SIR HUMPHREY GILBERT	ENGLAND	1583	X	ATTEMPT COLONY IN NEWFOUNDLAND
JOHN DAVIS	ENGLAND	1585	1587	3 EXPEDITIONS SEEKING NORTHWEST PASSAGE. REACH LABRADOR, BAFFIN BAY, AND NORTHEAST CANADA
SIR WALTER RALEIGH	ENGLAND	1585	1587	3 EXPEDITIONS TO ROANOKE ISLAND, NORTH CAROLINA, TO COLONIZE
JUAN DE ONATE	SPAIN	1598	X	EXPLORE FROM KANSAS TO GULF OF CALIFORNIA, DISCOVER SANTA FE 1609

SAMUEL DE CHAMPLAIN	FRANCE	1608	11 TRIPS	EXPLORES NORTH AMERICAN COAST, NEW YORK, EASTERN CANADA, FOUNDS QUEBEC CITY.
HENRY HUDSON	ENGLAND	1608	X	SEEKS NORTHWEST PASSAGE
HENRY HUDSON	HOLLAND	1609	X	SEEKS NORTHWEST PASSAGE, ENTERS NEW YORK HARBOR, EXPLORE NORTH ON HUDSON RIVER
HENRY HUDSON	ENGLAND	1610	1611	SEEK NORTHWEST PASSAGE, EXPLORE HUDSON BAY, JAMES BAY. ON WAY HOME IS SET ADRIFT BY OWN CREW, BELIEVED BY SOME HISTORIANS
DUTCH WEST INDIA CO.	HOLLAND	1621	1625	SETTLES NEW AMSTERDAM (NEW YORK CITY), COLONY OF NEW NETHERLAND (NEW YORK)
PETER MINUIT	SWEDEN	1638	X	SETTLES FORT CHRISTINA NEAR PRESENT-DAY WILMINGTON, DEL.
FATHER MARQUETTE & LOUIS JOLIET	FRANCE	1673	X	EXPLORES MISSISSIPPI RIVER VALLEY
SIEUR DE LA SALLE	FRANCE	1681	1687	CLAIMS MISSISSIPPI RIVER VALLEY FOR FRANCE

2c

E U R O P E A N   E X P L O R A T I O N S
(Sort by Sponsor Nation & Date)

EXPLORER	SPONSOR COUNTRY	DATES		EXPLORATION PURPOSE
JOHN CABOT	ENGLAND	1497	X	EXPLORES NORTH AMERICAN COAST, GIVES ENGLAND CLAIM TO NO. AMER.
JOHN CABOT	ENGLAND	1498	DIED	2ND TRIP SEEKS CIPANJU VIA NEWFOUNDLAND, DELAWARE BAY, AND CHESAPEAKE BAY
SEBASTIAN CABOT	ENGLAND	1509	X	CLAIMS TO REACH HUDSON BAY
MARTIN FROBISHER	ENGLAND	1576	X	SEEK NORTHWEST PASSAGE. VISITS GREENLAND, BAFFIN BAY. BELIEVES AREA IS NORTHWEST PASSAGE.
MARTIN FROBISHER	ENGLAND	1577	X	SAILS FOR MINING OPERATIONS IN BAFFIN BAY. RETURNS WITH ORE.
SIR FRANCIS DRAKE	ENGLAND	1577	1580	SEEKS NORTHWEST PASSAGE, CIRCUMNAVIGATES GLOBE, REACHES SAN FRANCISCO BAY.
SIR HUMPHREY GILBERT	ENGLAND	1583	X	ATTEMPT COLONY IN NEWFOUNDLAND
JOHN DAVIS	ENGLAND	1585	1587	3 EXPEDITIONS SEEKING NORTHWEST PASSAGE. REACH LABRADOR, BAFFIN BAY, AND NORTHEAST CANADA.
SIR WALTER RALEIGH	ENGLAND	1585	1587	3 EXPEDITIONS TO ROANOKE ISLAND, NORTH CAROLINA, TO COLONIZE.
HENRY HUDSON	ENGLAND	1608	X	SEEKS NORTHWEST PASSAGE
HENRY HUDSON	ENGLAND	1610	1611	SEEK NORTHWEST PASSAGE, EXPLORE HUDSON BAY AND JAMES BAY. ON WAY HOME IS SET ADRIFT BY OWN CREW, BELIEVED BY SOME HISTORIANS,
GIOVANNI VERAZZANO	FRANCE	1524	X	SEEK NORTHWEST PASSAGE. REACH NORTH CAROLINA COAST, NEW YORK HARBOR, NARRAGANSETT BAY, AND NOVA SCOTIA.
JACQUES CARTIER	FRANCE	1534	X	SEEKS NEWFOUNDLAND, DISCOVERS GASPE BAY, PRINCE EDWARD ISLAND

JACQUES CARTIER	FRANCE	1541	1542	SEEKS KINGDOM OF "SAQUENAY" FOR TREASURE. REACHES QUEBEC
SAMUEL DE CHAMPLAIN	FRANCE	1608	11 TRIPS	EXPLORES NORTH AMERICAN COAST, NEW YORK, EASTERN CANADA, FOUNDS QUEBEC CITY.
FATHER MARQUETTE & LOUIS JOLIET	FRANCE	1673	X	EXPLORES MISSISSIPPI RIVER VALLEY
SIEUR DE LA SALLE	FRANCE	1681	1687	CLAIMS MISSISSIPPI RIVER VALLEY FOR FRANCE
HENRY HUDSON	HOLLAND	1609	X	SEEKS NORTHWEST PASSAGE, ENTERS NEW YORK HARBOR, EXPLORE NORTH ON HUDSON RIVER
DUTCH WEST INDIA COMPANY	HOLLAND	1621	1625	SETTLES NEW AMSTERDAM (NEW YORK CITY), COLONY OF NEW NETHERLAND (NEW YORK)
PRINCE HENRY THE NAVIGATOR	PORTUGAL	1420	1460	DISCOVER ALL 8 ISLANDS OF THE AZORES ISLAND GROUP
C. COLUMBUS	PORTUGAL	1484	X	REQUESTS KING OF PORTUGAL TO SEEK CIPANJU (JAPAN). REJECTED.
BARTHOLOMEW DIAZ	PORTUGAL	1487	1488	SEEKS INDIA. DISCOVERS CAPE OF GOOD HOPE. FORCED BY CREW TO RETURN HOME.
VASCO DA GAMA	PORTUGAL	1498	1499	SEEKS INDIA VIA CAPE OF GOOD HOPE. RETURNS HOME WITH SPICES.
PEDRO ALVAREZ CABRAL	PORTUGAL	1500	X	SEEKS INDIA BUT DISCOVERS COAST OF BRAZIL
GASPAR CORTE-REAL	PORTUGAL	1500	1501	EXPLORES LABRADOR AND NEWFOUNDLAND. LOST AT SEA.
AMERIGO VESPUCCI	PORTUGAL	1503	X	VISITS BRAZIL. NEW WORLD NAMED "AMERICA" FOR HIM.

C. COLUMBUS	SPAIN	1492	1493	SEEKS ROUTE TO ASIA. REACHES BAHAMA'S, CUBA, HAITI.
C. COLUMBUS	SPAIN	1493	1496	2ND TRIP EXPLORE CANARY ISLANDS, PUERTO RICO, SANTO DOMINGO, AND JAMAICA.
AMERIGO VESPUCCI	SPAIN	1497	1498	EXPLORES SOUTH AMERICAN COAST NEAR BRAZIL
C. COLUMBUS	SPAIN	1498	1500	3RD TRIP TO TRINIDAD, COAST OF ARGENTINA.
AMERIGO VESPUCCI	SPAIN	1499	1500	2ND TRIP, EXPLORES VENEZUELA, RETURNS WITH PEARLS.
C. COLUMBUS	SPAIN	1502	1504	4TH TRIP VISITS MARTINIQUE, CANARY ISLANDS, HISPANIOLA, HONDURAN COAST & PANAMA.
SEBASTIAN DE OCAMPO	SPAIN	1508	X	CIRCUMNAVIGATE CUBA. PROVES IT NOT CONNECTED TO ASIA MAINLAND.
JUAN PONCE DE LEON	SPAIN	1513	X	AWARDED PUERTO RICO IF CONQUER. SEEKS "FOUNTAIN OF YOUTH". EXPLORES BOTH FLORIDA COASTS.
VASCO NUNEZ DE BALBOA	SPAIN	1513	X	DISCOVERS ISTHMUS OF PANAMA. CLAIMS PACIFIC OCEAN FOR SPAIN. THOUGHT IT WAS INDIAN OCEAN.
ALVAREZ PINEDA	SPAIN	1519	X	EXPLORES GULF OF MEXICO FROM FLORIDA TO VERA CRUZ, MEXICO
FERDINAND MAGELLAN	SPAIN	1519	1521	CIRCUMNAVIGATE GLOBE. DIES IN THE PHILLIPINES 1521.
HERNANDO CORTEZ	SPAIN	1519	1521	CAPTURES AZTECS OF MEXICO & CHIEF MONTEZUMA. SENDS TREASURES TO SPAIN.

FRANCISCO DE GORDILLO	SPAIN	1521	X	EXPLORE ATLANTIC COAST FROM FLORIDA TO SOUTH CAROLINA
PANFILO DE NARVAEZ	SPAIN	1527	1528	LANDS NEAR TAMPA, FLORIDA. SEND TROOPS TO TALLAHASSEE. SAILS FOR MEXICO, SHIP SUNK. 2 CREW MEMBERS SURVIVE AND REACH MEXICO.
CABEZA DE VACA	SPAIN	1528	1536	SURVIVES NARVAEZ EXPEDITION. REACH MEXICO CITY 1536.
FRANCISCO PIZARRO	SPAIN	1531	1535	BEGINS CONQUEST OF PERU & INCA INDIANS.
HERNANDO DE SOTO	SPAIN	1539	1542	EXPLORE FLORIDA, MISSISSIPPI RIVER VALLEY, ARKANSAS, OKLAHOMA.
FRANCISCO CORONADO	SPAIN	1540	1542	SEEKS MYTHICAL "7 CITIES OF GOLD" EXPLORES SOUTHWEST AMERICA, FOLLOWS ROUTE TO BE KNOWN AS "THE SANTA FE TRAIL" ON RETURN TO MEXICO. CLAIM LAND FOR SPAIN.
JUAN CABRILLO	SPAIN	1542	1543	EXPLORE CALIFORNIA COAST
BARTOLO FERRELO	SPAIN	1543	X	SUCCEEDS CABILLO, EXPLORES TO CALIFORNIA/OREGON BORDER.
P. MENENDEZ	SPAIN	1565	X	EXPLORE/SETTLE ST. AUGUSTINE, FL.
JUAN DE ONATE	SPAIN	1598	X	EXPLORE FROM KANSAS TO GULF OF CALIFORNIA, DISCOVER SANTA FE 1609

Chapter 3

Reasons for European Settlement & Colonization

A.   REASONS FOR EUROPEAN COLONIZATION

Each European nation had its own reasons for developing a colonization strategy, such as:

- **Political**

- **Religious**

- **Economic/profit**

- **Competition for commercial advantage as an instrument of national power**

- **Export their culture**

1. POLITICAL
   During the 17th century the struggle between the English Stuart Monarchs and Parliament for control of the government created considerable political conflict. It contributed to significant emigration to America. The same situation existed in France because of the absolute power of the French Monarchs.

2. RELIGIOUS
   Frequent religious wars and persecutions forced many people to immigrate to the New World for safety and freedom of worship. During this time, the 17th century, discrimination and

persecution in England were directed at Catholics, Quakers, and Puritans. Similarly, in 1649, members of the Anglican Church were also driven either into hiding or exile.

The Protestant Reformation created many diverse and dissenting Sects of Protestantism who sought to worship according to their own wishes and preferences rather than accept the religious conformity required by the Anglican Church. The non-conforming Sects were persecuted by the various governments.

3. ECONOMIC/PROFIT

Wealthy businessmen sought opportunities to invest money in "joint-stock" companies which sold shares of stock to adventurers allowing them to share in the expense and risk of founding colonies as business enterprises. As we learned, national mercantilism was the means of accumulating wealth. It also stressed the goal of economic self-sufficiency, producing their own raw materials rather than purchasing them from other nations while also creating overseas markets for their products.

4. COMMERCIAL DEVELOPMENT AS AN INSTRUMENT OF NATIONAL POWER

The competition for national wealth and power naturally led to competition for colonization, as well. In England, it was Sir Humphrey Gilbert who first recognized the benefit of using overseas colonies as bases from which to attack their rivals and diminish their national wealth.

The French participated in this activity as well by establishing Forts in the Mississippi river valley to counteract the Spanish influence. So, the Spanish did the same to the French in the lower Mississippi river valley, near the mouth of the river.

5. EXPORT THEIR CULTURE

England was very anxious to convert the Native Indians to Christianity, or, more specifically, to Protestantism before the Spanish and/or French, converted them to Roman Catholicism.

(Attachment 3a represents a comparison of the major European nations' colonization efforts.)

B. VARIOUS COUNTRIES' COLONIZATION EFFORTS

1. SPAIN

   Settlers brought to Haiti on the second Columbus voyage in 1493 founded the first permanent Spanish colony in the Americas. By 1515, Spain had also occupied Puerto Rico, Jamaica, and Cuba. These colonies served as bases for the extension of the Spanish empire to the mainland of America where the centers of Spanish control were established.

   To oppose the French occupation on the east coast of Florida, the Spanish founded the colony of St. Augustine in 1565 which was the first white settlement within the boundaries of America. This colony was near failure until the 1590's when the Franciscan and Jesuit missionaries established "missions" to convert and civilize the Indians. By 1606, the missionaries controlled the coast as far north as the Carolina's.

   Other settlement efforts in Florida included those of Fray Juan de Silva in 1595 with a number of missions in northern Florida, the Georgia and South Carolina coast, and the interior of Georgia. Hostilities with local Indians caused all of the missions north of St. Augustine to be abandoned. A retaliatory attack on the Indians produced a Peace Treaty in 1600. This period of peace brought the creation of more missions in the region. Despite another Indian uprising in 1647, 38 missions were established and approximately 26,000 Indians were at least partly converted by 1655.

Colonization efforts in the southwest included:

a. 1598 New Mexico

b. 1609 Santa Fe

Several missions were founded in the early 18th century to minimize French influence in Louisiana and Texas:

c. 1718 San Antonio became the center of Spanish influence in Texas

d. 1769 San Diego, California

The settlement of New Mexico occurred at the same time as the first permanent English colony in the New World, Jamestown, Virginia. Well before then, the Spanish had conquered almost all of South America. In one generation, Spain acquired more new territory than did Rome in 5 centuries and they organized whatever they conquered, including an Indian population more numerous and advanced than did the English and French, and managed to incorporate them into their society.

Spain had more than a century head-start on English and French colonization efforts and their results were the envy of Europe at the time. Spanish prestige reached its height in 1580 when King Philip succeeded to the Throne of Portugal as well as Spain, uniting the 2 empires which occupied a major part of the world. At that time, no other nation had placed a single permanent settler on the shores of the New World.

The authority of the Spanish King was supreme with a strict and highly regulated mercantilist policy strongly enforced. Foreigners were excluded from trade with the colonies and trade with Spain was under strict governmental control. Initially, the Spanish King entrusted the conquest and colonization of new lands to the "conquistadors", such as Hernando Cortez. Military leaders were given permission to establish economic and political control over the native populations by "grants of encomiendas" (huge landed estates). Later missions and military posts, or "presidio's", became the instrument for the extension of Spanish rule on the frontier. To govern their colonies, a "Council of the Indies" was created in Spain which placed the colonies under 2 "Viceroys", New Spain in 1535 and Peru in 1544. The Crown appointed all officials and governed autocratically. These territories were subdivided into provinces, "audiencias". Each had its own appointed Governor and an administrative-judicial tribunal. The laws of Spain were followed and all important decisions were made in Spain. Any action taken in the Spanish colonies could be reversed as no self-government was allowed in the colonies. Although the "Council of the Indies" handled political administration, the "House of Trade" (Casa de Contratacion) exerted tight control over commercial matters.

By 1600, before the English had made their first permanent settlement, Spanish colonists in the New World numbered about 200,000. Spain gave the New World her culture, notably her language and religion, Catholicism, and only Catholics were allowed to settle in its colonies where great Cathedrals and Church-related universities were built. Missionaries were active in attempting to convert the native Indians to Catholicism. Spanish settlers intermarried with Indians and their offspring were called "mestizo's". The Spanish introduced wheat, barley, and domestic animals such as horses and cattle and fruit-bearing trees. They also introduced the feudal European system of land-holding where the King granted large estates to Spanish noblemen. These estates were first worked by the Indians but, later, the large plantation owners used Negro slaves imported from Africa. Mestizo's were also used and often treated as slaves.

Colonial merchants were allowed to trade only with Spain, consistent with its mercantilist policy of using their colonies to develop and increase its national wealth. From her colonies, Spain obtained gold and silver which helped it become a national power during the 16th and most of the 17th centuries.

With the defeat of the Spanish Armada on 8/8/1588, Spain began to lose its national power and influence as well as the reduction of its' national wealth. But they did leave behind their culture, architecture, religion and language. Yet, its' successes led 3 other nations to acquire their own colonial possessions.

2. FRANCE

The Papal division of the world per the Treaty of Tordesillas between Spain & Portugal did little to stop other nations from exploration and colonization. The French King was among those who were not deterred.

Beginning in 1504 the French explored the Canadian & Newfoundland coasts to set up fishing and fur trading posts. The explorations of Verazzano and Cartier gave France access to the St. Lawrence River valley and gave France a claim to Canada. The fur trade led to the colonization of Quebec, founded by Champlain in 1608, which was the first permanent French settlement in Canada.

Previous attempts by the French to establish a permanent colony in the area were made on Saint Croix Island (Maine) in 1604 and at Port Royal, Nova Scotia, on the Bay of Fundy, in 1605. Both settlements were temporary but they mark the beginnings of a French presence in the area that the French called Acadie (Acadia) which today includes eastern Maine and the Canadian provinces of New Brunswick, Nova Scotia, and Prince Edward Island.

The 1604 expedition was led by a merchant adventurer named Sieur de Monts which included Samuel de Champlain. During the summer and early fall of 1604, Champlain explored the mid-Maine coast and up the Penobscot River in search of the mythical city of Norumbega. They settled at Saint Croix Island but a bitter winter caused them to abandon the site after the deaths of 35 settlers. During the summer of 1605 they sailed south as far as Cape Cod. On their return, they removed the settlement across the Bay of Fundy to Port-Royal where it was intended to be a significant trading post. During 1606/1607, Champlain continued to explore but just as the new colony at Port-Royal was beginning to succeed, the French Crown revoked De Monts' charter and later in the summer all of the settlers left for France. Unknown to the French, the English had already begun their settlement at Jamestown, Virginia, and would soon settle at Plymouth, Massachusetts in 1620.

Champlain founded Quebec 7/3/1608 and led another expedition in 1613 to re-occupy Port Royal as a fur-trading and missionary post but it was beyond repair so a missionary station was created in present-day Maine only to be destroyed later that year along with the total destruction of Port Royal.

In the St. Lawrence River valley the French and Dutch were in conflict over the fur-trade plus they were on opposite sides in the Indian rivalry between the Hurons and Iroquois.

Such was the tense situation among the European powers in North America during the early 17th century. It wasn't until many years later that settlements followed French explorers throughout the Great Lakes and Mississippi river valley. In the previous chapter we learned of the travels of Father Marquette and Louis Joliet in 1673 and the explorations of De la Salle in 1682.

By 1750 "New France", as their colonial territories were called, held only 80,000 white settlers primarily because no gold or silver was known to exist in their areas. France restricted emigration to Catholics only and their primary interest was in the fur-trade. The land did not lend itself to farming and the government of France did not promote the idea of self-government.

Throughout their vast areas of exploration they founded missions, trading posts, and agricultural settlements, established good relations with the Indians, primarily through the fur-trade, until Champlain angered the Iroquois when he supported the Algonquin tribe in an attack on the Iroquois in 1609. The Iroquois became allies of the Dutch and English and were used by those nations to help prevent French expansion south of Montreal.

France lost its possessions in North America as a result of the French-Indian war, 1754-1763, but, like the Spanish, much of their culture remained in Quebec and Louisiana.

3. HOLLAND

    Holland was a small but wealthy nation which meant that not many of their citizens felt the need to emigrate to a New World. In order to encourage settlement, the government supported the "patroon system" which granted large tracts of land to settlers who brought with them 50 families of tenants at their own expense. The "patroons" had full control over all government of the settlement including holding court. Holland did not restrict emigration to certain religious groups or impose other emigration restrictions.

In 1602, Dutch capitalists formed the Dutch West India Company to manage Holland's exploration and colonization efforts. They sponsored the 1609 voyage of Henry Hudson to explore the Hudson River valley which did not turn out to be the sought-after Northwest Passage but did become an important waterway to the richest fur-bearing region south of the St. Lawrence River.

By 1626, the Dutch settlements at New Amsterdam (New York) and New Netherlands were developing and by 1629 the government tried to encourage further settlement by issuing a "Charter of Privileges" which established more "Patroons" and land ownership.

Eventually, the directors of the West India Company claimed the best lands and power in the Hudson River valley and became the most influential people in the area.

Peter Stuyvesant was primarily responsible for enlarging New Netherland at the expense of his neighbors. In 1655 he annexed the colony of New Sweden, located near present-day Wilmington, Delaware.

The English were their chief rivals and the English felt the same way about the Dutch in the New World and especially along the Atlantic coast. In 1664 an English fleet appeared off New Amsterdam and ordered the Dutch to surrender. Governor Stuyvesant surrendered and New Netherland became New York under the English. The population of the city reached only 1500 and the entire colony less than 7000 under the Dutch. By the 1660's the colony contained settlers speaking 18 different languages although the total population did not exceed 10,000 at that time. Dutch influence is still seen in parts of New York in town names, architecture, and churches.

4. ENGLAND

England was motivated to colonize for many of the same reasons as were the other European nations. They began later than their rivals because of domestic issues and European conflicts which also spread to North America. They couldn't just set up their colonies wherever they wished because, for example, Spain dominated South America, Mexico, the West Indies, the American southwest and Florida. France had focused on major waterways of North America like the St. Lawrence, Mississippi, and upper Hudson River valleys. Also, dense forests and hostile Indians prevented settlers from moving west beyond the Appalachian Mountains. For this reason the original 13 colonies were located primarily along the Atlantic coast bordered by the mountains to the west.

King Henry VII, the first Monarch of the House of Tudor, had been second only to King Ferdinand and Queen Isabella of Spain in New World discovery so it may seem strange that England was so slow to follow up on their explorations. Cabot found no passage to Asia and reported nothing of value in the lands he discovered and England was fearful of Spain. The English Kings lacked revenues to sponsor extensive exploration and colonization efforts plus they were dependent upon Parliament with whom they were often in conflict for appropriations. They also needed time to accumulate venture capital so individuals could finance their own overseas enterprises.

During the reign of Queen Elizabeth I (1558-1603), England finally began a course of expansion, most of which failed. Conflict with Spain at sea, attacking their treasure ships, was seen as a higher priority than searching for routes to Asia or founding expensive colonies.

It was through the efforts of Sir Humphrey Gilbert and Sir Francis Drake who began the successful colonization efforts of England during the latter years of the 16th century.

Throughout the 17th century there was constant conflict between the powers of the Crown and those of Parliament. In succession, England experienced a Civil War (1642-1645), the beheading of King Charles I (1649), a Puritan military dictatorship under Oliver Cromwell (1649-1658), the Restoration of the Stuart Kings (1660), and then the final overthrow of the Stuart rule by the Glorius Revolution of 1688-1689 when William and Mary ascended to the throne.

The English government generally followed the theory of mercantilism, as did the other European nations, which believed that colonies existed for the purpose of enriching the mother country. If regulated along mercantilist lines, colonies would assure raw materials and markets for English manufacturers, trade for English merchants, and revenues for the English treasury.

It was a combination of these factors which led England to found 10 colonies along the Atlantic coast and also formed 3 colonies out of New Netherlands which she seized from the Dutch in 1664. These 13 colonies formed the basis of our country.

a.   *The Joint-Stock Company*

As we will examine in Chapter 4 the first English colonies in America were planned, financed, and settled by "joint-stock companies" which grouped many small investors into one joint or common-stock unit which was administered by a Governor, Treasurer, and other officers elected by the stockholders at quarterly meetings in London for the purpose of establishing overseas trading posts and colonies. The ultimate motive was profit and the secondary goal was the settlement on lands granted by the Kings. Some of these companies were:

1.   The Virginia Company (Includes the London Company and the Plymouth Company)
The "Virginia Company" refers collectively to a pair of English joint-stock companies chartered by King James I on 4/10/1606 for the purpose of establishing posts on the coast of North America.
The 2 companies were named the "Virginia Company of London" (The London Company) and the "Virginia Company

of Plymouth" (The Plymouth Company) and operated with identical charters but with differing territories. An area of overlapping territory was created and within that area, the 2 companies were not permitted to establish colonies within 100 miles of each other.

The charters of both companies called for a local council for each but with ultimate authority residing with the King through the Council of Virginia in England.

2. The London Company was permitted, by terms of the charter, to establish a colony of 100 square miles between the 34th and 41st latitude, or approximately from Cape Fear, North Carolina, to Long Island Sound.

3. The Plymouth Company was permitted, by terms of the charter, to establish settlements between the 38th and 45th latitude, roughly between the upper Chesapeake Bay and the current U.S.-Canada border. This company never fulfilled its charter and its territory later became New England which was also claimed by France.

4. The Massachusetts Bay Company was eventually responsible for the settlement and colonization of the Massachusetts Bay.

b. *Types of English Charters*

Many of the political institutions of England were transmitted to America through these company charters during the colonial period. The privileges of self-government granted by colonial charter combined with governmental neglect by England permitted the colonials to enjoy a relatively large degree of freedom. There were 3 types of colonies classified according to their charters which served as constitutions for the colonies. The English colonists in America retained the ancient rights and privileges of the King's subjects at home, as follows:

• ROYAL CHARTERS were created when the colonies were deprived of their earlier charters and brought directly under Royal administration. They were not used as an instrument for colonization since the King did not directly engage in establishing colonies. The governor plus the council (upper house) were appointed by the King while the voters elected the lower house, except for Massachusetts where they were appointed.

- PROPRIETARY CHARTERS were of 2 types, founded either by Joint-stock companies or by one or more individuals. Only 4 of the 13 colonies were begun as joint-stock companies but 7 were founded as proprietorships, including Georgia and New York. The Governor was appointed by the Proprietor and eligible voters elected by the colonial assembly.

  Pennsylvania, Maryland, and Delaware began with land grants from the English government. Individuals were awarded huge tracts of land to supervise and govern, usually in return for political or financial favors. They reported directly to the King.

- SELF-GOVERNING CHARTERS differed from the others in that they were held *in America* which gave the colonists greater local control of their political and financial affairs. The Governor and both houses of the legislature were elected directly or indirectly by the voters.

  Rhode Island and Connecticut were of this type of charter which was given to a joint-stock company which then set up its own government independent of the Crown although the King could revoke the charter at any time and convert it to a Royal colony.

c. *Undemocratic Aspects*

In Royal and Proprietary colonies the colonists had minimal voice in the selection of the Governor who retained the right of veto of laws passed by the Assembly plus the right to appoint lesser colonial officials. In the southern colonies the Governor appointed county agents and other local officials but the English Crown retained the right to review and reject any law passed in the colonies. In many colonies the voters had to meet certain religious qualifications and in all colonies the landless urban dwellers could not meet the property qualifications for voting. Frontier settlers living in danger and isolation found it difficult to vote and were under-represented in colonial assemblies. Membership in Assemblies were restricted to the well-to-do by the high property qualifications for office-holding.

d. *Democratic Aspects*

The legal rights of colonists were protected by colonial judges who followed English Common Law. They were protected against tyranny by the separation of governmental powers. The theory was that with power divided between the Royal Governor, which represented the Crown, and a Colonial Assembly which represented the settlers, neither branch could become too powerful. The colonial assembly was elected by the qualified voters and its' consent was necessary to enact laws such as to levy taxes and/or dispense funds. The assemblies had some control over the Executive by the "power of the purse", meaning the Assembly was responsible for raising revenues and writing legislation to spend those revenues. In fact, they were responsible for paying the Governor's salary.

e. *Colonial Government Organization*

The governments of all the colonies were generally similar. The office of the Governor was the executive head of the joint-stock business corporation but was transformed into a political position. The Governor was assisted by his "council" which was chosen in the same manner as the Governor, except in Massachusetts where the Council was chosen by the general court.

The Governor exercised the traditional powers of the Executive function. He enforced the laws, appointed officials and held veto power over acts of the colonial legislatures, and headed the militia. ***His position was very difficult since he had to execute the orders of those who appointed him but his salary and appropriations came from the local assemblies.***

There was no clear-cut separation of powers among the 3 branches of government. The Governor and his Council sat as the highest court. The Council sat as the upper house of the legislature while the Assembly, or lower House, consisted of members elected by the eligible voters.

The Assemblies engaged in periodic quarrels with the Governor and used their power of appropriations to force concessions from the Governor. Voting and office-holding qualifications were very restricted. Only males could vote and religious qualifications prevented many from participation. In spite of this, suffrage was broader than in England.

C. KEY DATES & SIGNIFICANT EVENTS

1565   First permanent European colony in North America founded at St. Augustine, Florida, by Spain.

1588   England defeats Spanish Armada

1609   Dutch East India Company sponsors a 7 month voyage of exploration to North America by Henry Hudson

1613   Dutch trading post established on lower Manhattan Island

1629   In England, King Charles I dissolves Parliament and attempts to rule as absolute Monarch causing many English to emigrate for America

1640   English Civil War and Cromwell period until 1660

1660   Charles I becomes King of England until 1685

1685   James II becomes King of England until 1688

1689   William & Mary assume the Throne. Pass Bill of Rights.

D.   REVIEW QUESTIONS

(Multiple Choice)

1. An important motive of English and other voyages of exploration in the 16th century was:
   a. the need for more geographic information
   b. the search for better agricultural lands
   c. scientific curiosity
   d. the desire for a direct water route westward from Europe to Asia

2. Early attempts of the English to colonize in America failed because of:
   a. war with Spain and a lack of experience
   b. early colonies were destroyed by Spain
   c. most colonizing expeditions were lost at sea
   d. recruits for the colonies could not be found

3. The 2 most important motives of English colonization of America were:
   a. love of adventure and religious rivalry with Spain
   b. the need to establish religious freedom and military bases against Spain
   c. the desire for religious freedom and economic opportunity
   d. the love of adventure and need to achieve a favorable balance of trade

4. English colonization differed from that of other colonizing nations in America because:
    a. English colonists enjoyed a greater degree of neglect and freedom from the Mother Country interference
    b. more attention was given to developing fishing and lumbering enterprises
    c. more aid was given by the Mother Country
    d. salutary regulation and helpful paternalism provided sound foundation

5. Which colonizing nation created the first permanent settlement in mainland America?
    a. England
    b. Holland
    c. Spain
    d. France

6. Which colonizing nation created the "Council of the Indies" to manage the political administration of its overseas possessions?
    a. France
    b. Holland
    c. Portugal
    d. Spain

7. Which French explorer founded Quebec?
    a. De La Salle
    b. Champlain
    c. Cartier
    d. Father Marquette & Louis Joliet

8. What did the Dutch "Patroon System" attempt to accomplish?
    a. Provide incentives to settlement
    b. Provide government in colonial possessions
    c. Establish trading relationships with the Indians
    d. Expand fur-trading ventures into New England

9. Which of the following English Monarchs was primarily responsible for English colonization?
   a. King Henry VII
   b. Queen Elizabeth I
   c. King Charles I
   d. William & Mary

10. Which type of government charter provided the King with the most direct control of the colonial settlements?
    a. Royal Charter
    b. Proprietary Charter
    c. Self-Governing Charter
    d. The Virginia Company

(True or False)

11. A single "Viceroy" ruled the Spanish colonies in America
    a. TRUE
    b. FALSE

12. The profitable fur-trade caused the French to spread rapidly over the area they came to control.
    a. TRUE
    b. FALSE

13. The Dutch settled in America to gain control of land for speculative purposes.
    a. TRUE
    b. FALSE

14. After Elizabeth I became Queen, the rivalry over religion and empire began in earnest between England and Spain.
    a. TRUE
    b. FALSE

15. Royal Charters were often used as instruments for initiating new colonies.
    a. TRUE
    b. FALSE

16. The office of the colonial Governor originated as the leading official of the Joint-Stock Corporation.
    a. TRUE
    b. FALSE

17. The England's long experience in ruling overseas colonies found her well prepared to successfully govern the American colonies.
    a. TRUE
    b. FALSE

E.   GLOSSARY

1. **Religious "sect"**   A smaller group which exists within a larger religion, a "section".

2. **Conquistadors**   16th century warriors and soldiers. The word means "conquerors".

CHAPTER 3 SUMMARY

REASONS FOR EUROPEAN SETTLEMENT & COLONIZATION

A. **PRIMARY MOTIVATION OF THE MAJOR EUROPEAN NATIONS**

1. Political

2. Religious

3. Economic/Profit

4. Commercial development as instrument of national power

5. Export their culture

B. **SPAIN**

1. Competition with Portugal and England, primarily

2. St. Augustine, 1565, the first permanent white settlement within America

3. Colonization led by "Conquistadors", military leaders with full governmental powers

4. King maintains control through a "Council of the Indies" with the colonies placed under the control of 2 "Viceroys" and a "House of Trade" controlled commercial matters

5. By 1600, Spanish Colonists in the new world numbered 200,000 before England had made their first permanent settlement

6. Spain began to lose its power and influence with defeat of Spanish Armada in 1588

C.   **FRANCE**

1. French King did not recognize authority of "Treaty of Tordesillas" between Spain and Portugal

2. Earliest settlements along Northeast Coast of Canada, 1604-1605 in present-day Nova Scotia

3. First permanent settlement at Quebec City 1608

4. Holland is primary fur-trade rival in St. Lawrence River Valley

5. By 1750, "New France" population of 80,000 white settlers; Government restricts immigration to Catholics only. Region does not lend itself to farming; fishing/fur-trading primary.

6. Maintain good Indian relations except for Iroquois because of Samuel de Champlain efforts

D.   **HOLLAND**

1. Small, wealthy nation, not many citizens feel need to immigrate

2. Holland uses "Patroon System" to encourage immigration, no restrictions on who could immigrate

3. Dutch capitalists form "Dutch West India Company" to manage nation's exploration and colonization efforts

4. Sponsor Henry Hudson exploration of Hudson River Valley and found Fort Orange (Albany) and New Amsterdam (New York)

5. Primary interest in fur trade; chief rival to England

6. Peter Stuyvesant significant in enlarging New Netherlands at the expense of other colonies

7. England takes control of New Netherland in 1644

E.   **ENGLAND**

1.   Began colonization efforts later than other nations due to national rivalries, domestic issues, Indian relations, financial problems, and difficult relations with parliament

2.   Queen Elizabeth primarily responsible for first attempt by English government to expand colonization, but fails

3.   Sir Humphrey Gilbert and Sir Francis Drake most responsible for successful colonization efforts; they followed the principles of "mercantilism" to justify their efforts

4.   Utilize the "Joint-stock Company" to begin colonization efforts through the Virginia Company

5.   3 types of Colonial Charters used: Royal, Proprietary, and Self-governing

Terrence Hagen

3a

COMPARATIVE COLONIZATION EFFORTS

CATEGORY	S P A I N	E N G L A N D	F R A N C E
EXTENT OF POSSESSIONS	MOST OF WEST INDIES, MEXICO, FLORIDA, CENTRAL AMERICA EXCEPT BRAZIL, SOUTHWEST AMERICA	LONG NARROW STRIP OF LAND ALONG ATLANTIC COAST FROM CAROLINA TO FLORIDA	HUDSON BAY REGION OF CANADA, GREAT LAKES REGION, MISSISSIPPI RIVER VALLEY TO NEW ORLEANS
MOTIVES	DEVELOP POWER THROUGH ACQUISITION OF TERRITORY, TRADE, AND GOLD	LOCATE BETTER ECONOMIC OPPORTUNITIES, FREEDOM FROM POLITICAL OPPRESSION, AND RELIGIOUS PERSECUTION	DEVELOP TRADE AND CONVERT THE INDIANS TO CATHOLICISM
GOVERNMENT	POLITICAL DESPOTISM DIRECTED BY CENTRAL GOVERNMENT OF SPAIN	LARGE MEASURE OF SELF-GOVERNMENT UNDER BRITISH GOVERNMENT CONTROL	PATERNALISTIC, ABSOLUTE RULE WITH NO SELF-GOVERNMENT
INDUSTRIES	MINES & LARGE PLANTATIONS, USE NEGRO & INDIAN SLAVES	MAINLY AGRICULTURAL PLUS OTHER ACTIVITIES SUCH AS FISHING, TRADING, AND SHIP-BUILDING	HUNTING, TRAPPING, FUR-TRADING. NO ATTEMPT AT PERMANENT SETTLEMENTS EXCEPT IN CANADA
SOCIAL CONDITIONS	ROMAN CATHOLIC RELIGION. SPANISH CULTURE EXTENDED THROUGH THE CHURCH AND PUBLICATION OF BOOKS	MINIMAL RELIGIOUS TOLERANCE TOWARD NON-ANGLICANS.	ROMAN CATHOLIC RELIGION. MINIMAL EFFORT AT EXTENDING FRENCH CULTURE

Chapter 4

17TH Century England

As stated in the Introduction, we cannot appreciate American colonial history without a basic understanding of British history during that period of time. Not only were a large percentage of the early settlers from England, but they brought with them their English customs, habits, and ideas about government and laws. Those English influences became imbedded within the American fabric.

A.   ORIGINS OF THE ENGLISH PEOPLE

The origin of the English people came from many sources: Stone-Age hunters, Celts, Romans, Anglo-Saxons, Vikings, Normans, and even the French for a brief period of time. By the 13th century, the rulers of England thought of themselves as Englishmen.

B.   THE TUDOR AGE (1485-1603)

RENAISSANCE, REFORMATION, AND A NEW WORLD

The social and economic order of the medieval period was beginning to break down with the rejection of authority of Kings and the Catholic Church. This was the period of the English Renaissance which produced a new form of Christianity known as Protestantism.

The two most famous Monarchs of this period were Henry VIII and Elizabeth I of the House of Tudor:

1. **HENRY VIII (1509-1547)**

   He created his own Church when the Pope refused to allow him to divorce his wife and marry Anne Boleyn. He was supported by a strong anti-Catholic attitude in England at the time so he assumed existing Church lands and buildings and gave much of its' wealth to friends. He ordered that Church services should be in English rather than in Latin and each Church should have an English Bible.

2. **QUEEN ELIZABETH I (1558-1603)**

   Henry's first daughter, Mary, was a Roman Catholic like her mother, Catherine, and tried to bring Catholicism back to England. When she died the next in line was Henry's 2nd daughter, Elizabeth, who became Queen Elizabeth I at age 25 and was a strong Protestant. When she assumed the Crown, England had no Army or police and a weak government bureaucracy. When she died in 1603, she left England as one of the most powerful nations on earth.

   In 1559, she made Protestantism the national religion by having Parliament pass the "Act of Supremacy" which made the Monarch the Supreme head of the Church of England.

   Her reign was a period of great economic growth for England which led to the beginning of the great age of exploration and discovery around the world.

C.   ENGLISH ROOTS OF AMERICAN DEMOCRACY

Attachment 4a summarizes the various English laws and documents which were passed along to the New World. We will see that the basic concept of rights and privileges dates back as far as the Magna Carta of 1215 when King John was forced to sign the document which limited his authority with regard to taxation and administration of justice. All 4 of these documents/practices show up in various American documents and traditions as well.

D.   SUMMARY OF BRITISH GOVERNMENT STRUCTURE

Attachment 4b summarizes the key characteristics of the British Government structure, composed primarily of:

1. Parliament

2. House of Lords

3. House of Commons

E.   CHRONOLOGY OF ENGLISH ACCESSION TO THE THRONE

Attachment 4c represents a chronology of the succession of 15 Monarchs during the years 1485 through 1820 with all but a few as members of the 3 primary ruling families.

F.   SUMMARY OF THE 3 PRIMARY RULING FAMILIES

Attachments 4d, e, and f summarize the Ruling family Monarchs:

- Tudor Monarchs from 1485 to 1603

- Stuart Monarchs from 1603 to 1714

- Hanover Monarchs from 1714 to 1820

G.   BACKGROUND FOR ENGLISH COLONIZATION

The motivation for early English settlement and colonization efforts came primarily from merchants seeking profits, as it was for other European nations as well. The Stuart Kings encouraged gentlemen to colonize although both King James I and King Charles I distrusted merchants, who gave them trouble while in Parliament and seemed eager to oppose Royal authority. They concluded that if colonies were to arise in the New World it would be best to have them in friendly hands. Land had always determined social status in England and the abundant lands of the New World, if properly distributed, might create a new nobility to strengthen the Crown against its opponents.

1. ENGLISH SOCIETY

When Elizabeth became Queen, England's population was 7 million with 12 different languages spoken throughout the British Isles. London was the primary city and seaport with a population of 250,000. Society deferred first to the King and then to the Nobility and then the Gentry who ran the countryside. The bulk of the House of Commons and the majority of the Justices of the Peace came from this class. The more prosperous farmers were called "yeomen" who usually owned their land outright, could vote, and were occasionally elected to minor governmental posts. Below the yeoman class was the great mass of "laboring poor" who didn't have much authority in the commonwealth. The poor of England lacked all rights.

The social hierarchy was clearly defined but the barriers between the classes were not beyond reach. Regardless of a man's class, the core of his life was the family which included all who lived beneath one roof whether blood-related or not. The male head of the family ruled absolutely and English women enjoyed no more freedom than those in Europe. No laws prevented them from marrying whom they wished and tradition was that the wife should share in all major decisions.

A child learned manners and morals at home, was taught to read by his mother, but if he appeared disinterested or unable to learn, he was sent to a tutor and its family. A 17th century child, either Puritan or Anglican, matured in a world that centered on religion. The Old Testament received particular interest as it was used to justify governmental decisions. For example, King James I emphasized that the relationship between Monarch and his people was that of an Old Testament patriarch to his children.

2. THE ECONOMY

From the time Gilbert first conceived of a colony and Jamestown was settled, England acquired the necessary power to take an active interest in the New World. It required an economic rebirth, revolution in agriculture and industry, a growing merchant class, and a new economic attitude on the part of government and business.

The first of these forces to impact England was that of "inflation". Goods from Asia and then from the New World gradually increased prices. The merchant gained the most since his wealth was invested in goods whose cash value constantly rose while the costs to produce the goods dropped. These events negatively impacted the personal wealth of the Crown who eventually had to ask Parliament for new taxes which were granted only after the Crown made concessions to Parliament. Inflation impacted everyone, the farmer, peasant, landowners, and even the Crown. The industrial revolution also impacted English life with an increase in coal, iron, and steel production.

Both Elizabeth and the Stuart Monarchs who followed her reign attempted to maintain order within the confusion of the times. The basis of wealth and power were to be found in trade and towns created barriers to protect their economic activity from rivals. Other policies included restrictions on the colonies by the English government, such as merchants could only export in English ships or foreign goods were prohibited to compete in competition with English products. The government regulated wages and working conditions to keep English industry competitive with outsiders.

These actions were consistent with the principles of "mercantilism" which we previously learned was intended to produce a "favorable balance of trade". The leading expert in this theory was Adam Smith who believed that a nation was strengthened by a highly regulated and self-sufficient economy. Mercantilism didn't arise in England until the merchants pushed themselves into the center of English life.

As world trade and competition grew, the merchants created the concept of the "joint-stock" company where members of these organizations pooled their resources in a common fund. Each member took a certain number of shares and all buying and selling was handled by company officials. The organization differed from a modern corporation in that each venture or voyage involved a separate investment and the "adventurers", or shareholders, might change with every venture. The joint-stock company operated under a charter like that of a regulated company, with the same privileges and responsibilities.

The greatest of the joint-stock companies was the "East India Company" established 12/31/1599. The charter gave it a world-wide trading opportunity. Members had the right to assemble and make all reasonable laws for their government not in opposition to the laws of England. They could punish offenders against these laws and customs duties were suspended until the company was solidified.

The company officers consisted of a Governor, deputy Governor, and 24 Assistants, all annually elected by the "general court", or assembly, of company members. All officers took an oath of allegiance to the Crown. In the beginning, each company venture was a separate investment by the stockholders. In 1609 and 1612 the Charter was revised and thereafter profits and losses from all ventures were pooled. With this revision, the transition from a medieval association to a modern corporation was completed.

3. THE LONDON COMPANY

This company would eventually settle Jamestown by following the charter and experience of the East India Company. Membership in both companies overlapped due to mainly London merchants financing both enterprises. Sir Thomas Smith was one of the most successful merchants of the day and was involved with both companies. He had 7 years experience with the East India Company which helped when he became involved with the Jamestown settlement. That experience was especially helpful since there were no English precedents to follow. No one dreamed in 1607 that when the London Company embarked on the colonization of Virginia the first great folk migration in history was about to begin.

4. THE "GREAT MIGRATION" BEGINS
    Historians generally believe the "Great Migration" to America began either in:

    - 1609 when the London Company sent a fleet of 600 settlers for Virginia

    - 1618 at the start of the "30 Years War"

    - 1630 with the migration of the Puritans to Massachusetts Bay

Regardless of when it happened, by 1641 there were 80,000 men, women, and children who had crossed the ocean to the West Indies, Bermuda, and the mainland of America. The English Civil War in 1642 temporarily slowed the pace of migration, most of which was voluntary but some came against their will, such as vagrants, orphans, paupers, criminals and prisoners.

They came from all parts of England and all classes of society although few of the laboring poor could afford to come. Most paid their way although servants traveled as members of a family. Indentured servants came and increased their numbers in America until they comprised at least one half of the total number of immigrants. In exchange for passage, a servant (indentured or bonded) committed to 4-5 years of servitude. Their rights were protected by a contract signed before departing England. The indenture system was viewed in the 17th century as a reasonable way of settling the colonies with people who had the will and energy to come but just lacked the funds.

Why did people emigrate? There were multiple reasons:

- Political discontent

- Religious discontent

- Economic discontent due to a depression and increasing unemployment in England

Dissatisfaction with the Church of England increased during the times of King Charles I reign (1625-1649) when Anglicans known as "Arminians" (favoring free will and an elaborate ritual), who favored Catholicism, dominated the Church and led to restrictions against Puritans.

The opportunities of the New World also appealed to adventurers and speculators seeking personal wealth and power.

The voyage itself followed the more northern route as opposed to the southern Columbus routes. The duration varied from 3-5 months by the southern route and 6-8 weeks by the more direct northern route in the summer but 12-14 weeks during the winter.

What they found when they arrived were thick forests, a mountain chain to the west, 50 miles inland in New England, about 150 miles inland in Pennsylvania, and about 300 miles inland in South Carolina. Occasional traders and trappers moved through gaps in the mountains but for the most part the settlers remained close to the sea, as in England. The land between the coast and mountains split into 2 regions:

- The "Tidewater Country" which comprised the lowlands which began in New Jersey and gradually spread inland to 150 miles at South Carolina

- The "Piedmont Region" comprised the rolling country that varies in width from 100 miles in Pennsylvania to 200 miles in South Carolina. It would take nearly a century before the settlers moved that far into the backcountry.

This is the background for the eventual settlement and colonization of the original 13 English colonies with each colony to be studied in subsequent chapters.

J.   EVOLUTION OF THE ENGLISH GOVERNMENT

In the early 17th century, English society was still undergoing its own changes at the same time as American colonization began. The King was the absolute ruler with the powers to order Parliament, appoint all officials, oversee justice, issue all charters, and protect all rights, as he defined them. He ruled by "Divine Right" and was considered above the law by virtue of his absolute power. But, the Monarchy lacked revenues and believed it needed some form of regular taxation if it were to maintain its power. The House of Commons, however, refused to approve such taxes so the Crown looked for ways around Parliament, such as raising customs duties and creating nobility titles for sale. *These actions only increased the natural friction between Crown and Parliament.*

The King's fight to maintain his power was aided by the Privy Council, his private advisory council. During the reign of King Charles I the Council numbered 40 and met daily to deal with problems which affected all aspects of life in England. Both Queen Elizabeth I and King James I (1603-1625) used it to oversee the colonization of Ireland, a precedent for American colonial affairs. It advised the King on foreign affairs, trading-company charters, and the quality of candidates for various government positions. A key role was that of moving the King's most important legislation through the Parliament. It worked to promote the welfare of the nation according to what the King determined that welfare to be.

The "Great Migration" spanned those years in the early 17th century when the House of Commons sought to impose its will on the King. Commons had previously won some privileges but the Crown was able to manipulate the debate through its Privy Council. Commons responded by use of committees which allowed decisions to be shaped informally off the floor, behind the scenes. Those who immigrated to America carried with them the memory of the battle between the

House of Commons and the Crown, the outcome of which left a permanent imprint on the development of colonial legislatures during the 17th century.

The Crown's legal and administrative system for the kingdom focused on the county. Government for the average Englishman centered on the village. The "justice of the peace" was a village Squire and the man who executed the Justice's orders was called the "constable" who apprehended thieves, chased vagrants, collected fines, and generally served as the village Police force.

English government authority filtered out and down from London and its strength pushed upward from the village. It was inefficient with many corrupt or inept officials and gave justice only to those with a stake in society. The King, in theory, remained absolute but, in fact, his success rested on the consent of the governed, although in this case, that meant only those who owned property.

For centuries, English society and government were impacted by the **battle between the Crown and Parliament**, right up to the day of the beginning of the American Revolutionary War, as we will see.

1. THE ENGLISH CIVIL WARS (First from 1642-1646, the Second from 1646-1648)

   The English Civil War was a dispute between King Charles I (1625-1649), his supporters, and the Long Parliament, led by Oliver Cromwell. It began in the summer of 1642 and continued until early 1649 when Charles I was tried and executed by members of Parliament. He dreamt of fulfilling his father's (King James I) dream of uniting all of the British Isles into a single Kingdom. He also shared his father's view of the power of the Crown which he also described as the "Divine Right of Kings". He demanded complete loyalty in return for "just rule" and tolerated no questioning of his authority or decisions. Prior to the Civil War, Parliament was not a permanent branch of the English government but just a group of temporary advisory committees summoned occasionally by the King whenever additional tax revenue, for example, was needed. The committees could also be dismissed at his will as well.

Because responsibility for collecting taxes was in the hands of the English Gentry, the Monarchs needed their support to rule and guarantee a steady flow of revenues into the Treasury. If the Gentry refused to collect the King's taxes, the King would be powerless to compel them.

The traditional conflict between Crown and Parliament was increased by the following:

a. King Charles I marriage to a Catholic, Henrietta Maria, shortly after his accession to the Throne in 1625, which angered the Puritan minority in Parliament which comprised about 1/3 of the membership.

b. He supported some of the wars in Europe but Parliament did not approve of the commander, the Duke of Buckingham. Parliament agreed to support the wars but only if they could recall Buckingham if he was not successful. Eventually, Parliament did dismiss Buckingham in 1626 which angered Charles who then dismissed the Parliament.

c. Having dismissed Parliament and being unable to raise money without them, the King then assembled another one in 1628 which included Oliver Cromwell who drew up the "Petition of Right" in 1628 which King Charles accepted.

The Petition stated that an English citizen should have:

- freedom from arbitrary arrest and imprisonment

- freedom from non-Parliamentary taxation

- freedom from the enforced billeting of troops

- freedom from martial law

NOTE THAT MANY OF THESE FREEDOMS EVENTUALLY APPEAR IN THE PATRIOT'S COMPLAINTS AGAINST THE BRITISH IN THE 1770's.

d. Charles was determined to rule without summoning another Parliament which required him to devise new means of raising revenues, many of which were opposed by the current

99

Parliament. He managed to avoid Parliament for a decade, to be known as the "11 Years Tyranny".

e. He involved England in a series of expensive wars in 1639-1640.

f. He and his Archbishop of Canterbury, William Laud, advocated reforms to the Church of England which many Puritans believed was a return to Catholicism. When they complained, Laud arrested them.

g. When he attempted to unify Scotland and England through a common Prayer Book, the Scots strongly reacted and rebelled in 1639. Charles fought them but failed and then decided to seek a truce, the "Pacification of Berwick", but was humiliated by being forced to agree not to interfere with religion in Scotland, which was strongly Presbyterian by this time.

h. He recalled Parliament in 1640 to seek their permission for revenues to pay for his wars. Parliament then took the opportunity to discuss their grievances against the King, so he dismissed them too, to be known as the "Short Parliament".

i. He called Parliament again in November, 1640, which came to be known as the "Long Parliament", who took up the grievances attempted by the Short Parliament. They passed a law stating that the Monarch could not dismiss Parliament and placed other restrictions on the authority of the Monarch.

j. Other wars were fought during the years from 1641-1645 which further eroded his popularity and support. He eventually fled the country in 1646 which ended the "First English Civil War". Even though he was being held prisoner he still managed to influence some events which caused further battles, which became known as the "Second English Civil War" which lasted through 1648. Eventually Charles and his supporters were defeated by Oliver Cromwell. A "Rump Parliament" was created and ordered to establish a high court of justice to try Charles for treason.

k. The 1648 Parliament found Charles guilty of treason by a vote of 68-67 and executed him in 1649. Many of those who supported his execution were themselves executed or imprisoned during the later "Restoration of the Monarchy" in 1660.

2. THE ENGLISH INTERREGNUM (Jan 1649–May 1660)
    The "Interregnum" refers to the period of Parliamentary &
    Military rule by the Lord Protector Oliver Cromwell under the
    Commonwealth of England after the English Civil Wars. It began
    with the overthrow and execution of King Charles I in January, 1649,
    and ended with the Restoration of King Charles II on 5/29/1660.
    This era of English history can be divided into 4 periods:

    a. First period of the Commonwealth of England   1649   1653
    b. Protectorate under Oliver Cromwell   1653   1658
    c. Protectorate under Richard Cromwell   1658   1659
    d. Second period of the Commonwealth   1659   1660

    After the Parliament victory in the Civil Wars, the Puritan views of
    the majority of Parliament and its supporters began to be imposed
    on the rest of the country. The Puritans favored a simple life and
    restricted what they saw as the excesses of the previous government.
    Holidays, such as Christmas and Easter, were suppressed. Life
    for both Irish and English Catholics was difficult and due to his
    subsequent actions against the Irish and Catholics, Oliver Cromwell
    is a despised person in Ireland to this day.

3. THE ENGLISH RESTORATION OF 1660
    The "English Restoration" of 1660 refers to the re-establishment
    of the Monarchy with the accession of King Charles II to the
    Throne after the execution of King Charles I and the collapse of the
    Commonwealth and Protectorate of the Cromwells. King Charles
    II, the son of the executed King Charles I, was offered the Throne
    by an influential group of Army officers in exchange for a promise
    of amnesty and toleration toward his father's former enemies. He
    was then crowned as King Charles II on 5/8/1660.
    While the Monarchy was eventually restored, the English Civil
    Wars set England on a path to become a Parliamentary Democracy.
    Future Monarchs became cautious of pushing Parliament too far.
    In 1662, Parliamentary factions became formal political parties,

known as "Tories" and "Whigs". The "Glorious Revolution" of 1688 and the "Act of Settlement" of 1701 gave Parliament the right to select the successor to the Throne.

K.   ENGLAND'S NEW IMPERIALISM (1650-1676)

Early English settlement and colonization efforts were led by non-government adventurers and merchants. It wasn't until the Cromwell government that England began to deal with the problems of Empire. The Dutch had replaced Spain as England's primary rival for world trade. By the mid-1600's, England had acquired 50 settlements around the world which then required some sort of unification policy in order to gain maximum advantage from those colonies. The State now had to assume responsibilities which it had previously ignored and also accept the principle of mercantilism, i.e., the purpose of colonies being to promote trade and increase the welfare of the Mother Country.

Parliament had tried during the English Civil Wars to gain the support of the colonies, against the Crown, by granting trading privileges and either reducing or eliminating tariffs. Three colonies did respond favorably by opening their ports to all ships, Virginia in 1643, Massachusetts in 1645, and Maryland in 1649. Once the Cromwell period began, in 1649, and the Puritans assumed leadership in England, those who had encouraged a tolerant attitude toward the colonies were eased out of power.

The new leadership introduced its policies through the Dutch who, by the mid-17th century, dominated world trade. It was estimated that 80% of the ships engaged in worldwide trade were owned by the Dutch. The Dutch East India Company had a near monopoly of the spice trade while the Dutch West India Company had captured over 500 Spanish vessels, occupied large parts of the coast of Brazil, and established settlements along the Delaware, Hudson, and Connecticut rivers in America.

By the early 1620's, as England was recovering from a serious economic depression, merchants and politicians started discussing trade policy. They came to the conclusion that in order to be an economically healthy country their exports should exceed their imports and the balance should be invested in military strength.

The Dutch advantage increased during the English Civil Wars which disrupted industry at home, forcing up production costs and the price of manufactured goods. Once the fighting ended, Puritan merchants in Parliament demanded something to be done to reduce Dutch influence in world trade. Cromwell and his supporters needed the Dutch as allies against Catholic Spain, whom Cromwell believed was their primary rival.

For the next 25-30 years the English Government passed a series of Acts of Trade and Navigation which were intended to replace the Dutch as the primary commercial traders, increase their own wealth, and protect their trade for and with the colonies. Those actions were:

1. THE NAVIGATION ACT 1651 (Also referred to as "British Acts of Trade")

    In 1650, Parliament passed an ordinance forbidding any foreign ships in the British colonies. The following year the Parliament, led by Oliver Cromwell, passed the first of multiple Navigation Acts. These laws were intended to protect British economic interests in colonial trade and to protect its industry against the rapidly growing Dutch trade. The Act subjected Virginia, Barbados, and Antigua to the laws of Parliament and required those who wished to deal with the colonies to obtain trading licenses from either Parliament or Cromwell's Council of State. It was Parliament's intent to block Holland from all trade with England or her colonies and attempted to change the commercial center of the world from Amsterdam to London.

    The terms of the Act were:

    a. No goods from America, Asia, or Africa could enter England, Ireland, or the colonies except in English ships;

    b. Coastal trading, whether between English or colonial ports, had to be in English ships,

    c. Goods from Europe had to be imported in English ships or ships of the country producing the goods.

    The effectiveness of this act was hard to judge because it was easy to evade due to the lack of enforcement measures. As the Act took effect, colonial merchants and producers were upset at the new restrictions. Trade in the West Indies, tobacco in Virginia, and fish in New England were growing industries for which the Dutch provided the best shipping rates. The unrest was so great in the colonies that England had to send troops to Virginia to deal with a growing rebellion.

2. THE FIRST ANGLO-DUTCH WAR (1652-1654) AND WAR WITH SPAIN

Soon after the Act was passed, war broke out between England and Holland even though Cromwell did not want a conflict with them. He pursued it with little enthusiasm and pulled his country out of it at the first honorable opportunity. The Peace of 1654 ended the war but failed to settle any of the underlying issues. It did, however, allow Cromwell to focus on his primary rival, Spain. He intended to spread the Puritan brand of Protestantism throughout the Indies and Caribbean region before they became Catholicized by the Spanish. His government needed revenues and targeted the considerable Spanish wealth in the region especially since their settlements were poorly defended and ripe for occupation.

3. THE NAVIGATION ACT 1660

The Restoration did impact the Navigation Acts because it shifted control over colonial affairs from Parliamentary committees back to Royal officials. Parliament quickly passed this Navigation Act when the new King, Charles II, ruled invalid all legislation passed under the Interregnum of 1649-1660.

The primary purpose of this Act was to tighten enforcement of previous Navigation Acts which had allowed the Dutch traders to continue their activities. The Act included an "enumerated clause" which listed products which must be shipped only to England or to another English colony. To enforce this clause all ship Captains were required to post a bond at their departure port which they could recover at their arrival port only after providing proof that they had complied with the law.

Enumerated items would eventually include all of the colonial products. This clause didn't hurt New England because their primary products, fish and lumber, were not enumerated. New England merchants could buy and sell where they wished as long as they shipped in English vessels.

The principle of enumeration marked a new step in the attempt to control colonial trade and hurt the Dutch and benefit the Crown, merchants, and English industry. The enumerated products paid customs duties which meant an increase in Royal revenues. European trade in enumerated items was closed to the colonies, giving English merchants a profitable monopoly in goods which formerly benefitted the Dutch.

4. THE NAVIGATION ACT 1662

The Act of 1660 became the foundation of English trade through the rest of the colonial period and most legislation passed afterward repaired defects of the previous Acts. A question was raised about English merchants owning foreign ships which were now prohibited from trade within the Empire. To fix this loophole the Navigation Act of 1662 declared that ships not of English construction should be considered foreign if they were not registered in England. This statute initiated the registration of ships.

5. THE STAPLE ACT 1663

Passed by the Crown and Parliament which basically completed the colonial economic dependence upon England. It dealt with colonial imports and declared that all goods from Europe to the colonies had to pass through England. Every ship which now entered the colonies had to prove that the goods it landed had been loaded in England. A few items of great demand in the colonies were exempted. The Act also declared that foreign goods passing through Europe could be taxed, thereby increasing their prices, which allowed English goods to undersell them overseas.

6. SECOND ANGLO-DUTCH WAR (1664-1667)

England provoked another war with Holland to complete its effort to dominate colonial trade by eliminating Dutch holdings on the American continent. Without firing a shot, they were able to capture New Netherlands from the Dutch. The "Treaty of Breda" ended this war in 1667 with these terms:

a. New Netherlands and Dutch slave-trading stations in Africa were ceded to England

b. France received Nova Scotia from England, thus depriving New England of a lucrative center of commerce, in return for ceding the islands of Antiqua, Montserrat, and the conquered half of St. Kitts Island.

This Treaty showed the colonists that their lives could be impacted by European Wars and treaties without any ability on their part to impact the agreements.

7. THIRD ANGLO-DUTCH WAR (1672-1674)

The Dutch recaptured New Amsterdam from the English in 1673 but the Peace Treaty of 1674 restored it again to England. The Treaty ended the Dutch presence in America. In the future, Holland confined its commercial efforts to Africa, Far East, and the Caribe region. During this war, England closed another loophole in their commercial system. The Act of 1660 had permitted coastwise trade between the colonies even of enumerated articles to be carried duty- free. Colonial merchants used this privilege to clear their home ports with goods supposedly bound for another colonial port but actually destined for a European market. The New England shippers were the greatest offenders. American goods in Europe brought prices equal to or better than those in England and with no commission going to English middle-men.

8. PLANTATION DUTY ACT (1673)

The Act was intended to eliminate another evasion of a previous Act. It levied a duty (tariff) at the point of departure on all enumerated articles bound to another colonial port. The Act was intended to impose English customs duties at the start rather than at the end of a voyage and directly primarily at regulating trade. This law also provided for the appointment of customs agents to enforce all of the Navigation Acts in the colonies and to collect the duties. While no one in the colonies welcomed the Act, Parliament's right to impose a duty on inter-colonial trade was unchallenged.

9. SUMMARY OF THE VARIOUS NAVIGATION ACTS
    The underlying principles of the Navigation Acts of 1651, 1660, 1662, 1663, and 1673 governed the economic structure of the Empire for over a century. The effect of these Acts on the economy of England seemed to have an immediate and positive impact. Merchant shipping doubled between 1660 and 1688, while the Dutch lost their lead in world commerce, as was the English plan. Colonial goods imported and then re-exported accounted for 5% of England's trade in 1640 and increased to 25% by the end of the century. A variety of refining and finishing industries arose while this protective navigation system kept cheaper foreign goods away from the Empire.

L. THE GLORIOUS REVOLUTION 1688-1689 (Reign 1689-1702)

The Glorious Revolution of 1688-1689 replaced the reigning King James II with the joint-Monarchy of his Protestant daughter, Mary, and her Dutch husband, William of Orange. It established the supremacy of Parliament over the Crown, setting England on the path towards a Constitutional Monarchy and Parliamentary democracy.

The primary cause of the Glorious Revolution was, once again, fear of Catholicism and the strong suspicion that Catholics were actively plotting the overthrow of the government in favor of a Catholic tyranny. King James II assumed the throne in February, 1685, and immediately promised to defend the existing government and Anglican Church. He also promised that he would not impose his personal faith, Catholicism, on the country. But, he slowly began to remove obstacles to Catholics holding key government positions. Concern grew as he appointed Catholic officers to the Army. In April, 1687, he issued a "Declaration of Indulgence" suspending penal laws against Catholics. Later, he dissolved the Parliament which further aroused existing suspicions.

In May, 1688, seven leading Protestant Bishops refused to follow an order and were arrested for seditious libel but were later acquitted and released. Soon, some Protestant leaders contacted William of Orange, a Dutch leader who was urged to intervene militarily when it became known that King James' II wife gave birth to a male heir, James Edward Stuart, on 6/10/1688. Now the fear and suspicions became more real, there was a legal Catholic heir and successor to the Throne and the possibility of a Catholic dynasty in England.

William agreed to intervene not only because of the succession issue but also because he wanted to involve England in the war against France. He landed a military force in England on 11/5/1688 and the news of this military force began a series of anti-Catholic rioting in cities and towns across England. At the same time, many of the King's army were beginning to defect and even his daughter, Princess Anne, joined the Protestant forces.

King James II feared for his life and attempted to escape but was captured on 12/11/1688 but, somehow, managed to escape on 12/23/1688 to France. A new Parliament, the "Convention Parliament" met on 1/22/1689 and agreed that William & Mary should jointly assume the Throne. On 2/13/1689, they formally accepted but before they were crowned, however, they were presented with a document known as "The Declaration of Rights" which affirmed some Constitutional principles such as the prohibition of taxation without Parliamentary consent and the need for regular Parliamentary meetings.

Pressure from William also ensured the passage of the "Toleration Act" of May, 1689, granting Protestant groups freedom of worship. Unfortunately, this "toleration" did not include the same rights for Catholics.

As a result of this Revolution, Parliament gained powers over taxation, Royal succession, appointments, and the right of the Crown to wage War independent of Parliament. Oddly, in one way, the Revolution represented not the broadening of freedom but the expansion of servitude by promoting the growth of slavery by ending the Royal African Company's monopoly on the slave trade in 1698.

M.   THE EMPIRE TAKES SHAPE (1689-1713) (After William & Mary)

After 1689, the Crown steadily tightened its control and created a uniform administration of the colonies. The period from 1689-1713 included 2 wars which began in Europe but impacted America. The colonists failed to see at the time that Europe had imposed these wars on them and it was Thomas Paine who was the first to declare that to separate from England would also mean separating from European "entanglements". As far as the colonists were concerned, France was still the primary menace to their security.

1.   DEVELOPMENT OF IMPERIAL CONTROL
The rise of New France under King Louis XIV did much to awaken England to the inadequacy of its own Imperial efforts. From 1660-1675, England constructed a framework to control the trade of the Empire that, to a large degree reflected a respect for Colbert's French Imperial design. Two wars had shown that the colonies were unable to cope with New France on their own. England was forced, through self-preservation, to assume the task of providing an adequate military defense which further engaged it into colonial politics. First the Crown, and then the Crown with Parliament struggled with the problem of how to control America without ruining England's political traditions.

2.   THE CROWN AND THE COLONIES
The Crown controlled colonial affairs as indicated by King James I in 1624 stating that Parliament should not "concern

itself" with colonial matters. Even in the 18th century, when Parliament was beginning to assert its authority, the King had not given up much of its power over the colonies. He could still:

a. make colonial appointments

b. issue instructions and commissions

c. disallow colonial laws

d. hear appeals from colonial courts

He delegated most of his powers to his staff, such as the Secretary of State for the Southern Department, who assumed responsibility for colonial matters in addition to the same for Southern Europe. It wasn't until 1768 that a new Secretarial post was created solely for colonial matters. Other departments involved in colonial affairs were the Treasury, the Commissioners of Customs, to enforce the Navigation Acts, the Admiralty or Navy Department, and the Admiralty Courts. The heads of these departments formed the "Privy Council" which was the King's Chief advisory board.

The history of the oversight of colonial affairs included:

a. 1622 King James I created a subcommittee of the Privy Council to specialize on colonial matters.

b. 1634 King Charles I replaced it with a "Commission for Regulating Plantations" headed by Archbishop Laud who used it to bring the Massachusetts Bay colony under Royal supervision. It was ended by the English Civil Wars.

c. 1643 Parliament created a "Commissions for the Plantations" making its Chairman, the Earl of Warwick, the Governor-in-Chief of the American Colonies.

d. 1649 The "Rump Parliament" created the Commonwealth of Cromwell and extended its authority to Dominions and Territories of the Empire. A sub-committee of the Council of State, Parliament's Executive body, was assigned to oversee imperial trade.

e. 1655 A separate board for colonial matters was created.

f. 1660 King Charles II replaced the Parliamentary committee on trade with 2 new committee's:

- Council of Trade

- Council for Foreign Plantations

g. 1672 "Joint Council for Trade and Plantations", directed by the Earl of Shaftesbury, was only a fact-finding body with no decision-making authority.

h. 1675 The new Treasurer, Earl of Danby, replaced the Joint Council with the Committee of the Privy Council on Trade and Plantations, unofficially known as the "Lords of Trade", which had the power to make and enforce decisions.

3. THE LORDS OF TRADE

Its' goal was to create uniform governments subservient to the wishes of the Crown throughout the colonies. It forced colonial governors to adhere to policies established in London, which was now getting better colonial information than ever because of the diligence of the Earl of Shaftesbury. From this information it prepared the Governor's instructions, issued dispatches, wrote the King's proclamations affecting the colonies, and worked toward a stronger central administration of the Empire. Some of its accomplishments were:

a. It separated New Hampshire from Massachusetts Bay colony control in 1679 and converted it into a Royal colony.

b. It won annulments of the Massachusetts Bay and Bermuda Company charters in 1684.

c. It limited the Proprietary power in the King's grant to William Penn.

d. It strengthened Royal government in Virginia in 1683 by sending over a new, strong, Governor, Lord Howard of Effingham.

e. It created the Dominion of New England

It lost some power during the reign of King James II (1685-1689) when it reverted to just an advisory body and the real authority over the colonies returned to the Privy Council. During the early years of King William III reign (1689) he restricted the authority of many of the colonial proprietors, such as William Penn and Lord Baltimore, and issued a new charter to Massachusetts in 1691 which transformed it into a Royal province Governor with authority to appoint judges and justices of the peace.

Parliament's role in managing the colonies was strengthened with the reign of King William III. By 1695, the War with France plus illegal trade and smuggling, caused the Crown and Parliament to pass in 1696 "An Act for Preventing Frauds and Regulating Abuses in the Plantation Trade". It was also known as the "Navigation Act" of 1696 which basically once again tightened control over trade. Its' terms were:

4. THE NAVIGATION ACT OF 1696

    a. Defined English ships as those with crews at least 3/4 Englishmen

    b. Demanded that bonds be posted on enumerated articles even when a duty was paid in a colonial port to ensure their being kept within the Empire

    c. Established a more effective procedure for ship registration

    d. Declared that any colonial laws in any way "repugnant" to this act were to be declared as illegal, null, and void

    e. Governors of all colonies must have Royal approval before assuming office and must also take an oath of office to enforce the Acts of Trade

    f. Established Vice-Admiralty Courts in America plus a customs organization with the same powers as held in England.

5. OTHER ACTS OF CONTROL

    1699 "An Act for the More Effectual Suppression of Piracy" allowed the King to establish special courts to offenders without juries.

    1699 "Woolen Act" intended to help the struggling cloth industry in England. It forbade the exportation of all wool or woolen cloth produced in America. This permitted wool to be produced for home use and legally blocked the growth of a large-scale colonial commercial woolen industry.

6. THE BOARD OF TRADE

(Officially known as the "Lords Commissioners of Trade and Plantations", or "BOT")

It differed from the former "Lords of Trade" in the following ways:

a. Included members of Parliament as opposed to the Lords of Trade which was composed only of Privy Council members

b. Although still only an advisory board, the King's backing gave its advice the impact of a Royal command

c. Anything having to do with colonial matters came within the board's scope of authority

d. It recommended legislation to Parliament that related to the colonies

e. It had strong input into selecting Royal governors

f. It examined colonial laws and its recommendations were generally followed

g. It judged religious matters

Soon after it was created, it conducted a survey of the colonies and decided that before any centralized, uniform control could be developed, all Proprietary colonies had to be converted into Royal colonies. In 1701, the "BOT" and Customs Commissioners introduced in the House of Lords a Bill designed to deprive all Proprietors of their right to govern. It was opposed by William Penn with enough support to defeat it in the Parliament. Failure to pass this "Reunification Bill" marked a turning point in colonial history because the narrow margin of defeat frightened many Proprietors. Those who owned New Jersey surrendered their government in 1702 and some other Proprietors became unsure of their power.

The key significance of the failure of the "Reunification Bill", however, was that its failure blocked the Crown's long-range plan to make all colonies conform to a single political system.

The "BOT" was most effective during its first decade but then gradually lost power. Queen Anne showed minimal interest in their efforts. During the 1720's, the Secretary of State retrieved full control over colonial patronage and paid little attention to the BOT recommendations. From 1730-1748 the BOT was just a shadow of its former self and it was not until Lord Halifax as President of the "BOT" that it returned to power although it never controlled colonial affairs as fully as it wished. It had difficulty making effective decisions because it feared advancing a recommendation until all government officials had bought into the idea. This division of authority would continue to cause trouble for England's management of colonial affairs right up to the Revolution and also during the military battles.

The "BOT" had 2 avenues to the colonies:

a. The colonial agent in London who represented the interests of the colony as well as communicated Crown information to the colonies.

b. The colonial Governor who was required to enforce the Crown's decrees.

N.   IMPERIAL RELATIONS 1713-1763

For most of the time after 1713, control of Imperial Affairs was led by Sir Robert Walpole, the King's Chief advisor and administrator between 1721 and 1742, and also the Duke of Newcastle, Walpole's Secretary of State for the Southern department. This period was known as *"The Period of Salutary Neglect". They argued that the government should avoid interfering in colonial affairs.* "Neglect" is an incorrect term because neither Walpole nor Newcastle neglected or were ignorant of colonial matters. Newcastle controlled the appointment of a majority of Royal officials in America and tended to pick men who were efficient managers. *Walpole and Newcastle opposed both the "BOT" and Parliament in their efforts to tighten control over the colonies.*

1. PARLIAMENT AND THE COLONIES

As we have learned, Parliament gradually increased its interest in the colonies, with the passage of all the Navigation Acts between 1660-1696. By 1753, Parliament had passed 80+ Acts relative to colonial trade with the cumulative effect of this activity being to challenge the power of the Crown regarding colonial matters and make Parliament a partner in the regulation of imperial affairs.

Most of the regulation was intended to control colonial trade to benefit England, such as the following Acts beginning in 1705 and aimed at the northern colonies:

a. White Pines Act of 1711, strengthened in 1722 & 1729

b. Hat and Felt Act 1732

c. Sugar Act 1733 (Molasses Act) aimed at French dominance of the Sugar and Molasses Trade

d. Iron Act 1750

e. Currency Act 1751 which forbade the further issuance as legal tender of any paper bills or bills of credit; It hurt the New England merchants the most

These acts caused the colonists to resent Parliament.

2. CROWN AND THE COLONIES

Despite Parliament's growing involvement with the colonies, most colonists felt a strong bond to the Crown, for the following reasons:

a. the Crown legalized their existence by granting their original charters

b. all British officials in the colonies were Crown-appointed officers

c. oaths were to be taken to the Crown such as jury duty and prayers for the King's health, etc.

Loyalty to the King was always tempered with self-interest as authorities of the Crown learned that the colonists would hesitate at every effort to uphold the King's prerogative or to enforce Parliamentary legislation.

d. *the Crown's permissive attitude toward the colonists began to change in 1748 primarily because of the appointment of Earl of Halifax as President of the "BOT".* The Board of Trade had been declining in importance but Halifax now campaigned to increase its influence again. He campaigned for a specific American department with Cabinet rank and was partially successful in 1752 although he left office in 1761. The terms of his 1752 "compromise" were:

- The "BOT" would have the authority to nominate men to colonial offices with the Secretary of State for the southern department losing control over colonial affairs.

- Halifax was granted permission to attend all sessions of the Privy Council dealing with colonial affairs.

- Governors were to send their papers directly to the "BOT".

Colonial Governors learned that they were to respond now to the "BOT" rather than to the Secretary of State. It also extended its influence over the specific colonies of New York and Pennsylvania.

With the resignation of Halifax in 1761, the "BOT" again lost influence such as its nominating power for colonial offices which then reverted back to the Secretary of State and, by 1762, it had been reduced again to a board of reporting with minimal direct authority over colonial affairs. Even though it was losing its power, it didn't stop its attempt to tighten control over the colonies.

O. TROUBLE AHEAD

1760 was a significant year for both England and America. King George II died after 34 years on the Throne. His son became King George III on 10/25/1760 at the age of 22. It also marked the beginning of economic troubles for the colonies, mostly in the north because of British attacks on the illegal colonial trade and smuggling with France.

England used the technique of ***"writs of assistance"*** to stop illegal trade. These were general warrants which allowed officials to search private property without offering proof of suspicion. They had been in use since 1751 without much opposition but, in 1760, Boston merchants protested their use and were represented by James Otis, a Boston Attorney, who was opposed by Massachusetts Chief Justice Thomas Hutchinson, whom Otis personally detested.

Otis argued that the "writs" should be declared null and void because they were contrary to the basic principles of the English Constitution. His argument was dismissed and the legality of the Writs were upheld. There wasn't much of an impact at the time but, after a number of years, his arguments became more known and supported. At about the same time Patrick Henry also defended the "2 Penny Act" passed by the Virginia House of Burgesses in 1759-1760 after it had been disallowed by the Crown.

Neither Otis nor Henry won their cases but their arguments did *lay the foundation for later resistance to Parliament and the Crown's control over the colonies. John Adams later stated that the "child, Independence, was born" at that time.* Henry's attack on the King's right to disallow colonial statutes was later expanded into an attack on the Royal prerogative in general.

One other event hinted at future trouble for England. William Pitt objected to the King's prosecution of the "7 Years War" (French & Indian War in America) by resigning from the Cabinet in October, 1761. By resigning, he removed himself from the leadership of the House of Commons. At the same time, the Duke of Newcastle also retired in 1762. *Some historians believe that if Newcastle had been in office he would have opposed the provocative colonial measures from 1763-1765. The Newcastle retirement meant, however, that the Treasury position was assumed by George Grenville who would play a significant, and anti-colonial, role in the future events which led to the American Revolution.*

P.   ACHIEVEMENTS OF THE MONARCHS DURING COLONIZATION PERIOD

ELIZABETH I 1558-1603

- Last of the Tudor Monarchs who practiced absolute Monarchy
- Absolute Monarch but governed with support of Parliament
- Defeated Spanish Armada and ended Spanish threat to England
- Confirmed Anglican Religion as Church of England

JAMES I 1603-1625

- Stuart family

- Poor relationship with Parliament over issue of authority to tax

- Indecisive ruler

- Made peace with Spain in 1604 but eventually declared war against them in 1618

- United England and Scotland

- Jamestown colony founded

- Plymouth colony founded

CHARLES I 1625-1649

- Stuart family

- Parliament drafts the Petition of Rights in 1628 in reaction to King Charles collecting taxes without Parliamentary approval

- Dissolves multiple Parliaments and rules on his own authority for 11 years, 1629-1640

- Appoints Archbishop Laud to enforce Anglicanism on the country, persecutes Puritans

- 20,000 Puritans leave England between 1617-1640

- Tries to impose Anglicanism on Scotland who rebels and defeats Charles

- Creates the "Long Parliament" in 1640 to reform England but they eventually turn on him and approve his execution

- Parliament victory over the Crown

- English Civil War

- Eventually tried for treason and executed

OLIVER CROMWELL 1653-1658

- Presided over a Republic

- Puritan dominance in government although population opposed Puritanism

CHARLES II 1660-1685

- Stuart family

- Acceptable relationship with Parliament

JAMES II 1685-1689

- Stuart family

- Tried to subvert Parliament by packing it with friends

- Catholic, accused of trying to convert England back to Catholicism, overthrown and replaced by William & Mary

WILLIAM & MARY 1689-1694 (William of Orange)
WILLIAM III 1694-1702

- Glorious Revolution

- Represents the ultimate supremacy of Parliament over the Crown; Placed limits on William & Mary authority

- Wanted to involve England in war with France, to support the Dutch

- Passage of Bill of Rights, Toleration Act, Mutiny Act which forced the Monarchs to accept Parliament authority

ANNE 1702-1714

- Last of the Stuart Monarchs

GEORGE I 1714-1727

- First of the Hanover (German) family

- Did not speak English, Government run by Sir Robert Walpole, Prime Minister

- Devoted as much time to ruling Hanover as England

GEORGE II 1727-1760

- Hanover family

- Also not fluent in speaking English

GEORGE III 1760-1820

- Presided over the loss of the American colonies

Q. BRITISH PRIME MINISTERS

DATES	PRIME MINISTER	REIGN OF
1721-1742	Sir Robert Walpole	King George I & King George II
1742-1743	Sir Spencer Compton	King George II
1743-1754	Henry Pelham	King George II
1754-1756	Duke of Newcastle	King George II
1756-1757	Sir William Cavendish	King George II
1757-1762	Duke of Newcastle	King George II & King George III
1762-1763	The Earl of Bute	King George III
1763-1765	Sir George Grenville	King George III
1765-1766	The Marquess of Rockingham	King George III
1766-1768	William Pitt/Earl of Chatham	King George III
1768-1770	The Duke of Grafton	King George III
1770-1782	Lord North	King George III
1783-1801	William Pitt Jr .	King George III

R. KEY DATES & SIGNIFICANT EVENTS

1215	Magna Carta
1295	Model Parliament
1509	King Henry VIII assumes the Throne
1558	Queen Elizabeth I assumes the Throne
1559	Act of Supremacy makes Monarch the Supreme head of the Church of England
1603	King James I assumes the Throne
1625	King Charles I assumes the Throne
1628	Petition of Right
1642	English Civil War
1649	The Interregnum
1651	First Navigation Act
1652	First Anglo-Dutch War
1660	King Charles II assumes the Throne, the Restoration
1660	Second Navigation Act
1662	Third Navigation Act
1663	Staple Act
1664	Second Anglo-Dutch War
1672	Third Anglo-Dutch War
1673	Plantation Duty Act
1685	King James II assumes the Throne
1689	English Bill of Rights

1689	The Glorious Revolution, William & Mary assume the Throne
1696	Navigation Act
1701	Act of Settlement gives Parliament the right to select who should succeed to the Throne
1702	Queen Anne assumes the Throne
1714	King George I assumes the Throne
1727	King George II assumes the Throne
1760	King George III assumes the Throne

S.   REVIEW QUESTIONS

(Multiple Choice)

1. The Navigation Acts:
    a. greatly hurt the economic prosperity of the colonies
    b. had minimal impact on the colonies
    c. created both benefits and restrictions
    d. account for the rapid growth of colonial prosperity

2. Which European country contributed the primary roots of American democracy?
    a. France
    b. England
    c. Spain
    d. All of the above

3. What was the date of the Magna Carta?
    a. 1200
    b. 1315
    c. 1492
    d. 1215

4. What did the Magna Carta declare?
    a. The Divine Right of Kings
    b. Freedom of the Press
    c. Limited the authority of the King
    d. Provided for large land grants to Nobles

5. Which of the ruling Monarchy families was the first to govern England?
    a. Tudor
    b. Stuart
    c. Hanover
    d. Saxons

6. To which ruling family did Queen Elizabeth I belong?
    a. Stuart
    b. Saxon
    c. Tudor
    d. Hanover

7. The English Civil War of 1642-1646 was a dispute between:
    a. King James I and King Charles II
    b. Queen Elizabeth I and King James II
    a. King Charles I and the Long Parliament led by Oliver Cromwell
    b. King Henry VIII and Queen Anne

8. During what years did the English Interregnum occur?
    a. 1649-1660
    b. 1653-1659
    c. 1649-1658
    d. 1658-1660

9. Which nation did England conduct war against the most in the mid–1650's?
    a. France
    b. Spain
    c. Portugal
    d. Holland

10. What does the term "The Restoration" mean?
    a. Restored King James I to the Throne
    b. Restored Queen Elizabeth I to the Throne
    c. Placed Oliver Cromwell on the Throne
    d. Restored King Charles II to the Throne

(True or False)

11. After Elizabeth became Queen, the rivalry over religion and empire began in earnest between England and Spain.
    a. TRUE
    b. FALSE

12. Wealthy English businessmen avoided investment in colony-founding ventures as too risky.
    a. TRUE
    b. FALSE

13. In English King James I ruled before King George III.
    a. TRUE
    b. FALSE

14. The law-abiding trait of Englishmen made the enforcement of England's trade regulations easy in the colonies.
    a. TRUE
    b. FALSE

15. The leading objective in a mercantile economy was the achievement of a favorable balance of trade.
    a. TRUE
    b. FALSE

16. The primary English laws regulating colonial trade were the Navigation Acts.
    a. TRUE
    b. FALSE

17. Goods which could be sold anywhere in the world were known as "enumerated articles".
    a. TRUE
    b. FALSE

18. General search warrants were known as "Writs of Assistance".
    a. TRUE
    b. FALSE

19. The English Parliament consists of the House of Lords and the Senate.
    a. TRUE
    b. FALSE

20. The Petition of Right (1628) confirmed, among other things, that taxes can be levied only by Parliament.
    a. TRUE
    b. FALSE

T.   GLOSSARY

1. **Indenture system**   A contract binding one person to work for another for a specified period of time in return for payment of some sort, such as travel expenses to a different location.

2. **English Tories**   British political party which generally favored the retention of the social and/or political order. They generally supported the Monarchy and also, during the American Revolutionary War, the colonists who supported the English were known as "Tories".

3. **English Whigs**   British political party which generally favored a limited Monarchy and represented the aristocracy and upper middle class. They also were regarded as political dissenters, even supporting the American colonists in their Revolutionary War.

CHAPTER 4 SUMMARY

17TH CENTURY ENGLAND

A. BRITISH HISTORY OUTLINE TO 1750

1. Stone-Age Britain   5000 BC – 55 BC

2. The Celts   800-600 BC &
                                          Roman Occupation

3. Roman Britain   55 BC – 440 AD

4. Anglo-Saxon & Viking period   440 AD – 1066 AD

5. Early Middle-Ages   1066 AD – 1290 AD

6. Later Middle-Ages   1290 AD – 1485 AD

7. Tudor Period   1485 AD – 1603 AD

8. Stuart Period   1603 AD – 1714 AD

9. Georgian Period   1714 AD – 1837 AD

B. ENGLISH ROOTS OF AMERICAN DEMOCRACY

1. Magna-Carta   1215

2. Model Parliament   1295

3. Petition of Right   1628

4. English Bill of Rights   1689

C. SUMMARY OF BRITISH GOVERNMENT STRUCTURE

1. PARLIAMENT

- Supreme Legislative Body of British Empire

- Headed by a Monarch

- Formed in 1707 from a Treaty of Union (England & Scotland)

- Bicameral;

- Upper House/House of Lords

- Lower House/House of Commons

- Developed from "The Great Council" which advised the King during Medieval times

- First Parliament to be known as "The Model Parliament" of 1295

- Conflicts between Parliament and the Crown lead to the English Civil Wars of the 1640's

2. HOUSE OF LORDS

- Upper House of the Parliament

- Primary purpose to review all legislation proposed by the House of Commons

- Members are not democratically elected

- Number of members not fixed

3. HOUSE OF COMMONS

- Lower House of Parliament

- 650 members elected from electoral districts known as "Constituencies"

- Originally less powerful than House of Lords but now more powerful

- Prime Minister not elected by House of Commons but needs their support to retain office

D.   THE THREE MAJOR RULING FAMILIES

1. House of Tudor   1485- 1603
2. House of Stuart   1603-1714
3. House of Hanover   1714-1820

E.   ENGLISH CIVIL WAR 1642-1649

- Main issues were religious toleration for Puritans and other Protestant groups and more power for Parliament. Puritans supported Parliament against the Monarchs.

- Left England as the only European country without a Monarch

F.   THE ENGLISH INTERREGNUM 1649-1660

1. The Commonwealth of England   1649-1653
2. The Protectorate under Oliver Cromwel   1653-1658
3. The Protectorate under Richard Cromwell   1658-1659
4. The Second period of the Commonwealth   1659-1660

G.   THE RESTORATION 1660

- The people became tired of the Puritan form of Government of the Cromwells

- King Charles II assumes the Throne

- The power and wealth of the middle classes increased

- A time of great commercial success

- The beginning of the period known as the "English Enlightenment"

- The King no longer had absolute power but now was required to share with Parliament

H.   NEW IMPERIALISM 1650-1676

- Cromwell begins to deal with the problems of Empire

- 3 Wars with Holland, 1652-1654, 1664-1667, 1672-1674

- A series of Navigation Acts to regulate trade with the colonies and reduce the commercial influence of the Dutch

I.   GLORIOUS REVOLUTION 1689

- King James II assumes the Throne in 1685 and desires to re-establish Catholicism in England. The people revolted. Has a son/heir causing the people to fear a Catholic succession and dynasty.

- Prominent Protestants invite William of Orange, who is James son-in-law, to assume the Throne. King James flees to France and Parliament offers the Throne to William and his wife, Mary as joint-Monarchs.

- It represents a significant Parliamentary victory over the Monarchy.

J.   EMPIRE TAKES SHAPE 1689-1713

- A uniform administration of the colonies is created

K.   CROWN ATTITUDE HARDENS TOWARD COLONIES 1748

- The appointment of Earl of Halifax as President of the Board of Trade

L.   KING GEORGE III 1760

- Succeeds his father at age 22

- The Crown cracks down on illegal colonial trade with France

- "Writs of Assistance" are used against the colonials, causing unrest

- William Pitt and the Duke of Newcastle are supporters of the colonists but they resign which opens the door to George Grenville who becomes an opponent of the colonists.

Terrence Hagen

4a

ENGLISH ROOTS OF AMERICAN DEMOCRACY

English traditions & practices of liberty brought by the settlers to the New World

1. ***ENGLISH MAGNA-CARTA***   1215

    King John of England was forced to approve a document which limited the authority of the King with regard to taxation and the administration of justice.

    It established the right to trial by one's peers and allowed taxation only with the consent of those to be taxed. It also included a provision which protected the English Church from Royal interference especially in the election of Bishops

    It's influence on American political documents can be seen in Article 21 of the Maryland Constitution of 1776 and other subsequent colonial documents.

    The specific language was, "that no freeman ought to be taken, imprisoned, or dis-seized of his freehold, liberties, or privileges, or deprived of his life, liberty, or property but by the judgment of his peers or by the law of the land."

2. ***THE MODEL PARLIAMENT***   1295

    The Parliament of King Edward I consisted of members of the Clergy and Aristocracy as well as representatives from the various counties and boroughs. Each county sent 2 Knights. 2 Burgesses were elected from each borough and each city provided 2 citizens. This composition became the "model" for future Parliaments.

3. ***THE PETITION OF RIGHT***   1628

    Produced by the English Parliament and approved by King Charles I. It was most notable for its' confirmation that taxes may be levied only by Parliament and that Martial Law may not be imposed in time of peace. It also stated that prisoners must be able to challenge the legitimacy of their detention through "Writ of Habeas Corpus". It also included a ban on the billeting of troops which was eventually reflected in the 3rd Amendment of the United States Constitution.

    "Habeas Corpus" was defined as freedom from arbitrary and unjust arrest.

4. ***ENGLISH BILL OF RIGHTS***   1689

    Restated in statutory form the "Declaration of Rights" of 1628. It limited the powers of the King and established the rights of Parliament, the rules for freedom of speech in Parliament, the requirement for regular elections to Parliament, and the right to petition the King without fear of retribution.

    These ideas about "rights" reflected the political thinking of English Philosopher John Locke.

4b

SUMMARY OF THE BRITISH GOVERNMENT STRUCTURE

PARLIAMENT;

1. SUPREME LEGISLATIVE BODY OF THE BRITISH EMPIRE POSSESSING LEGISLATIVE SUPREMACY AND POWER OVER ALL OTHER POLITICAL BODIES OF THE EMPIRE.

2. LED BY THE MONARCH/SOVEREIGN.

3. BICAMERAL, WITH AN UPPER HOUSE (HOUSE OF LORDS) AND LOWER HOUSE (HOUSE OF COMMONS)

    a. BILLS COULD BE INTRODUCED IN EITHER HOUSE

4. FORMED IN 1707 FOLLOWING THE RATIFICATION OF THE TREATY OF UNION BETWEEN ENGLAND & SCOTLAND.

5. DEVELOPED FROM THE "MAGNUM CONCILIUM" (THE GREAT COUNCIL) WHICH ADVISED THE KING DURING MEDIEVAL TIMES.

6. THE FIRST PARLIAMENT IS OFTEN REFERRED TO AS "THE MODEL PARLIAMENT" OF 1295 WHICH INCLUDED ARCHBISHOPS, BISHOPS, ABBOTS, EARLS, BARONS, AND REPRESENTATIVES OF THE SHIRES & BURROUGHS.

7. THE POWER OF PARLIAMENT GREW SLOWLY AND WAS CLOSELY TIED TO THE STRENGTH OF THE MONARCHY.

    a. DURING THE REIGN OF KING EDWARD II (1307-1327) THE NOBILITY WAS SUPREME AND THE CROWN WAS WEAK.

    b. IN 1569 THE AUTHORITY OF PARLIAMENT WAS RECOGNIZED FOR THE FIRST TIME BY STATUTE AND PASSED BY THE PARLIAMENT ITSELF.

    c.   THE CROWN WAS AT THE HEIGHT OF ITS' POWER DURING THE REIGN OF

           KING HENRY VIII (1508-1547)

8.   CONFLICTS BETWEEN KING & PARLIAMENT, MOSTLY THE HOUSE OF COMMONS,

    LED TO THE ENGLISH CIVIL WARS OF THE 1640'S.

HOUSE OF LORDS;

1.   UPPER HOUSE OF PARLIAMENT.

2.   TWO DIFFERENT TYPES OF MEMBERS;

    a.   LORDS SPIRITUAL, MEMBERSHIP BASED ON AN ECCLESIASTICAL

           ROLE IN THE CHURCH OF ENGLAND. THERE WERE 26 SENIOR BISHOPS.

    b.   LORDS TEMPORAL, THE MAJORITY OF WHICH WERE "LIFE PEERS",

           APPOINTED BY THE MONARCH ON THE ADVICE OF THE PRIME MINISTER.

    c.   THE NUMBER OF MEMBERS WAS NOT FIXED BUT AS OF 2011 THERE WERE

           789 WITH 38 ON LEAVE OF ABSENCE.

3.   PRIMARY PURPOSE TO REVIEW ALL LEGISLATION PROPOSED BY THE

    HOUSE OF COMMONS. IT COULD PROPOSE AMENDMENTS.

4.   MEMBERS ARE NOT DEMOCRATICALLY ELECTED.

5.   ITS' POWER WAS REDUCED IN 1649 UNDER LORD CROMWELL AND THE

    HOUSE OF COMMONS. ON 3/19/1649 THE HOUSE OF LORDS WAS ABOLISHED

    BY AN ACT OF PARLIAMENT AND DID NOT ASSEMBLE AGAIN UNTIL 1660

    WHEN THE MONARCHY WAS RESTORED. IT THEN RETURNED TO BEING THE

    MORE POWERFUL AND INFLUENTIAL CHAMBER OF PARLIAMENT.

4b

HOUSE OF COMMONS;

1. LOWER HOUSE OF PARLIAMENT.

2. DEMOCRATICALLY ELECTED CONSISTING OF 650 MEMBERS (AS OF 2010 ELECTION) KNOWN AS MP'S (MEMBERS OF PARLIAMENT). THEY ARE ELECTED FROM DISTRICTS KNOWN AS CONSTITUENCIES AND HOLD THEIR SEATS UNTIL PARLIAMENT IS DISSOLVED, A MAXIMUM OF 5 YEARS AFTER THE PRECEEDING ELECTION.

3. COMPOSED OF 2 KNIGHTS OR GENTLEMEN FROM EACH COUNTY AND 1 OR 2 BURGESSES FROM EACH OF NEARLY 300 BURROUGHS;

    a. THERE WAS NO ATTEMPT TO MAKE THE HOUSE OF COMMONS SYSTEM OF REPRESENTATION EQUAL OR DEMOCRATIC.

    b. MEMBERS FROM THE COUNTIES WERE ELECTED BY THOSE HOLDING A "40 SHILLING" FREEHOLD, OR, THOSE WHO OWNED OR RENTED LAND FOR THAT AMOUNT.

    c. THEY REPRESENTED ONLY THE PROPERTIED CLASSES AND WHEN THEY SPOKE OF "RIGHTS" THEY MEANT ONLY THE RIGHTS OF THE PROPERTIED PEOPLE.

4. IT EVOLVED DURING THE 14TH CENTURY.

5. IT WAS ORIGINALLY LESS POWERFUL THAN THE HOUSE OF LORDS BUT CURRENTLY ITS' LEGISLATIVE POWERS EXCEED THOSE OF THE HOUSE OF LORDS, SINCE THE MID-17TH CENTURY.

6. THE GOVERNMENT IS PRIMARILY RESPONSIBLE TO THE HOUSE OF COMMONS AS THE PRIME MINISTER REMAINS IN OFFICE ONLY AS LONG AS HE/SHE RETAINS THE SUPPORT OF THE HOUSE OF COMMONS.

7. ALMOST ALL GOVERNMENT MINISTERS ARE DRAWN FROM THE HOUSE OF COMMONS AS WELL AS ALL PRIME MINISTERS WITH ONE EXCEPTION SINCE 1902.

8. IT DOES NOT FORMALLY ELECT THE PRIME MINISTER BUT THE PRIME MINISTER IS ANSWERABLE TO AND MUST MAINTAIN THE SUPPORT OF THE COMMONS.

4c

CHRONOLOGY OF ENGLISH ACCESSION TO THE THRONE			
1.	HENRY VII	1485	1509
2.	HENRY VIII	1509	1547
3.	EDWARD VI	1547	1553
4.	MARY I	1553	1558
5.	ELIZABETH I	1558	1603
6.	JAMES I	1603	1625
7.	CHARLES I	1625	1649
8.	OLIVER CROMWELL *	1649	1660
9.	KING CHARLES II **	1660	1685
10.	KING JAMES II	1685	1689
11.	WILLIAM III & MARY II ***	1689	1702
12.	QUEEN ANNE	1702	1714
13.	KING GEORGE I	1714	1727
14.	KING GEORGE II	1727	1760
15.	KING GEORGE III	1760	1820

FOOTNOTES:

* *Known as the "Interregnum". Cromwell title was*
"Lord Protector of the Commonwealth of England"

** *Known as the "Restoration"*

*** *Known as the "Glorious Revolution".*
William of Orange and Mary Stuart, co-Monarchs.

TUDOR MONARCH'S OF ENGLAND (1485-1603)

NAME	CLAIM TO THRONE	BIRTH	CROWN	DEATH	MARRIAGE(S)
HENRY VII	Descended from King Edward III	1/28/1457	10/30/1485	4/21/1509	Elizabeth of York
HENRY VIII	Son of King Henry VII	6/28/1491	6/24/1509	1/28/1547	Six
EDWARD VI	Son of King Henry VIII & Jane Seymour	10/12/1537	2/20/1547	7/6/1553	None
MARY I	Daughter of King Henry VIII by Catherine of Aragon	2/18/1516	10/1/1553	11/18/1558	King Philip II of Spain
ELIZABETH I	Daughter of King Henry VIII by Anne Boleyn	9/7/1533	11/17/1558	3/24/1603	None

STUART MONARCH'S OF ENGLAND (1603-1714)

NAME	CLAIM TO THRONE	BIRTH	CROWN	UNTIL	MARRIAGE(S)
JAMES I	Son of Mary, Queen of Scots, and Henry Stuart	6/19/1566	3/24/1603	3/27/1625	Princess Anne of Denmark
CHARLES I	Son of King James I	11/19/1600	3/27/1625	1/30/1649 Executed	Princess Henrietta Maria (France)
CHARLES II	Son of King Charles I Jane Seymour	5/29/1630	5/29/1660 (Records changed)	2/6/1685	Catherine of Braganza
JAMES II	Brother of King Charles II Son of King Charles I	10/14/1633	2/6/1685	2/13/1689	Anne Hyde 1659 Mary of Modena 1673
MARY II	Daughter of King James II Co-Monarch with William of Orange	4/30/1662	2/13/1689	12/28/1694	William III (Orange)
ANNE	Sister of Queen Mary II Daughter of King James II	2/6/1665	3/8/1702	8/1/1714	Prince George of Denmark
***	WILLIAM OF ORANGE RULES AS SOLE MONARCH 1694-1702				

141

4f

HANOVER MONARCHS OF ENGLAND (1714-1820)

NAME	BIRTH	CROWN	UNTIL	MARRIAGE(S)
GEORGE I	1660	1714	1727	Sophia Dorothea of Celle
GEORGE II	11/10/1683	1727	1760	Caroline of Ansbach
GEORGE III	6/4/1738	1760	1820	Charlotte of Mecklenburg-Strelitz

Chapter 5

The Virginia Colony

This chapter will be the first of 13 to deal with each of the original English colonies.

Attachment 5a summarizes the 13 Original English colonies by region; New England, Middle Atlantic, and Southern, in terms of their basic characteristics.

Attachment 5b summarizes the 13 original colonies, the site and date of the original settlement, the date in which that colony ratified the new Federal Constitution, the order in which ratification occurred and the number of years from the date of the original settlement to the date of its ratification.

The purpose of this chart is to show that it took the United States 169 years from the first settlement to the Declaration of Independence and another 12-14 years to ratify the first Federal Constitution of the United States.

A.   BACKGROUND

Our examination of the history of the Virginia colony will fall into 7 sections:

- The vision of Sir Humphrey Gilbert and Sir Walter Raleigh

- The formation of an English settlement and colonization policy

- The first settlement at Jamestown

- The significance of the Charter of 1618

- Becoming a Royal Colony in 1624

- The Parliament threat of 1650

- Frontier unrest

B.   THE VISION OF SIR HUMPHREY GILBERT & SIR WALTER RALEIGH

The history of the Virginia colony actually begins in present-day North Carolina due to the efforts of 2 half-brothers, Sir Humphrey Gilbert and Sir Walter Raleigh.

1.   SIR HUMPHREY GILBERT (1539-1583)

He was born in England and served Queen Elizabeth I in a variety of governmental positions where he became a strong supporter of state-sponsored exploration of North America to find the Northwest Passage to Asia. He was knighted in 1570, entered Parliament in 1571, and sought Royal permission to explore North America. He eventually obtained a Charter from Queen Elizabeth I on 6/11/1578 to discover and occupy new, unclaimed lands and extend the rights of Englishmen to those who joined in his venture. *This Charter was significant because it established the principle that "a freeborn Englishman lost no rights by moving overseas" and the Monarch could not rule as a dictator but must follow English law. This principle appears again in the pre-Revolutionary war debates among the colonists about their "rights of Englishmen".*

Gilbert had dreamed of reproducing in the New World the England he knew, a land of great estates ruled by Nobles over tenants and freeholders, almost like the Kings of the countryside. The Crown shaped Gilbert's Charter to fit his dream by giving him a grant of Lordship to all of the land he settled. He financed his voyages by distributing, for a fee, huge parcels of land to those who shared his vision.

2. **SIR WALTER RALEIGH (1552-1618)**

There is some question about his actual birth date with some historians claiming it as 1554 while others claim it to be 1552. He was a half-brother to Sir Humphrey Gilbert and also related to Sir Richard Grenville and Sir Francis Drake. In 1580 he helped defeat an Irish rebellion and was Knighted by Queen Elizabeth I and became one of her favorites. In 1586, he helped discover the plot to assassinate Queen Elizabeth I and replace her with Mary Queen of Scots. This was called the "Babington Plot" and his role in defeating the plot further endeared him to the Queen.

Raleigh shared the same vision for America as did Gilbert and received the same generous terms from the Crown for his voyages which he also personally financed.

3. **EARLY EXPLORATIONS AND SETTLEMENT ATTEMPTS**

Merchants backed both men's ventures because commerce and colonization could not be completely separated. The "gentleman adventurer" was motivated by the profit, prestige, and power which came with the land although the merchants were primarily interested in profits and wealth accumulation.

The following summarizes the early English efforts to colonize the New World:

a. THE FIRST EXPEDITION OF 11/12/1578

Sir Humphrey Gilbert obtained his charter from the Queen on 6/11/1578 to discover and occupy unclaimed lands in North America. As previously mentioned, this Charter was significant because it established the precedent that freeborn Englishmen lost no rights by moving overseas and that the Monarch could not rule as a dictator but must follow English law.

b. THE SECOND EXPEDITION OF 6/11/1583

Gilbert sent 5 ships to colonize somewhere between Cape Hatteras and the mouth of the Hudson River. It landed in St. John harbor, Newfoundland. After some explorations, it was decided to return home but Gilbert vanished somewhere near the Azore Islands in 8/1583.

c. THE ROANOKE ISLAND VOYAGES

In 1584, Sir Walter Raleigh hired 2 navigators, Phillip Amadas and Arthur Barlowe, to lead an exploration to the New World with the Chesapeake Bay as its' original destination because of its perceived milder climate than the northern regions. Also, it was outside the influence of the Spanish in Florida. They targeted an area off the coast of present-day North Carolina and south of Albemarle Sound as the likely site for a new colony.

Raleigh received a grant from Queen Elizabeth I on 3/15/1584 for all the North American lands he could occupy. He was given 7 years to either succeed or lose his right to colonize. His expedition left England on 4/27/1584, eventually sighted the North Carolina coast on 7/4/1584, and landed at Roanoke Island on 7/13/1584. After brief explorations they returned to England and recommended Roanoke Island as the site of a new colony.

On 4/9/1585, Raleigh sent 7 ships from Plymouth, England, to Virginia, led by Sir Richard Grenville and Sir Ralph Lane with 600 settlers. In early August, they landed on Roanoke Island and began building houses and fortifications. Lane assumed command as the Governor of the colony on 8/17/1585. Raleigh named the colony "Virginia" after a Queen Elizabeth I nickname, "The Virgin Queen".

After a small settlement was established, the settlers became disappointed and asked to return to England in 1586 with Sir Francis Drake who had just stopped at the site after a naval expedition against Spanish shipping. The settlement was failing because they landed too late in the season for planting and their supplies were rapidly diminishing. To make matters worse, Lane, a military officer, angered the neighboring Indians by killing their Chief Wingina over a stolen cup.

The settlement was abandoned but the Fort was left, which can be seen today at the "Fort Raleigh National Historic Site". Ironically, a supply ship from England arrived at Roanoke Island less than a week later and, finding the island deserted, the leader left behind 15 men who were apparently attacked by the local Indians and either killed, captured, or fled without a trace of them being found.

Raleigh was angry with Lane but decided on another attempt at a more self-sufficient and permanent settlement. On 5/8/1587 another 3 ships left Plymouth, England, for Virginia with 119 colonists, 9 assistants, the appointed Governor, John White, and his pregnant daughter Eleanor Dare and son-in-law Annanias Dare, and the Indian Chief Manteo who had become an ally while in England. They reached the mainland of Virginia on 7/16/1587 and then Roanoke Island on 7/22/1587 but found no sign of the settlers. They began rebuilding the settlement plus constructed new facilities and planted self-sustaining crops.

On 8/18/1587, Virginia Dare became the first English child born in the New World. It was also during August that relations with the Indians began to worsen and the settlers began thinking of returning home. Eventually, Governor White agreed to return to England with the unsatisfied settlers and request additional supplies for another attempt at colonization.

He arrived in England on 11/5/1587 and met with Raleigh to request additional supplies or, if not, to end the colonization effort there. Raleigh failed to resupply the effort partly because Queen Elizabeth I issued a "stay of shipping" because of the impending war with Spain and its threat to English shipping. Because of the war with Spain, White was forced to remain in England for 3 years.

When he finally returned on 8/18/1590 he found no sign of the settlers and the entire colony had vanished. He eventually returned to England and was never again able to raise the funding and resources to return to the colony. Although there have been many theories about the "Lost Colony", none have been substantiated.

C. FORMATION OF ENGLISH SETTLEMENT & COLONIZATION POLICY

King James I succeeded Queen Elizabeth I upon her death in 1603 and immediately made peace with Spain in the "Treaty of London" (8/18/1604). The Treaty was also known as the "Somerset House Conference" negotiated with King Phillip III of Spain who had also inherited the war from his father and predecessor, King Phillip II.

The end of the war with Spain allowed England to return its' attention to colonization and settlement. The 16th century ended without England having created a single colony or trading post in the New World. Even though the war retarded their colonization efforts, there were the following benefits:

- the defeat of the Spanish Armada increased the national confidence in the Royal Navy;

- the Naval conflicts allowed them to improve their ship design and navigation methods;

- the improved Naval and commercial shipping skills greatly increased their national wealth and world influence. England also learned from the failed colonization efforts of Gilbert and Raleigh.

- the colonies must create their own wealth through agriculture rather than depending on the exploitation of the environment or trade with the local Indians;

- the wealth of no individual would be sufficient to sustain a colony to a profitable result.

As a result of this knowledge, future efforts would be led by "joint-stock companies" which would sell stock to individual investors (adventurers) which shifted control of overseas expansion from the individualistic noble class to a rising middle class.

By the early 1600's, England was in a good position to continue their colonization efforts not only through what they had learned from the

Gilbert and Raleigh efforts, but from recent events in Europe which also helped stimulate the conditions for expansion and development, such as:

- the Protestant Reformation caused Englishmen to desire to convert the American Indians to Protestantism before the Spanish could convert them to Catholicism;

- the Reformation also created numerous dissenting Protestant Sects whose members wanted to worship their religion as they chose;

- population density and overcrowding in England led to economic problems which caused many citizens to look at the New World for opportunities to better their lives;

- there was a growing spirit of adventure as well as the lure of wealth. England's commercial and industrial enterprises had created surplus capital for which there were no home markets;

- under the prevailing "mercantilism system" every nation sought to export more than it imported. But, England was forced to import sugar, tobacco, and lumber. Colonies could provide her with these items thus allowing her to keep her wealth at home;

- England's woolen manufacturers were unable to sell cloth in Europe because most nations forbade imports as an effort to protect their competitive industries.

This was the world facing England as it began to develop its existing colonies and settle new ones. The competition for wealth and power led the European nations to compete with one another. In England's case it was Sir Humphrey Gilbert who foresaw the benefit of using overseas colonies as bases from which to attack its rivals/enemies and diminish their national wealth. France had established forts in the Mississippi river valley to block Spanish expansion and the Spanish did the same in the lower Mississippi river valley against French expansion.

1. **THE FIRST CHARTER FOR THE VIRGINIA COLONY (4/10/1606)**

A charter was issued by King James I to the Virginia Company of London which was composed of the London and Plymouth companies. It assigned land rights to colonists for the purpose of expanding the Christian religion and the land was described as Coastal Virginia which ranged from present-day South Carolina to Canada. The company was effectively managed by Sir Thomas Smith as Treasurer.

The land itself would remain the property of the King with the London Company as the King's tenant and the settlers as sub-tenants. The colony's government, at first, consisted of a Council residing in London, which designated the London Company as responsible for financing the project, recruiting potential settlers, and providing for their transport and supplies.

The significance of this charter, similar to the one granted to Gilbert in 1578, was that it granted that all settlers within the colonies would have the same rights and privileges as if they had never left England. It also granted that all those to be born in the colonies would also have the rights of English citizens. In effect, this was an extension of the charter granted to Gilbert.

The Charter was subject to the Royal Council used by the King to provide for government of the colonies. Its members were chosen by the King and they controlled all matters of government, such as choosing and instructing subsidiary councils to directly rule over the colonies. In theory, the Crown governed the colonies and held all political power. In reality, however, the Royal Council was composed primarily of Company leaders so they actually ran their own ventures but in the name of the Crown.

Eventually, control of the colonies would pass from the King to Company leaders, then to the Parliament, colonial governors, and then to colonial assemblies.

At first, the London Company intended only to establish a small settlement but company officials decided that the first group of settlers would set up a base and then report back to recommend a pattern of settlement. The company would then slowly develop the base to prepare for integrating the new settlers and additional supplies.

D.　FIRST SETTLEMENT AT JAMESTOWN (5/14/1607)

On 12/20/1606, 3 ships, the "Susan Constant, Godspeed, and Discovery", sailed from England with 144 settlers. Captain Christopher Newport was in overall command until they landed and then they would read the governing orders from the Royal Council which required a majority of 7 to take charge of the colony. They arrived off the coast of Virginia 4/26/1607 but during the 4 months at sea, 39 settlers died while others were involved in a mutiny, including Captain John Smith who was to be the military officer of the settlement. He was placed in jail but the governing orders included Smith as one of the 7 leaders. The governing charter also included a provision that the council could depose any member by a majority vote, so Smith was expelled.

The settlement plan intended to avoid the same mistakes made at Roanoke Island. They suggested a site easily defended along a large river with access to the backcountry and a wide area for native trade plus it suggested settlement far enough inland to avoid a surprise attack from the sea. After searching for a month, the council selected land near the James River, 30 miles inland from the sea. The settlers went ashore 5/14/1607 and were divided into 3 work groups to:

- build a fort and housing within it;

- clear the ground for planting and erect a warning post on the seacoast

- explore the river for a possible passage to Asia.

The plan was for a self-sustaining settlement for a long period of time. Trouble with the Indians began almost immediately when, on 5/26/1607, they were forced to defend themselves from an Indian attack. In late June, Captain Newport returned to England for supplies but the settlers realized that it would be at least 6 months before they would be re-supplied from England. The settlement population in June was 104 but within 6 months, 51 died of starvation and disease.

In October, 1608, Captain Newport returned with more settlers and supplies. In spite of two reinforcements, Jamestown remained just a fortified trading post where employees of the company worked for their absentee stockholders. No private property was allowed, which diminished individual incentive. As previously mentioned, the Company was managed by a Council elected and managed in London which did not provide local direction. This lack of local direction allowed the settlers to waste time searching for gold and failed to produce the necessary provisions to sustain them. They became sick on the local food they had bought from friendly Indians and also caught malaria from the mosquito's and many died.

1. **EARLY INDIAN RELATIONS AND CAPTAIN JOHN SMITH**

   At the time of Jamestown, there were 200,000 Indians east of the Mississippi river. Language differences were the primary differential among the tribes. Although we will devote a later chapter to Indian relations, for now we will just identify two of the major Indian tribes which may have impacted the Jamestown settlers.

   a. The Algonquin Tribe was the largest language group east of the Mississippi river which controlled most of Canada, the Ohio valley, all of New England, and scattered southward through eastern Pennsylvania, New Jersey, Maryland, and Virginia.

   b. The Powhatan Confederacy was a branch of the Algonquins who greeted the Jamestown settlers. Others greeted the colonists at Plymouth, Boston, and parts of Canada. They were semi-nomadic and lived in bark-covered huts, and were known for their enterprise and for the birch-bark canoes they invented.

   The Confederacy focused on the Tidewater Virginia region and eastern shore of the Chesapeake Bay. Wahunsonacock, or Powhatan, as the English called him, was the leader of the Confederacy when Jamestown was settled in 1607. The Powhatan were said to have been driven north into Virginia by the Spanish where their Chief, Powhatan's father, subjugated 5 other Virginia tribes. They were sedentary people with 200 settlements throughout eastern Virginia. They cultivated corn, fished, hunted, and located their capital at present-day Puritan Bay on the east shore of the York River near present-day Gloucester, Virginia.

It was in this eastern region of Virginia where John Smith first met Chief Powhatan. Beginning in 1608, English settlers began seizing the best Indian lands which caused unrest with the Indians. To appease the Chief, the English gave him a Crown and a Coronation ceremony performed by Captain Newport in 1609. Relations were up and down until the Chief's daughter, Pocahontas, married John Rolfe, a successful local planter.

After being expelled from the Council, Smith was free of official duties so in the summer of 1608, he explored and mapped the Chesapeake Bay region. When he returned to Jamestown, he found the settlers searching for gold rather than working on developing the settlement. He left again to explore for food and other supplies, returning in September with some provisions. 3 days later the Council decided to make him President of the Council. When Captain Newport returned from England with 70 new settlers and more supplies he was impressed with the improvements made by Smith. That winter less than a dozen settlers out of 200 died and, by the summer of 1609, it seemed as if Jamestown would survive even though it was clear that further improvements were needed, such as:

- A profitable cash crop;

- A system of land-holding which would give the colonists a financial stake in the colony;

- Strong leadership and discipline.

Among the colony leaders, Smith was the most successful in dealing with the Indians. He became expert in their customs and explored the surrounding region. He was successful with the Nansemond Indians who located near the Nansemond River near present-day Suffolk, west of Norfolk, Virginia.

After one of the re-supply efforts of Captain Newport, Smith felt the colony was secure enough to attempt another peace effort with the Powhatan Chief. Some historians claim that it was during this time that Pocahontas saved him from capture by Opechancanough, thought to be the brother of the Powhatan Chief. The improving Indian relations, because of Pocahontas, didn't last long. After a fire destroyed much of the settlement, which caused the settlers to rely even more on the Indians, Chief Powhatan decided it was time to end the truce, stop all trade with the colonists, and drive them out of Virginia.

John Ratcliffe, Captain of the ship "Discovery", tried his hand at making peace with the Indians but was captured and tortured to death, leaving the colony without strong leadership at a time when Indian attacks were increasing.

2. THE SECOND CHARTER FOR THE VIRGINIA COLONY (5/23/1609)

A new charter was approved which created a "joint-stock company" which included the following:

- revision of the boundaries to include 400 miles along the coast with the interior running west and northwest;

- provision for the governing Council in England to be elected by the stockholders;

- replaced the squabbling local Council with a Governor.

The newly-elected Treasurer, Sir Thomas Smith, persuaded the Council to revise the government along autocratic lines like that of the home office in London. The ineffective local council and its President were replaced by a Governor with complete control over the colony. He might choose a Council of Advisors but was not required to agree with their advice. This change of government was influenced by the success of John Smith while he was President, combined with the overall English government suspicion of popular representation. This joint-stock plan was designed to end in 1616 at which time all of the accumulated profits would be divided among shareholders and the cleared land would be divided with the settlers receiving at least 100 acres.

The major significance of the 2nd Charter was the replacement of the local council with a Governor.

3. **THE FIRST GREAT MIGRATION**

Six ships commanded by Sir Thomas Gates left England in May, 1609, with 600 settlers. Three other ships joined them in Plymouth, England, and was the largest emigration to Virginia to date. On the way, one ship was lost at sea while another with the 3 leaders of the expedition, Gates, Newport, and George Somers, who commanded the fleet, was wrecked on the island of Bermuda. The remaining 7 ships arrived at Jamestown with 400 new settlers to meet the remaining 100 original settlers. No housing had been prepared and no food crops planted. John Smith had no authority in the new charter to manage the settlers, so he left for more supplies.

In spite of their best planning efforts, Jamestown's chances for survival for the first few winters didn't look very good. Their food supplies quickly diminished because the settlers didn't promptly plant their food crops. The combination of malaria and hostile Indians made life difficult. By mid-September, 46 settlers had died, mostly from famine. This was at the time that John Smith had returned to England for supplies plus the Indians were beginning to refuse to trade with the settlers plus had launched some attacks outside of the fort. All of these efforts caused a severe food shortage. Various attempts at farming led to kidnappings and murder by the Powhatans while peace efforts resulted in either the emissaries being killed, captured, or just not successful in securing a truce. The Indians, led by Powhatan, planned to starve the colonists out of Virginia. Eventually, all of these factors led to the almost total collapse of the colony. This period, the winter of 1609-1610, was to be known as "The Starving Time".

In May, 1610, Gates and the Bermuda survivors arrived in Jamestown with 175 settlers to add to the settlement which was still starving and having discipline problems. It was decided that Jamestown should be abandoned but left intact rather than burnt down. As they boarded their ships to return to England and began drifting downstream they saw Lord De La Warr's relief fleet which was bringing supplies and more settlers.

De La Warr assumed control and sent ships to Bermuda to secure a cargo of pork as well as return Gates and Newport to England to discuss the long-term situation with the Company. He introduced discipline which gradually ended the starving time but didn't solve all of the problems. Some settlers continued to die and De La Warr himself became ill and returned to England in March, 1611. Fortunately, at the same time, Sir Thomas Smith raised enough money to finance two more relief expeditions. The first of these, with 3 ships and 300 settlers, sailed under Thomas Dale in March, 1611, and the second expedition in May was led by Gates with 6 ships, 300 settlers, and a large supply of cattle, swine, and poultry.

4. **THE THIRD CHARTER FOR THE VIRGINIA COLONY (3/12/1612)**

In 1612, the colony requested and received a new charter which relieved their financial problems by allowing it to run lotteries to raise revenues. The company was awarded a 7 year exemption on all customs duties in England. The Virginia boundary was extended to include Bermuda, which, with Jamestown, was treated as a single part of the Company until 1615 when Bermuda received its' own charter.

The negative impression of adventurers toward Virginia caused the Crown to abandon their attempt to control Virginia. It returned to the trading-company charter of pre-colonization days where company members managed their own affairs. Power was now shifted from a Council, responsible to the Crown, to a "Court and Assembly". The charter also authorized 4 great courts to be held annually and to include all members of the Company to determine matters of policy. Lesser matters were handled by an "ordinary court" which met weekly. Though the charter of 1612 gave adventurers in England control over company affairs, it made no changes in the management of the government of Virginia.

5. **GROWING INDIAN PROBLEMS**

After his arrival, De La Warr launched a counter-attack against the Indian raids which produced another, but short, truce. Even the marriage of John Rolfe and Pocahontas in 1614 wasn't able to sustain long-term peace between the Indians and colonists. When the colonists attempted to expand their settlements beyond Jamestown, the Indians reacted against additional land invasions by the settlers. Opechancanough decided to attack and, for once and for all, drive them out of the area. The death of Pocahontas in 1617 hurt the peace effort because she was no longer a force for peace and unity. The attacks continued until 3/22/1622 when Indian attacks killed 347 settlers, including John Rolfe.

Another massacre of women and children caused the settlers to retreat into their protected stockades and live in crowded conditions which were already made worse by the inclusion of 340 new settlers. During the year, 500 settlers died from all causes and Indian relations were at an all-time low. Fighting continued until 1644 when Opechancanough led the last uprising where he was captured and killed at Jamestown. In 1646 the Confederacy yielded much of its territory and, beginning in 1665, its Chiefs were appointed by the Governor. After the Iroquois, traditional enemies of the Powhatan, agreed to cease their attacks in the "Treaty of Albany", the tribes were scattered, mixed with settlers, and all semblance of the Powhatan Confederacy disappeared. The prolonged warfare with the Powhatan changed the initial viewpoint of the settlers of the Indians as "noble savages" which represented a shift in attitude which occurred in every American colony before the end of the 17th century.

6. **GATES AND THOMAS DALE REPLACE DE LA WARR**

Gates arrived at Jamestown with 220 new settlers and governed from 8/16/1611 to 1614 before returning home. Although Gates was the Chief Executive it was Thomas Dale who actually managed the settlement during this time. He arrived with his relief expedition 3 months prior to Gates and enforced strict rules, known as "Dale's Laws", which Gates approved. The colony expanded under their strict management with both serving a term as Governor. Dale explored 40 miles up the James River in 1611 and founded the town of Henrico. He enclosed 7 acres of land within a stockade and built within it a storehouse, church, and 3 rows of houses. Enough land was cleared to raise grain for the entire colony.

By 1616 there were 6 similar settlements along the river although Jamestown continued as the "seat of government" but over half of the colony's population of 381 was scattered in stockades above the town and along the mouth of the James River, leaving Jamestown nearly a deserted village.

All of the new settlements were cooperative projects. Dale and Gates continued the communal management of the colony's life that had begun in 1609 and was to continue until 1616 at which time the hoped-for profits would be divided among planters and adventurers. Both men feared that some would not work for the overall interest of the many and just fail to do their share. In 1613-1614 they modified the communal plan by giving the most senior settlers 3 acres of cleared land in return for which they devoted one month's service to the colony and 2 1/2 barrels of grain to the company storehouse. The incentive of free land was successful when it appeared that the Virginia soil might provide settlers with more than food.

In 1616 and until 1619 the Joint-Stock system was terminated and the land divided among private owners to give the colonists a greater incentive to produce. The labor supply of the colony increased as indentured servants were imported. "Indentured servants" were those who sold their services for a period of 4-7 years to the farmer who paid their way to America. To encourage their importation the company granted a "head-right" of 50 acres of land to anyone paying the passage of a servant. This process transferred more land to private hands, further stimulating self-sufficient production.

7. **TOBACCO**

Its' value for export was first discovered in 1613 when John Rolfe imported seed from the West Indies, crossed it with the local-grown tobacco, and produced a smooth smoke which captured the English market. Virginia then became "tobacco-mad" even growing it in the streets of Jamestown. As early as 1618, Virginia exported 50,000 pounds weight of tobacco to England. Although this encouraged more would-be settlers, it also made the colony more dependent on England for supplies. To keep Virginia supplied with food a special organization was formed, "The Magazine", by wealthy members of the Company. It distributed food supplies and, in return, received the monopoly of selling Virginia tobacco in England.

Dale returned home in 1616 with John Rolfe and his wife, Pocahontas, who had been converted to Christianity, plus a small group of Indians. The Company praised Dale for his success in Virginia but enthusiasm for the Virginia experiment was decreasing because of the cost and loss of so many lives. Only 351 settlers had survived and the 7 year period of joint-stock was about to end without any profits to distribute. The hoped-for cash crop, tobacco, could not compete with the Spanish tobacco which the English preferred because of a better taste. Even Virginia settlers were not optimistic about their future. Trading was monopolized by a London-controlled group which dumped their over-priced and useless goods on the settlers in return for their tobacco and other goods.

E.   THE SIGNIFICANCE OF THE CHARTER OF 1618 (11/18/1618)

Combined with the plan to reinforce the settlement was a desire to change the form of local government to deal with an increasing number of new settlements along the James River. New ways had to be found to entice new groups of settlers who would finance themselves to Virginia for settlement. In 1618, new instructions were given to the new Governor, George Yeardley, who had replaced Dale. Yeardley announced new laws called *the "Great Charter of 1618"* which were identical to those of citizens living in England.

The key element in the new charter was the distribution of land to be used to attract settlers. The Company promised a minimum of 100 acres to all adventurers and pre-1616 planters. Those carried at company-expense would work the company lands (public estate) at half-rent for 7 years and then be free at the end of that time to set out on their own. Those who left for Virginia at their own expense would receive a "head-right" of at least 50 acres and additional grants for every person they brought with them. This system became fixed in Virginia tradition and, in one form or another, was adopted by all colonies in time.

The Charter also created 4 "Borough's", James City, Charles City, Henrico, and Kecoughtan, and within each the tenants would work the company's 3000 acres of land while the rest remained in private hands. The income from these lands would be used to ease all the inhabitants of Virginia forever of all taxes and public burdens as much as possible and to also pay dividends to the adventurers back home in England.

The private plantations had presented a tricky problem for the Company. They often represented the investment of influential men, the sort the Company wanted to attract to Virginia but also the sort who would resist interference in their affairs. Yet, to allow these private "corporations" a free hand would create a chaotic diversity in the colony. The issue was resolved by requiring the same company management in Virginia as in London.

The significance of the Great Charter of 1618 was that it was created to govern an expanding number of settlements beyond Jamestown and it also gave birth to the House of Burgesses. (Attachment 5c represents a Map of Virginia settlements in 1632)

1. **ORIGINS OF THE HOUSE OF BURGESSES**

   The Virginia House of Burgesses derives from the "Great Charter of 1618" which required that annually 2 members from each corporation and borough would be chosen on the local level to assemble in Jamestown to meet as a "House of Burgesses". The creation of this colonial Assembly was similar to the company Assembly in London which completed the equality between the Virginia planter and the London adventurer.

   The first Assembly met in Jamestown on 7/30/1619 with the Governor, his Council, and 22 Representatives, known as "Burgesses". The session lasted 6 days with laws passed dealing with a variety of issues, such as:

   - Indian affairs

   - Morals and religion of the settlers

   - Encouragement of agricultural experiments

   - Contracts with tenants and servants

   - Maintenance of the company storehouse

   - Provision for their own salaries

   - A tax of one pound of tobacco on every man over the age of 16

   They agreed that the Company could disallow their laws but requested a reciprocal right on company ordinances. The Great Charter of 1618, which was the genesis of the House of Burgesses, had been produced while Sir Thomas Smith still led the Company but was aided by Sir Edwin Sandys who strongly opposed the King's power while a member of the English

Parliament. Smith and Sandys worked effectively together for over a decade when Sandys became the Company Treasurer in 1619. Eventually, they disagreed not over policy but how policy was to be implemented. The election of Sandys as Treasurer angered the tyrannical King James I who was already annoyed by a conflict over the collection of customs duties on tobacco. Sandys proved to be a strong leader who managed to persuade over 4000 new colonists to emigrate to Virginia from England over the next 4 years.

He assumed the Treasurer position after years of facing tough problems with debt and taxes. One solution was to broaden the industry base beyond tobacco, seeking to develop an iron industry, erect and operate a sawmill, experiment with cotton, sugar-cane, and other potential crops. He was working on a variety of efforts to increase self-sufficiency at the time of the great Indian massacre of 1622 which changed the focus of the government back to self-defense.

F.   FAILURE OF THE LONDON COMPANY LEADS TO VIRGINIA BECOMING A ROYAL COLONY IN 1624

The Indian massacre of 1622 changed Sandys plans. Approaching bankruptcy produced opposition to Sandys from within the Company. Any thought of expansion and experimentation must wait until the colony regained its strength and tobacco was once again identified as the cash-crop to improve their financial situation. He negotiated the "Tobacco Contract of 1622" in which the company received a monopoly to handle all tobacco brought into England, and the King, in return, received a fixed revenue on every pound imported plus a percentage of the Company's overall profits. This was not popular and opposition to him grew.

Those who controlled private plantations in Bermuda and Virginia opposed having to market their crop through the Company when they might do better on the open market. Opposition became so strong that the Tobacco Contract of 1622 was voided in 1623. Soon afterward, the

English Privy Council took over the management of Company affairs in London while a 5-man commission traveled to Virginia to investigate the situation.

1. **FAILURE OF THE LONDON COMPANY**

    The commission did not receive much cooperation although they learned enough to know that the colony had problems. The Crown offered a compromise in the form of a new charter patterned after the 1606 charter which would give the government some control over company affairs. This was rejected by the Company so the government then ordered them to appear in a London court to justify its claims to a privilege or liberty. In mid-1624, the Company lost the case and was ordered divested of its privileges under the Charter of 1612.

    The Company failed because it went bankrupt and also because of dissatisfaction over the failure to pay dividends from the profits, as promised, the increasing Indian troubles since 1622, plus there were too many settlers unwilling or unable to do physical work. Even though the company failed, there were some positives:

    - the company created a colony in the wilderness which survived 17 years

    - the settlers learned how to sustain themselves and produce a cash-crop (tobacco)

    - they had established a form of representative government

2. **VIRGINIA BECOMES A ROYAL COLONY IN 1624**

    Virginia now became a Crown colony, with a Governor and Council appointed by the King. The colonists agreed with this change because the Representative Assembly (House of Burgesses) was retained and under King Charles I, who succeeded his father, King James I, in 1625, a period of prosperity began. *The King retained the right to veto acts of the Assembly but the people enjoyed a large degree of self-government especially after*

1624 when the Governor was forbidden to levy taxes without the consent of the House of Burgesses. During the Puritan Revolution in England, 1642-1660, the colony virtually ruled itself.

3. **GOVERNOR FRANCIS WYATT (1624)**

The English Privy Council sent Francis Wyatt as the new Governor. Even though his instructions did not require an Assembly or Council, which suggests that the Crown (still King James I in 1624 and until 1625) wanted to return to an autocratic rule, he soon learned that he needed the counsel of those who knew the local situation.

From this effort came the Governor's Council with a form and functions which would persist through the colonial period. In 1625, Wyatt wanted the advice and support of all interests in the colony and since he lacked the formal authority to convene an assembly, he called for a "convention" (The Virginia Convention) of former assembly delegates. This group indicated how the Americans throughout the colonial period would create new political machinery to deal with extraordinary conditions demanding prompt attention.

While the Virginia Convention deliberated, the new King Charles I announced that Virginia would be managed by the Crown ALONE but did not explain how the local government was to function. However, in 1627, he ordered Governor Wyatt to convene an assembly to resolve a particular problem about tobacco. This was significant because in the past the colonists had gathered on their own each year to discuss local affairs and to petition the King to grant them the right of Assembly which they held under the terms of the company charter. He neither agreed nor disagreed to the repeated requests and as the Governors came and went their instructions essentially remained the same as the company had written for its Governor.

Throughout this period of indecision the Governor's Council became the most effective opposition to arbitrary authority. In 1634, it rebuked Governor Harvey for exceeding his authority. The following year the Council arrested Harvey and returned him to England and elected one of their own, John West, but the King forced Harvey back upon the Virginians. But, once the point had been made that a Crown representative could not be maltreated, Harvey was recalled and Governor Wyatt reappointed to his old post bringing with him news that the annual assemblies might begin again.

G.   PARLIAMENT THREAT OF 1650

The impact of the "Interregnum" was also felt in the colonies. The English Parliament threatened Virginia and Maryland with a trade boycott unless they accepted the Puritan regime in England. The next year they supported that threat with a military expedition to force Virginia to accept their demand. Governor Berkeley resisted at first but eventually gave up the government to the English Commonwealth commissioners on 3/12/1652. *The Articles of Surrender required the Virginians to acknowledge the authority of the Commonwealth but they still had the privileges of free-born Englishmen. They did retain the right to govern themselves* and soon the people of England began to look upon Virginia as an attractive place to emigrate. The Virginia Assembly then selected Richard Bennett to succeed Berkeley who had previously driven Bennett out of Virginia.

Throughout the Commonwealth period, 1649-1660, this agreement served as the basis of Virginia's government and the Burgesses retained the substance of power in their hands. They selected both the Governor and his Council which led them to gradually assume the position of a separate House of Government.

In 1658, Sir William Berkeley was asked by local leaders to serve as "unofficial acting Governor". With the English Restoration in 1660 the Virginia Assembly commissioned him to represent their interests to the Crown in London. He departed in 1661 with instructions to request trained Ministers, urge the founding of a college, and promote the revival of subsidized experimental projects.

While Berkeley was in England, the Virginia Assembly worked to revise and codify the laws of the previous 50 years. *The work was completed by men who were raised in America, not England, so they were better able to reflect an American perspective rather than an English perspective.* Berkeley was warmly received by King Charles II, an old friend, who re-appointed him as Governor. He then returned to Virginia in 1664 and ran the government for the next 25 years. He was well-liked as Governor since he was a planter and protected their interests. A steady influx of immigrants added to growing colonial prosperity and helped ease the labor shortage prior to slavery. By the mid-1660's, the areas around the James, York, and Rappahannock rivers were occupied by 30,000 settlers.

H.   FRONTIER UNREST

Governor Berkeley's favoritism toward the planters of eastern Virginia caused some neglect of the interests of settlers on the western frontier. They became so angry at the failure of the government to protect them from continuing Indian attacks that they formed an expedition, without the Governor's knowledge or authority, to punish the Indians.

1.   BACON'S REBELLION 1676

By the end of the 1660's, the new immigrants had begun to disturb the peace but in 1670 a new law tightened the suffrage requirements to block the influence of the new immigrants and their possible rise to power in the Assembly. *By the 1670's, the combination of Berkeley's autocratic style, an economic depression, and Indian attacks finally forced the colonists into "Bacon's Rebellion".* Nathaniel Bacon was a well-educated and recent immigrant from England. He was also a Council member and it was he who led the un-authorized expedition against the Indians at the Roanoke River. He was declared a traitor on 5/26/1676 and arrested when he tried to take his seat in the Burgesses, to which he had been elected, but was eventually freed upon admitting to his offense and pardoned by the Governor. He led another expedition to Jamestown and forced Governor Berkeley to sign his commission.

The Assembly then passed on 7/29/1676 some democratic reforms against the wishes of the Governor who again declared Bacon a rebel and attempted to raise a force to attack Bacon. He failed to raise a sufficient force and then decided to flee from office. The large planters in the area then took an oath of support to Bacon and joined his army in the attack on Jamestown, which they burned the next day. Bacon then suddenly died which caused the disintegration of his army who began surrendering under the promise of amnesty.

Two commissioners from England arrived on 1/29/1677, John Berry and Francis Moryson, to investigate the uprising. A few days later, Colonel Herbert Jeffreys arrived to restore order. He provided Royal pardons for the rebels which the Governor nullified. 23 rebels were hanged before Jeffreys could assume control of the government. Governor Berkeley was subsequently recalled to England in disgrace.

This event was significant because it contained some of the same grievances as those later claimed by the Patriots against the English, such as arbitrary autocratic rule by the English government or their representatives. Jeffreys and his successors, Sir Henry Chichester and Lord Culpepper, enjoyed peaceful administrations. The administration of Lord Howard of Effingham was marked by a struggle between the Governor and the Assembly during the years of 1683-1689. A list of grievances was presented to King James II on 9/16/1688 but, before it could be acted upon, William and Mary assumed the Throne as a result of the "Glorious Revolution" on 2/13/1689 and Howard was removed as Governor.

2. **THE SUSQUEHANNOCK WAR 1673**

From the earliest days of exploration the coastal Virginia area had been inhabited by a powerful, warlike tribe known as the "Susquehannock". When they were first encountered by Captain John Smith in 1608 he described them as "the most noble and heroic nation of Indians that dwell upon the confines of America". Although related to the Iroquois, the Susquehannocks carried out constant warfare with them. At the time they were one of the most formidable tribes in the mid–Atlantic region and dominated the large area between the Potomac River in northern Virginia to southern New York. They used canoes for their transport and their war parties routinely attacked the Delaware tribes along the Delaware River and also traveled down the Susquehanna River where they terrorized other tribes including the Powhatan's living in the Chesapeake Bay area.

The west shore of the Potomac River was the last of the Virginia's Tidewater area to be settled. In 1669, Governor Berkeley granted Robert Howsing 6000 acres of land to settle the west side of the river. Captain John Alexander who had surveyed this tract of land, including the site of Alexandria, bought the Howsing grant the next year which launched some settlements.

Bands of Susquehannock Indians, fleeing more powerful tribes to the north, crossed the Potomac River and attacked the settlers. A joint-force of Marylanders and Virginians failed to defeat them at Piscatawy Creek on 9/27/1675. The Indians were further angered when, during a temporary truce, Maryland forces killed the Indian peace negotiator causing the Susquehannocks to expand their attacks southward and arouse other Indians to also attack. In one day, 36 settlers were killed but Governor Berkeley, who had been accused of protecting the fur-trade from which he personally benefitted, refused to retaliate against the Indians.

The Susquehannock War was the beginning of the end for the tribe which was almost entirely destroyed by the Iroquois in 1675. The remaining survivors joined the Nottoway tribe and later formed a new tribe called the Meherrin which eventually became known as the Conestoga tribe. The 17th century ended before the Indians were driven out and permanent settlements established.

For many years the survivors lived with the Oneida tribe in New York but eventually they were permitted to return along with remnants of other tribes which had been defeated by the Iroquois. Epidemics reduced their population and by 1763 the last 20 were massacred by a party of rioters known as the "Paxton Boys" seeking revenge for Indian atrocities in the western regions.

I.   MISCELLANEOUS

Virginia population growth:

1617	1,000	
1624	1,100	
1648	15,000	300 Negro slaves
1671	45,000	
1681	75,000	3,000 Blacks

The "head-right" system:

The prospective settler obtained from the colonial Secretary a warrant entitling him to 50 acres of un-granted land for himself and for each person brought to America at his own expense. He received another 50 acres for every other person brought in later.

All head rights did not have to be converted into land at once, they could be saved for future use, inherited by his heirs, or even sold. But, if he chose to start a plantation promptly, he had to find a site for it, lay it out with an official surveyor, record it at the county court, and then develop it. After that, he received a deed and the land was his to have subject to a quit-rent to the Crown.

Slavery in Virginia did not become significant until after 1681.

(Attachment 5d represents a list of Virginia Governors.)

J.   KEY DATES & SIGNIFICANT EVENTS

6/11	1578	Sir Humphrey Gilbert obtains a charter from Queen Elizabeth I to discover and occupy new, unclaimed lands in North America.
Nov	1578	Gilbert's first voyage, 7 ships, purpose to establish a colony on the southern coast of North America, expedition fails.
6/11	1583	Gilbert's second voyage, 5 ships, purpose to colonize between Cape Hatteras and mouth of Hudson River. Lands in Newfoundland, some exploration but ships return home although Gilbert lost at sea near the Azore Islands.
3/25	1584	Raleigh receives grant from Queen Elizabeth I for an exploratory expedition.
4/27	1584	Raleigh leads expedition to Chesapeake Bay. Primary interest in locating rich minerals. Navigators recommend Roanoke Island for settlement.
7/13	1584	Settlers go ashore Roanoke Island and claim territory for Queen Elizabeth I and England.
4/9	1585	Raleigh sends 7 ships from England to Virginia territory led by Sir Richard Grenville and Sir Ralph Lane with 600 settlers.
8/17	1585	Ralph Lane becomes Governor of the colony of 108 settlers. Named "Virginia" after Queen Elizabeth I knick-name. Sir Francis Drake stops at Roanoke Island after naval raid against Spanish fleet. Settlers ask that he take them back to England and leave behind a Fort, today known as "Fort Raleigh National Historical Site".
7/15	1586	Sir Richard Grenville fleet arrives at the Outer Banks, North Carolina, and finds the Roanoke settlement deserted. Leaves 15 men and supplies for 2 years and returns to England.

Sep	1586	Grenville's 15 men on Roanoke Island apparently attacked by the Indians, some killed and some captured or escaped and never found.
5/8	1587	3 ships leave Plymouth, England, for Virginia with 119 colonists, 9 assistants, and the appointed Governor, John White.
7/22	1587	Settlers land at Roanoke Island but find no sign of the original settlement.
8/18	1587	First English child born in America, Virginia Dare.
8/18	1590	Governor John White returns to Roanoke Island but finds no trace of original settlement.
Mar	1602	Raleigh final expedition to search for survivors of Roanoke Island but no sign of the "Lost Colony"
3/24	1603	Death of Queen Elizabeth I, succeeded by King James I
8/18	1604	Treaty of London (Somerset House Conference) settles English–Spanish War. Allows England to re-focus on colonization.
4/10	1606	First Charter for Virginia issued by King James I to the Virginia Company to establish the Christian religion. Significance, declared that all settlers would have same rights as if they had never left England. Charter creates Governing Council with all members chosen by the King
12/20	1606	3 ships leave England for Virginia with 144 settlers
4/26	1607	Ships arrive off coast of Virginia, 39 die during voyage
5/14	1607	Settlers go ashore at Jamestown
5/26	1607	Jamestown settlers defend selves against Indians
Oct	1608	Captain Newport returns from England with more settlers and supplies

5/23	1609	2nd Virginia Charter creates Joint-Stock company
June	1609	6 ships leave England for Virginia with 600 settlers led by Sir Thomas Gates
Winter	1609	"The Starving Times"
May	1610	Sir Thomas Gates and survivors of Bermuda shipwreck arrive at Jamestown with 175 additional settlers
Aug	1611	Governor Sir Thomas Gates to 1614
	1612	"The Dale Codes"
3/12	1612	3rd Virginia Charter replaces the Governing Council with a "Court and Assembly" by creating 4 great courts to handle all civil matters.
	1613	John Rolfe discovers tobacco as valuable export crop
4/14	1614	John Rolfe married Pocahontas
	1618	Sir Edwin Sandys leads Virginia Company
	1618	Virginia exports 50,000 pounds of tobacco to England
11/18	1618	The Great Charter of Virginia issued by King James I authorizes a General Assembly which becomes the first Representative Legislative body in America, to be known as the "House of Burgesses"
7/30	1619	First House of Burgesses Assembly meets in Jamestown
	1619	First slaves sold in Jamestown
3/22	1622	Indian massacre at Jamestown
July	1623	English Privy Council assumes management of the Virginia Company
5/24	1624	Company Charter revoked by King and Virginia becomes a Royal Colony
3/30	1628	Call for a General Assembly
3/18	1644	Indian wars end with capture and death of Chief Opechancanough

	1646	Indian Chiefs cede territory to Virginia
Oct	1650	English Parliament passes law imposing blockade on Virginia for refusing to accept the new Puritan government in England.
3/12	1652	Governor Berkeley gives in to English demands
	1673	Susquehannock Indian war
5/10	1676	Bacon's Rebellion

K.   REVIEW QUESTIONS

(Multiple Choice)

1. Virginia's early problems as a colony were due to all of the following EXCEPT:
   a. the poor choice of location for the settlement of Jamestown
   b. the poor choice of colonists for such an enterprise
   c. the loss of time due to Spanish interference
   d. the loss of time due to searching for gold and a water passage to Asia

2. When the economic success of the Jamestown settlement was finally won it was due to:
   a. the opening of the fur-trade with the Indians
   b. subsidies by the English government
   c. the introduction of a more marketable variety of tobacco
   d. the finding of gold

3. Bacon's Rebellion is significant primarily because:
   a. It was caused by some of the same conflicts of interest which were associated with the American Revolution
   b. It showed that westerners would fight the Indians on the slightest provocation
   c. It was planned to overthrow English rule
   d. It's success encouraged other rebellions

4. Which was the Indian's greatest contribution to American civilization?
   a. corn, tobacco, white potatoes
   b. several types of domesticated animals
   c. many geographic names
   d. methods of warfare

5. Who was the first English explorer to support state-sponsored exploration of North America?
   a. Sir Francis Drake
   b. Sir Humphrey Gilbert
   c. Sir Walter Raleigh
   d. Captain John Smith

6. Which of the following world events created the conditions for England to renew its interest in colonization?
   a. growing spirit of adventure and lure of wealth
   b. population density in England led to economic problems which caused people to look for other opportunities to make a decent living
   c. the Protestant Reformation made Englishmen anxious to convert the American Indians to Christianity
   d. All of the above

7. Which Indian tribe met the settlers at Jamestown?
   a. Iroquois
   b. Hurons
   c. Powhatan Confederacy
   d. Mohicans

(True or False)

8. John Smith contributed very little to the success of the Jamestown colony.
   a. TRUE
   b. FALSE

9. The First Representative legislature in the colonies was held in Virginia.
    a. TRUE
    b. FALSE

10. The leading cause of Bacon's Rebellion was extremely high taxes levied by the Jamestown ruling group.
    a. TRUE
    b. FALSE

11. The First Representative Assembly in Virginia was called the "House of Burgesses".
    a. TRUE
    b. FALSE

M. GLOSSARY

1. **Sedentary**   Characterized by sitting, taking little exercise, remaining or living in a single area, not migratory.

2. **Cash-Crop**   A crop for direct sale in a market as distinguished from a crop for use as livestock feed or other purposes. A crop which is easily marketable.

3. **Opechancanough**   Became Chief of the Powhatan Confederacy upon the death of his brother, Wahunsonacock. The Confederacy existed in eastern Virginia and was composed of the Pamunkey, Mattapony, and Chickahominy tribes. He led many attacks on the Virginia Settlers but was eventually killed in 1644.

CHAPTER 5 SUMMARY

The Virginia Colony

1. The creation and development of the Virginia colony actually began with an expedition to present-day North Carolina, Roanoke Island, known as the "Lost Colony".

2. Sir Humphrey Gilbert and Sir Walter Raleigh opened the door for subsequent expeditions which settled Virginia.

3. King James I succeeded Queen Elizabeth I in 1603 and made peace with Spain which allowed England to re-focus its efforts on colonization.

4. Jamestown was settled 5/14/1607 as a result of the "First Charter of Virginia of 1606" issued by King James I to the Virginia Company for the purpose of expanding the Christian religion in the Coastal Virginia area. *This charter established the precedent that all settlers within the colony would have the same rights as if they had never left England. The charter also created a Governing Council residing in London.*

5. The "Second Charter of Virginia" of 5/23/1609 created a "Joint Stock Company" which replaced the Council with a Governor. It was a communal plan with the purpose to share all accumulated profits with the shareholders after 7 years.

6. The first great migration to Virginia occurred in 5/1609 with 600 settlers.

7. The "3rd Charter of Virginia" of 3/12/1612 allowed the colony to operate lotteries to raise revenues. Power was now shifted to a Court and Assembly to share power with the Governor.

8. Indian problems from 1608 through 1644 with a great massacre of settlers in 1622.

9. By 1616 there are 6 similar settlements along the James River with Jamestown the seat of government.

10. Tobacco became the primary cash-crop and a valuable and profitable export product.

11. The "Great Charter of 1618" was intended to integrate the various settlements. It used available land as an inducement for additional emigration to Virginia. It created 4 "Borough's" and also established a procedure for annual elections of members to a "House of Burgesses" which met for the first time on 7/30/1619 at Jamestown.

12. In 1624 the London Company was failing and refused a compromise from the Crown so the Crown divested the Company of its charter and made Virginia a "Royal Colony" with the Governor and Council appointed by the King.

13. Virginia was threatened by the English Parliament in 1650 with a trade boycott if it did not accept the new Puritan regime in England as a result of the "Interregnum" beginning in 1649. Governor Berkeley resisted at first but eventually surrendered to the pressure from England. Virginians were forced to accept the authority of the Commonwealth although they retained the right to govern themselves and enjoy the privileges of free-born Englishmen.

14. "Bacon's Rebellion" was caused primarily by Indian attacks and the settlers dissatisfaction with the government's inability to protect them.

5a

ENGLISH COLONIES

CATEGORY	NEW ENGLAND	SOUTHERN	MIDDLE ATLANTIC
LOCATIONS	NEW HAMPSHIRE MASSACHUSETTS CONNECTICUT RHODE ISLAND	VIRGINIA NORTH CAROLINA SOUTH CAROLINA GEORGIA	NEW YORK NEW JERSEY PENNSYLVANIA DELAWARE MARYLAND
MOTIVES	PRIMARILY FREEDOM FROM POLITICAL & RELIGIOUS PERSECUTION	DESIRE TO DEVELOP TRADE AND EARN A BETTER LIVELIHOOD	PRIMARILY FOR TRADE AND FREEDOM FROM PERSECUTION
GEOGRAPHY	POOR SOIL SWIFT-FLOWING RIVERS GOOD NATURAL HARBORS	A LEVEL, FERTILE REGION WITH NAVIGABLE RIVERS, WARM CLIMATE	RICH, FERTILE, LEVEL SOIL NAVIGABLE RIVERS EXCELLENT HARBORS
PEOPLE	PREDOMINANTLY ENGLISH PURITANS	PREDOMINANTLY ENGLISH COURTIER'S ASSOCIATED WITH COURT PRESENCE	MIXTURE OF ENGLISH, DUTCH, SWEDES, IRISH
OCCUPATIONAL LIFE	SMALL FARMS, VARIED CROPS FISHING, HUNTING SHIP-BUILDING COMMERCE	LARGE PLANTATIONS USING SLAVES TO RAISE FEW CROPS SUCH AS TOBACCO, RICE, COTTON, INDIGO	COMBINATION OF LARGE AND SMALL FARMS KNOWN AS "BREAD COLONIES" CROPS SUCH AS, WHEAT, OATS, BARLEY, SHIPS, LIVESTOCK, FURS, LUMBER TO ENGLAND
COMMUNITY LIFE	STRONG, CENTERS AROUND COMPACT VILLAGES	UNDEVELOPED, EACH PLANTATION SOMEWHAT ISOLATED	DEVELOPED ALONG NEW ENGLAND TYPE
SOCIAL LIFE	SIMPLE, SIGNIFICANT CLASS DISTINCTIONS RIGID MORALS DOMINANCE OF CHURCH	STRONG CLASS DISTINCTIONS LESS RIGID MORALS THAN NEW ENGLAND MINIMAL CHURCH INFLUENCE	SIMILAR TO SOUTH LESS SIGNIFICANT CLASS DISTINCTIONS
EDUCATION	SYSTEM OF FREE PUBLIC EDUCATION	NO PUBLIC EDUCATION PRIVATE SCHOOLS FOR RICH	SIMILAR TO NEW ENGLAND
LOCAL GOVERNMENT	DIRECT DEMOCRACY OF THE TOWNSHIPS	COUNTY GOVERNMENT CONTROLLED BY STATE GOVERNOR	MIXED WITH BOTH COUNTIES AND TOWNSHIPS

5b

ORIGINAL COLONIES, SETTLEMENTS, RATIFICATION

O R I G I N A L 13 E N G L I S H C O L O N I E S							
S E T T L E M E N T S			FEDERAL CONSTITUTION RATIFIED				
COLONY	STATE	FOUNDED	MO.	DATE	YR	# ORD	# YRS*
JAMESTOWN	VIRGINIA	1607	JUNE	25	1788	10	181
PLYMOUTH	MASSACHUSETTS	1620	FEB	6	1788	6	168
PORTSMOUTH	NEW HAMPSHIRE	1631	JUNE	21	1788	9	157
HARTFORD	CONNECTICUT	1633	JAN	9	1788	5	155
ST. MARY'S	MARYLAND	1634	APRIL	28	1788	7	154
PROVIDENCE PLANTATIONS	RHODE ISLAND	1636	MAY	29	1790	13	154
WILMINGTON	DELAWARE	1638	DEC	7	1787	1	149
ALBEMARLE	NORTH CAROLINA	1663	NOV	21	1789	12	126
CHARLESTON	SOUTH CAROLINA	1663	MAY	23	1788	8	125
NEW YORK	NEW YORK	1664	JULY	26	1788	11	124
FORT NASSAU	NEW JERSEY	1664	DEC	18	1787	3	123
PHILADELPHIA	PENNSYLVANIA	1681	DEC	12	1787	2	106
SAVANNAH	GEORGIA	1732	JAN	2	1788	4	56

* # OF YEARS FROM COLONIAL CHARTER TO FEDERAL CONSTITUTION RATIFICATION

5c

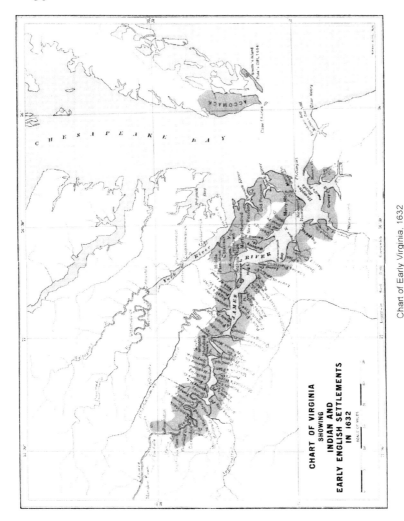

5d

5d		VIRGINIA GOVERNORS
DATES	**DATES**	**NAME & TITLE**
1610		LT & DEPUTY GOV SIR THOMAS GATES
1610	1611	GOV THOMAS LORD DE LA WARR
1611		DEP GOV GEORGE PERCY
1611	1614	ACTING GOV SIR THOMAS GATES
1614	1616	ACTING GOV SIR THOMAS DALE
1616	1617	LT GOV GEORGE YEARDLEY
1617	1619	LT GOV SAMUEL ARGALL
1619	1621	GOV SIR GEORGE YEARDLEY
1621	1626	GOV SIR FRANCIS WYATT
1626	1627	GOV SIR GEORGE YEARDLEY
1630	1635	GOV SIR JOHN HARVEY
1637	1639	X
1639	1642	GOV SIR FRANCIS WYATT
1642	1644	GOV SIR WILLIAM BERKELEY
1645	1652	X
1652	1655	ACTING GOV RICHARD BENNETT
1662	1677	GOV SIR WILLIAM BERKELEY
1677	1678	LT GOV SIR HERBERT JEFFREYS
1678	1680	DEP GOV SIR HENRY CHICHELEY
1680	1682	X
1684	1688	LT GOV FRANCIS HOWARD
1688	1690	X
1690	1692	LT GOV FRANCIS NICHOLSON
1692	1698	GOV SIR EDMUND ANDROS
1698	1705	LT GOV FRANCIS NICHOLSON
1705	1710	X
1710	1722	LT GOV ALEXANDER SPOTSWOOD
1722	1726	LT GOV HUGH DRYSDALE
1726	1727	X
1727	1740	LT GOV WILLIAM GOOCH
1740	1751	X
1751	1758	LT GOV ROBERT DINWIDDIE
1758	1763	LT GOV FRANCIS FAUQUIER
1763	1768	GOV IN CHIEF SIR JEFFREY AMHERST
1768	1770	GOV IN CHIEF NORBORNE BERKELEY
1770	1771	X
1771	1775	GOV IN CHIEF EARL OF DUNMORE
1775		CHAIRMAN OF THE COMMITTEE OF SAFETY
1776		EDMUND PENDLETON
1776	1779	PATRICK HENRY
1779	1781	THOMAS JEFFERSON
1781	1784	BENJAMIN HARRISON
1784	1786	PATRICK HENRY
1786	1788	EDMUND RANDOLPH

Chapter 6

Massachusetts Colony

The History of the development of the Massachusetts colonies is complex and inter-connected, with initial settlements at Plymouth, Salem, Boston, and Dorchester before merging into the Massachusetts Bay colony and then the State of Massachusetts.

A.   PILGRIMS, PURITANS, AND SEPARATISTS

In the 16th century, England broke away from the Catholic Church and created a new "Church of England", (Anglican). Everyone in England was required to belong to that religion. It came to be known as "The State Religion". There was a group of people called "separatists" who wanted to separate from the Anglican Church. They were led by William Bradford, a Minister, and wanted to leave England and start their own settlement where they could freely practice their religion. At this time, all those who were dissatisfied with the Church of England were known as "Puritans" but within that category there were various sects and beliefs.

The majority of Puritans remained members of the established Church and worked from within for a "second Reformation" which would cleanse or purify the Church by ridding it of its Catholic influences. Other Puritans broke away from the Church of England and formed churches of their own which was viewed as a criminal act making them the victims of arrests, fines, imprisonment, and sometimes even death.

1. WHAT WAS THE DIFFERENCE BETWEEN PURITANS AND PILGRIMS

The Puritans wanted to "purify" the Church and the term "Pilgrim" referred to those who left England to freely practice their religion. The Pilgrims who settled Plymouth were Puritans seeking to reform their Church. According to William Bradford, Puritanism was a movement seeking to return to the virtues of primitive Christianity. There was nothing revolutionary in its doctrine. Its innovating principle was in the idea that the Bible, rather than any established religious hierarchy, was the final authority. Therefore, every individual had direct access to the Word of God. It was the Puritan's aim to reconstruct and purify not only the Church but individual conduct as well.

Because it was an extension of the government, the English Church was as subject to political abuse and favoritism as any other governmental agency. Some Parish Ministry's were given as political favors but in many cases those Ministers did not even serve in those Parishes and the members had no way to oppose these abuses and just had to accept whatever the Church hierarchy imposed on them.

The initial Puritan movement came first from a highly enlightened brain trust and, as the movement grew, it began to break into different sects. The least radical Puritans were committed to purifying their Church from within with as little upheaval as possible. They were referred to as "non-conformists". They were okay with the idea of a State Church but aware that a challenge to it could be viewed as an Act of Treason. Therefore, they sought to bring about change from within the structure of the Church. The change they most wanted was to establish the Bible, not the Church hierarchy, as the ultimate authority. Membership in the movement was to be by choice and limited to those who had at least some degree of religious motivation, and an active clergy who carried out some educational as well as liturgical functions.

There was another group which wanted to retain the Church of England identity but reform its organizational structure, to give each Congregation control over its own affairs. They were a small minority in the Church of England and were known as "Congregationalists".

There was another group known as the "separatists" who had given up any hope of major reform from within the Church. They sought to separate from the Church and start their own churches. Most of the separatists who remained in England favored a structured form of church organization called "Presbyterianism" which was already established in Scotland.

To summarize, *there were 4 distinct groups resulting from the protests against Catholicism:*

a. Separatists - those seeking a complete break from the Anglican Church and practice their own religion

b. Non-Conformists - those seeking purification of the Church from within the Church structure

c. Congregationalists - those wanting to give each local Congregation control over their own affairs

d. Presbyterianism - those "separatists" remaining in England who favored a structured form of Church organization. This sect was already strong in Scotland.

B.   THE COLONIZATION OF PLYMOUTH

Captain John Smith of Virginia did much to spark the creation of New England through his influence. While in England he was hired by two London merchants to hunt whales off the American coast. He found no whales but returned with many fish and impressions of the North American east-coast. In 1616, he published "A Description of New England" with a map which was a big seller in England and caught the attention of Pilgrims and Puritans.

1.   SEPARATISTS LEAVE ENGLAND FOR AMERICA

William Brewster was a successful member of the gentry in the town of Scrooby located in the southern part of Yorkshire, England. He had been exposed to Puritanism while studying at Cambridge after he had left the Anglican Church. Soon, he and some neighbors were worshipping with another Cambridge man, Reverend John Robinson, whose membership did not seek to reform the Church of England, they just wanted to be left alone to worship as they pleased, forming their own Church in 1606. They were accused of treason so, during 1607-1608, a majority of the Scrooby Separatists left for Holland which tolerated all shades of Protestantism. Brewster sold his property to finance the trip and, after two false starts, 125 of the Congregation left for Amsterdam where they joined a group of London separatists, later to move to the town of Leyden. They worshipped as they pleased for awhile but were still uneasy because of the more liberal lifestyle in Holland as well as the fear that Spain was ready to control Holland and create its own religious persecution, Catholicism.

Brewster knew Sir Edwin Sandys who was then involved in developing Virginia. Two representatives of the Scrooby group went to London to speak with Sandys who welcomed their desire to emigrate but questioned how the King would react to Separatists populating the colony. Reverend Robinson drafted the "Leyden Agreement" of 1618 which pledged their loyalty to the Crown in return for the Crown agreeing to not persecute the Separatists as long as they acted peacefully.

The London Company granted a charter on 2/2/1620 for a town/plantation in the name of John Pierce, one of their London friends but they had a financing problem. The London Company didn't offer enough money but a local group of merchants did offer their support. They were led by Thomas Weston, who turned out to be a dishonest self-promoter interested only in his own success. The terms were the same as offered to the Jamestown settlers and ignored all the lessons learned from that experience since 1607. They decided to form a joint-stock company where, at the end of 7 years, all property and profits, held in common up to then, would be divided among the adventurers and planters. Management of the plantation's affairs, as in early Virginia, would be split between London and America. This arrangement spelled future trouble because it seemed odd that a business group focused only on profits would make a deal with a religious group seeking a pure and simple existence. In spite of this potential problem, the Separatists believed that a bad deal was better than no deal at all and just wanted to move elsewhere.

A group of 50 settlers made the trip from Holland to England and, of those, only 35 continued on to America. By sailing time, 2/3 of the party were "strangers" (Non-Puritans) including John Alden and Miles Standish, the military officer. Based on what they knew about the Virginia experience, they realized that the initial colony would, by necessity, be a military outpost. They declined Captain John Smith's offer to serve as military officer.

They departed from Plymouth, England, on 9/6/1620, although April was their first choice so they could plant a fall harvest. They left in two ships, "Speedwell and Mayflower". The Speedwell was unable to make the trip and their passengers were taken onboard the Mayflower. They departed with 102 settlers during the worst time of the year in the stormy Atlantic Ocean. They brought with them no cattle or livestock and would land at the beginning of winter. They traveled 2750 miles in 66 days and sighted land-fall at what is today Provincetown, Massachusetts, on 11/11/1620. Winter was too close to sail for the Hudson river area, their first choice, and they did not want to sail to Nova Scotia and spend the winter with their hated Catholic rivals, so they explored the Cape Code region and eventually decided to settle at Plymouth where they sailed to and anchored their ship on 12/11/1620.

2. **THE MAYFLOWER COMPACT 11/20/1620**

On the last day at sea, someone suggested drafting a *"Compact of Laws"* to govern the colony, similar to a Church covenant, which became known as the *"Mayflower Compact"*. *It pledged*

loyalty to King James I, framed a body of laws and appointed officers. It was signed by 41 Pilgrims who promised "obedience to the laws and officers thus enacted". All signers, even those who were servants, automatically became freemen with the right to share in the government to be formed.

The "compact" was not a Constitution nor did it have legal validity because they were settling in a place where they had no right to be. It was a temporary expedient designed to give the "saints" control over any mutinous strangers. It provided a basis for order and authority at a time when the Pilgrims had been thrust into a new environment and intended to serve only until the settlement obtained a patent/charter from the "Council for New England". Under the authority of the Compact the new freemen, with the Saints in a majority of one, elected John Carver as Governor. He was 44 and the wealthiest of the passengers who had used his own wealth to pay what the merchants and Thomas Weston had failed to pay.

3. **PILGRIMS LAND AT PLYMOUTH 12/21/1620**

They landed at the worst possible time of the year, in terms of weather, and by spring almost half of the settlers had died, including Governor Carver, whose position was filled by William Bradford. The survivors endured a "starving time" similar to Jamestown except for the Indian menace primarily because the local Indians had mostly been wiped out by a small pox epidemic shortly before their arrival. They were befriended by one particular Indian named "Squanto", who taught them how to plant corn, showed them the best streams for fishing, and served as an emissary with local Tribes.

The Pilgrims gathered in October, 1621, to give thanks to God for their first harvest as they had little else for which to be grateful. No relief ships had arrived except for 35 new settlers sent by Weston who brought nothing but their appetites. The Mayflower soon left England with a cargo of goods to pay off their debts but it was captured by a French warship. Weston continued to exploit the settlers, sending new settlers to be housed and fed but not sending any food or supplies. Weston opposed Bradford's plan to discontinue the communal plan ahead of schedule and give each family its own land which proved a great incentive to self-sufficiency. Eventually, in 1627 the settlers bought out the London investors and paid off the debt in 17 years, taking that long because Weston and the management group had so badly cheated the colony.

4. **PLYMOUTH POLITICAL SITUATION**

The Plymouth colony was legalized by a charter from the Council for New England in 1621 which did not satisfy Governor Bradford who preferred a Royal charter which would make the colony responsible to the Crown alone. The colony had always conducted its business respectful of England laws and customs but was never granted a Royal charter to protect their rights. This led to their eventual absorption by the Massachusetts Bay colony.

(The Council for New England replaced the former Plymouth Company in 1620 led by Sir Fernando Gorges)

The issue of who should share in Plymouth's government was settled on an impromptu basis. The Mayflower Compact disposed only temporarily of the traditional English voting requirement of a 40 shilling "freehold". Plymouth struggled with the issue of who could vote. The liberality of the early years disappeared once the colony began to grow and old English customs took over. Even the old English habit of choosing leaders from among the elite remained strong. Elections occurred annually but rarely produced a leadership change. Governor Bradford ruled most of the time from 1620-1657.

By Bradford's death in 1657, Plymouth and its local settlements were no longer dominant since Boston, once it began to develop, possessed a better harbor for commercial trade. The Pilgrims were okay with Plymouth not developing into a major city since they preferred a simple life and quiet place to worship.

5. **EARLY PLYMOUTH GOVERNMENT AND COURT SYSTEM**

The Plymouth colony lived by the Mayflower Compact for a number of years in the absence of a Royal charter outlining the provisions for establishing a government. In 1636, when the population was less than 3,000 people, a committee of the General Court *composed a Legal Code, the first produced in North America.*

It was called the "General Fundamentals" or the "Declaration of Rights" of 1636 and contained a rudimentary "Bill of Rights" which guaranteed trial by jury and that laws were to be made with the consent of the freemen of the colony. It was upgraded in 1671 to include that "no person shall be endamaged in respect of life, limb, liberty, good name or estate but by virtue of some express law of the General Court of the this colony". These "General Fundamentals" have been viewed by historians as one of the earliest forms of a demand for "representative government" and individual rights within the American colonies.

The specifics of the "General Fundamentals" of 1636 were:

a. Laws to be made by the freemen or their representatives

b. Representatives chosen annually by the freemen

c. Justice to be equally and speedily administered

d. None to suffer but according to the Law and by due course and process of the law

e. All trials to be with a jury with the liberty to challenge any of the jury

f. The Churches of Christ are to be protected and the Ministers of the Gospel to be provided for

g. All of the foregoing Fundamentals are inviolably to be preserved.

C.   CREATION OF THE MASSACHUSETTS BAY COLONY

The Massachusetts Bay Colony actually began its formation with a settlement at Cape Ann in 1623 when several merchants inspired by

Reverend John White had organized themselves into the Dorchester Company and secured a patent from the Council for New England to found a fishing settlement. The plan was to send settlers who would grow food for the fishing crews and then double as fishermen in-season. It didn't take long for the Dorchester Company to collapse in 1626 but several of the fishermen-planters then moved to Salem (named "Naumkeag" by the Indians) led by Reverend White. *Early in 1628, a new group of Puritan merchants took out a patent from the Council for New England for the land between the Merrimac and Charles rivers. It was to become known as the "New England Company"* with 40 settlers departing for Salem in June 1628 led by John Endicott with orders to prepare the way for others to follow.

1. **MASSACHUSETTS BAY CHARTER 3/14/1629**
    While Endicott developed Salem, Puritan leaders in England converted their charter into a Royal charter and the New England Company was incorporated into the Massachusetts Bay Colony. The charter confirmed the original land grant and, in addition, gave the company all rights of government over any colony it created. It formed 26 investors into a corporation which controlled all company property and the right to administer its affairs. Members would meet quarterly in a General Court to decide important business. The Court could pass any laws it deemed necessary as long as they did not conflict with English law.

    (There was no provision that the Charter and company headquarters remain in England, which would become very important in the future.)

    The charter was well-planned, financed, and provisioned, and with a clear goal of creating a refuge for persecuted Puritans.

    Meanwhile, things were also happening in England which had an impact on the colonies. King Charles I had dissolved Parliament two weeks before the Massachusetts Bay colony received its charter, leaving the King and his Archbishop Laud free to persecute English Puritans without restraint. *By 1629 it was clear that the Puritans would have to leave for America to practice their religion free from persecution. Not only would they go but they would take their Company with them and merge it in New England with the colonial government.* It bothered them that the charter had created an open corporation allowing non-Puritans to buy into control of the company. John Winthrop, a wealthy Puritan, agreed with fellow members that they must transfer their government of the plantation/colony to those in America. They were aware of the Crown's efforts to revoke the Virginia charter and wanted to protect against a similar experience.

On 8/29/1629 the "Cambridge Agreement" was created which stated that all company members who did not wish to emigrate to America could sell-out their interests to those who did choose to emigrate and the company charter was turned over to them to carry to America as long as it could be done legally. A subordinate government for financial affairs only was maintained in London and worked so well that the Crown was not even aware that the Charter had been taken to America until 1634 when Archbishop Laud learned of it and tried to get it annulled. John Winthrop was chosen to head the new venture and plans proceeded to send out the greatest fleet of colonists to ever leave for America.

In March, 1630, a fleet of 11 ships with 700 passengers, livestock, and supplies left for New England. The date allowed for an early planting on arrival. Some differences did exist between this effort and previous ones in Virginia. For example, religion gave a unity of purpose and strength to the Puritan venture which was not the case in Virginia. Also, the machinery for governing the colony was different with the Charter actually residing in America rather than in England. John Winthrop announced the intention to be a "City Upon a Hill" with the eyes of all people upon them with a mission to build a "Holy Commonwealth" out of a trading company.

The fleet arrived in June, 1630, in time to plant a crop for fall harvest. John Endicott met them at Salem with housing and food waiting for them. *Within a few weeks it had been agreed that the center of the new colony should be a few miles south of*

Salem, in Boston, with its better harbor. During the summer
of 1630, the development of Boston and some villages around
it began. The first winter was tough with 200 deaths. A relief
ship in February, 1631 helped, but, upon its return to England,
it took 80 settlers who wished to return home.

By the end of summer 1631 there were 2,000 Puritans who
had arrived in Massachusetts Bay. The great arrival of new
immigrants also helped boost the local economy and the
eventual growth of the colony.

2. THE CHURCH

30 of 200 settlers at Salem joined together to announce a
"covenant" to one another and to God. A year after the Salem
covenant a half dozen other covenanted communities arose
along the Massachusetts coast and a decade later nearly 30
others were scattered throughout the Bay Colony, New Haven,
Connecticut, and Plymouth. The Church within each town had
complete liberty to stand alone. The entire community made
up the Congregation but the Church consisted solely of "saints".
Previously, "saint" was defined as one who professed faith and
repentance and lived free from scandal. New England Puritans
now claimed that one must prove that they had been "reborn".
Once they had created the Church within the community,
they would choose a Pastor and teacher, who, together, would
spread and teach the Word of God. The "elders" were chosen
by members of the Church to serve as disciplinarians, punish
the sinners, and prevent the corruption of the Church.

The Clergy's power in colonial New England emerged from the
authority of their office but even more from the quality of the
men who occupied their offices. John Cotton was considered
as their greatest intellectual who "could not err". Their religion
demanded much of the people and when the people fell short,
the Ministers turned for support to their civil rulers. The
Church knit together the Saints and set the tone of society and
the State enforced this tone.

3. **THE GOVERNMENT**

The Puritan's chief problem was to change a trading company into a colonial government without letting power slip from the hands of the Saints and without doing harm to their charter. The Bible's vagueness about civil institutions left them uncommitted to any particular form of government but the charter appeared to impose certain limitations. The power of the government was placed in the hands of the freemen or shareholders of the company who were to assemble four times a year as a General Court to elect all officers and pass all ordinances and laws.

When the first General Court met in October, 1630, they voted to transfer the right to select all company officers and to make all laws to the Governor's Court of Assistants who had concentrated all executive, legislative, and judicial power in their and the Governor's hands.

Once Winthrop and his supporters had the colony somewhat established, they called a 2nd meeting of the General Court in May, 1631, at which time they admitted an additional 118 freemen who declared that no man shall be admitted to freeman-status unless they were members of one of the local churches. They further decreed that all settlers must take an oath of loyalty to the Massachusetts government. The oath made no mention of allegiance to the Crown.

Winthrop kept tight control of he colony for four years *until a complaint was raised in 1632 when his assistants levied a colony-wide tax. A Minister at Watertown opposed the tax on the basis that the colonists had not consented. Winthrop was able to quiet the fuss but the door to "representative government" had been opened.* The General Court declared that in the next election, two men from every town should be appointed to advise the Governor and his assistants. It was also agreed that the election of the Governor should be transferred from the Assistants to the freemen of the colony.

Two years later a group of deputies to the General Court led by Thomas Dudley, who thought Winthrop was too lenient and wished to oust him from office, asked the Governor to see the Charter. From it they learned that the General Court should make all laws and that it should consist of all freemen. They demanded that the charter be followed strictly. Winthrop proposed his previous compromise which called for each town to send 2 deputies to the General Court which now became a representative assembly consisting of 20 deputies, a governor, deputy-governor, and sitting together. ***The evolution of a trading company into a colonial constitution had now been completed.***

Winthrop wanted laws resulting from judicial decisions rather than by legislation. He believed that laws would impose rigidity on the colony just when they needed flexibility to govern. He fought a losing battle primarily because the clergy refused to support him, fearing excessive Executive power, just like England, which they escaped for many of the same reasons.

The Puritans suspected power and whoever held it. They combined their Church and government into specific spheres of action and tolerated no overstepping the boundaries. ***This was an early attempt at the concept of "separation of Church and State" although they were still combined for now.*** The Church had no power in government and Ministers were forbidden to hold public office. The government refused to allow actions of any Congregation to affect civil or political rights. But, the state saw to it that the Church was supported by local taxation. It passed laws to protect Ministers against insults and it enforced compulsory attendance. The Church condemned political radicals and denied people the right of revolution on the grounds that it violated one of God's institutions. State and Church cooperated to excommunicate and banish all political and religious heretics.

D.   DIFFERENCES BETWEEN PLYMOUTH AND THE MASSACHUSETTS BAY COLONIES

The Pilgrims at Plymouth were Separatists and the Puritans at Massachusetts Bay were not. One of the greatest concerns of Governor Winthrop was the fear that in New England his supporters would be attracted to the Separatists of the Plymouth colony. Puritanism was a shared commitment that did more to draw the 2 New England colonies together than to force them apart in spite of the following minor differences:

1. **SIZE**

   When the Mayflower arrived at Plymouth it brought 102 settlers. Ten years later, 17 ships with 1000 settlers arrived at Salem. After another decade, the population of Plymouth was 2,500 while Massachusetts Bay was 20,000.

2. **ECONOMIC AND SOCIAL STATUS**

   The Plymouth Pilgrims were primarily working people. There was not even a Minister. The Massachusetts Bay colonists were better educated and more economically and socially successful, and brought with them an educated clergy to give leadership to both the Church and community. William Bradford the Governor whose leadership shaped the Plymouth colony had been a cloth-worker while Governor Winthrop of Massachusetts Bay was a trained lawyer.

3. **CONCEPT OF "COVENANT"**

   The Separatists who first fled to Holland accepted the concept of "covenant", the voluntary but sacred agreements by which they understood themselves bound together in Church and community. This highly developed idea of covenant tends to separate the Pilgrims of Plymouth from the Puritans of Massachusetts Bay in the following ways:

Colonial Government

In Plymouth, the "Mayflower Compact" made everyone equal in their eyes including those who signed the Compact aboard the ship as well as those who they chose to represent them in the community. The Plymouth government came closer to being a true democracy with its elected officers deriving their powers by the consent of the governed within the terms of their convenant.

In Massachusetts Bay they followed a more English model. The Governor, deputy Governor, Assistants, and other officers were chosen by the people but, once chosen, they understood themselves to be ruling with divine authority.

Role of Religion

Massachusetts Bay has been described as a "theocracy" because the leaders believed the Church should dominate government in order to enforce its religious principles. This was according to the teachings of the Reformation theologian John Calvin. Only members of the Church were permitted to vote and participate in government. According to the colony charter only "freemen" (of which there were only 12 in 1630) were to choose the Court of Assistants to the Governor. The base of the government was broadened in the fall of 1630 when 109 members of the Church won the right to become "freemen".

Relationship of Church and State

The Puritans were certain that God had prescribed the terms of that relationship but in England they were one, from Crown down to the Parish. In Massachusetts Bay the Puritans drew a firmer line. The State was still responsible for supporting and protecting the Church, such as punishing heresy. But, in prosecuting heresy it did not operate as an agent of the Church. It formed its own judgments with the aid of a jury or sat in judgment with the Magistrates. The Church had no authority in the government and the government was careful to not allow the actions of any Church to affect civil and political rights.

At Plymouth, Church and State were more separated. They maintained that what Scripture did not claim as a religious function remained a civil one. The best-known result of that thinking was the belief in Plymouth that marriage was a civil rite, not a religious one. It has been said that what Bradford wanted was to create a Christian commonwealth in which Scripture should be the guide but with civil and religious functions clearly separate.

E.   THE FATHER OF NEW ENGLAND

Some historians refer to ***Archbishop Laud*** as the "Father of New England". He became King Charles I Archbishop of Canterbury in 1633, the same year that 700 Puritans immigrated to New England, double the total for the two previous years. Laud directly opposed the principles of Puritanism and believed the English Anglican Church perpetuated the true Catholic faith and that once Rome had been purified, the old union would return. ***He sought to reform without separating, directly opposite of the Puritans, who sought to separate from the Anglican Church.*** Laud wanted to retain some less offensive aspects of Catholicism.

Laud's attempts at reform clashed with the Puritan efforts at reform, especially his attempts to improve the Church's economic position and the quality of the clergy. King Henry VIII had undermined the church's economic foundation by giving much of its landed wealth to the nobility. By the 17th century the church's inability to support its clergy had led to "pluralism", the holding of several jobs in order for a Minister to earn enough income to make a decent living. But, this led to numerous Parishes being occupied by absentee Ministers. This led to an inability to attract able, well-trained, men into the pulpit, thus many poorly trained Ministers.

Puritanism had thrived on the Church's economic problems. Wealthy Puritans had offered to endow a local pulpit if they could choose the Minister and the offer was often accepted. Laud attempted to correct these abuses. He encouraged able young men to enter the Ministry and searched for ways to increase church revenues. He also removed Puritans from pulpits wherever he found them. ***When opposed, he reacted so violently that the English Puritans found it better to emigrate from England and start anew. Laud even attempted to oppose them in America, too.***

1.   COMMISSION FOR REGULATING PLANTATIONS (1634)

Laud found the cause for involving himself in New England Puritanism. Sir Fernando Gorges, who had been involved in various efforts to colonize Maine allied himself with colonists banished from the Massachusetts Bay Colony who claimed that the issuance of the Royal Charter in 1632 from the Council for New England was illegal. He forwarded his claims to the Privy Council of King Charles I. *Even though his efforts were unsuccessful they created enough animosity between the Crown and the Massachusetts government that it led to the eventual repeal of the Bay Charter in 1684.*

In 1634, King Charles I created the "Commission for Regulating Plantations" composed of the Privy Council members and headed by Bishop Laud for the *purpose of retrieving the Massachusetts Bay colony's charter.*

In Massachusetts the General Court reacted defensively to the threat. It drew up plans to physically resist an invasion plus worked to eliminate the "sins" which brought the threat. *Bishop Laud learned of the transfer of the charter to New England and directed his attorney-general to open suit for its repeal. In 1635 the Courts declared it revoked and appointed Sir Ferdinando Gorges the Royal Governor.* King Charles was too occupied with unruly Puritans at home to enforce the decree and Sir Gorges was too old and weak to travel across the Ocean to assume the Governor position.

Governor Winthrop immediately announced that he would not relinquish the charter. The local clergy sided with Winthrop who was also supported by 3,000 new settlers during the summer of 1638. *This successful resistance to the Crown emboldened Massachusetts and probably explains the later resistance of Boston in leading up to the Revolutionary War.*

F.   "THE BODY OF LIBERTIES" (1641)

In 1641 the General Court approved a *"Body of Liberties" which codified a number of offenses and punishments for the citizens of the colony. It was the first legal code established by European colonists for all of New England, by expanding the 1636 Declaration of Rights which had been developed for the Plymouth colony.* It was drafted by a Puritan Minister Nathaniel Ward and established by the Massachusetts General Court.

Terms: Established the right of the General Court to legislate and dictate authority. ***Many of these rights eventually became part of our Bill of Rights, such as; freedom of speech, right to bail, right to jury trial, right against cruel and unusual punishment, the right against double jeopardy, the right to notice and hearings before the court (due process), the prohibition of a compulsory draft except for territorial defense, and the prohibition of an estate tax.***

After 1644 the deputies and assistants began to meet separately and thus originated a two- house Legislature which not only levied taxes but passed laws. The government was still far from democratic as only selected members of the church were allowed to be "freemen". Those who disagreed with the ruling Puritan theocracy were forced into exile or they voluntarily left Boston. The outstanding leader among the Boston Puritans was John Winthrop, who served as Governor most of the years from 1630–1650.

H.   DISSENT WITHIN DISSENT. ("THE HIVINGS OUT")

In its early years, the Bay Colony was active, it argued among itself about who should hold power within the government, then joined together to oppose the Crown plus deal with Indian problems. It was also during this time that Roger Williams and Anne Hutchinson were banished from Massachusetts, along with their followers, for opposing Puritan doctrine. There were other defections from the Puritan solidarity which caused considerable unrest in the colony at this time.

The "Separatist" was an idealist who just wanted to worship God as he pleased but this made him want to rebel against authority and the established Church. His threat to the state made him intolerable to Puritan Massachusetts. In spite of the separatist movement in New England, there was no concerted government or Church effort to harass them into moving elsewhere, as was the case in England.

1. **ROGER WILLIAMS**

   He was born in 1603 and studied at Cambridge University where, in the 1620's, he was exposed to Puritan ideas and influential Puritans. Eventually, the Bishop Laud campaign to harass Puritans caused him to leave for Massachusetts in 1630. He first arrived in Boston, then moved to Salem and Plymouth where he was eventually asked to leave because some of his ideas were inconsistent with theirs. He contacted the Plymouth Indians and began to develop the belief that the Plymouth and Massachusetts Bay charters were invalid because the King had no right to give away land which belonged to the Indians. His challenge to the validity of the charter came at the same time as the Crown was also developing plans to recall it and send a Royal Governor.

He wrote the King on the issue and when the Puritans learned of his activities they turned against him although no effort was made to forcibly banish him. It wasn't until April 1635 that the General Court noticed his activities after he had stated that no man should take an oath to an "unregenerated man", a comment which challenged the entire foundation of the Holy Commonwealth. He had stated that oaths were sacred and Magistrates must keep hands off all sacred things. They could punish civil offenses, but those against God must be punished by the Church alone. He strongly believed that Church and State must be kept separate.

The foundation for his beliefs was that the link between Church and State corrupted the Church. Government, said Williams, is man-made and designed to order the lives of all, regenerate and unregenerate alike. To tie this unholy institution to the Church defiled the Church. In his mind they were totally different societies and the gulf between them can never be closed.

He had no argument with most Puritan doctrines. He believed in predestination and the absolute authority of the Bible. He broke with his brethren on the bond between Church and State, on the issue of forced worship, and on the question of religious liberty. These divergences challenged the authority of the Holy Commonwealth. After repeated efforts to persuade him to either change his views or keep silent, the Magistrates in October, 1635, ordered his banishment. They based their decision on a provision in the charter that allowed the settlers to expel anyone who became a detriment or annoyance to the community. Soon after the sentence had been passed, friends in England commended Winthrop for disclaiming Williams views. The Magistrates planned to send him back to England but when the time came he had escaped into the wilderness, aided by a secret letter from Winthrop urging him to seek Narragansett Bay. Winthrop didn't have the heart to track him down and deport him so he secretly aided him.

2. **ANNE HUTCHINSON**

She arrived in Boston with her husband in 1634. She came as a devout supporter of John Cotton with the purpose of disrupting the Holy Commonwealth. She soon was holding Thursday evening prayer meetings in her home interpreting the previous Sunday sermons for women who were unable to attend. Soon, she went beyond interpretation and began to question established doctrine. She suggested that just because man "acted sanctified" and lived an outwardly devout life it did not mean that he was "saved". His "inner life" must also be changed, also preached by Cotton, a view preached by earlier English Puritans. Her attacks on the importance of regular church attendance, moral purity and modest dress weakened a weapon the Church used to discipline its people. She further maintained that the "Holy Spirit illumines the heart of every true believer" and every "saved" individual can commune directly with God. This opposed the Orthodox Puritan view that God had spoken to man once and for all time in the Scriptures and these alone were the source for inspiration and instruction. Her doctrine that God could and did reveal Himself could cause problems within the Bay Colony and lead to a lawless society.

Her influence expanded throughout the area so that, by 1636, all of Boston was divided into one of two camps. Those who supported her views were called "Antinomians" (against law).

Many of her supporters were just anti-government but the merchants, for example, opposed the government because of economic restrictions on them, young people also supported her, plus those extremely devout who believed that some of the spirit had waned from Puritanism. In general, she appealed to the discontented of society. John Cotton's sermons kept the issue alive.

The Antiomians were strong enough to elect Henry Vane, a supporter, as Governor in 1636, defeating John Winthrop. But, in 1637 Winthrop was able to reclaim the Governorship. He immediately set out to unify the colony but first had to show where Mrs. Hutchinson had been wrong. During the summer of 1637 he called a Synod of 25 Ministers to define heresy, hoping to split the Antinomian movement. A long list of doctrinal errors were identified and condemned. John Cotton recanted one opinion and modified some others but refused to sign the record. The Synod rebuked Mrs. Hutchinson and ordered Rev. Wheelwright to recant, which he also refused to do. He was banished by Governor Winthrop in November, 1637, as were those who signed a petition supporting him. He and his supporters moved north to found the town of Exeter, New Hampshire.

In spite of her personal popularity, Mrs. Hutchinson was found guilty of sedition and contempt, in a two-day trial, and ordered banished. She received a reprieve while Cotton attempted to convince her to recant. She prepared a confession which did not satisfy the Clergy. After the Boston Church had excommunicated her in March, 1638, the sentence was carried out. She left with her family for Aquidneck, as the Indians called it, where Roger Williams had already established a colony. Her husband died while in Rhode Island so she settled northeast of New Amsterdam where she and her family were killed by Indians in the fall of 1643.

I.   INDIANS AND THE PEQUOT WAR

New England began with few enemies to fear. The Spanish were far to the south, the French had yet to build up strength in Canada, and the Indians were not considered a threat. *The Puritans came expecting to make the Indians over in their own image. When the Indians resisted this effort the Puritans adopted a "get-tough" policy which lasted throughout the colonial period.* As the Puritans began to take Indian lands they justified it as "the Lord's waste", it was land not being utilized to its maximum, therefore okay for the taking.

This was the first full-scale war in New England. Its roots go back to a dispute between the Dutch fur traders and Plymouth officials. Both sides claimed deeds to land along the Connecticut River valley purchased, they said, from the Pequot Indians. A land-rush occurred as settlers from Massachusetts Bay and Plymouth tried to beat the Dutch in settling the area. *This settlement activity negatively impacted the Pequot Indians since it was originally their lands. Other Indians tribes, who opposed the Pequot, sided with the English.* The event which began the war was the capture of a boat and the murder of its Captain, John Oldham, in 1636, an event blamed on the allies of the Pequots. In April, 1637, a raid on a Pequot village by John Endicott led to a retaliatory raid by the Pequot warriors on the town of Weathersfield, Connecticut, where 30 English settlers were killed. This led to further retaliation with a raid by Captain John Underhill and John Mason which burned a Pequot village in May, 1637, near present-day Mystic, Connecticut, killing 300 Pequot Indians. Plymouth colony played a minor role in the fighting. After reinforcements were sent from Massachusetts, the Pequots were tracked down and killed, enslaved, or sold to the West Indies as slaves.

In September, 1638, Roger Williams, who had befriended the Indians, was called in to meet with the Narragansett and Mohegan Indians (the Pequots had been virtually eliminated) to negotiate a peace settlement. The Indians did not cause any further trouble until King Philip's War in 1675.

J.   THE NEW ENGLAND CONFEDERATION (5/29/1643)

(Also known as the "United Colonies of New England)

When it appeared the war would resume, four of the New England colonies, Massachusetts Bay, Connecticut, New Haven, and Plymouth formed a defensive compact known as the *"United Colonies of New England"* led by Edward Winslow. *John Adams later considered the United Colonies to be the prototype for the Articles of Confederation which was the first attempt at a national government.*

This was the first attempt to combine the colonies into any common effort in response to a variety of threats, Indian, Dutch, and French. It endured until 1684 but was mostly ineffective after 1665. The colony members each sent 2 representatives to determine Indian policy, deal with foreign powers, and settle differences among themselves. Lack of cooperation from Massachusetts led to its failure.

K.   IMPACT OF THE RESTORATION ON THE MASSACHUSETTS BAY COLONY

Something of the Massachusetts Bay colony aggressiveness toward the Crown died in 1649 with John Winthrop Sr., whose passing symbolized the diminishing power of the first generation settlers. Political power was now drifting into the hands of those who set the economic and social tone of the colony, the merchants, which upset the religious class who saw a fundamental clash of values between mercantilism and piety. The religious class saw a diminished role for the Church at the same time they began to see a drop-off in Church attendance and membership. In 1657, they gathered to devise a way to increase Church influence again and created the "Half-way Covenant" which allowed the children of the "saints" who held to the forms of Godliness (lived upright lives but had failed to receive God's grace) to become Church members simply by professing their faith. These half-way members were deprived only of the right to share in the Lord's Supper and of a vote in Church affairs.

It failed and marked the end of the "holy experiment" as Winthrop, Cotton, and their associates had conceived it some 25 years earlier. For awhile, it did spread throughout New England as distinctions between full and half-way members vanished in many communities.

The well-to-do merchants in Massachusetts shunned this easy entry into the Church. Puritanism had become unfashionable in Restoration England and the merchants hoped they and the Crown might totally remove the Puritan Orthodoxy from power. This conflict of power created unrest in the colony and soon word of it reached London. A Royal Commission was created in 1664 with the purposes of recapturing New Netherlands from the Dutch and investigate conditions in New England. The commission was ordered that once the Dutch had been evicted they were to focus on insisting that all English liberties, secular and religious, be maintained in Massachusetts.

The commission was further ordered to check on colonial obedience to the Navigation Acts of 1660, to sit as a Royal Court of appeal, and to hear and determine grievances. It was warned to not sit in judgment on any matter within the jurisdiction of the colonies except those proceedings contrary to English Law. The group was headed by Richard Nicholls and three others including the source of the friction, Samuel Maverick of Massachusetts, who was the bitterest critic of Bay Colony authorities and the prime instigator in the creation of the commission.

Before the commission visited Massachusetts, it visited Connecticut and made some boundary changes which were approved by all parties. They did not arrive in the Bay Colony until 1665 and by then rumors were already circulating that they planned to establish the Church of England, impose a stiff land tax, and, in general, assume strong control over the Bay Colony's way of life. The General Court of the colony blocked the commission by refusing to allow it to meet within the boundaries of the colony. The commissioners then moved on to New Hampshire but achieved little because Massachusetts controlled the settlements there and obstructed its efforts.

Maine was unhappy under Massachusetts' domination and warmly greeted the commissioners. They ordered Maine to be made a temporary province of the Crown, taking it away from Massachusetts, and appointed Justices of the Peace and left the final determination to the Crown.

The commissioners' final report to the Crown suggested that the Massachusetts Charter be revoked and turned into a Royal Colony. The recommendation died on paper because by the time the Crown received it other troubles had surfaced in England, including a Plague of 1665, the Great Fire of 1666, another Anglo-Dutch War, and internal government changes, all of which left the Crown with little energy to spare for events in Massachusetts. The Bay Colony then resumed its control of Maine.

1. **MAINE**

    The history of Maine actually precedes the Pilgrims landing at Plymouth in 1620. An English explorer, Martin Pring, explored the coast of Maine in 1603. There were landings on the island of St. Croix, below Calais, in 1604. A group of English explorers traveled the St. George's river in 1605 and settlers led by John Popham and Sir Ferdinando Gorges settled at the mouth of the Kennebec river in 1607. Severe weather forced a return to England in 1608 thus allowing Jamestown to be the first permanent American settlement. There were also Jesuit colonists on the Penobscot River in 1611 and at Mount Desert in 1613.

    Much of the 17th century in Maine was marked by ongoing land disputes. Gorges and his heirs based their claims on rights extended to them by the Council for New England. The competing claim was from resident colonists who wanted to ally with Massachusetts.

    In the 1620's and 1630's, English settlers became interested in the vast lands and limitless supplies of lumber, fish, and fur in the extreme northern areas of America. They settled along the coast on land which had been granted to them in 1622 by the regional proprietor, Sir Ferdinando Gorges, who had been a leader in the Council for New England, which was a group of English officials interested in colonizing what is today known as New England.

    Settlement growth in Maine was very slow, especially compared to the rapid growth of Bay Colony settlements. The Bay colony was united by its homogenous puritanical and Protestant roots whereas people in Maine were a more diverse compilation of people from many different areas of England with no strong religious or political bonds. In fact, there were groups of Anglicans, Puritans, Quakers, and Antinomians in Maine, something unheard of in Massachusetts.

Also, settlements in and around Massachusetts Bay were centrally located and interconnected, therefore easier to unite and control. By contrast, Maine settlements were scattered all along a rocky coast making it hard to unify them into a single unit.

Another factor in the different growth rates in those colonies was the radical transformation occurring in England, a shift towards Protestant control over the government. This shift favored the puritanical Bay Colony over the Anglican centered settlements of Maine.

While the Bay Colony was growing in population and power, there were two provinces created in northern New England to try and establish self-governing states:

- The Province of Lygonia

- The Province of Maine

In 1642 an English settler named George Cleeves sailed to England to appeal to Sir Ferdinando Gorges for land. With the support of a prominent English merchant named Edward Rigby, they managed to secure a land grant to be known as the "Plough Patent" which covered the territory from the Kennebec river to Cape Porpus, near Kennebunk. This tract of land became known as the "Province of Lygonia". By 1647, with the official support of the English Parliament, Cleeves secured his authority in the region by appointing some old foes to high offices, holding frequent general assemblies, issuing grants to new settlers, and reconfirming old deeds. Cleeves policies and actions brought stability to the region.

Settlers living outside of Lygonia had minimal official support from other proprietors in England. In 1649, Thomas Gorges, cousin of Ferdinando, plus the inhabitants of Wells, York, and

Kittery formed an independent "Province of Maine" to try to protect their land claims and bring some sense of order to the area. A man named Edward Godfrey of York was appointed governor of the new province.

In 1651, the Province of Maine attempted to obtain official recognition from the English Parliament. The Bay colony opposed this effort because they were interested in obtaining the Province of Maine. They used a clever interpretation of the Bay Colony original charter by claiming that their northern boundary already included all of the Province of Maine to which Parliament agreed. Since Oliver Cromwell had become Lord Protector of England in 1649 he would, as a devout Protestant himself, support and defend the large Protestant population in the area. In November, 1652, the Bay Colony absorbed Kittery and York. The following summer the Bay Colony annexed other settlements to the south and west of Lygonia's boundary. In the fall of 1653, George Cleeves returned from England and reasserted his claim to the Province of Lygonia and for the next few years was able to hold off the Bay Colony's attempts at a takeover. The Bay Colony decided to hold off until conditions suited an annexation effort. Parliament couldn't concern itself with the sovereignty of a minor American colony with other English problems needing resolution. Eventually, in 1658 the entire Province of Lygonia was annexed by the Massachusetts Bay Colony.

As it absorbed the territories of Maine and Lygonia, the Bay Colony granted its newest citizens generous terms. Land titles were secured, local leaders would remain in charge of administration, and, in general, Maine settlers would enjoy the same protection, favor, and justice enjoyed by other Massachusetts residents.

There was peace in the area for a few areas but with the Restoration of the English Monarchy in 1660 (King Charles II) Ferdinando Gorges, grandson of Sir Ferdinando, made several attempts to persuade individual towns to pledge allegiance to his administration. However, Massachusetts was able to defeat his attempts and retain their control of Maine.

At the same time, other settlements were created along the northern coast of Maine, outside of the territories annexed by the Bay Colony. These settlements were controlled by the Duke of York who sent a royal commission to Maine in 1665 to help establish and control the area. However, the inhabitants of the area petitioned the Massachusetts General Court asking to be brought into the Bay Colony. On July 27, 1674, this region, known as Devonshire County, opened court under Massachusetts jurisdiction ***bringing all of Maine under Massachusetts authority.***

The purchase of Maine by Massachusetts did not truly settle the ownership question since the area was also claimed by France. A series of wars into the mid–18th century occurred between the English colonists and the French and their Indian allies. Much of the warfare consisted of raids on white or Indian villages. A high point for Maine residents occurred in 1745 when colonial forces captured the French Fort at Louisbourg in Nova Scotia. The French then surrendered their claim to the region as part of the terms of the Treaty of Paris of 1763 ending the 7 Years War, or, the French-Indian War.

Maine remained part of Massachusetts until it achieved statehood under the provisions of the Missouri Compromise in 1820.

2. NEW HAMPSHIRE

New Hampshire was technically a part of Massachusetts from 1641 until 1679 when the King separated them. They were joined together again in 1686 through the Dominion of New England, created by the Crown, but were again finally separated in 1691 with New Hampshire becoming a Royal province with the President and his Council appointed by the Crown and the Assembly elected by the people. Until 1741, however, the Governor was subordinate to the Governor of Massachusetts.

L.   DEFINITIONS/EXPLANATIONS

"The Council for New England" was the reorganized Plymouth branch of the Virginia Company and was incorporated by a charter issued by King James I on 11/3/1620 for the "planting, ruling, and governing of New England, in America". The Council was granted all the land, from sea to sea, within the 40 & 48 North Latitude and controlled the area by issuing all orders, commissions, patents, and grants of land for the purposes of division at a profit.

(Attachment 6a represents a List of Massachusetts Governors.)

M. KEY SUMMARY POINTS TO REMEMBER

1. The settlement of Massachusetts was triggered by Puritan "separatists" who refused to become members of the Church of England and chose to immigrate to the New World to create their own settlements and freely practice their own form of religion.

2. The Pilgrims who settled at Plymouth were Puritan Separatists who left England on 9/6/1620 and sighted land-fall at Provincetown, Massachusetts, on 11/11/1620.

3. On the last day at sea the settlers agreed to draft a "Compact of Laws" to govern the colony. It was to become known as the "Mayflower Compact" which pledged loyalty to King James I and was signed by 41 of the Pilgrims.

4. They then sailed over to Plymouth where they landed on 12/21/1620. They were initially welcomed by the Indians and, in the following October, 1621, they gathered to give thanks to God for their first harvest.

5. The Plymouth colony was legalized by a patent from the Council for New England in 1621 although the new Governor, Bradford, preferred a Royal charter.

6. In 1623 a group of merchants settled at Cape Ann and organized themselves into the Dorchester Company and secured a patent/charter from the Council for New England to locate a fishing settlement.

7. The Dorchester Company failed in 1626 and some of their fishermen/planters remained in New England but moved to Salem, Massachusetts. Some Puritan merchants secured a patent/charter from the Council of New England in 1628 which awarded them land between the Merrirmac and Charles Rivers. It was to be called "The New England Company" which then financed a group of 40 settlers to leave for Salem, led by John Endicott.

8. During the first half of the 17th century religious and political oppression in England grew worse. In 1628 the Puritans received approval from the English government to leave England and settle north of Plymouth on the condition that they would retain political control over their colony. They wanted it to become a "theocracy"

9. While Endicott built up Salem, the New England Company was converted into the "Massachusetts Bay Colony" on 3/14/1629 with government authority over any and all colonies it created. There was no condition attached which required the Company headquarters to be located in London, which would prove significant in the future. Early efforts at forming a government occurred in late 1630 and early 1631.

10. On 3/30/1630 a large fleet of 11 ships and 700 passengers left for New England, arriving in Salem in June, 1630, greeted by John Endicott. Soon they decided to center the colony at Boston which possessed a better harbor. After a rough start by summer 1631 roughly 2,000 Puritans had arrived in Massachusetts Bay.

11. In 1636 a committee of the General Court composed a legal code, the first produced in America, considered as a preview of the "Bill of Rights", called the ***"General Fundamentals"***. It was broadened in 1671.

12. By 1657, Plymouth and its local settlements were no longer dominant since Boston had now become more developed and important.

13. ***Key differences between the Plymouth and Massachusetts Bay settlements were;***
    a. Plymouth settlers were Separatists, Massachusetts Bay settlers were not.
    b. Size…………..Plymouth was originally settled by 102 persons whereas by 1630 there were 1,000 settlers at Salem. After another decade the population was 2,500 and that of Massachusetts Bay was 20,000.

c. Economic and social status......Plymouth Pilgrims were primarily working people. The Massachusetts Bay settlers were better educated and more economically and socially successful.

d. Government....In Plymouth, the *"Mayflower Compact"* made everyone equal and more of a true democracy. In Massachusetts Bay their government leaders were chosen by the people to represent them.

e. Church and State....In Plymouth, Church and State were separate. They maintained that what Scripture did not claim as a religious function remained a civil one. In the Bay Colony the State was responsible for supporting and protecting the Church.

14. The "New England Way" meant that the Puritan settlers faced fewer obstacles than Puritans in England because they could create new institutions in the wilderness without first having to tear down existing ones. If something didn't work, they could try something else or move to another location and try again. This became known as the "New England Way".

15. In 1632, something happened which created the precedent for "representative government" in the Bay Colony. A group of unelected "Magistrates" passed a colony-wide tax. A local Minister opposed the tax on the grounds that the colonists had not given their consent. The General Court then declared that there would be an election calling for two men from each town to be appointed to advise the Governor and Magistrates on public matters. The Court then agreed that the election of the Governor should be transferred from the Magistrates to the freemen of the colony.

16. In 1634 a group of deputies to the General Court challenged Governor Winthrop to make the original charter available for review. It declared that laws must be made by ALL FREEMEN. Winthrop proposed a compromise calling for a "Representative Legislative Assembly".

17. London learned of the dispute over the legality of the Charter so in 1634 King Charles I and Bishop Laud created a "Commission for Regulating Plantations" intended to revoke the Bay Colony's charter. The King was too preoccupied with other problems and failed to enforce the decree at the same time that Governor Winthrop refused to surrender the charter. The successful resistance to the Crown emboldened Massachusetts and probably explains the later resistance of Boston in leading to the Revolutionary War.

18. The Pequot War was fought from 1634-1638 resulting from the Puritans efforts to convert the Indians, who resisted. This was the first full-scale Indian war in New England which began with the settlers taking over Indian lands. In September, 1638, Roger Williams helped negotiate a peace settlement which generally lasted until King Philip's War in 1675.

19. In 1641 the General Court approved a "Body of Liberties" which was the first legal code established by European colonists in New England. It established the exclusive right of the General Court to legislate and dictate authority. After 1644 the deputies and assistants began to meet separately which basically created a two- House Legislature which not only levied taxes but passed laws.

20. The New England Confederation (United Colonies of New England) was formed on 5/29/1643 to defend themselves against external threats from a variety of sources; Indians, Dutch, and French. The colonies who formed this compact were Massachusetts Bay, Connecticut, New Haven, and Plymouth. This represented the first attempt by the colonies to form a common bond. It endured until 1684 and was mostly ineffective after 1665. Lack of cooperation from the Massachusetts Bay Colony led to its failure.

N.   KEY DATES & EVENTS

	X	***Considered as part of the Plymouth Colony***
May	1609	50 Scrooby Separatists leave Holland for England
	1618	Leyden Agreement - London Separatists wishing to immigrate to Virginia were required to pledge loyalty to the King, in order to receive a grant to Virginia land.
2/2	1620	London Company issues a charter for settlement in America
9/6	1620	102 settlers leave for America including 35 Scrooby Separatists originating in Holland
11/9	1620	Site land off Cape Cod
11/11	1620	Mayflower Pilgrims anchor at Provincetown, Massachusetts. 41 sign "Mayflower Compact"
11/13	1620	Go ashore at Provincetown
12/21	1620	First landing party ashore at Plymouth
	1621	Plymouth Colony legalized by a patent/charter from the Council for New England; Town of Plymouth begins being built
	1623	Dorchester Company organized by several merchants at Cape Ann. Receive patent/charter from the Council for New England to locate a fishing settlement
	1626	Dorchester Company fails. Some of the fishermen/planters move to Salem
June	1628	A group of Puritan merchants at Salem receive a patent/charter from the Council for New England, called the "New England Company"; Company finances a group of 40 settlers who depart for Salem
3/14	1629	Massachusetts Bay Colony created and Salem merged with it; Charter contains no condition that company headquarters must remain in London…significant
April	1629	400 new settlers leave England for Salem for purpose of creating a refuge for persecuted Puritans

June	1629	King Charles I dissolves Parliament which allows him and Archbishop Laud free to harass the Puritans; Puritans realize that if they want religious freedom they will have to emigrate to America
8/26	1629	Cambridge Agreement states that all Company members who did not wish to emigrate to America could sell their shares to those who did and the company Charter was turned over to them to carry to America; John Winthrop named to head the new venture
3/30	1630	Fleet of 11 ships & 700 settlers leave England for Massachusetts led by John Winthrop
6/16	1630	Fleet arrives in Salem and a few weeks later they agree to move to Boston which possesses a better harbor; Boston begins to grow with nearby settlements .
Oct	1630	First General Court of Salem meets. Passes some laws which violate the true intent of the Charter
May	1631	2nd meeting of the General Court of Salem further distorts meaning of the charter
Aug	1631	By end of summer there are 2,000 Puritans in Massachusetts Bay
	1632	Salem Magistrates pass colony-wide tax. A Minister at Watertown warns that it was wrong to pay taxes to which they had not consented and introduces concept of "representative government".
	1633	The first town government in the colonies is organized in Dorchester, Massachusetts
	1634	The General Court then agreed that the next election would broaden representation
	1634	King Charles I creates the "Commission for Regulating Plantations", its purpose to retrieve the Bay Colony's charter

	1635	English Courts revoke Massachusetts Bay Colony charter. Governor Winthrop of Massachusetts Bay refuses to give up the Charter. England doesn't enforce. This successful resistance to the Crown emboldened Massachusetts for its later actions.
	1635	Settlement of Concord
	1635	Roger Williams banished from Massachusetts
	1636	The General Fundamentals of Plymouth Colony defined a legal code which led to a "Bill of Rights", updated in 1671, also known as "Declaration of Rights"
1636		Harvard University founded
X	1636	Settlement of Scituate
1637		Anne Hutchinson banished from Massachusetts
X	1637	Settlement of Duxbury
4/16	1637	Beginning of "Pequot War"
X	1638	Settlement of Yarmouth
X	1639	Settlement of Sandwich
X	1639	Settlement of Barnstable
	1640	Settlement of Bedford
X	1641	General Court approves the General Fundamentals as the "Body of Liberties"; Becomes the first legal code established by European colonists in New England
5/29	1643	New England Confederation formed for mutual defense. Consists of Massachusetts Bay, Connecticut, New Haven, and Plymouth; also known as "United Colonies of New England"
X	1643	Settlement of Nauset
	1646	In Massachusetts, the General Court approves laws making religious heresy punishable by death
X	1650	Settlement of Rexham
	1657	Plymouth no longer the dominant colony in Massachusetts due to growth of Boston
	1675	King Philip's War begins at Swansea, Massachusetts

	1684	Crown revokes Massachusetts Charter.
May	1686	Dominion of New England begun
	1686	Plymouth is made part of the Dominion of New England
Mar	1687	New England Royal Governor Sir Edmund Andros orders Boston's Old South Meeting House to be converted into an Anglican Church
	1691	Plymouth eventually absorbed by the Massachusetts Bay Colony; Massachusetts becomes a Royal Colony
	1692	Salem Witchcraft trials
6/17	1700	Massachusetts passes law ordering all Roman Catholic priests to leave the colony within 3 months upon penalty of life imprisonment or execution; New York passes similar law
	1704	Boston "News Letter", the first regular newspaper, began publication
	1727	King George II assumes Throne of England
	1731	Boundary line between New York and Massachusetts settled
	1760	King George III assumes Throne of England
	1775	English Parliament declares Massachusetts to be in Rebellion
	1788	Massachusetts becomes a State

O.   REVIEW QUESTIONS

(Multiple Choice)

1. The Mayflower Compact:
   a.   provided a detailed framework of government
   b.   was disallowed by the Privy Council
   c.   went into effect in Boston in 1630
   d.   provided for rule by the majority at Plymouth

2. The term "theocracy" is synonymous with:
   a.   the divine right of kings
   b.   the establishment of a single government church
   c.   the rule by a few
   d.   an oligarchy of religious leaders

3. The Massachusetts Bay Colony was founded because:
   a.   the Mayflower was blown off course by a storm
   b.   it's founders sought religious freedom and opportunities for economic improvement
   c.   the English Separatists were being persecuted by Bishop Laud
   d.   the English King sought to banish all Puritans and Catholics

4. The Confederation of New England was organized:
   a.   for joint measures of defense against common enemies
   b.   but never put into operation because of disapproval of legislatures of the separated colonies
   c.   in spite of the disapproval of the English King
   d.   in 1686

(True or False)

5. In Massachusetts, representative government began when outlying towns demanded the right to send deputies to the General Court before paying taxes.
    a. TRUE
    b. FALSE

6. Puritanism assured uniformity of opinion and prevented disagreement among the settlers who came to Boston.
    a. TRUE
    b. FALSE

7. The Mayflower Compact was a Constitution with legal validity.
    a. TRUE
    b. FALSE

R.   GLOSSARY

8. **Covenant**   A binding agreement, a compact. A formal sealed agreement or contract. In the Bible, God's promise to the Human Race. To come together to make an agreement.

9. **Theocracy**   A government ruled by or subject to religious authority

10. **Heresy**   An opinion or a doctrine at variance with established religious beliefs. Adherence to a dissenting opinion or doctrine. A controversial or unorthodox opinion or doctrine.

11. **Pre-destination**   The doctrine that God has fore-ordained all things, especially that God has elected certain souls to either eternal salvation or damnation. Doctrine associated with John Calvin.

12. **Council for New England** Sir Fernando Gorges tries to revive the failed Plymouth Company under a new name. The Council received a grant from the Crown to settle and control all the land from the 40th to 48th parallel (southern boundary of present-day Pennsylvania to just beyond the northern tip of Maine)

CHAPTER 6 SUMMARY

Massachusetts Colony

1. Massachusetts Bay Colony created from the settlements at Plymouth, Salem, Boston, and Dorchester

2. Settlement started by Puritan "Separatists" who refused to become members of the Church of England and preferred to immigrate to the New World to create their own settlements and freely practice their own religion.

3. "Mayflower Compact signed by 41 pilgrims on board the Mayflower which was a compact of laws to govern their colony until a more complete government could be created.

4. Pilgrims landed at Plymouth on 12/21/1620. Colony legalized by a patent from the council for New England 1621.

5. 1623 a group of merchants receive grant from council for New England to create the Dorchester Company.

6. 1628 English puritans receive permission to settle north of Plymouth. Council for New England grants charter to "New England Company" to settle Salem.

7. 1629 Massachusetts Bay Company receives charter and eventually settles Boston. Significance...no requirement for charter to remain in England.

8. 1630 a group of 900 puritans emigrate to Massachusetts to settle Boston.

9. By summer 1631 population of 2,000 Puritans in Massachusetts Bay.

10. 1634 King Charles I and Archbishop Laud create "Commission for Regulating Plantations" to be used to revoke the Bay Colony Charter.

11. Pequot War 1634–1638 with most of the fighting during the years of 1636–1637.

12. 1636 "General Fundamentals of Plymouth Colony" creates first attempt at a Bill of Rights.

13. 1641 "Body of Liberties" creates first legal code established by European Colonists in New England. (98 specific laws)

14. 1643 New England Confederation (United Colonies of New England) formed for self-defense.

15. By 1657, Boston becomes predominant Colony.

6a

DATES		MASSACHUSETTS GOVERNORS	
		COLONY	INCUMBENT
1620	1621	PLYMOUTH	JOHN CARVER
1621	1632	PLYMOUTH	WILLIAM BRADFORD
1633	1634	PLYMOUTH	EDWARD WINSLOW
1634	1635	PLYMOUTH	THOMAS PRENCE
1635	1636	PLYMOUTH	WILLIAM BRADFORD
1636	1637	PLYMOUTH	EDWARD WINSLOW
1637	1638	PLYMOUTH	WILLIAM BRADFORD
1638	1639	PLYMOUTH	THOMAS PRENCE
1639	1644	PLYMOUTH	WILLIAM BRADFORD
1644	1645	PLYMOUTH	EDWARD WINSLOW
1645	1657	PLYMOUTH	WILLIAM BRADFORD
1657	1673	PLYMOUTH	THOMAS PRENCE
1673	1680	PLYMOUTH	JOSIAH WINSLOW
1680	1692	PLYMOUTH	THOMAS HINCKLEY
			(Plymouth absorbed into Massachusetts Bay by New Charter issued to Bay Colony in 1691)
1629	1630	MASS BAY	JOHN ENDECOTT
1630	1633	MASS BAY	JOHN WINTHROP
1634	1635	MASS BAY	THOMAS DUDLEY
1635	1636	MASS BAY	JOHN HAYNES
1636	1637	MASS BAY	SIR HENRY VANE
1637	1640	MASS BAY	JOHN WINTHROP
1640	1641	MASS BAY	THOMAS DUDLEY
1641	1642	MASS BAY	RICHARD BELLINGHAM
1642	1644	MASS BAY	JOHN WINTHROP
1644	1645	MASS BAY	JOHN ENDECOTT
1645	1646	MASS BAY	THOMAS DUDLEY
1646	1649	MASS BAY	JOHN WINTHROP
1649	1650	MASS BAY	JOHN ENDECOTT
1650	1651	MASS BAY	THOMAS DUDLEY
1651	1654	MASS BAY	JOHN ENDECOTT
1654	1655	MASS BAY	RICHARD BELLINGHAM
1655	1665	MASS BAY	JOHN ENDECOTT
1665	1672	MASS BAY	RICHARD BELLINGHAM
1672	1679	MASS BAY	JOHN LEVERETT
1679	1685	MASS BAY	SIMON BRADSTREET
1686	X	MASS BAY	JOSEPH DUDLEY
1687	1689	MASS BAY	SIR EDMUND ANDROS
1689	1691	MASS BAY	SIMON BRADSTREET
1691	1694	MASS BAY	SIR WILLIAM PHIPS
1694	1699	MASS BAY	LT. GOV. WILLIAM STOUGHTON
1699	1700	MASS BAY	RICHARD COOTE, EARL OF BELLOMONT
1700	1701	MASS BAY	LT. GOV. WILLIAM STOUGHTON
1701	1702	MASS BAY	THE COUNCIL
1702	1714	MASS BAY	JOSEPH DUDLEY
1715	1716	MASS BAY	LT. GOV. WILLIAM TAILER
1716	1722	MASS BAY	SAMUEL SHUTE
1722	1727	MASS BAY	LT. GOV. WILLIAM DUMMER
1727	1729	MASS BAY	WILLIAM BURNET
1729	1730	MASS BAY	LT. GOV. WILLIAM DUMMER
1730	1741	MASS BAY	JONATHAN BELCHER
1741	1757	MASS BAY	WILLIAM SHIRLEY
1757	1760	MASS BAY	LT. GOV. THOMAS HUTCHINSON
1760	1769	MASS BAY	SIR FRANCIS BERNARD
1769	1774	MASS BAY	ACTING GOV THOMAS HUTCHINSON
1774	1775	MASS BAY	GENERAL THOMAS GAGE
1775	1780	MASS BAY	*GOVERNED BY COMMITTEES DURING THE REVOLUTION*
1780	1785	MASSACHUSETTS	JOHN HANCOCK
1785	1787	MASSACHUSETTS	JAMES BOWDOIN
1787	1793	MASSACHUSETTS	JOHN HANCOCK

Chapter 7

Maryland

A. SIR GEORGE CALVERT, THE FIRST LORD BALTIMORE

1. BACKGROUND

He was the first person to dream of a colony in America where Catholics and Protestants could prosper together. He was born in Yorkshire, England, and studied at Trinity College at Oxford, England. He was initially hired to work for Sir Robert Cecil as a clerk to the Privy Council in 1608 and then became a member of the Council for New England. In 1617, King James I anointed him as Sir George Calvert, one of the principal Secretaries of State.

By the time King James I died and was succeeded by his son, King Charles I, Calvert had distinguished himself as a statesman and loyal subject. He served several terms as a member of Parliament and received gifts of land in Ireland and acquired great wealth. But, he had a problem. Although forced to become an Anglican at age 12, by 1624 he had returned to Catholicism which made him ineligible for high government office.

In 1625, Calvert informed the King of his return to Catholicism and resigned his job but the King liked him so much that he created a new title for him, "Baron of Baltimore in the County of Longford". He now had a new and higher status in society and could support himself and his family.

2. **BECOMES INTERESTED IN EXPLORATION**

He became interested in the exploration of the New World and the eventual creation of English colonies so he invested money in both the New England and Virginia companies. He had previously purchased land in Newfoundland in 1620 and sent Captain Edward Wynne to Newfoundland to lead some settlers and serve as their Governor. He also received permission from King James I to establish a larger colony called the "Province of Avalon" in Newfoundland where George lived from 1627-1629. But, Newfoundland's climate was cold and the settlers had trouble surviving there. In the spring he sent his children home and sailed with his wife to Jamestown in October.

3. **TWO NEW CHARTERS 1630**

When he appeared before Governor Harvey and his Council, he was asked to take an oath to the King and did so. But, when he was asked to accept the King as the leader of the Church, he refused. The Governor then sent him back to England from which he returned to Virginia in 1630 with a new charter from King Charles I for land south of the James River which the Virginia Company strongly opposed because the King had granted it without consulting Virginia. Calvert then requested another charter north and east of the Potomac river which included the Chesapeake Bay, which he had explored. Part of the reason for the King granting this land north of Virginia was to pacify Virginia who didn't like having any portion of its territory given to a potential Catholic colony. When the King asked him what name he would give to the new territory, he deferred to the King who then suggested "Terra Maria" (Mary Land) to honor Queen Henrietta Mary. Before the King could make the charter official, Calvert died in London.

B.   CECILUS CALVERT, THE 2ND LORD BALTIMORE 8/5/1605-11/30/1675)
(Charter of 6/20/1632)

Cecilus, age 26, was the oldest son of George who assumed the charter for his father on 6/20/1632. He was given the title of "Absolute Lord of Maryland and Avalon". It was his original intention to travel to America with the colonists but there were many enemies of his colonial project in England, so he sent his brothers, Leonard and George Jr. to lead the expedition. The enemies were primarily members of the London Company who did everything in their power to defeat his objectives. They claimed that the charter interfered with the grant of land to the Virginia company and would therefore draw colonists away from the other colonies, thus weakening them. His charter covered territory from the 40th latitude to the mouth of the Potomac River and west along the line of that river.

This new charter was similar to one granted by King Charles I to his Attorney-General, Sir Robert Heath, for "Carolina", a territory south of the Roanoke River. It provided greater democratic privileges to the settler than any yet issued by any company or Monarch. It stated that future settlers were exempted from taxation by the Crown except by their own consent. It allowed religious toleration without establishing a State Church, leaving that issue up to the Legislature. This toleration was a wise gesture because it helped promote growth of the colony by offering a refuge from religious persecution.

With this charter, Cecilus began the colonization process but not for the same reason as his father, as a refuge from religious persecution, but for his own financial gain. He appointed his half-brother, Leonard, as Governor and on 11/22/1633 he led 300 settlers from the Isle of Wight, England, in two ships, the "Ark" and "Dove". Cecilus stayed in England to defend the charter.

Cecilus paid for the expedition and provided the transportation and provisions costs. The colony was so well prepared that it was determined that the new colony made as much progress in the first six months as did Virginia in the first few years. Although he intended to eventually join his colonists in Maryland, events in England prevented him from ever making it to Maryland.

The voyage took the southern route by way of the Canary and West Indies islands but the ships encountered a severe storm for three days. The "Ark", however, managed to arrive in Barbados, followed shortly by the "Dove", after a separation of six weeks. This round-about voyage took four months in all.

Leonard was appointed as Governor, and given instructions on how to establish the first elected assembly and provide a set of laws for the Colony.

C.   LEONARD CALVERT 1606-1647

The Calverts and most of the would-be settlers were Roman Catholics but most of those who followed were Protestants who took an oath of supremacy before leaving England. He appealed for more settlers regardless of religion, realizing that he would not be able to build a successful colony with Catholics only. Learning from the Virginia experiences he used land to attract new settlers, offering special inducements to first-comers. He offered 100 acres for each settler, his wife, and every servant plus 50 acres for each child under age 16. He offered 2,000 acres for every settler who brought 5 others with him, with the right to erect a "manor" with the same terms as those in England. He published a list of things a settler would need to survive. He sought to avoid Jamestown's "starving time" by requiring food provisions planted before other projects were done. When Maryland became too tobacco-focused, a law modeled on the Virginia "Two-Acres Act" of 1624 ordered planters to also plant and tend two acres of corn. The effort to copy the success of Virginia paid off, Maryland was initially successful.

The Maryland charter boundaries proved less generous than the King had planned. The northern boundary ran west from the Delaware Bay along the 40th latitude including all of the present-day Delmarva Peninsula. Virginia demanded the southern tip since it had settlers there plus it also wanted to control both sides of the mouth of the Chesapeake Bay. The King approved but gave Lord Baltimore the southern bank of the Potomac river, then west to the river's first "fountain", not knowing that the river moved northwest which hemmed in Maryland, making it one of the smallest colonies.

Boundary problems persisted. William Penn later claimed and received part of the Delmarva Peninsula for Delaware. Later, Maryland lost part of its northern boundary to Pennsylvania. With Virginia receiving both sides of the mouth of the Chesapeake Bay and Maryland receiving all of the Potomac River, it created questions about navigation rights which were not settled until the eventual creation of the Federal Constitution in 1787.

Lord Baltimore possessed 10 million acres and the charter made him absolute Lord and Proprietor with full authority to pass along to his heirs. He held all land in his name, not the King's, and controlled all branches of government. He could appoint all officers and judges, establish courts, and try all cases both civil and criminal. He could erect towns, boroughs, cities, and bestow titles. The people were entitled to give advice and consent to the laws but only the Proprietor could initiate laws except those in conflict with English law. The Crown reserved the right to control war, trade, and most of the gold and silver found in the province.

In spite of having all of this authority, the settlers, who were accustomed to the liberties of Englishmen, restrained him. Plus, they saw the liberties enjoyed by Virginians, also restrained by distance from home and the realities of the frontier, which caused the settlers to seek unique solutions to unique problems not ordinarily found in England.

D.   ST. MARY'S COLONY 3/27/1634

1.   FIRST SETTLERS ARRIVE

The first settlers arrived in Virginia in February 1634 and traveled to Jamestown where their Royal letters borne by Calvert were given a friendly reception by Governor Harvey. They stayed there nine days and then moved to the Chesapeake Bay and Potomac river. They sailed up the Potomac to the Heron Islands and were met by various Indian groups. On the Feast of the Annunciation, March 25, the Priests performed religious services for the first time in that Indian region. Their celebration and procession were watched by the local Indians of the Piscataway tribe who ruled over several small principalities.

Calvert tried to make peace with the local Indians, meeting with one Chief at Mount Vernon, who pledged peace. After exploration of the Potomac and Chesapeake areas they selected present-day St. Mary's on 3/27/1634 for their capital city, supported by friendly Indians.

The King of the Piscataway Tribe became sick and was treated by the Priest, Father White. He recovered and was so grateful for his survival that he asked to be Baptized along with his Queen, daughter, and a few of his Chiefs. So, St. Mary's began in harmony although the colony did experience some growing pains along the way.

2. **PROBLEMS WITH VIRGINIA**

While St. Mary's was attempting to prosper, other events worked against its' success. One problem was the arrival of William Claiborne in 1621 from England. Between 1627-1629 he explored the upper part of the Chesapeake Bay. Virginia sent him to England to oppose the pending Lord Baltimore charter. While in England, he received permission to engage in fur-trade on the Chesapeake Bay. In 1631 he led 100 settlers to establish a trading post on Kent Island in the Bay. This happened before Cecilus Calvert assumed the charter on behalf of his father in 1632 so Claiborne believed he had a solid legal claim to the territory.

Clairborne's trading post tapped the rich fur-trade up the Susquehanna River that Governor Calvert had hoped to exploit for Maryland. He was also trying to turn the Indians against the Catholics and other Maryland settlers but only succeeded in making the Virginia and Maryland conflict worse. While Claiborne was in England, in 1637, Calvert captured Kent Island. In 1638, the Maryland Assembly passed a "Bill of Attainder" against Claiborne which deprived him of his property within the colony.

3. **THE COLONY GROWS**

Meanwhile, in February 1635, the first Assembly passed laws which were rejected by Lord Baltimore because he believed they infringed on his rights. Then, in 1637, the Assembly passed another set of laws which he reluctantly approved but retained his right to veto. The new assembly was the product of a growing colonial population plus some emigration but, in 1638, the settlers objected to having laws handed down to them from the Proprietor or England. The opposition was led by Thomas Cornwallis, a member of the Governor's Council. He suggested another set of laws and awaited a response from England. Governor Calvert opposed those laws but agreed to establish a committee to draft new laws. *By August, he had agreed to allow the legislature some role in drafting legislation. The people were allowed to send as many delegates as they pleased._Then they founded the Republican Commonwealth of Maryland in 1639.*

4. **REPUBLICAN COMMONWEALTH OF MARYLAND 1639**

In that first Representative Assembly the people asserted their rights. The Proprietor presented to the Legislature a system of laws which he had framed. The Representatives of the people, feeling that the inherent right to make laws resided in their constituents, rejected the entire system. They adopted a Declaration of Rights, defining the powers and duties of each branch of the government, and set to work to pass bills for the security to the people of every privilege that belonged to a British subject.

This popular sovereignty was opposed by Lord Baltimore with vetoes or refusals to sign such bills. After vetoing more than 40, and finding the people firm in their attitudes, the proprietor gave up the contest and gracefully yielded to the popular will. Prior to this Assembly the colony was without any laws so this was a significant achievement.

E.   CHESAPEAKE SOCIETY

In spite of frequent conflict between Virginia and Maryland, they managed to co-exist because they did have much in common. Chesapeake Bay stretched nearly 200 miles in length, 3-22 miles wide. There were 150 rivers, creeks, and branches which fed into it. Ships could travel upstream in some rivers almost 100 miles. The total shoreline has been estimated at 5,600 miles which explains why the area was so receptive to tobacco, even more than the soil itself. This encouraged the growth of tobacco in the Chesapeake Bay area. Tobacco was heavy and expensive to transport overland but the many waterways made it easy to load and unload at the planter's sources. The Bay shoreline explains why no large towns developed and those which did were located at the head of major waterways, such as, Baltimore on the Patapsco River, Fredericksburg on the Appomattox river, and often the trader sailed to the planter's backdoor. Every planter desired an outlet on a navigable stream. The choice sites were taken up in Jamestown or St. Mary's so they searched elsewhere for well-watered lands. Within a few years the desire for lots near water had shattered the village pattern of life. The farm soon replaced the village throughout the Chesapeake area. By 1640 the land and economic realities created a pattern of life alien to the English experience.

The population of the colony grew rapidly due to large numbers of immigrants, especially those who brought 10-20 settlers with them who were then given manors, plantations, and/or farms. Most of the work on the plantations was done by indentured white servants. Negro slavery existed in Maryland from the beginning but not in large numbers until after 1700. Food was abundant because of the great wildlife such as deer, turkeys, and wild pigeons.

Because so much of the population was located on plantations and farms there were very few towns created. Even St. Mary's as late as 1678 was not really a town but a string of 30 houses along 5 miles of shoreline. The Chesapeake Bay, with its many rivers, creeks, inlets, etc, provided great water communications between farms and plantations.

As Maryland grew and dispersed, local government became more important at the expense of the Governor and his Council. County Officers became more important, serving warrants, making arrests, and collecting taxes.

During the "Interregnum" period of 1649-1660 the Legislatures of Maryland and Virginia became bi-cameral. An Act of 1650 called for separation between the council and deputies but it was not recognized as the "Upper House" until 1659.

F.   RELIGIOUS CONFLICT

Eventually, the Protestants gained a majority in the Assembly and passed laws against the Catholics. The growing unrest and future conflict began in 1644 and reached its peak in 1647 when the Catholic Governor arrested Richard Ingle, a Protestant, for treasonable comments which caused a small civil war which ended with the expulsion of Governor Calvert. He returned in March, 1652, and forced Protestant Governor Stone and his Council from power and installed his own people. English authorities overturned his actions and reinstated Stone but then devised a compromise which caused even more unrest.

Lord Baltimore then ordered settlers to take an oath of loyalty to him, that "writs" be issued in his name, and that failure to accept these orders would mean loss of land, but *civil war still broke out again in Maryland. Puritans,* who had settled by invitation at Providence (near Annapolis) after their ejection from Virginia, *led the opposition.* Governor Stone, defeated in battle at the Severn River in 1655 was imprisoned and William Fuller, a Puritan, was made Governor. *A Puritan-dominated Assembly repudiated the Proprietor and repealed his statute of religious toleration, and deprived Catholics of all legal protections.* Puritans ran the colony for 3 years until 1658 when Lord

Baltimore regained power and made Josias Fendall Governor. Baltimore believed he held absolute authority but Fendall disagreed and sided with the Assembly when they demanded authority in 1660 at the time of the English Restoration. This was referred to as "Fendall's Rebellion". The King supported Lord Baltimore who, a few months later, sent his brother Philip to rule as Governor.

During this time the Maryland colony was growing with 5,000 settlers in the 1660's and the Proprietor's tight control over the land meant that he was making money through quit-rents from land holdings. Baltimore solidified his support of the planters by careful distribution of political appointments and a tight control of the land office. A major part of Maryland's elite were tied to his family, either through marriage or blood. From this group came the Governor's Council and many of the Assembly's upper House. Some historians believe Maryland more closely represented the English peerage and House of Lords than any other colony.

Despite this tight control from above, there was no pressure from below for several years after the Restoration. Then, in 1669 members of the Assembly submitted a list of grievances which the Governor resisted and ignored. But it marked the beginning of a long struggle between the Proprietor and Assembly.

1. **TOLERATION ACT (4/21/1649)**

   On April 2, 1649, at St. Mary's city, then the capital of Maryland, freemen gathered for a meeting of the General Assembly in Governor Stone's home. Acting as representatives of the people they were to consider 16 bills for possible approval as laws of the province. ***On April 21, 1649, the freemen voted into law 12 of the proposed bills, including "An Act Concerning Religion".***

   It was intended to guarantee a degree of religious liberty, especially freedom of conscience, to all Christians. Religious toleration was not new to the people of Maryland. The original charter intended the province to be a haven for persecuted Catholics and eventually the goal expanded when the second Lord Baltimore, Cecilus, warned those ready to leave for America to "get along". For 15 years the settlers generally co-existed peacefully.

Once they landed in Maryland they shared a single chapel building at St. Mary's. The earliest religious dispute occurred in 1638 when a Catholic was found guilty of abusing his authority to advocate his religion to a Protestant servant. What was significant was that he was found guilty by a predominantly Catholic court. In 1641 there was a similar case and result.

When William Stone, a Protestant, had become Lord Baltimore's Governor in 1648 he was required to take an oath to not persecute anyone believing in Jesus Christ. ***This was the background to the passing of the Toleration Act of 1649 which stated that "no person or persons whatsoever within this province professing to believe in Jesus Christ shall henceforth be in any ways troubled, molested, or discountenanced for or in respect of his or her religion, nor in the free exercise therefore".*** This act of religious toleration, like Lord Baltimore's policy of separating church and state, was far ahead of its time.

This religious unrest in Maryland was happening at the same time as a religious civil war in England which had begun in 1642 and ended with the execution of King Charles I on 1/30/1649. Charles had defied the will of Parliament , had been tried, condemned, and beheaded. The King's concept of government had been that the subjects' lives were in the sovereign's hand, the Englishmen who had executed Charles, however, had asserted the principle that, once he undertook to destroy their liberty, the sovereign's life was in the hands of the subjects. This was an attack on the idea of absolute Monarchy. The English were beginning to realize how a climate of ideas of English freedom were spreading to the New World.

When King Charles I was executed, Lord Baltimore lost his protector and now the authority of his charter was weakened. No longer were Lord Baltimore edicts strong enough to support the government which he had imposed on Maryland. The consent of the people of Maryland had become a necessity.

Toleration in Maryland lasted only until 1654 when the conflict in England ended. Cromwell, a Puritan, was in power so Maryland Puritans swept away the Toleration Act and harshly persecuted Catholics, Jews, and Quakers.

In 1661, after Cromwell's death and the Monarchy had been restored, Marylanders repealed all the laws of the Puritan regime and basically reinstated the Toleration Act of 1649 (1661) where it remained in force until 1692 when it was replaced by the new English government of William & Mary who sought to re-establish the Anglican Church throughout the Empire.

The Toleration Act played a role in the eventual First Amendment to the Federal Constitution which states that Congress shall make no law respecting the establishment of religion or prohibition of the free exercise of religion. It had the effect of separating Church and State. True religious freedom did not arrive until the State Constitution of 1867 where it stated that religion could not be used as a test for public office although provisions were made to accommodate non-Christians as office holders in 1825.

G.   ROYAL GOVERNMENT

Political and religious conflicts led a group of angry Protestants to revolt against Lord Baltimore in 1689. The Crown appointed Royal Governors and they moved the capital of the colony from St. Mary's to Annapolis in 1695. The old colonial statehouse was turned into an Anglican Church in 1695 and then, *in 1704, the principle of liberty of conscience was overturned when all Catholic Church's and schools were closed in accordance with the "Act to Prevent the Growth of Popery within this Province".* The town was gradually abandoned and died, leaving very little evidence of its existence.

H.   GLOSSARY

The difference between a "manor" and an ordinary "landed estate" is that the Lord of the Manor had judicial powers, such as in Maryland.

"Servant" in the colonial era was really equivalent to an "employee" in today's terminology. A servant's passage was paid or assisted in return for working a certain number of years (4-5 for an adult). When released from this apprenticeship the servant became a "freeman".

"Indentured servant" was one who had a specific contract with his employer, called an "indenture". This system of exchanging cost of passage for a few years of labor was the primary means of settling the colonies.

After 1650 the Maryland government contained two Houses; (1) Council appointed by Lord Baltimore, (2) Elected House of Burgesses. The Governor and Council retained the right to legislate and the Burgesses could not introduce Bills. With the Restoration in 1660 the Proprietor assumed supreme authority again.

The "Delmarva Peninsula" is the significant peninsula on the eastern coastline of the United States occupied by the entire State of Delaware and portions of Maryland and Virginia, thus, "Del Mar Va".

I.   KEY DATES & EVENTS

	1608	Captain John Smith explores Chesapeake Bay
	1629	George Calvert, 1st Lord Baltimore, sails from Newfoundland to Virginia
	1631	Kent Island trading post and farming settlement established by William Claiborne, member of the Virginia Council. Becomes Maryland's first permanent English settlement.
6/20	1632	Maryland charter granted to Cecilus Calvert, 2nd Lord Baltimore, by King Charles I
	1632	Colony named for Queen Henrietta Maria, wife of King Charles I
11/22	1633	English settlers on the ships "Ark" and "Dove" set sail from Cowes, England, for Maryland
3/25	1634	200 settlers land at St. Clements Island. Calvert party celebrates Feast of the Annunciation and later purchased Indian land and built a fort at St. Mary's City
1634 –	1635	First General Assembly of freemen meet at St. Mary's City
	1635	Virginians and Marylanders fought over territorial rights to Kent Island
	1637	St. Mary's County first cited in provincial records
	1638	Assembly claims protections of English law
	1644	Leonard Calvert, Governor
2/14	1645	Richard Ingle leads rebellion against the proprietary government
	1649	Governor Stone invites Virginia Puritans to settle in Maryland
4/21	1649	Maryland Act of Toleration passed
	1649	King Charles I beheaded

7/5	1652	Susquehannock Indians sign peace treaty at Severn River ceding the Chesapeake Bay Eastern and Western shore-lands to the English, except Kent Island & Palmer Island.
	1654	Patuxent County (later Calvert County) formed by order of the Council
3/25	1655	Puritans from Virginia defeat Gov Stone's forces at the Battle of the Severn
11/30	1657	Oliver Cromwell restores Maryland colony back to the Calverts which reaffirms Lord Baltimore's claims to Maryland. Lord Baltimore re-establishes Proprietary Government.
	1658	The Lower House of the Assembly voted to compose itself of 4 delegates per county, elected by freemen.
	1658	Charles County created by order of the Council
	1660	Monarchy restored in England to King Charles II
Jan	1660	Baltimore County established
	1663	Augustine Herrman, first naturalized citizen of Maryland
	1664	Slavery sanctioned by law, slaves to serve for life
	1667	St. Mary's City incorporated
	1670	Voting restricted by the Governor to planters with a 50-acre freehold or property worth 40 pounds. Officeholding restricted to owners of 1,000 acres.
	1677	Maryland & Virginia war against Susquehannock Indians
	1684	Presbyterians under Francis Makemie built a church at Snow Hill, the first in the colonies
July	1689	Maryland Revolution. Protestant's overthrow Proprietary officers

	1692	Crown Rule......William & Mary declare Maryland a Royal colony and appoint Sir Lionel Copley Governor. Maryland governed as a Royal Colony rather than as a Proprietary province.
	1692	Church of England (Anglican) made the established Church. Crown approves Church financially supported by taxation imposed on all free men, male servants, and slaves.
2/5	1694	Capital of Maryland moved from St. Mary's City to Anne Arundel Town
May	1695	Anne Arundel Town renamed Annapolis
	1698	Monopoly of slave trade abolished by English Parliament. Slave imports greatly increased.
	1704	New State House built and later burned down
	1715	Crown restores Proprietary rights to Benedict Leonard Calvert, 4th Lord Baltimore
	1718	***Catholics disenfranchised by Assembly***
	1727	First newspaper in Chesapeake area, "Maryland Gazette", published at Annapolis
	1730	Baltimore founded
	1732	Establishment of a boundary line with the 3 lower counties of Pennsylvania, which later become Delaware
	1742	First Baptist Church in Maryland established at Chestnut Ridge, Baltimore County
	1743	First Lutheran Church in Maryland built at Monocacy River
6/30	1744	Indian Chiefs of the Six Nations cede by treaty all claims to land in Maryland. The Assembly purchases the last Indian land claims in Maryland.
	1750	Ohio Company establishes a trading post at Will's Creek on the Potomac River
	1754	Fort Cumberland built

	1755	General Edward Braddock leads expedition through Maryland to the west. French & Indians defeat his forces near Fort Duquesne. Indians begin attacking western settlers
	1755	French-speaking Catholics begin arriving in Baltimore from Nova Scotia
	1765	Daniel Dulany Jr. denounces the Stamp Act in Annapolis. Stamp Act resistance at Frederick.
	1766	Sons of Liberty organized in Baltimore County
	1769	Maryland merchants adopt policy of "non-importation" of British goods
3/28	1772	Cornerstone laid for new State House in Annapolis
6/22	1774	First Provincial Convention meets at Annapolis and sends delegates to First Continental Congress
10/19	1774	Mob burns the British ship "Peggy Stewart" in Annapolis harbor
3/22	1775	"Bush Declaration" signed at Bush River, Hartford County, call for Independence.
8/29	1775	Council of Safety organized
Dec	1775	Association of Freemen begins recruiting troops
6/26	1776	Departure of Robert Eden, Maryland's last Colonial governor
7/4	1776	Declaration of Independence adopted in Philadelphia
7/6	1776	Maryland Convention declares Independence from England
11/3	1776	Declaration of Rights (Maryland's Bill of Rights) adopted by 9th Provincial Convention. Church of England disestablished.
12/20	1776	Continental Congress meets at Baltimore until 3/4/1777
2/5	1777	First General Assembly elected under the new State Constitution of 1776 meets at Annapolis

3/21	1777	Inauguration of Thomas Johnson, the first Governor elected by the General Assembly. The Council of Safety is disbanded.
2/2	1781	Property of Maryland Loyalists and British subjects confiscated
3/1	1781	Maryland votes to ratify the Articles of Confederation, its' vote making the Articles effective.
11/26	1783	Annapolis serves as Capital of new nation when the Continental Congress met at Annapolis; Meets until 6/3/1784.
12/23	1783	George Washington resigns Commission as Commander-in-Chief at the State House in Annapolis
1/14	1784	Treaty of Paris, ending Revolutionary War, ratified by Congress at Annapolis State House.
3/28	1785	Mt. Vernon Compact serves as agreement on navigation and fishing in the tidewaters of the Potomac River and Chesapeake Bay.
3/12	1786	Mt. Vernon Compact ratified by Maryland
9/11	1786	Annapolis Convention of delegates from several states meet at Mann'sTavern, Annapolis, to discuss revisions to the Articles of Confederation. Maryland sends no delegates.
9/17	1787	U.S. Constitution signed by Maryland delegates at Philadelphia
4/28	1788	Maryland Convention ratifies U.S. Constitution making Maryland the 7th state to do so; the convention adjourns without recommending amendments.
11/6	1789	Pope Pius VI appoints John Carroll as the first Catholic Bishop in the United States
12/19	1789	Maryland ratifies Federal Bill of Rights, the first 10 Constitutional Amendments.

12/19	1791	Maryland cedes land for the Federal District of Columbia
12/26	1794	Maryland ratifies the 11th Amendment to the Constitution
	1796	Maryland law forbade import of slaves for sale and permitted voluntary slave emancipation

J.   REVIEW QUESTIONS

(Multiple Choice)

1.   The Toleration Act in Maryland was passed:
     a.   to encourage immigration
     b.   because of imminent danger of a religious uprising
     c.   because Catholic settlers had become a minority in danger of losing religious freedom
     d.   after King James II was overthrown in England

2.   Who was the first Calvert to dream of a colony in America where Protestants and Catholics could live peacefully together:
     a.   George Calvert
     b.   Cecilius Calvert
     c.   Leonard Calvert
     d.   all of the above

3.   What settlement became the first Capital of Maryland?
     a.   Baltimore
     b.   St. Mary's
     c.   Annapolis
     d.   Kent Island

4.   Where did the name "Maryland" come from?
     a.   To honor Queen Elizabeth I
     b.   To honor King Charles I
     c.   To honor Queen Henrietta Mary
     d.   None of the above

(True or False)

5. Maryland is a prominent example of a Proprietary colony.
   a. TRUE
   b. FALSE

6. The name "Maryland" was derived from "Terra Maria" (Mary Land).
   a. TRUE
   b. FALSE

(Attachment 7a List of Maryland Governors)

CHAPTER 7 SUMMARY

Maryland

1. George Calvert was the first Lord Baltimore and first person to plan for a colony where Catholics and Protestants could live together peacefully.

2. He was raised Roman Catholic but forced to become Anglican at age 12. He returned to Catholicism in 1624.

3. He invested in explorations and colonial settlements in America although his initial interest was in Newfoundland.

4. In 1630 he received a Charter from King Charles I for the territory south of the James River. But, the King had already offered that territory to someone else so he received another Charter for the area north of Virginia, including the Chesapeake Bay.

5. His son, Cecilus, the 2nd Lord Baltimore, assumed his fathers' Charter in 1632. He wasn't able to leave for Maryland so he sent his brothers, Leonard and George Jr. The Charter included democratic privileges such as exemption from taxes without their consent and offered religious toleration. His goal was that of financial gain and not as a haven from religious persecution as was his fathers' goal.

6. In 1633 Leonard leads 300 settlers in two ships, the "Ark" and "Dove". The initial colony was successful following the lessons learned from the Virginia experience. Leonard was appointed

as the first Governor. Most of the initial settlers were Catholic but more of the later settlers were Protestant. The availability of land was used to attract settlers.

7. Initial boundary problems with Virginia and Pennsylvania. The Virginia Secretary of State William Claiborne was sent to England to oppose the Maryland Charter. In 1631 he opened a fur-trade outpost on Kent Island, Maryland. It leads to a considerable dispute between Virginia and Maryland.

8. Settlers arrive in Virginia in 1634 and eventually settle at St. Mary's City, Maryland, which becomes their Capital on 3/27/1634. The colony grows rapidly until religious conflicts in 1689 cause the city to lose its influence and importance..

9. During 1637-1638 the Maryland Assembly opposes the Proprietor simply handing down laws from England without their input or consent. Eventually a small degree of self-government is allowed.

10. From 1644-1647 there is considerable conflict between Catholics and Protestants.

11. The "Toleration Act" of 1649 guarantees religious freedom for all Christians. It happens at the same time as the religious Civil War in England.

12. ***William Fuller, a Puritan, becomes Governor in 1655. The Puritan Assembly repeals the Toleration Act of 1649 and persecutes Catholics.*** The Puritans lead the colony until 1658, when Lord Baltimore regains power and appoints his brother, Philip, as Governor in 1660.

13. In 1661, after the English Restoration, the Maryland Assembly repeals all of the laws of the Puritan government and reinstates the Toleration Act. This provision for religious toleration plays a future role in the First Amendment to the Federal Constitution regarding the establishment of and free exercise of religion.

14. The population of the Colony is 5,000 in the 1660's

15. In 1695 the new English government appoints Royal Governors who move the Capital to Annapolis.

16. ***In 1704 there is an "Act to Prevent the Growth of Popery within this Province" which closes all Catholic Churches and Schools.*** St. Mary's City is eventually abandoned.

7a

MARYLAND   GOVERNORS

MARYLAND GOVERNORS & CHIEF EXECUTIVES		
DATES		**NAME AND TITLE**
1634	1647	LEONARD CALVERT
1647	1649	THOMAS GREENE
1649	1655	WILLIAM STONE
1655	1658	WILLIAM FULLER (PURITAN)
1658	1660	JOSIAS FENDALL
1660		PHILIP CALVERT
1661	1675	CHARLES CALVERT
1675	1692	MULTIPLE
1692	1693	SIR LIONEL COPLEY
1693	1698	SIR FRANCIS NICHOLSON
1698	1702	NATHANIEL BLAKISTON
1704	1709	JOHN SEYMOUR
1713	1720	JOHN HART
1720	1727	CHARLES CALVERT
1727	1731	BENEDICT LEONARD CALVERT
1731	1742	SAMUEL OGLE
1742	1747	THOMAS BLADEN
1747	1752	SAMUEL OGLE
1752	1753	BENJAMIN TASKER
1753	1769	HORATIO SHARPE
1769	1776	ROBERT EDEN
1774	1777	COMMITTEES & CONVENTIONS
1777	1779	THOMAS JOHNSON
1779	1782	THOMAS SIM LEE
1782	1785	WILLIAM PACA
1785	1788	WILLIAM SMALLWOOD

Chapter 8

Rhode Island

A. SETTLEMENT (1636)

The story of the founding of the Rhode Island colony actually begins in Massachusetts. The undemocratic government of Massachusetts bred many rebels who founded other colonies. In addition to Roger Williams, who left Massachusetts to found Rhode Island, there was also Anne Hutchinson who followed him there.

Some historians suggest that Rhode Island was the "Vinland" associated with the Norse explorers in the year 1000. Adriaen Block, the Dutch navigator, explored the area in 1614. Dutch traders, afterwards, referred to the marshy estuaries with red cranberries as "Roode Eyelandt" (red island)..

1. ROGER WILLIAMS (1603–1683)

Roger Williams was a Church Minister in Salem, Massachusetts, who challenged the Puritan leadership in that colony. He was born in 1603 and first exposed to Puritan ideas while studying at Cambridge, England, during the 1620's. He left England for Massachusetts in 1630 due to persecution by Archbishop Laud. He refused an offer to become a Church Minister in Boston, moved to Salem where he ran into conflict, then to Plymouth where he was asked to leave because of his "strange opinions". He made friends with the Indians near Plymouth and began to challenge the King's authority to give away Indian lands, thereby declaring that such charters were invalid.

In April 1635 a General Court noticed him when he refused to take an oath which he believed were Sacred with the government having no role in such events. He believed the link between government and the Church corrupted the Church, not the other way around. He denied the right of the Massachusetts government to interfere in religious matters.

Williams had no disagreement with Puritan doctrine but broke with them over the relationship of Church and State. He opposed forced worship and challenged the entire concept of the "Holy Commonwealth". He refused to be quiet and change his views. Local magistrates finally ordered his banishment in October, 1635, which they justified by a provision in the charter allowing expulsion of anyone of "detriment" to the colony. They planned to return him to England but when it came time to execute the order, they couldn't find him. John Winthrop, the Governor of Massachusetts, secretly helped him by referring him to the Narragansett Bay Indians for protection.

In 1636, Williams purchased land from the Narragansett Chiefs and established a settlement at Providence. He selected the name in gratitude for "God's merciful providence" that the Narragansetts granted him title to the site. There was almost immediate dissension in the colony. He regarded himself as a "Proprietor" similar to Lord Baltimore of Maryland. He had bought the land, dispensed it as he saw fit but not with rights of ownership. He was not a big believer in democracy but accepted all settlers even though he retained all political power. He was opposed by William Harris from the beginning. ***Harris founded Pautuxet in 1638.***

While Williams and Harris argued over land policy, two others, William Coddington, a merchant, and Samuel Gorton, a self-promoting speculator who had been expelled from Plymouth, were also involved in local settlements. ***In 1639 Coddington founded the village of Newport*** and in ***1640 he united Newport with***

Portsmouth which had been settled by the Hutchinsons. Gorton, meanwhile, was expelled once again but in **1643 he settled Warrick**. The villages of Providence, Portsmouth, Newport, and Warrick were totally independent of one another but were united by their dislike for, and fear of, the Massachusetts Bay colony.

2. **SUMMARY OF SETTLEMENTS:**
1636 Providence

- During its first 40 years it was exclusively a fishing and farming village.

- It was mostly destroyed during King Philip's War.

- In the years following, some commercial activity began and new or farming families moved outward to the town's remote lands bordering upon Connecticut to the west and Massachusetts to the north.

- Despite this growth the entire population of Providence in 1708 was only 1,446. By 1730 the population was 3,916 and so many farmers had moved into the "outlands" of Providence from which three large towns were created in 1731 from which area, Scituate, Glocester, and Smithfield. Before the end of the colonial period, three more towns were created, Cranston, Johnston, and North Providence.

- The entire Rhode Island census as of 1774 was 3,950.

1637 Pocasset (Portsmouth)
1638 Pautuxet
1639 Newport
1640 Newport united with Portsmouth
1643 Warrick

3. **EXPANDING SETTLEMENTS (5/19/1647)**

Gorton's outpost at Warrick was eventually annexed by Massachusetts Bay in 1643. Williams returned to England in 1643 to obtain a charter to protect his colony from being absorbed by other colonies. *He returned in 1644 with a charter to unite the settlements known as the "Providence Plantations in Narragansett Bay".* He established a trading post at present-day North Kingstown where he traded with the local Indians. *The Commonwealth of Rhode Island was established although the new government did not go into effect until the first General Assembly, composed of the freemen of several plantations, met at Portsmouth on 5/19/1647 to establish a code of laws for government.* In 1651 he sold the trading post and returned to England to confirm the charter.

The charter was confirmed by Cromwell in 1655 and a new one obtained from King Charles II on 7/15/1663 which would govern the Commonwealth for 180 years. It not only separated Rhode Island from the Massachusetts colonies but it combined the Rhode Island and Providence Plantations together as a single colony. It provided for self-government through the creation of a General Assembly with the authority to enact all necessary laws for the government of the colony. It also guaranteed complete religious freedom.

Its reputation for religious freedom attracted dissenters from all over Europe and the other colonies. The first Baptist church in America was formed in Providence in 1639. Quakers arrived in Aquidneck in 1657 and became a significant force in the colony. A Jewish Congregation was formed in Newport in 1658 while French Huguenots/Calvinists settled East Greenwich in 1686.

Roger Williams was Governor of Rhode Island from 1654-1658.

4. **FORMATION OF THE COMMONWEALTH OF RHODE ISLAND**

1643 Warrick annexed by Massachusetts Bay. Williams's returns to England to obtain a new charter to prevent further annexations

1644 New charter unites the settlements at Providence, to be known as the "Providence Plantations".

1647 Commonwealth established and begins operations with first General Assembly

1655 Charter confirmed by Cromwell

1663 New charter obtained from King Charles II governs Commonwealth of Rhode Island for 180 years

5. **ANNE HUTCHINSON (1591-1643)**

After she was banished from the Massachusetts Bay colony, she and her husband plus 13 of their children and 60 followers settled in the land of the Narragansett, from whose Chief, Miantonmah, they purchased the island of Aquidneck (Peaceable Island), now part of Rhode Island. In early 1638 she moved to Pocasset (Portsmouth) and helped the colony develop its first civil government with a Compact for the new colony on 3/7/1638. In 1640 her husband, William, was elected as an assistant to Governor Coddington but after his death in 1642 she took all but two of her children to New Amsterdam where she and all but one of her children were killed in an Indian raid in 1643.

B.   KING PHILIP'S WAR (1675-1676)

The most significant event in Rhode Island was King Philip's War 1675-1676 ending four decades of declining Indian-Colonial relations. Although Roger Williams maintained good relations with the Narragansett Indians, in 1637 they formed an alliance with England against the Pequot Indians. By 1670 even the Indians friendly to Williams began to turn against the colonists.

Clashes in culture, appropriation of Indian lands by settlers, and hostility between King Philip/Metacom, the Wampanoag Chief, and the Plymouth colony government caused "King Philip's War". It began in Swansea, Plymouth colony, in June 1675, and soon spread throughout New England. In December, King Philip's winter quarters in Rhode Island's "great swamp" were destroyed by the settlers. By June 1676 the tide of war had turned against the Indians who were short of food, manpower, and arms. King Philip was eventually killed in August 1676 by a Wampanoag Indian fighting on the side of the settlers.

The war was devastating for the Indians. Entire families were sold into slavery and many others forced to work as servants in various New England towns. The remaining Narragansett Indians united with the Wampanoags plus a few surviving Pequot Indians to become the new Narragansett tribe.

C. GROWTH OF THE COMMONWEALTH

In 1686, Rhode Island joined the Dominion of New England.

Governor Samuel Cranston (1698-1727) established unity and developed a better working relationship with England. During this period the colony experienced significant growth. By the 1740's a system of two-party politics emerged. Opposing groups led by Samuel Ward, Stephen Hopkins, and merchants and farmers from Newport and South County supported Ward against their counterparts in Providence for control of the legislature.

A major boundary dispute with Connecticut was settled in 1726-7 plus another settlement with Massachusetts in 1746-7 resulted in the annexation of Cumberland and several East Bay towns.

By 1750 the large farm plantations of South County, utilizing the labor of black and Indian slaves, reached peak prosperity. Colonial farmers raised livestock and cultivated commodities such as apples, onions, flax, and dairy products. Forests yielded lumber and the sea provided an abundance of fish for food and fertilizer. Most of these items became valuable exports for Rhode Island.

In the 1760's, England tightened its' enforcement of the Navigation Acts and the imposition of new controls threatened the colony's prosperity and autonomy. ***Rhode Island, therefore, became a leader in resisting extreme governmental pressure.***

By 1774, the colony population was 59,707 who lived in 29 incorporated towns.

(Attachment 8a List of Rhode Island Governors.)

D.   KEY DATES & EVENTS

	1524	Giovanni Verrazano employed by France discovers Rhode Island
	1609	Henry Hudson explores the area on behalf of the Dutch
	1614	Adriaen Block visits the island now named after him
	1634	William Blackstone is the first Rhode Island settler
	1636	Roger Williams founded Providence settlement
3/7	1638	First Portsmouth Compact signed by 19 potential settlers
4/30	1639	Second Portsmouth Compact signed by 29 potential settlers
April	1639	Newport Compact signed as the basis of the settlement
	1643	Samuel Gorton founded Shawomet as 4th settlement. Renamed Warwick in honor of Earl of Warwick a few years later
	1643	Name of Aquidneck changed to "The Isles of Rhodes" (Rhode Island)
5/19	1647	Commonwealth of Rhode Island established.
	1661	Block Island first settled. Becomes part of Rhode Island 1663 under the Charter
7/15	1663	King Charles II grants the Royal Charter of Rhode Island; remains Constitution until 1842
	1677	King Philip's War. Final struggle by Native Americans in Rhode Island
	1708	First census population 7,181
	1724	Rhode Island establishes property ownership qualification for voters
	1730	Census population 17,935
	1748	Census population 32,773
	1755	Census population 40,414
	1772	British trade restrictions anger colonists, burned English revenue cutters "Liberty & Gaspee".

	1774	Census population 57,707
	1774	Connecticut and Rhode Island colonies prohibited further importation of slaves
5/4	1776	Colony declares its Independence
	1779	Newport occupied by the British
Oct	1779	British troops evacuate Rhode Island
	1782	Census population 52,347
	1784	Emancipation Act passed providing for gradual abolition of slavery. All children born after 3/1/1784 were free.
5/29	1790	Rhode Island 13th State to be admitted to the Union

E.   REVIEW QUESTIONS

(Multiple Choice)

1. What was the primary reason for the settlement of Rhode Island?
    a. Religious freedom
    b. Fur-trading benefits
    c. Fishing benefits
    d. Convert the Indians

2. Which is the correct group of the leaders in the founding of Rhode Island?
    s. Roger Williams, Anne Hutchinson, Thomas Hooker, John Davenport
    b. Roger Williams, Anne Hutchinson, Samuel Gorton, William Coddington
    c. Roger Williams, Samuel Gorton, Thomas Hooker, William Coddington
    d. Roger Williams, Thomas Hooker, Theophilus Eaton, John Davenport

3. Which of the following settlements did NOT become part of the Commonwealth of Rhode Island?
    a. Warrick
    b. Newport
    c. Hartford
    d. Providence

4. In what year was Providence founded by Roger Williams?
    a. 1640
    b. 1636
    c. 1655
    d. 1638

5. In what year did the Commonwealth of Rhode Island government begin to function?
    a. 1636
    b. 1644
    c. 1647
    d. 1663

6. In what years was Roger Williams Governor of Rhode Island?
    a. 1644–1647
    b. 1647–1653
    c. 1654–1658
    d. 1655–1673

(True or False)

7. Rhode Island was a part of Connecticut.
    a. TRUE
    b. FALSE

8. Roger Williams was a former Governor of the Massachusetts Bay colony.
    a. TRUE
    b. FALSE

9. Roger Williams purchased land from the Indians which became his settlement at Providence.
    a. TRUE
    b. FALSE

10. "King Philip's War" was mostly fought in Rhode Island and Massachusetts.
    a. TRUE
    b. FALSE

CHAPTER 8 SUMMARY

Rhode Island

1. Roger Williams was the founder of Providence in 1636. He was a religious exile from the Massacusetts Bay Colony. He denied the right of the Massachusetts government to interfere in religious matters. Ann Hutchinson was also an exile from the Massachusetts Bay Colony who arrived in Rhode Island in 1638.

2. Other founders and settlements were; Anne Hutchinson, Pocasset, 1638 (became Portsmouth). William Coddington, Newport, 1639, and Samuel Gorton, Shawomet, 1643 (became Warwick).

3. In 1644 a Charter was received which united the "Providence Plantations in Narragansett Bay".

4. A new Charter is granted by King Charles II in 1663 creating the "Commonwealth of Rhode Island". It granted complete religious freedom and established self-government. It was considered the most liberal Charter granted by England during the entire Colonial period. It served as the basis of government for more than 180 years.

5. The colony's reputation for religious freedom attracts dissenters from all over Europe and also the other colonies.

6. Roger Williams serves as Governor from 1654-1658 before the confirmation of the Commonwealth in 1663

7. King Philip's War of 1675-1676 was fought primarily in Rhode Island and Massachusetts. It basically ended Indian Wars in the Colony.

8. In 1686 Rhode Island joins the "Dominion of New England".

9. Governor Samuel Cranston (1698-1727) established unity and economic growth. By the 1740's a system of two-party politics emerged.

10. Boundary disputes settled with Connecticut in 1726-1727 and Massachusetts in 1746-1747

11. In the 1760's England tightened enforcement of the Navigation Acts and the imposition of these new controls threatened colonial prosperity and autonomy. Rhode Island becomes a leader in opposing extreme British government pressure.

12. In 1774 the population of the Rhode Island colony was 59,707 living in 29 incorporated towns.

13. In 1774 both Connecticut and Rhode Island prohibited further importation of slaves.

14. In 1784 an "Emancipation Act" provided for the gradual abolition of slavery. It also declared that all children born after 3/1/1784 are free.

15. In 1790 Rhode Island was admitted as the 13th State to the Union.

8a

RHODE ISLAND GOVERNORS & CHIEF EXECUTIVES		
DATES		NAME AND TITLE
1663	1666	BENEDICT ARNOLD
1666	1669	WILLIAM BRENTON
1669	1672	BENEDICT ARNOLD
1672	1674	NICHOLAS EASTON
1674	1676	WILLIAM CODDINGTON
1676	1677	WALTER CLARKE
1677	1678	BENEDICT ARNOLD
1678		WILLIAM CODDINGTON
1678	1680	JOHN CRANSTON
1680	1683	PELEG STANFORD
1683	1685	WILLIAM CODDINGTON JR
1685	1686	HENRY BULL
1687	1689	SIR EDMUND ANDROS
1689	1690	DEPUTY GOVERNOR JOHN COGGESHALL
1690	1695	JOHN EASTON
1696	1698	WALTER CLARKE
1698	1727	SAMUEL CRANSTON
1727	1732	JOSEPH JENCKES
1732	1733	WILLIAM WANTON
1734	1740	JOHN WANTON
1740	1743	RICHARD WARD
1743	1745	WILLIAM GREENE
1745	1746	GIDEON WANTON
1746	1747	WILLIAM GREENE
1747	1748	GIDEON WANTON
1748	1755	WILLIAM GREENE
1755	1757	STEPHEN HOPKINS
1757	1758	WILLIAM GREENE
1758	1762	STEPHEN HOPKINS
1762	1763	SAMUEL WARD
1763	1765	STEPHEN HOPKINS
1765	1767	SAMUEL WARD
1767	1768	STEPHEN HOPKINS
1768	1769	JOSIAS LYNDON
1769	1775	JOSEPH WANTON
1775	1778	NICHOLAS COOKE
1778	1786	WILLIAM GREENE JR
1786	1790	JOHN COLLINS

Chapter 9

Connecticut

A. BACKGROUND

Connecticut was first explored by the Dutch as early as 1614 when Adriaen Block explored the Connecticut River valley. During the 1630's there were other efforts by English Puritans and Massachusetts settlers in the region. At the same time the Dutch decided to focus their attention in New Netherlands (New York) and didn't make serious efforts to expand their efforts into Connecticut after the 1630's.

1. **EARLY SETTLEMENTS**

In 1632, English Puritans received a grant of land from the Earl of Warwick, President of the Council for New England, stretching 120 miles along the coast. Some of the early settlements were:

a. *In 1633*, the Dutch purchased land from the Pequot Indians, erected a Fort (The House of Good Hope) on the *future site of Hartford*, and established a trading post at Windsor.

b. *In 1634*, John Oldham and other Massachusetts settlers founded *Wethersfield* which became the oldest settlement in the state.

c. *In 1635*, the first English settlers arrived in Windsor and erected a Fort at *Saybrook*, soon to be joined by settlers from Dorchester, Massachusetts.

d. ***In 1636***, Reverend Thomas Hooker led a group of 100 settlers west from Boston to settle ***Hartford***. By the end of 1636 there were nearly 800 settlers along the Connecticut River in the three towns of ***Windsor, Hartford, and Westerfield.***

The settlements which developed along the Connecticut river in the 1630's were the result of a search for fertile farmland and a lucrative fur trade more than a search for religious freedom. Controversies over religious and political matters were of secondary importance. By the end of 1636, more than 800 settlers had moved from Massachusetts to Connecticut. The Pequot War in 1637 briefly interfered with settlement but didn't totally stop the efforts.

e. ***In 1638***, a colony was established at ***New Haven*** by London Puritans led by Reverend John Davenport and a merchant named Theophilius Eaton. ***By 1643, the New Haven colony included the settlements of Milford, Guilford, and Stamford.***

f. On ***1/14/1639***, Reverend Thomas Hooker plus two friends, Josh Haynes and Roger Ludlow, drafted the ***"Fundamental Orders"*** which was a ***plan for the Government of Connecticut. It became the first written Constitution in America and was adopted by the freemen of Hartford, Wethersfield, and Windsor.***

2. **OTHER KEY DATES AND SIGNIFICANT EVENTS**
   a. On ***5/19/1643 the "New England Confederation" was formed. (Also known as the "United Colonies of New England.)*** At the end of the Pequot War, Connecticut proposed a ***mutual defense alliance of New England colonies*** to protect their interests against continuing Indian raids as well as Dutch, French, and English interference in Connecticut's colonization efforts. After several years of negotiations, representatives of Connecticut, Massachusetts Bay, Plymouth, and New Haven met in Boston to draft 12 Articles of Confederation for mutual defense and inter-colonial cooperation. Each colony was to send two Representatives, for a total of eight, requiring six votes to make a binding decision. Annual sessions were held until 1664 although it did suffer from lack of cooperation at

times by Massachusetts Bay, the largest of the colonies, which refused to accept any decision which they deemed harmful to their interests, regardless of the vote.

Failure of the Confederation was predicted when Massachusetts Bay failed to accept the decision of the Confederation to participate in the Anglo-Dutch War of the 1650's in defense of Connecticut, which lived in the shadow of the Dutch in nearby New Netherlands. The Confederation did play a role in King Philip's War of 1675-1676 but, by 1684, it was no longer effective and finally terminated.

The Confederation was a small first step toward formal cooperation among the colonies. In 1686, the Crown would create the "Dominion of New England" which was a highly unpopular merger of New York and New Jersey with the New England colonies.

b. In *1646, New London* was founded by John Winthrop Jr.

c. In May, 1650, a Code of Laws was drafted and adopted by the Legislature, known as "Ludlow's Code.

d. In *1651, Middletown was founded.*

e. In *1659, Norwich was founded.*

f. In 1662, John Winthrop Jr. obtains a Royal Charter from King Charles II.

g. In *1665, New Haven joins Connecticut*

From 1665 to 1687, Connecticut was generally free from conflict and the colony was growing both in size and prosperity.

h. In 1687, King James revoked the Connecticut charter and Sir Edmund Andros, the Royal Governor, assumed the rule of Connecticut.

i. In 1689, Connecticut resumed government under its charter after the Glorious Revolution of William and Mary.

j. In 1702, Queen Anne's War doesn't impact Connecticut.

k. In 1774, Silas Deane, Eliphalet Dyer, and Roger Sherman represent Connecticut at the First Continental Congress.

l. In 1776, Samuel Huntington, Roger Sherman, William Williams, and Oliver Wolcott sign the Declaration of Independence for Connecticut.

m. In 1784, an Act is passed providing for emancipation at age 25 for all negroes born after March, 1784.

n. In 1787, Oliver Ellsworth, William Samuel Johnson, and Roger Sherman serve as Connecticut's Representatives at the Philadelphia Constitutional Convention.

o. In 1788, the Convention at Hartford approves the Federal Constitution by a 128-40 vote.

p. In 1789, Oliver Ellsworth and William Samuel Johnson begin service as the first U.S. Senators from Connecticut.

(Attachment 9a List of Connecticut Governors)

B.   REVIEW QUESTIONS

(Multiple Choice)

1. The first European exploration of the Connecticut area was by which country:
    a. Spain
    b. France
    c. Holland
    d. England

2. Which group(s) of settlers formed the core of early Connecticut?
    a. Dutch
    b. English Puritans
    c. Dissatisfied Massachusetts settlers
    d. All of the above

3. What was the primary attraction of Connecticut to the early settlers?
    a. Religious freedom
    b. Political opportunity
    c. Rich farmland and potential fur trade
    d. None of the above

4. Which was the first major Connecticut settlement?
    a. Windsor
    b. Hartford
    c. Saybrook
    d. New Haven

5. In which year were the "Fundamental Orders" drafted
    a. 1632
    b   1636
    c   1639
    d. 1643

6. Which colonies formed the Confederation of New England?
    a. Plymouth and New Haven
    b. Massachusetts and Connecticut
    c. Massachusetts, New Haven, Connecticut
    d. Connecticut, Plymouth, New Haven, Massachusetts

7. The Confederation of New England was also called:
    a. Albany Plan of Union
    b. United Colonies of New England
    c. Dominion of New England
    d. Articles of Confederation

(True or False)

8. The Puritans founded Connecticut for religious freedom.
    a. TRUE
    b. FALSE

9. Reverend Thomas Hooker led the first group of settlers to found Hartford.
    a. TRUE
    b. FALSE

10. The Fundamental Orders of Connecticut represented the first written Constitution in North America.

    a. TRUE
    b. FALSE

11. The Confederation of New England was formed to become a Central Government of New England.
    a. TRUE
    b. FALSE

12. Connecticut received the Royal Charter from King Charles II in 1665.
    a. TRUE
    b. FALSE

CHAPTER 9 SUMMARY

Connecticut

1. First exploration of the Connecticut river valley by the Dutch explorer Adriaen Block in 1614.

2. The earliest settlers were the Dutch, English Puritans, and dissatisfied Massachusetts citizens. Their primary motivation was to search for good farmland and a lucrative fur trade, not religious or political freedom.

3. The earliest settlements were;

   - Windsor   1633

   - Wethersfield   1634

   - Fort Saybrook   1635

   - Hartford   1636

   - New Haven   1637–1638
     By 1643 it included Milford, Guilford, and Stamford.

   - New London   1646

   - Middletown   1651

   - Norwich   1659

4. By the end of 1636 more than 800 settlers had moved from the Massachusetts Bay Colony.

5. In 1637 the Pequot War briefly interrupted settlement and colonization efforts.

6. In 1639 the "Fundamental Orders" were drafted and approved as the colonial plan for government. It becomes the first written Constitution in America. It was adopted in Hartford, Wethersfield, and Windsor.

7. In 1643 Connecticut jons the New England Confederation with Masachusetts, Plymouth, and New Haven.

8. In 1650 a Code of Laws was adopted by the Colonial Legislature.

9. In 1662 John Winthrop Jr obtains a Royal Charter from King Charles II. Connecticut is officially recognized by England.

10. In 1665 New Haven joins the colony of Connecticut.

11. In 1687 King James II revokes the Connecticut Charter and Sir Edmund Andros assumes the rule of Connecticut.

12. In 1689 Connecticut resumes government under its Charter.

9a

DATES		NAME AND TITLE
CONNECTICUT GOVERNORS & CHIEF EXECUTIVES		
NEW HAVEN		
1639	1657	THEOPHILUS EATON
1658	1660	FRANCIS NEWMAN
1660	1662	WILLIAM LEETE
	1662	NEW HAVEN ABSORBED INTO CONNECTICUT COLONY
CONNECTICUT		
1639	1640	JOHN HAYNES
1640	1641	EDWARD HOPKINS
1642	1643	GEORGE WYLLYS
1643	1644	JOHN HAYNES
1644	1645	EDWARD HOPKINS
1645	1646	JOHN HAYNES
1646	1647	EDWARD HOPKINS
1647	1648	JOHN HAYNES
1648	1649	EDWARD HOPKINS
1649	1650	JOHN HAYNES
1650	1651	EDWARD HOPKINS
1651	1652	JOHN HAYNES
1652	1653	EDWARD HOPKINS
1653	1654	JOHN HAYNES
1654	1655	EDWARD HOPKINS
1655	1656	THOMAS WELLES
1656	1657	JOHN WEBSTER
1657	1658	JOHN WINTHROP JR
1658	1659	THOMAS WELLES
1659	1676	JOHN WINTHROP JR
1676	1683	WILLIAM LEETE
1683	1687	ROBERT TREAT
1687	1689	SIR EDMUND ANDROS
1689	1698	ROBERT TREAT
1698	1707	FITZ JOHN WINTHROP
1707	1724	GURDON SALTONSTALL
1724	1741	JOSEPH TALCOTT
1741	1750	JONATHAN LAW
1750	1754	ROGER WOLCOTT
1754	1766	THOMAS FITCH
1766	1769	WILLIAM PITKIN
1769	1784	JONATHAN TRUMBULL
1784	1786	MATTHEW GRISWOLD
1786	1796	SAMUEL HUNTINGTON

Chapter 10

New Hampshire

A.   BACKGROUND

New Hampshire derives its name from Hampshire County in England in honor of Captain John Mason, one of the future proprietors.

It differed from other New England colonies in that it was not founded by religious dissenters but was intended from the beginning to be a commercial venture. The primary attraction was fishing but timber and fur became important segments of the economy.

Early European explorers include Englishman Martin Pring who explored the Portsmouth area around 1603 and France's Samuel de Champlain who mapped the coastline in 1605. Captain John Smith, of Jamestown history, surveyed the coast of New Hampshire in 1614 seeing the great fishing potential.

The territory which eventually became known as New Hampshire was included in a grant of land in 1622 by the Council of New England to Sir Ferdinando Gorges and John Mason. It extended from the Merrimac river to the Kennebec river. Both proprietors proved ineffective. Many settlements were attempted such as Pannaway (present-day Rye) while another settled Northam (present-day Dover). Other towns were developed at Kittery, York, and Portsmouth, all being done independently of the efforts and intentions of Mason and Gorges. The migration of unhappy Puritans from Massachusetts and Connecticut added to the area's population at Hampton and Exeter.

1. EARLY SETTLEMENTS

The first settlement was called "Hilton's Point" after the Hilton brothers, William and Edward, who founded it at Dover Point in 1623. While the settlement was led by Edward, it was called "Pascataqua" or "Newichwannock" as the Indians called it, meaning, "place of wigwams". Some of the early settlers came from Bristol, England and in *1633 they renamed it "Bristol", which remained until 1637 when Reverend George Burdett became Governor and changed the name to "Dover", then renamed Northam in 1639 and formally incorporated in 1641 as Dover.*

In 1629, the "Laconia Company" was formed in England which sent a vessel in 1630 to the mouth of the Piscataqua River with a colony of settlers led by Captain Neal as Governor. *Portsmouth, first called "Strawberry Bank", was settled in 1631* while Governor Neal explored the local area. He returned to England with a negative report about the area and the settlement was allowed to expire.

The two Proprietors of Laconia had in 1629 divided their possessions. Mason received the portion which became New Hampshire and Gorges the eastern portion which became Maine. The Laconia patent was a grant of land from the Council for New England and not a Royal charter. In 1639 Gorges received from King Charles I a Royal charter for Maine. In 1677, the heirs of Gorges sold their rights to Massachusetts and the area called the "District of Maine" and was governed under Massachusetts until the "1820 Compromise" which admitted both Maine and Missouri to the Union.

In *1638 a settlement was made at Exeter* between the Piscataqua and Merrimac rivers by John Wheelwright who had been banished from Massachusetts. These towns were settled independent of the others and none with a stable form of government which created constant conflict. In 1639, the towns formed an agreement to unite, *but since Massachusetts claimed this territory, the towns eventually agreed to come under its jurisdiction.* The Union was formed in 1641 with the people of the settlements retaining their liberty to manage their own town affairs. Each town was permitted to send a delegate to the General Court at Boston. *So, New Hampshire officially became part of Massachusetts in 1641.*

New Hampshire remained part of Massachusetts until 1679 when King Charles II granted it a Royal charter and made it a separate colony. The King rejoined them in 1686 through the Dominion of New England but then they were finally separated in 1691 with New Hampshire again becoming a Royal province. The President and Council were appointed by the Crown and the Assembly was to be elected by the people. Until 1741, however, the Governor was subordinate to the Governor of Massachusetts.

New Hampshire grew slowly for years because the heirs of Mason claimed the land and their constant legal battles slowed emigration into the area. It wasn't until 1759 that the Mason heirs were satisfied with the purchase of their claims.

In *1719, a colony of Scotch-Irish immigrants settled the town of Londonderry*, named after their home town in Ireland. They were thrifty and began an industry learned in Ireland, the raising of flax and manufacturing of linen goods.

2. **VERMONT**

After the middle of the 18th century there was a bitter dispute with New York over the territory west of the Connecticut River with it being claimed by both colonies. One of New Hampshire's previous Governors had laid out 140 townships in the disputed region, called the *"New Hampshire Grants"*. But, in 1765 the King decided in favor of New York when the Governor of that colony ordered a few thousand settlers to re-purchase their lands. This caused a rebellion led by Ethan Allen and Seth Warner who eventually defeated the New Yorkers and in *1777 they declared the "New Hampshire Grants" an independent state under the name of Vermont. 14 years later Vermont became the 14th state of the new Union.*

B.   KEY DATES AND SIGNIFICANT EVENTS

Native Indians of New Hampshire were the Abnaki, Malecite, Passamaquoddy, and Pennacook.

	1602	Bartholomew Gosnold explored for English merchants the coast of New England from southern Maine to Buzzards Bay.
	1603	Martin Pring sent by Sir Walter Raleigh on trading exploration and discovers Cape Cod. Explores the rivers, islands, and harbors of New England.
Mar	1622	King James 1 grants the region between the Salem and Merrimac rivers under the name of Mariana, to John Mason and Sir Fernando Gorges.
8/10	1622	King James I grants region between Merrimac and Kennebec rivers for 60 miles inland, under the name of the Province of Maine, to Sir Fernando Gorges and John Mason.
	1623	First settlement called "Hilton's Point" after the Hilton brothers founded it at Dover Point in 1623. It went through a number of name changes with the current name of Dover dating from 1641.
11/7	1629	John Mason receives a grant of that portion of the Province of Maine which lay between the Merrimac and Piscataqua rivers under the name of New Hampshire
	1629	Company called the "Laconia Company" formed in England which sent a ship in 1630 to the mouth of the Piscataqua river with settlers led by Captain Neal as Governor.

1629   The two Proprietors of Laconia divided their possessions: Mason received the portion which became New Hampshire Gorges received the portion which became Maine The Laconia Patent was a land-grant from the Council for New England and not a Royal charter from the King.

1631   Portsmouth, first called "Strawberry Bank", was settled while Governor Neal explored the area.

1638   Settlement at Exeter by John Wheelwright who had been banished from Massachusetts

1639   Gorges received from King Charles I a Royal Charter for Maine but in 1677 the heirs of Gorges sold their rights to Massachusetts and the area called "The District of Maine" was governed by Massachusetts until the 1820 Compromise which admitted both Maine and Missouri to the Union.

1641   Massachusetts colony gains control of New Hampshire until 1679 when the King separated them. He joined them again in 1686 through the Dominion of New England but they were finally separated in 1691 with New Hampshire becoming a Royal Province. Until 1741 the Governor was subordinate to the Governor of Massachusetts.

1675   King favors New York claim to the area known as the "New Hampshire grants" but Ethan Allen and Seth Warner led a local rebellion which defeated the New Yorker's and in 1777 declared the "Hampshire Grants" an independent state under the name of Vermont.

1679   King Charles II grants a Royal Charter making it a separate colony

1686   King rejoins New Hampshire with Massachusetts through the Dominion of New England

	1691	Final separation from Massachusetts with New Hampshire becoming a Royal Province although, until 1741, the Governor was subordinate to the Governor of Massachusetts.
	1719	A colony of Scotch-Irish immigrants settled Londonderry, named after their home town in Ireland.
	1722	Royal charter for Nottingham granted by King George
	1749	Governor Benning Wentworth makes the first New Hampshire grant for Bennington.
	1774	New Hampshire Grants declared an independent State named Vermont.
6/21	1788	New Hampshire becomes 9th state admitted to Union; Federal Constitution ratified at convention at Exeter

(Attachment 10a List of New Hampshire Governors)

C.   REVIEW QUESTIONS

(Multiple Choice)

1. What was the primary reason for its settlement?
    a. religious freedom
    b. political freedom
    c. commercial opportunities through fishing, timber, and fur trade
    d. none of the above

2. By which of these names was Dover New Hampshire known;
    a. Hilton's Point
    b. Pascataqua
    c. Bristol
    d. Northam
    e. All of the above

3. What year was the first land-grant made for the New Hampshire territory?
    a. 1605
    b. 1614
    c. 1622
    d. 1629

4. What was the first settlement in New Hampshire?
    a. Hilton Point
    b. Strawberry Point
    c. Portsmouth
    d. Exeter

5. In what year did New Hampshire unify under the colony of
    Massachusetts?
    a. 1623
    b. 1629
    c. 1638
    d. 1641

6. In what year did New Hampshire finally become independent
    of Massachusetts?
    a. 1641
    b. 1679
    c. 1686
    d. 1691

7. What state eventually became the "New Hampshire Grants"?
    a. New Hampshire
    b. Vermont
    c. New York
    d. Massachusetts

(True or False)

8. New Hampshire derives its name from France.
    a. TRUE
    b. FALSE

9. Early settlers came from England, Massachusetts, and Scotch-
    Irish.
    a. TRUE
    b. FALSE

10. The colony of Portsmouth was first called "Strawberry Point".
    a. TRUE
    b. FALSE

11. The 2 Proprietors of Laconia divided their possessions into New Hampshire and Maine.
    a. TRUE
    b. FALSE

12. The various towns of New Hampshire were unified under Massachusetts in 1639.
    a. TRUE
    b. FALSE

13. New Hampshire first became part of Massachusetts in 1641.
    a. TRUE
    b. FALSE

14. In 1686 the Dominion of New England separated the colonies of New Hampshire and Massachusetts.
    a. TRUE
    b. FALSE

15. Bartholomew Gosnold was an English merchant who explored the coast of New England for England.
    a. TRUE
    b. FALSE

CHAPTER 10 SUMMARY

New Hampshire

1. Differed from most New England colonies because the settlement motivation was not religious freedom but commercial success.

2. The first land grant was made in 1622 by the Council for New England to Sir Fernando Gorges and John Mason.

3. The first settlement was made at "Hilton's Point" in 1623 and was eventually incorporated as "Dover" in 1641.

4. Portsmouth was settled in 1631 but it was first called "Strawberry Point".

5. Exeter was founded in 1638 by John Wheelwright who was an exile from the Massachusetts Bay Colony.

6. In 1641 various New Hampshire settlements were unified as part of the Massachusetts Bay Colony.

7. In 1675 the King supported the New York colony in a conflict with New Hampshire over the "New Hampshire Grants". A rebellion led by Ethan Allen and Seth Warner led to the area eventually becoming the State of Vermont.

8. New Hampshire is a part of the Massachusetts Bay Colony until 1679 when King Charles II granted a Royal Charter and made it a separate colony. The King then rejoined them in 1686 through the "Dominion of New England" but finally it was separated in 1691 with New Hampshire again becoming a Royal Province.

Until 1741 the New Hampshire Governor was subordinate to the Massachusetts Governor.

9. In 1719 a group of Scotch–Irish founded the town of Londonderry.

10. In 1722 King George granted a Royal Charter to the town of Nottingham.

10a

NEW HAMPSHIRE GOVERNORS *****		
DATES		NAME AND TITLE
1680	1681	JOHN CUTT, PRESIDENT OF THE COUNCIL
1681	1682	RICHARD WALDRON, PRESIDENT OF THE COUNCIL
1682	1685	LT GOVERNOR EDWARD CRANFIELD
1685	1686	DEPUTY GOVERNOR WALTER BAREFOOTE
1686	1687	JOSEPH DUDLEY
1687	1689	SIR EDMUND ANDROS
1689	1692	SIMON BRADSTREET
1692	1697	LT GOVERNOR JOHN USHER
1697	1698	LT GOVERNOR WILLIAM PARTRIDGE
1698	1699	SAMUEL ALLEN
1699	1702	LT GOVERNOR WILLIAM PARTRIDGE
1702	1715	LT GOVERNOR JOHN USHER
1715	1716	LT GOVERNOR GEORGE VAUGHAN
1717	1730	LT GOVERNOR JOHN WENTWORTH
1731	1741	LT GOVERNOR DANIEL DUNBAR
1741	1766	BENNING WENTWORTH
1766	1785	MESHECH WARE
1785	1786	JOHN LANGDON
1786	1788	JOHN SULLIVAN
1788	1789	JOHN LANGDON

*****

THE GOVERNOR OF MASSACHUSETTS SERVED AS THE CHIEF EXECUTIVE OFFICER OF NEW HAMPSHIRE FROM 1641 -1679 WHEN IT BECAME A ROYAL PROVINCE. BETWEEN 1680-1741, WHEN THE ROYAL GOVERNOR RESIDED IN MASSACHUSETTS, THE LIEUTENTANT GOVERNOR ACTED AS CHIEF EXECUTIVE OFFICER

Chapter 11

South Carolina

A.   BACKGROUND

The territory of present-day North and South Carolina was known by the name of "Carolina" at the time of the earliest explorations. It was first called "Carolana" after King Charles I of England and it derived from "Carolus" which means Charles in Latin. In 1663, King Charles II changed the spelling to "Carolina". *The area was explored, settled, and governed as a single entity until 1712 when "Carolina" was officially split into North and South Carolina even though each section had its own Governor until 1691.*

The history of the South Carolina colony can be viewed through 9 phases:

1. EARLY EXPLORATIONS

2. SETTLEMENT ACTIVITY BEFORE THE CHARTER OF 1663

3. SETTLEMENT ACTIVITY AFTER THE CHARTER OF 1663

4. FUNDAMENTAL CONSTITUTIONS OF 1669

5. SUCCESS

6. IMPACT OF THE GLORIOUS REVOLUTION

7. SOUTH CAROLINA BECOMES A ROYAL COLONY

8. COLONIAL DEVELOPMENT

9. CHARLESTON

B.   EARLY EXPLORATIONS

From 1497 to 1526, England, France, and Spain sent explorers to the area but no settlement attempts were made.

In 1526, L. Vasquez de Ayllon of Spain sponsored a settlement effort at present-day Myrtle Beach but poor weather and sickness forced a return to Santo Domingo. Years later Spain established new bases in Florida and then built a string of forts further north.

In 1562, Jean Ribault led an expedition of French Huguenots to present-day Parris Island where they built "Charles-Fort" which failed within a year. Part of the reason for the failure was because the Spanish built many forts to discourage other settlements.

C.   SETTLEMENT ACTIVITY BEFORE THE CHARTER OF 1663

England became involved when a charter was given to Sir Robert Heath in 1623 for the Carolina territory but it was never used. *Another grant was given to Heath in 1629 for the territory from 31–36 degrees north latitude extending from Albemarle Sound, North Carolina, to Jekyll Island off the Georgia coast.* It sought to encourage settlement by granting exemptions from English customs duties on wines, silks, olives, and other subtropical products for 7 years after experimental tests had been completed. *It allowed settlers the right to worship as they wished, only requiring that they worship.*

Settlement lagged due to the absence of a good harbor in the north but, in 1653, Roger Green led a group of persecuted Presbyterians from Jamestown to a land-grant he had secured of 10,000 acres near present-day Edenton, North Carolina, near the Chowan river and Albemarle Sound. He promised the first 100 settlers 1,000 acres each. Historians are not certain as to the success or duration of this colony. Other settlers followed with some Puritans arriving in the Cape Fear river area in 1661 to purchase land from the Indians. They were planting the seeds of a colony when news arrived that King Charles II had given the entire region to 8 of his supporters, calling it "Carolina". Many of them left for other parts of the area, though, and the colony never fully developed. *(Attachment 11a represents a map of early Carolina from 1565–1733)*

D. SETTLEMENT AFTER THE CHARTER OF 3/24/1663

Over the years much information about the potential of the Carolina's had gotten back to England causing some adventurers to think of exploration and settlement. Sir John Colleton was one of the first to think about a full-scale colony in the area. After a brief career as a planter and speculator he had become a member of the Privy Council and Committee for Foreign Plantations. It was from this key position that he was able to proclaim the potential benefits of a venture to the area. He persuaded the Berkeley brothers, Sir William and Lord John, to seek out other influential men to propose an expedition to King Charles II.

They formed a group of 8 key members of the English nobility who would receive a charter from the King to establish (1663) the colony of Carolina. They were known as the "Lords Proprietors of Carolina" who would become the landlords of the colony. They were:

- Sir John Colleton

- Edward Hyde (The Earl of Clarendon)

- George Monck (The Duke of Albemarle)

- Lord William Craven

- Lord John Berkeley

- Sir William Berkeley

- Lord Anthony Ashley Cooper (Later to become the Earl of Shaftesbury)

- Sir George Carteret

They sought to follow Gilbert and Raleigh's dream, to make money for themselves and promote the welfare of England. They planned to follow an earlier plan to encourage agricultural experiments leading to products England could not grow. They differed from Gilbert and Raleigh, however, in that they did not intend to personally invest in the effort. They didn't think it was wise to carry out costly colonization from England when the New World was already populated with many people seeking free land. The Proprietors, then, would draw from those who had already made the trip and gained some immunity to New World diseases, using land to attract them from New England, Virginia, and the Barbados islands.

King Charles II, the "Merry Monarch", was the most popular King ever in England. He generally chose to leave the colonies alone. No English subsidies increased the prices of colonial products, no Royal bounty assisted the colonists when they were starving, and there were no Royal troops to defend them. Only 1 colony gave him trouble, Massachusetts Bay. The colonies were generally allowed to grow as they wished and were able. Historians believe he never had a firm colonial policy and just reacted from day to day. Eventually, tighter control of the colonies would become necessary because of trade and commercial matters affecting both the colonists and England. He liked to reward his friends and punish his enemies which caused many to seek colonial charters for the rewards. Six of the original 13 colonies were founded during his reign and all as Proprietary grants.

England used the "Proprietary Colony" during the 1660–1690 period to award land in the New World to resourceful groups or individuals with the intent for it to be developed by them. These colonies were owned by an individual proprietor or a group of proprietors under a charter from the Monarch who used this approach to meet demands for territorial expansion and to also raise funds to repay his debts. The awarded Proprietors were normally Feudal Lords with the right of absolute rule but remained subject to their Monarch who could, at any time, remove their privileges. They collected quit-rents from settlers to whom they granted the land, for their own profit.

As part of a promotional campaign the Proprietors issued *"A Declaration and Proposals to All That Will Plant in Carolina"* where *they promised settlers as much if not more political freedom than they might get elsewhere in America. An Assembly was authorized to make all laws, subject only to the consent of the Governor and possible disallowance by the Proprietors.* In addition to religious freedom, generous land grants would be dispensed to all settlers, including servants at the end of their indenture. The only charge on the settlers would be a small quit-rent to underwrite administrative costs.

There was some conflict with Governor Berkeley of Virginia when the Proprietors were authorized to extend their authority over the few settlers on the Chowan river. So they organized a separate government in 1663-1664 calling it the "Albemarle County Colony", named after one of the Proprietors, George Monck, the Duke of Albemarle. He appointed William Drummond as Governor. Settlement was slow because the northern section had little to offer that Virginia could not grant on better terms. The lack of a harbor forced most supplies to enter and exports to leave through Virginia, anyway. Quit-rents were less there and the land grants as generous. Albemarle settlers demanded, at once, the right to hold land upon the same terms and conditions as was held by inhabitants of Virginia.

Two years later more emigrants arrived and bought land from the Indians along the Cape Fear river, near present-day Wilmington, North Carolina, and founded a settlement with Sir John Yeamans as Governor. It was organized and called the "Clarendon County Colony", and named after another of the Proprietors, Edward Hyde, the Earl of Clarendon. Yeaman's jurisdiction extended from the Cape Fear river to the St. John's river in Florida. *This settlement became permanent which formed the foundation of the Commonwealth of North Carolina.*

While Berkeley worked to promote the Albemarle settlements, the other Proprietors worked on the southern part of the grant. William Hilton of Barbados had explored the Cape Fear region in 1663 and his report created interest in Barbados among the small planters who had been suffering economically.

To encourage further settlement, the Proprietors in 1665 expanded their earlier "Declaration and Proposals" with a long document entitled, "Concessions and Agreements" which, in addition to detailing the settler's privileges, divided Carolina into 3 counties, each with its own Assembly, Governor, and Council:

- Albemarle in the north

- Clarendon and Craven in the south

Settlers arrived in 1670 and established the first permanent settlement in Albemarle. They were anxious to secure Carolina against Spanish attacks from St. Augustine, Florida, and to do so they needed to attract more colonists. They offered inducements such as religious toleration, political representation in an Assembly, exemption from quit-rents, and large land grants. They created a "headright system" by granting 150 acres of land to each member of a family, postponed the collection of quit-rents until 1689, and allowed an indentured male servant who served his term to receive his freedom and 100 acres of land. These incentives drew 6,600 colonists to the colony by 1700 compared with only 1,500 in the Spanish colony of Florida.

In 1670, another colony was created, called the "Carteret County colony", after Sir George Carteret, another Proprietor. The settlers were joined by Governor Sayle who had previously explored the coast.

From 1663 the Proprietary government was ineffective due to incompetent and dishonest governors combined with domestic conflicts. The future of creating a colony in Carolina, independent of Virginia, wasn't optimistic. All efforts had failed even in the south where the magnet of a good harbor had attracted a greater effort. The leaders of the colony were ready to abandon further attempts at settlement until Sir Ashley Cooper, soon to be the Earl of Shaftesbury, became involved.

E.   "FUNDAMENTAL CONSTITUTIONS" OF 1669

Cooper persuaded some investors to pledge funds to launch a new effort for a four year duration. Three ships left England in late summer 1669 with settlers and supplies. They stopped at Barbados to pick up various seeds to try out in the Carolina climate and soil. He instructed the settlers to first plant provisions and then begin their agricultural experiments. To encourage the experiments and give the settlers a financial boost he offered to purchase all crops at London prices. With help from John Locke, his physician, they drafted the "Fundamental Constitutions" of 1669. The purpose was to create a pattern of orderly settlement of Carolina. The land was to be surveyed into giant squares of 12,000 acres each. 40 of these squares (480,000 acres) comprised a county. In every county 8 squares (96,000 acres) were "seignories" of the Proprietors, 8 became "baronies" for an American nobility, and the remaining 24 (288,000 acres) were called "colonies" which were further subdivided into 4 "precincts" (72,000 acres) which would be settled by freeholders. Manors of the English type could be erected inside a colony but it was expected that most of the land would go to small planters. As settlement advanced each new county would be laid out in this grid pattern.

He proposed this method to attract the "well-to-do gentlemen" and at the same time give the small planter a voice in local affairs. Every county was designated to put 3/5 of the land and power in the hands of the ordinary settlers and 2/5 for the nobility. He believed that society functioned best when factions were checked and balanced, that power followed property and that a nobility was the very life and soul of society except, when it ruled unrestrained, it became destructive of society.

The form of government resembled that of early Virginia and Massachusetts. Proprietors, nobles, and deputies of the freeholders sat together in a one-house "Parliament". The "Grand Council" comprised of the Proprietors or their deputies prepared all bills and Parliament merely approved or disapproved them.

Several features of the Constitutions were devised to fit American conditions, such as providing for the registration of all births, marriages, deaths and land titles and that deputies should live in the district they represented. They foresaw the shortage of labor on the large estates and to overcome this they encouraged the development of slavery. They also made liberal use of land as an inducement, offering 100–150 acres for the first settlers and the amount diminishing to 60 for later settlers.

The Fundamental Constitutions were cumbersome and after four revisions and 30 years of trial, they were dropped. They failed mainly because they attempted to impose orderly settlement on a people who preferred to move when and where they wished.

F.   SUCCESS

Cooper (Shaftesbury) set the stage for eventual success in South Carolina. His small fleet arrived at Port Royal in April, 1670, after a difficult 8 month trip. They believed they were too close to the Spanish at St. Augustine, Florida, so they moved north and built a fort on Albemarle Point, 25 miles inland on the Ashley river, which along with the Cooper river, was named after Lord Shaftesbury, Ashley Cooper. This spot was safer from attack but still subject to attempts by the Spanish. Soon a relief ship arrived to get the settlers through the first winter. By 1672 there were 200 colonists and in 1680 were supplemented by 45 French Huguenots. Eventually they resettled along the Ashley and Cooper rivers above Charleston.

In 1680 this settlement was abandoned for Oyster Point which became the present city of Charles Town. This was the beginning of the South Carolina colony.

Few of Shaftesbury's plans survived long in the wilderness because soon the settlers began drifting away from the preferred "grid" pattern of settlement and moved inland, generally following the waterways and choosing sites on the two rivers. Only Charles Town, founded in 1680 at the junction of the two rivers, remained to remind posterity of his orderly settlement pattern. Eventually, Charleston, as it was to be called, followed Philadelphia and New Haven in being laid out in this grid pattern.

By the late 1680's the colony was becoming prosperous especially in the coastal areas. The economic base depended initially on the fur trade which produced good relations with the Indians. Tobacco production was briefly successful but eventually supplanted by rice. Years later indigo was introduced and it became the 2nd most important product. Both products depended on slave labor and elaborate plantation systems. Black slaves soon outnumbered whites which caused greater efforts to recruit white settlers. In the early 18th century thousands of Germans, Swiss, Welsh, and Scotch-Irish arrived in South Carolina.

By the end of century some 3,000 people had settled around Albemarle Sound in the northern part of Carolina and some 5,000 had spread out from Charlestown in the south. The northern part remained dependent on Virginia. Settlers lived on small farms and grew tobacco as a cash crop and lived isolated from their neighbors. They had their own Governor and Assembly and the county was the basic unit of government. Little distinguished their lives from those who farmed in Virginia.

G.   IMPACT OF THE GLORIOUS REVOLUTION (1688-1689)

Carolina absorbed the news of the Glorious Revolution quietly. The Proprietor's order to proclaim the new Monarchs produced no demonstrations although South Carolina was already in turmoil. They objected to high quit-rents, to the inappropriateness of the Fundamental Constitutions, to the lack of the right to initiate legislation, and to Governor John Colleton's arbitrary rule. But the opposition lacked strength and a leader and failed to use the Glorious Revolution as an excuse to stage a revolt of its own. Carolina grumbled but endured its grievances even when Governor Colleton dissolved the Assembly and ruled by decree.

H.   SOUTH CAROLINA REQUESTS ROYAL COLONY STATUS

Troubles began in 1703 with Sir Nathaniel Johnson becoming Governor. His first act was to pass a law excluding all dissenters, who comprised 2/3 of the population, from the Assembly. The next Assembly voted to repeal the law but Johnson refused so the Assembly then appealed to the Proprietors who upheld the Governor. The Assembly then appealed to the English House of Lords and won their case. The Proprietors yielded when the Governor's Act was vetoed by Queen Anne and the threat of losing their charter.

The next obstacle to growth was the Yamassee Indian War in 1715. At one time they were allies of the settlers in their fight against the Tuscarora Tribe in North Carolina. The Yamassee were urged by the Spanish to disrupt the English settlements. The war lasted 10 months with the Indians totally destroyed but it caused financial problems for the colony.

Those problems created another friction between the settlers and the Lords Proprietors who had received a financial profit from the quit-rents paid to them. The settlers asked them to share in bearing the expenses of the war but the Proprietors refused. They even refused to allow the assembly to raise the revenues by import duties or by selling the vacated Yamassee lands. They also refused to allow the rural freemen the right to vote in their own districts thus requiring them to travel to Charleston to vote.

In 1712 the two Carolina's were separated and in 1719 South Carolina requested to become a Royal colony because the Proprietors could no longer govern. The Charter was terminated and the King sent Francis Nicholson as their first Governor. From that time South Carolina began to grow through the remaining half-century of the colonial era. However, the people still resisted many efforts of the Royal Governors.

I.   COLONIAL DEVELOPMENT

The earliest important product of the colony was rice although it required a hundred years to bring the industry to perfection. Within a few years the Carolina's rivaled Egypt and Lombardy in furnishing rice for Southern Europe. By the middle of the 18th century, indigo became a strong rival of rice with many other products, such as, grain, furs, and cattle being exported. Later, cotton became predominant.

Expansion into the back-country was retarded by the presence of the Cherokee until 1755 when they made a treaty ceding this territory to the Crown. Soon after there was a considerable westward movement.

The character of society in the two Carolina's differed, except in the back-country. South Carolina possessed a major seaport while North Carolina did not. That seaport allowed for greater exposure to other cultures and trade opportunities.

In less than a century, South Carolina grew from a struggling settlement to one of the wealthiest colonies in the British Empire. The South Carolina low-country was the richest society in North America. The population of the low-country is usually divided into four groups:

- Elite/Aristocracy

- Middle Class

- Working class

- Slaves

Elite Aristocracy

The greatest fortunes were made by rice and indigo planters while some Charleston merchants, physicians, and lawyers also achieved great wealth.

Middle Class

The artisans, cabinetmakers, carpenters, bricklayers, and silversmiths formed the bulk of this class. Small shopkeepers and some Physicians, lawyers, and teachers also formed part of this class. Society did allow for movement between the classes.

Working Class

Consisted of journeymen and apprentices, day laborers, and sailors.

Slaves

Comprised about 80% of the population of the low-country with the vast majority serving as field hands on rice and indigo plantations, but some were house servants.

J.   CHARLESTON

Charleston was the only major seaport in the Southern colonies. The city's merchants developed regular trade patterns with the West Indies, northern colonies, Portugal, England, and it became the center for the export of rice and indigo.

Life in the south focused on Charleston. Economic ties as well as the origin of many early settlers oriented Charleston toward the West Indies rather than toward the other continental colonies. Farmers up the Ashley and Cooper rivers floated their crops down to town and from there their products were carried to Barbados. Charleston ships sold their cargoes at Barbados and reloaded with sugar and ginger, which was exchanged in England for manufactured goods which were sold back in Charleston. This "triangular trade" pattern seldom overlapped the trade lines of other American colonies.

A lucrative fur trade and traffic in Indian slaves flowed through Charleston from the inland trading centers like Savannah Town, known today as Augusta, South Carolina. Carolina traders pushed their frontier westward faster and farther than any other English settlers. By the end of the century they had reached the Mississippi river. Their expansion had also created turmoil with the Indians who allied with both the English and French settlers. Carolina's Indian trade, with its collision with French and Spanish traders would involve the colony in every imperial war of the next generation.

The primary occupations were raising livestock, cutting timber for export to the West Indies, trading for furs and deerskins with the Catawba and Cherokee Indians. They also bought captives taken by the Indians and sold them as slaves in other colonies. Most of the initial settlers were poor whites from Barbados and not much was accomplished in the early years.

The backcountry, for all of the wealth it sent eastward, remained a social, commercial, and political appendage of Charleston. The dominance of Charleston forced a form of government on southern Carolina different from what had taken shape in the Chesapeake region. Charleston delegated minimal political authority to interior communities which would eventually cause unrest.

The frontier did not lend itself to plantations and was settled primarily by subsistence farmers. In the early 1700's there was increasing tension between the settlers and the Proprietors due to a series of crises that the settlers complained were not adequately resolved by the Proprietors, such as:

- Incursions by the French and Spanish south of the colony

- Indian conflicts, primarily the Yamasee War in 1715-1718, which resulted in hundreds of deaths

- Pirate raids on coastal shipping and communities

As previously stated, in 1719, the South Carolina Assembly sent a petition to England requesting that the Proprietors be replaced with Crown administrators. King George I then appointed Royal Governors for each of North and South Carolina, whereby England ruled the colony but allowed the people self-government.

In 1729 the Crown bought out 7 of the 8 Proprietors for what they had invested in the colony. The 8th Proprietor, John Carteret (Lord Granville) refused to sell and retained title to the lands and quit-rents in the northern third of North Carolina. ***1729 marks the date that South Carolina officially became a Royal colony.***

K. KEY DATES AND SIGNIFICANT EVENTS

Native Indians of South Carolina include the Bear River Indians, Cape Fear Indians, Catawba, Cheraw, Cherokee, Chowanoc, Machapunga, Moratok, Natchez, Occaneechi, Saponi, Shakori, Tuscarora, and Waccamaw tribes.

	1497	English exploration by John Cabot but no settlement attempt
6/24	1521	Francisco Gordillo explores the Carolina coast for Spain but no settlement attempted
	1524	Giovanni Verrazano explores Cape Fear and the Carolina coast for France
Aug	1526	Lucas Vasquez de Ayllon attempted a settlement of several hundred colonists in the Winyah Bay area (present-day Myrtle Beach) but unfavorable weather and sickness forced them to return to Santo Domingo.
	1562	Jean Ribault leads expedition of French Huguenots to Parris Island but it failed within a year because of Spanish power in nearby Florida. French build a fort named "Charles-Fort".
	1566	Spain decides to build coastal forts to discourage French settlements
	1623	First charter for Carolina Colony granted to Sir Robert Heath but would never be used
	1629	Grant to Sir Robert Heath for all of present-day North and South Carolina. No settlement attempt was made. The Grant includes territory from 31–36 North Latitude from Albemarle Sound, North Carolina, to Jekyll Island off the coast of Georgia.
	1650	First settlements near Albemarle Sound, present-day North Carolina

3/24	1663	King Charles II grant to eight of his most loyal supporters, the "Lords Proprietors". Charter includes Albemarle Sound settlements.
	1665	The Lords Proprietors expanded their 1663 "Declaration and Proposals" with another document called "Concessions and Agreements" which divided Carolina into 3 counties, each with its own Governor, Council, and Assembly.
	1666	Captain Robert Sanford explores and names the Ashley River and takes formal possession of Carolina for England and the Proprietors.
	1669	Lord Anthony Ashley Cooper drafted "Fundamental Constitutions of Carolina", a feudal scheme calling for a nobility. Guarantees religious freedom which leads to immigration of French Huguenots and Sephardic Jews.
April	1670	Cooper fleet arrives at Port Royal but move north because of Spanish threat and build a Fort on Albemarle Point 25 miles inland on the Ashley River.
	1680	Charles Town moved to Oyster Point, its current site, from Albemarle Point and becomes Charles Town.
	1691	The area assumes the name of South Carolina which is derived from the Latin name "Carolus" (Charles). The territory is named in honor of King Charles IX of France and then King Charles I and King Charles II of England.
	1693	Liberty of Conscience is confirmed reaffirming the right to worship as one pleases
	1700	Charles Town grows into major trading center with population estimated at 6,600
	1704	Church of England is official Church until 1778
	1706	French & Spain attack Charles Town during Queen Anne's War
	1712	Carolina split into 2 colonies, North and South

	1715	Yamasee War until 1718
	1719	Citizens petition the King to take over the Government of the Colony.
7/25	1729	7 Lord's Proprietors surrender their rights to King George II and South Carolina officially becomes a Royal colony.
	1742	Spanish prevented from capturing Charles Town in "Battle of Bloody Marsh". Town population estimated at 6,800.
	1760	Population estimated at 150,000 with 3/4 as slaves. Cherokee War until 1761.
	1761	Cherokee War ends, Treaty opens land for settlement. Bounty Act offers public land tax free for 10 years in the Up-Country, settlers begin to move in.
	1775	South Carolina first provincial Congress meets and Charles Town population estimated at 12,000.
8/13	1783	Charleston is officially incorporated as the name of the town.
5/23	1788	South Carolina becomes 8th state admitted to Union.

L. REVIEW QUESTIONS

(Multiple Choice

1. Which country attempted the first settlement of South Carolina?
   a. England
   b. France
   c. Spain

2. The Charter of 1663 was granted by:
   a. King Louis XIV of France
   b. King Charles II of England
   c. King George II of England
   d. none of the above

3. In what year was the first permanent English settlement in Carolina?
   a. 1623
   b. 1629
   c. 1650
   d. 1670

4. The Fundamental Constitutions of South Carolina were intended to:
   a. create a Representative Assembly
   b. establish a system for orderly settlement
   c. create a Legal Code
   d. none of the above

5. The growing prosperity of South Carolina in the 1680's was due to which products:
    a. fur trade
    b. tobacco
    c. rice
    d. indigo
    e. all of the above

6. In what year did South Carolina become a separate colony from North Carolina?
    a. 1703
    b. 1715
    c. 1719
    d. 1729

(True or False)

7. North and South Carolina were given different charters for settlement.
    a. TRUE
    b. FALSE

8. "Charles-Fort" was built by the Spanish to protect against the English.
    a. TRUE
    b. FALSE

9. South Carolina quickly developed economically because of its good harbor.
    a. TRUE
    b. FALSE

10. The Lords Proprietors were involved in a plan to settle in Carolina country.
    a. TRUE
    b. FALSE

11. The Earl of Craven was one of the 8 original Lords Proprietors.
    a. TRUE
    b. FALSE

12. The document "Concessions and Agreements" was created by the French to create a settlement strategy.
    a. TRUE
    b. FALSE

13. The "Fundamental Constitutions" was successful in settling South Carolina.
    a. TRUE
    b. FALSE

14. North and South Carolina were separated in 1719.
    a. TRUE
    b. FALSE

M.   GLOSSARY

1. **Quit-Rents**   A small fixed annual rent whose payment released a tenant from manorial services.

2. **Triangular Trade**   Trade among 3 ports or regions.

(Attachment 11b lists the South Carolina Governors from 1669-1719, Royal Governors until 1776, and State Governors to 1789)

CHAPTER 11 SUMMARY

South Carolina

1. Early explorations of the Carolina coast by France and Spain in the 1520's.

2. The first English Charter was granted to Sir Robert Heath in 1629 but it was never used.

3. The first attempted settlement was by Roger Green who led a group of persecuted Virginia Presbyterians to a site near present-day Edenton, North Carolina. Historians are uncertain of the settlement duration.

4. In 1663 King Charles II approved a Grant to eight "Lords Proprietors" to colonize the Carolina territory. The Proprietors controlled the colony until 1729.

5. The "Fundamental Constitutions" of 1669 were an attempt to regulate settlement but it failed.

6. The first permanent English settlement is made at Albemarle Point on the Ashley River in 1670. It eventually becomes known as Charleston after it is moved to Oyster Point, its' current Site.

7. By the late 1680's, the colony becomes prosperous due to a successful fur trade, rice, and idigo.

8. In 1703 there are political troubles with Governor Sir Nathaniel Johnson.

9. During the period from 1692–1712 the colonies of North and South Carolina existed as a single governmental unit. In 1712 it was formally divided into North and South Carolina.

10. The Yamassee War was fought from 1715–1718.

11. In 1719 South Carolina requests that Royal Administrators replace the Proprietors.

12. In 1729 the 7 remaining "Lords Proprietors" surrendered their rights to King George II. South Carolina officially became a Royal Colony.

13. The Cherokee War ends in 1761. The Treaty opens land for settlement. The "Bounty Act" offers public land tax-free for 10 years in the up-country, which provides a boost for expansion.

14. In 1775 the first South Carolina Provincial Congress meets.

15. In 1788 South Carolina becomes the 8th State admitted to the Union.

11a

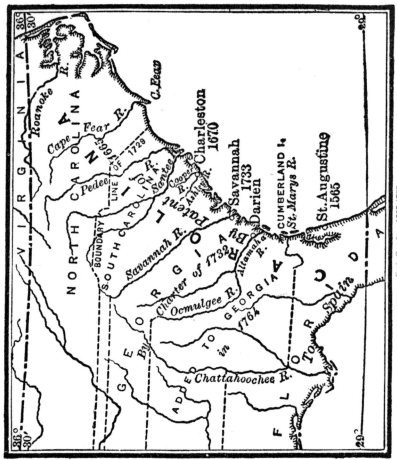

11b

SOUTH CAROLINA GOVERNORS	
DATES	**NAME AND TITLE**
1669 1670	WILLIAM SAYLE *(a)*
1670 1672	JOSEPH WEST *(b)*
1672 1674	SIR JOHN YEAMANS
1674 1682	JOSEPH WEST
1682 1684	JOSEPH MORTON
1684 1685	JOSEPH WEST & ROBERT QUARY *(b)*
1685 1686	JOSEPH MORTON
1686 1690	JOHN COLLETON
1690 1691	SETH SOTHEL
1691 1693	PHILIP LUDWELL
1693 1694	THOMAS SMITH
1694 1696	JOHN ARCHDALE
1696 1700	DEPUTY GOV JOSEPH BLAKE
1700 1702	JAMES MOORE *(b)*
1702 1708	SIR NATHANIEL JOHNSON
1708 1709	COLONEL EDWARD TYNTE
1709 1712	ROBERT GIBBES
1712 1716	CHARLES CRAVEN
1716 1717	DEPUTY GOV ROBERT DANIEL
1717 1719	ROBERT JOHNSON
ROYAL GOVERNORS	
1719 1721	JAMES MOORE
1721 1724	SIR FRANCIS NICHOLSON
1724 1729	ARTHUR MIDDLETON *(c)*
1729 1735	ROBERT JOHNSON
1735 1737	LT GOV THOMAS BROUGHTON
1738 1743	LT GOV WILLIAM BULL *(c)*
1743 1756	JAMES GLEN
1756 1760	WILLIAM HENRY LYTTLETON
1760 1761	LT GOV WILLIAM BULL II
1761 1764	THOMAS BOONE
1764 1766	LT GOV WILLIAM BULL II
1766 1773	LORD CHARLES GREVILLE MONTAGU
1773 1775	LT GOV WILLIAM BULL II
1775 1776	LORD WILLIAM CAMPBELL
GOVERNORS OF THE STATE	
1776 1778	PRESIDENT JOHN RUTLEDGE
1778 1779	PRESIDENT RAWLINS LOWNDES
1779 1782	JOHN RANDOLPH
1782 1783	JOHN MATHEWS
1783 1785	BENJAMIN GUERARD
1785 1787	WILLIAM MOULTRIE
1787 1789	THOMAS PINCKNEY
(a) 1st Gov of the colony established on the Ashley River	
(b) Chosen by the Council	
(c) President of the Council	

Chapter 12

North Carolina

The territory of present-day North and South Carolina was known by the name of "Carolina" at the time of the earliest explorations. It was first called "Carolana" after King Charles I of England and it derived from "Carolus" which means Charles in Latin. In 1663, King Charles II changed the spelling to "Carolina". *The area was explored, settled, and governed as a single entity until 1712 when "Carolina" was officially split into North and South Carolina even though each section had its own Governor until 1691.*

The history of the North Carolina colony can be viewed through 6 phases:

1. EARLY EXPLORATIONS
2. SETTLEMENT ACTIVITY BEFORE THE CHARTER OF 1663
3. SETTLEMENT ACTIVITY AFTER THE CHARTER OF 1663
4. COLONIAL UNREST
5. COLONIAL DEVELOPMENT
6. THE ROYAL PERIOD

A.   EARLY EXPLORATIONS

From1497 to 1526, England, France, and Spain sent explorers to the area but no settlement attempts were made.

Excluding the exploration by John Cabot in 1497 of the coastline, England didn't become seriously interested in the area until the ill-fated effort to settle at Roanoke Island in 1584. It was almost another century before others were able to realize the dreams of Raleigh.

B.   SETTLEMENT ACTIVITY BEFORE THE CHARTER OF 1663

England became involved when a charter was given to Sir Robert Heath in 1623 for the Carolina territory but it was never used. *Another grant was given to Heath in 1629 for the territory from 31-36 degrees north latitude extending from Albemarle Sound, North Carolina, to Jekyll Island off the Georgia coast.* It sought to encourage settlement by granting exemptions from English customs duties on wines, silks, olives, and other subtropical products for 7 years after experimental tests had been completed. *It allowed settlers the right to worship as they wished, only requiring that they worship.*

Settlement lagged due to the absence of a good harbor in the north but, in 1653, Roger Green led a group of persecuted Presbyterians from Jamestown to a land-grant he had secured of 10,000 acres near present-day Edenton, North Carolina, near the Chowan river and Albemarle Sound. He promised the first 100 settlers 1,000 acres each. Historians are not certain as to the success or duration of this colony. Other settlers followed with some Puritans arriving in the Cape Fear river area in 1661 to purchase land from the Indians. They were planting the seeds of a colony when news arrived that King Charles II had given the entire region to 8 of his supporters, calling it "Carolina". Many of them left for other parts of the area, though, and the colony never fully developed. *(See Attachment 12a for a map of early Carolina from 1565-1733)*

C.   SETTLEMENT AFTER THE CHARTER OF 3/24/1663

Over the years much information about the potential of the Carolina's had gotten back to England causing some adventurers to think of exploration and settlement. Sir John Colleton was one of the first to think about a full-scale colony in the area. After a brief career as a planter and speculator he had become a member of the Privy Council and Committee for Foreign Plantations. It was from this key position that he was able to proclaim the potential benefits of a venture to the area. He persuaded the Berkeley brothers, Sir William and Lord John, to seek out other influential men to propose an expedition to King Charles II.

They formed a group of 8 key members of the English nobility who would receive a charter from the King to establish (1663) the colony of Carolina. They were known as the "Lords Proprietors of Carolina" who would become the landlords of the colony. They were:

- Sir John Colleton

- Edward Hyde (The Earl of Clarendon)

- George Monck (The Duke of Albemarle)

- Lord William Craven

- Lord John Berkeley

- Sir William Berkeley

- Lord Anthony Ashley Cooper (Later to become the Earl of Shaftesbury)

- Sir George Carteret

They sought to follow Gilbert and Raleigh's dream, to make money for themselves and promote the welfare of England. They planned to follow an earlier plan to encourage agricultural experiments leading to products England could not grow. They differed from Gilbert and Raleigh, however, in that they did not intend to personally invest in the effort. They didn't think it was wise to carry out costly colonization from England when the New World was already populated with many people seeking free land. The Proprietors, then, would draw from those who had already made the trip and gained some immunity to New World diseases, using land to attract them from New England, Virginia, and the Barbados islands.

King Charles II, the "Merry Monarch", was the most popular King ever in England. He generally chose to leave the colonies alone. No English subsidies increased the prices of colonial products, no Royal bounty assisted the colonists when they were starving, and there were no Royal troops to defend them. Only 1 colony gave him trouble, Massachusetts Bay. The colonies were generally allowed to grow as they wished and were able. Historians believe he never had a firm colonial policy and just reacted from day to day. Eventually, tighter control of the colonies would become necessary because of trade and commercial matters affecting both the colonists and England. He liked to reward his friends and punish his enemies which caused many to seek colonial charters for the rewards. 6 of the original 13 colonies were founded during his reign and all as Proprietary grants.

England used the "Proprietary Colony" during the 1660-1690 period to award land in the New World to resourceful groups or individuals with the intent for it to be developed by them. These colonies were owned by an individual proprietor or a group of proprietors under a charter from the Monarch who used this approach to meet demands for territorial expansion and to also raise funds to repay his debts. The awarded Proprietors were normally Feudal Lords with the right of absolute rule but remained subject to their Monarch who could, at any time, remove their privileges. They collected quit-rents from settlers to whom they granted the land, for their own profit.

As part of a promotional campaign the Proprietors issued *"A Declaration and Proposals to All That Will Plant in Carolina" where they promised settlers as much if not more political freedom than they might get elsewhere in America. An Assembly was authorized to make all laws, subject only to the consent of the Governor and possible disallowance by the Proprietors.* In addition to religious freedom, generous land grants would be dispensed to all settlers, including servants at the end of their indenture. The only charge on the settlers would be a small quit-rent to underwrite administrative costs.

There was some conflict with Governor Berkeley of Virginia when the Proprietors were authorized to extend their authority over the few settlers on the Chowan river and then they organized a separate government in 1663-1664 calling it the "Albemarle County Colony", they named after one of the Proprietors, George Monck, the Duke of Albemarle. He appointed William Drummond as Governor. Settlement was slow because the northern section had little to offer that Virginia could not grant on better terms. The lack of a harbor forced most supplies to enter and exports to leave through Virginia, anyway. Quit-rents were less there and the land grants as generous. Albemarle settlers demanded, at once, the right to hold land upon the same terms and conditions as was held by inhabitants of Virginia.

Two years later more emigrants arrived and bought land from the Indians along the Cape Fear river, near present-day Wilmington, North Carolina, and founded a settlement with Sir John Yeamans as Governor. It was organized politically and called the "Clarendon County Colony", and named after another of the Proprietors, Edward Hyde, the Earl of Clarendon. Yeaman's jurisdiction extended from the Cape Fear River to the St. John's River in Florida. ***This settlement became permanent which formed the foundation of the Commonwealth of North Carolina. In 1674 the population was about 4,000.***

While Berkeley worked to promote the Albemarle settlements, the other Proprietors worked on the southern part of the grant. William Hilton of Barbados had explored the Cape Fear region in 1663 and his report created interest in Barbados among the small planters who had been suffering economically.

To encourage further settlement, the Proprietors in 1665 expanded their earlier "Declaration and Proposals" with a long document entitled, "Concessions and Agreements" which, in addition to detailing the settler's privileges, divided Carolina into 3 counties, each with its own Assembly, Governor, and Council:

- Albemarle in the north

- Clarendon and Craven in the south

Settlers arrived in 1670 and established the first permanent settlement in Albemarle. They were anxious to secure Carolina against Spanish attacks from St. Augustine, Florida, and to do so they needed to attract more colonists. They offered inducements such as religious toleration, political representation in an Assembly, exemption from quit-rents, and large land grants. They created a "headright system" by granting 150 acres of land to each member of a family, postponed the collection of quit-rents until 1689, and allowed an indentured male servant who served his term to receive his freedom and 100 acres of land.

D.   EARLY COLONIAL DEVELOPMENT

From 1692-1712, the colonies of North and South Carolina existed as a single unit of government although until 1691 each had its own Governor. In 1712 the province was officially divided into 2 separate colonies.

In 1714, the Lords Proprietors sent Charles Eden as Governor and he proved to be the best and most able Governor the colony ever had. But, on his death in 1722, unrest returned. Beginning about 1719 settlers began moving westward thus almost creating two different societies, the coastal and the western frontier with different living conditions and way of life. The "back-country" was non-slaveholding while the coastal settlements were slaveholding.

The first products of the colony were tobacco along the Virginia border, rice on the Cape Fear river, and grain, cattle, and swine in both of these sections. Eventually the great pine forests began to yield their wealth and before the Revolution, tar, turpentine, and lumber became the chief products of North Carolina.

Of all the 13 colonies, North Carolina was the least commercial, the most provincial, the farthest removed from European influences and its wild forest life the most unrestrained. Every colony had a frontier, its borderland between civilization and savagery, but North Carolina was composed entirely of frontier. The people were impatient of legal restraints and opposed the paying of taxes. They were mostly farmers and woodsmen, lived far apart and scattered throughout the wilderness. Their highways were the rivers and bays with their homes connected by narrow trails winding among the trees. Yet, the people were happy in their freedom and content with their lonely isolation

As the settlers colonized the area, they gave new names to the places they settled, sometimes retaining Indian place-names or they created Anglicized versions of the Indian words. The names of local tribes were often used, such as Chowan county, Currituck county, Pasquotank county, and Perquimans county which were all formed in 1672 and named after tribes who had lived in the northeast portion of the colony.

Some colonial areas were named after local geographic features. Other places were called by the last names of their earliest settlers. A few towns were named for European cities such as Salisbury which took its name for Salisbury, England, while the Swiss Baron Christoph von Graffenried named New Bern, for the capital of his homeland, Bern, Switzerland. Perhaps the most popular way to name towns and counties was after famous people. For example, all eight of the "Lords Proprietors" had districts, counties, or towns named for them.

The northeastern part of the colony, where European settlement initially began, was known as "The Albemarle" after the Duke of Albemarle. Between 1664 and 1667 the Cape Fear river was called Clarendon river and the land around the mouth of the river was called Clarendon county, both named after Edward Hyde, the Earl of Clarendon.

Craven county was named for the Earl of Craven, while Sir George Carteret gave his name to Carteret Precinct which existed between 1671 and 1684 and to Carteret county founded in 1722.

Shaftesbury precinct (1671-1684) which later became Chowan county was named for Anthony Ashley Cooper, the Earl of Shaftesbury, who played a significant role in the development of South Carolina as well.

E. COLONIAL UNREST

From 1663 the Proprietary government was viewed as ineffective due to incompetent or dishonest governors who were also unable to protect them from frequent Indian attacks. This led to many domestic conflicts, such as the:

- Culpeper Rebellion   1677 – 1679

- Cary Rebellion   1711

- Tuscarora War   1711 – 1715

- Regulator Movement 1760's

Beginning with the Culpepper Rebellion in 1677, the region experienced considerable unrest due to the combination of ineffective government, religious issues due to repeated efforts to establish the Church of England at the expense of the Quakers, and constant Indian conflicts.

During the first decade of the 18th century, immigration increased considerably with Huguenots from France who settled at Bath near Pamlico Sound and the Germans and Swiss from the Rhine river region who founded New Bern. The white population was about 5,000 and the Albemarle settlement extended many miles into the forest, encroaching on the soil of the Indians and sowing the seeds of future Indian conflicts.

Because the Proprietors ruled from their homes in England, they were out of touch with the daily lives of the colonists. They tried, mostly unsuccessfully, to run the colony as a profitable business. They did their best to encourage settlement, but for many years Carolina was an unruly place. Epidemics, disease, hurricanes, droughts, crop failures, political turmoil, religious dissension, and Indian conflicts added to the challenge of settling in a new land.

1. **CULPEPER REBELLION**

    This was an uprising against the Proprietary rule in the Albemarle region of northern Carolina. It was caused by the efforts of Proprietary government to enforce the British Navigation Acts which denied the colonists markets outside of England and placed heavy duties on commodities.

    The colonists focused their displeasure on the Deputy Governor, Thomas Miller, who was also the Customs collector. The uprising was led by John Culpeper and George Durant. They imprisoned Miller and other officials and then convened a legislature of their own, elected Culpeper as Governor, and for 2 years they ran their own government. Culpeper was finally removed by the Proprietors and tried for treason and embezzlement but never punished.

2. **CARY'S REBELLION**

The event which led to this rebellion was primarily a religious conflict. In 1672, George Fox, the founder of the "Society of Friends" (Quakers), visited Albemarle county and established his Church. In succeeding years this Church grew and became strongly entrenched in the colony where for several decades it was the sole representative of organized religion.

In 1694, a Quaker named John Archdale, was appointed as Governor which led to the domination of all branches of government by the Quaker Church. This produced a reaction from the Anglicans who believed they were being discriminated against.

Things changed when Henderson Walker, an Anglican, became Governor in 1699. The next year he persuaded the General Assembly to pass an Act establishing the Church of England as the colony's official Church, to be supported by taxes upon the colonists. At the same time, Queen Anne came to the Throne on 3/8/1702 upon the death of King William II and required oaths of loyalty by the colony's officials and assemblymen. The Quakers were unable to swear an oath, per their religious beliefs, but offered to affirm their loyalty, as they had done in the past, but the Anglicans in power refused to accept their offer. They barred all Quakers from public office which led to the colony splitting into those who supported the Anglican establishment, called the "Church Party", against the Quakers, which caused great friction in the colony.

In 1705, Thomas Cary, a supporter of the "Church Party", was named Governor which caused the Quakers to send Emanuel Low to England to secure his removal from office. He succeeded but when he returned to the colony, he found Cary in South Carolina and William Glover, President of the

Council, acting for him. He soon found that Glover was a more ardent supporter of the Anglican party so he withheld the order from the Proprietor's removing Cary from office, since Glover would have been worse for the Quakers than Cary. Meanwhile, Cary had a conversion to the Quaker cause and, in 1708, he managed to oust Glover from office and forced him and his supporters to move to Virginia. From 1708-1710, Cary and the Quaker party ran the colony.

In January, 1711, Edward Hyde arrived in North Carolina claiming the Governorship. At first, Cary and the Quakers worked with him but eventually Hyde pursued policies against the Quakers. Cary refused to recognize him and claimed the Governorship for himself until Hyde could prove that he had been officially commissioned as Governor.

This further split the colony into open hostilities. The Pamlico regions and town of Bath were viewed as the headquarters of Cary and the center of his support. Governor Hyde then declared him in open rebellion and planned to seize him by force. Hyde assembled an army in present-day Bertie County and on 5/27/1711 led a force to the home of Cary who had already fled a few miles down the Pamlico river. Hyde's force attacked them there but failed to capture Cary. Hyde then returned to Albemarle on 6/1/1711.

Hyde's failure encouraged Cary's supporters who had grown in number. Cary declared himself as Governor and attacked Hyde's forces on 6/30/1711 but they also failed, and retreated. Hyde then attacked and again failed to capture Cary.

Meanwhile, Governor Spotswood of Virginia, decided to support Hyde and prepared an army which caused the Cary forces to refuse to fight them and flee to Virginia where they were captured and sent in chains to England. Somehow, Cary's friends in England were able to free him to return to Carolina where he was never heard of again.

The rebellion left a permanent scar on the Pamlico region which continued to experience constant unrest.

3. **THE TUSCARORA WAR (1711-1715)**

The Tuscarora's were part of the Iroquois Nation closely connected with the "5 Nations Confederacy" in New York. The movement of settlers into Bath County and up the Pamlico and Neuse rivers upset the Indians because it disturbed their favorite hunting and fishing regions and destroyed their villages.

They lived in peace with the settlers for the first 50 years of the Carolina colony. There were two major factions within the Tribe;

a. Northern group led by Chief Tom Blunt, near present-day Bertie County on the Roanoke River.
b. Southern group led by Chief Hancock, near present-day New Bern south of the Pamlico river.

North Carolina was growing in the early 18th century but its troubles continued. There was still unhappiness over the presence of Quakers in the colonial government and disputes over religious freedom, plus constant Indian problems.

Both Indian groups were negatively impacted by the arrival of the European settlers who took their lands, kidnapped their people, and sold them into slavery. Chief Hancock decided to retaliate on 9/22/1711 by attacking the planters on the Roanoke river. Governor Hyde called out the militia and also received assistance from the South Carolina colony and attacked the Indians in 1712, killing more than 300 and taking another 100 as prisoners who were eventually sold into slavery. Chief Blunt then helped the colonists capture and execute Chief Hancock in 1712. After that, many southern Tuscarora were also killed or captured while others escaped to New York. The remaining Tuscarora signed a Peace Treaty in June, 1718. The Indians ceded a tract of land on the Roanoke river in what is now Bertie County. The remaining southern Tuscarora were removed from their homes on the Pamlico river and required to move to Bertie County in 1722. Over the next few decades the remaining Tuscarora lands were almost totally sold or given to the settlers.

4. **THE REGULATOR MOVEMENT (1764-1771)**

This movement occurred in both North and South Carolina but the uprising in western North Carolina was led by small farmers protesting the corruption of local sheriffs and court officials. They first petitioned the Assembly in 1764-1765 to recall the local officials. When this failed, they formed an "Association" in 1768 and pledged to pay only legal taxes and abide only by the will of the majority. They won control of the Provincial Assembly in 1769 but with the Governor, William Tryon, the Provincial Council, and the Courts against them, they were unable to secure relief. They eventually resorted to violence after Edmund Fanning, a particularly despised official was allowed to go unpunished. The violence alienated some of their support among the large property holders and the clergy. On 5/16/1771, Governor Tryon's militia defeated a force of "The Regulators" in the "Battle of Alamance Creek". Seven of the leaders were executed which ended the movement. One group of Regulators moved west to Tennessee but most surrendered. Tension remained for a number of years between the western farmers and the coastal and tidewater aristocracy.

F.   THE ROYAL PERIOD (1729-1776)

1.   GOVERNMENT

Between 1663 and 1719, North Carolina was under the control of the Lords Proprietors and their descendants, who commissioned colonial officials and authorized the Governor and his Council to grant lands in the name of the Lords Proprietors.

In 1719, the Proprietary government was terminated and replaced with a Provincial Royal Governor because of considerable colonial unrest. By 1729 most of the Proprietors were tired of dealing with their colonial problems so all but one sold their shares back to King of England.

On 5/14/1729 both North and South Carolina officially became Royal colonies with all political functions now to be controlled by the Crown until 1775. As previously noted, the colonies had already been officially separated in 1712.

During the Royal period, North Carolinian's received minimal Royal supervision of the colony until the mid-1760's at the end of the final French-Indian Wars (1756-1763). *Britain had borrowed large sums of money from the Dutch to finance the war and many in England felt the colonists should contribute a greater portion to repay the debt since it was the colonists who were receiving the benefits. As the British began to pass laws to have the colonists contribute more for their own defense, the settlers began to believe that they would be better off governing themselves rather than submit to new invasions of their perceived liberties.*

This was happening at a time when the colonists were exhausted from Indian conflicts, conflicts with other settlers, frontiersmen, coastal colonists, etc, plus the normal tensions arising from recent immigration and the mixing of various ethnic groups. *All of these events were stirring up tensions which would eventually lead to the pre-Revolutionary period of the early 1770's.*

2. **POPULATION AND COLONIAL GROWTH**

North Carolina's population increased from 30,000 in 1730 to more than 265,000 in 1775. For example, in 1729 there were only seven permanently settled towns in the colony:

a. Bath
b. New Bern
c. Fort Settlement
d. Edenton
e. Perquimans Court House
f. Beaufort
g. Brunswick

During the period from 1729-1775 there were 18 new counties created, which generally followed the westward expansion. Newcomers found minimal land available along the coast so they went where land was still unclaimed, in the west. So, in the 1730's, the pace of westward expansion greatly increased because the lands were excellent for farming. Travel from the west to the coast was difficult and, in the absence of roads, they used the rivers for their major movement.

The "King's Highway" was constructed in North Carolina between 1732-1734, following the Neuse-Cape Fear road, which had been completed in 1724. In 1732 this road was widened and extended to the Virginia border in the north and to the South Carolina border in the south. Those living in the Albemarle region could now trade with those in the growing Cape Fear river region.

By 1775 there were 53 more towns with settlement patterns shifting westward from the coastal plain toward the Piedmont and foothills. Thousands of incoming families traveled down the "Great Wagon Road" from Pennsylvania and other northern colonies while other new immigrants arrived from Europe. Farmers from Virginia migrated to settle in North Carolina because it had a warm climate and good soil.

Terrence Hagen

3. **IMMIGRATION**

The largest group of immigrants were the Scots-Irish. They were the first to settle along the Pennsylvania and Virginia frontiers and were also the first to be attacked by the French-inspired Indians in the 1740's and 1750's. Other large groups of immigrants were the Germans, Moravians, and French Huguenots which tended to congregate only with their own at first but eventually they began to mix with the predominantly English settlers.

In the late 1740's, the newcomers began to settle the Piedmont area from the north instead of from the coast. By 1760, the foothills of the Appalachian Mountains were beginning to be settled. The central and western parts of the colony were growing faster than the coastal areas, for the first time in the colony's history. By the end of the Royal period most of the Piedmont up to the Appalachian Mountains was fairly well inhabited and the land virtually covered from seacoast to mountains by people of various ethnic backgrounds and points of origin.

4. **FRONTIER TENSIONS**

External influences were not as significant as had been experienced during the rule of the Proprietors. King George's War (1739-1748) brought with it a prolonged harassment by French and Spanish Privateers along the North Carolina coast, but rarely did this harassment result in the loss of its' citizens lives.

Much of the frontier tension occurred in the areas of the most recent growth, along the Pennsylvania and Virginia frontiers. *These rising tensions would eventually lead to the final French-Indian War of 1756-1763.*

5. **PRE-REVOLUTIONARY PERIOD**

The seeds of the Revolution began to appear in North Carolina as early as 1769 when the Assembly denied the right of Parliament to tax the colonists without their consent. In 1774, North Carolina sent its delegates to the First Continental Congress, an association was formed in Mecklenburg county for its defense, and in *May, 1775, they virtually declared themselves independent of England.* Alarmed at the escalation of public opinion, the

326

Royal Governor (Martin) abdicated and took refuge on an English ship in the Cape Fear river. A Provisional Convention assumed the government and organized a body of troops, a militia. *A State Constitution was adopted in a Congress at Halifax, North Carolina, on 12/18/1776, with the government led by a Provincial Congress and Committee of Safety until 1777 when Richard Caswell was chosen as the first State Governor.*

G. KEY DATES AND SIGNIFICANT EVENTS

The native Indians of North Carolina included the Bear River and Cape Fear tribes, Catawba, Cheraw, Cherokee, Chowanoc, Machapunga, Mortok, Natchez, Occaneechi, Saponi, Shakori, Tuscarora, and Waccamaw tribes.

6/24	1521	Francisco Gordillo explores the Carolina coast for Spain but no settlement attempted.
	1524	Giovanni Verrazano explores Cape Fear and the Carolina coast for France
Aug	1526	Spain established a small settlement led by Lucas Vasquez de Ayllon at Cape Fear but it failed because of disease and lack of food.
	1623	First charter for Carolina Colony granted to Sir Robert Heath but would never be used
	1629	Grant to Sir Robert Heath for all of present-day North and South Carolina. No settlement attempt was made. The Grant includes territory from 31-36 North Latitude from Albemarle Sound, North Carolina, to Jekyll Island off the coast of Georgia.
July	1653	Roger Green leads a group of persecuted Virginia Presbyterians from Jamestown to a land-grant he was given for 10,000 acres near the present-day site of Edenton, near the Chowan river and Albemarle Sound. Historians are not certain of long the settlement survived.
3/24	1663	King Charles II grant to eight of his most loyal supporters, the "Lords Proprietors". Charter includes Albemarle Sound settlements.

1665   The Lords Proprietors expanded their 1663 "Declaration and Proposals" with another document called "Concessions and Agreements" which divided Carolina into 3 counties, each with its own Governor, Council, and Assembly.

1665   Sir John Yeamans established a permanent colony on the Cape Fear river near present-day Wilmington, North Carolina.

1672   George Fox, founder of "The Society of Friends", (Quakers) visits Albemarle country and established his Church which grew in strength for several decades.

1677   Culpeper Rebellion until 1679

1691   Area assumes the name of North Carolina.

1694   John Archdale, a Quaker, appointed as Governor which led to domination of all government branches by the Quaker Church. This produces a reaction from Anglicans who believed they were victims of discrimination.

1699   Henderson Walker, an Anglican, becomes Governor. Passes a law making the Anglican Church the official Church of the colony to be supported by taxes on the colonists. The Quakers refused and were barred from public office. This conflict splits the colony into 2 major factions, the Church party and the Quakers.

1704   Unrest developed over the ineffective Proprietary Governors and religious issues over constant efforts to impose the Anglican Church of England at the expense of the Quakers.

1705   Thomas Cary becomes Governor, supports the Anglican Party. Quakers send representatives to London to have Cary removed from office. They succeed but the replacement would have been worse for the Quakers so they hold off removing Cary. Eventually Cary converts to Quaker faith and from 1708-1710 Cary and the Quaker party control the colony.

	1710	Germans and Swiss establish a settlement on the Neuse River.
	1711	Cary Rebellion. Edward Hyde arrives claiming Governorship and creates policies against the Quakers. Cary resists until Hyde can prove he was officially commissioned as Governor. Open rebellion and fighting. Virginia Governor supports Hyde, causing Cary supporters to quit the fight. Rebellion ends.
	1711	Tuscarora War until 1715 and Peace Treaty of 1718.
	1712	Carolina split into 2 colonies, North and South
	1714	"Lords Proprietors" send Charles Eden as Governor who is very successful but, with his death in 1722, unrest re-appears.
	1715	Yamasee War until 1718
	1719	Settlers begin moving westward
	1719	Citizens petition the King to take over the Government of the Colony.
7/25	1729	Seven Lord's Proprietors surrender their rights to King George II and North and South Carolina officially become separate Royal colonies.
	1764	"Regulator Movement" in western North Carolina protest corruption of local sheriffs and court officials. Defeated by Governor's militia in 1771 and most surrendered.
	1769	Assembly of North Carolina denied the right of Parliament to tax the colonists without their consent.
11/21	1789	North Carolina 12th State admitted to Union.

(See Attachment 12b for a List of North Carolina Proprietary, Royal, and State Governors)

H.   REVIEW QUESTIONS

(Multiple Choice)

1. Which of the following geographic regions were NOT part of colonial Carolina?
    a.   Coastal Plain
    b.   Appalachian Piedmont
    c.   Tidewater
    d.   Appalachian Mountains

2. Which religious groups were most often in conflict in North Carolina?
    a.   Quakers and Puritans
    b.   Puritans and Anglicans
    c.   Presbyterians and Puritans
    d.   Quakers and Anglicans

3. The Culpeper Rebellion occurred during which years?
    a.   1711–1715
    b.   1677–1679
    c.   1758–1760
    d.   1729–1760

4. Cary's Rebellion was due to which issue(s)?
    a.   Economic
    b.   Legal
    c.   Religious
    d.   All of the above

5. In which year did North Carolina officially become a Royal
    Colony ?
    a. 1712
    b. 1719
    c. 1729
    d. 1760

6. The first settlements in the Carolina region were by the:
    a. Swedish
    b. Spanish
    c. Virginians
    d. French Huguenots

(True or False)

7. The territory "Carolana" was named for King Charles II of
    England.
    a. TRUE
    b. FALSE

8. 1584 was the year of the first permanent settlement in North
    Carolina.
    a. TRUE
    b. FALSE

9. North and South Carolina were governed together until the
    year 1729.
    a. TRUE
    b. FALSE

10. There was considerable unrest in the colony between Quakers
    and Anglicans.
    a. TRUE
    b. FALSE

11. The Tuscarora War was fought primarily because the Indians were upset at the settlers taking their lands.
    a. TRUE
    b. FALSE

12. North Carolina was under Proprietary rule from 1663-1723.
    a. TRUE
    b. FALSE

13. North Carolina's population increase from 30,000 in 1730 to 265,000 in 1775.
    a. TRUE
    b. FALSE

14. North and South Carolina were separated in 1719.
    a. TRUE
    b. FALSE

15. In 1769, the Assembly of North Carolina denied the right of Parliament to tax the colonists without their consent.
    a. TRUE
    b. FALSE

CHAPTER 12 SUMMARY

North Carolina

1. Early explorations of the Carolina coast by France and Spain in the 1520's.

2. The first English Charter was granted to Sir Robert Heath in 1629 but it was never used.

3. The first attempted settlement was by Roger Green who led a group of persecuted Virginia Presbyterians to a site near present-day Edenton, North Carolina. Historians are uncertain of the settlement duration.

4. In 1663 King Charles II approved a Grant to eight "Lord Proprietors" to colonize the Carolina territory. The Proprietors controlled the colony until 1729.

5. Considerable domestic unrest between 1677 and the 1760's;

    • CULPEPPER REBELLION • 1677 - 1679 • resist enforcement of the Navigation Acts

    • CARY REBELLION • 1711 • power struggle between Quakers and Anglicans.

    • TUSCARORA WAR • 1711 - 1715 Indian War

    • REGULATOR MOVEMENT • 1760+ • protest against back-country government corruption.

6. During the period from 1692-1712 the colonies of North and South Carolina existed as a single governmental unit. In 1712 it was formally divided into North and South Carolina.

7. The Carolina's became Royal Colonies in 1729. During the Royal period from 1729-1763 the Crown and Parliament exercised minimal interference in governing the colony. There was significant economic and population growth during this period, adding 18 new counties, reflecting westward expansion. All political functions were under control of the Crown until 1775.

8. In 1769 the North Carolina Assembly denies the right of Parliament to tax the colonists without their consent.

9. North Carolina is admitted as the 12th State on 11/21/1789.

10. There is significant population growth from 30,000 in 1730 to 265,000 in 1775.

12a

Early Carolina, 1565-1733
Robert Hall, Harriet Smither, and Clarence Ousley, A History of the United States (Dallas, TX: The Southern Publishing Company, 1920)
Downloaded from *Maps ETC*, on the web at http://etc.usf.edu/maps   [map #05275]

12b

NORTH CAROLINA GOVERNORS		
DATES		**NAME AND TITLE**
GOVERNORS OF ALBEMARLE COUNTY UNDER THE LORDS PROPRIETORS		
1663	1667	WILLIAM DRUMMOND
1667	1669	SAMUEL STEPHENS
1670	1673	PETER CARTERET
1673	1676	JOHN JENKINS *(c)*
1676	1678	THOMAS EASTCHURCH
1678		SETH SOTHEL
1679	1681	JOHN JENKINS *(c)*
1682	1689	SETH SOTHEL
GOVERNORS OF CAROLINA NORTH & EAST OF CAPE FEAR		
1689	1691	DEPUTY GOV PHILIP LUDWELL
1691	1694	DEPUTY GOV THOMAS JARVIS
1694	1699	DEPUTY GOV THOMAS HARVEY
1699	1704	HENDERSON WALKER *(c)*
1704	1705	DEPUTY GOV ROBERT DANIEL
1705	1706	DEPUTY GOV THOMAS CARY
1706	1708	WILLIAM GLOVER *(c)*
1708	1710	THOMAS CARY *(c)*
1710	1712	EDWARD HYDE
GOVERNORS OF NORTH CAROLINA UNDER LORDS PROPRIETORS		
1712	1714	THOMAS POLLOCK *(c)*
1714	1722	CHARLES EDEN
1722	1724	WILLIAM REED *(c)*
1724	1725	GEORGE BURRINGTON
1725	1729	RICHARD EVERARD

		ROYAL GOVERNORS
1729	1731	RICHARD EVERARD
1731	1734	GEORGE BURRINGTON
1734	1752	GABRIEL JOHNSTON
1752	1753	NATHANIEL RICE *(c)*
1753	1754	MATTHEW ROWAN *(c)*
1754	1765	ARTHUR DOBBS
1765	1771	WILLIAM TRYON
1771	1775	JOSIAH MARTIN

		PRESIDENTS OF THE COUNCIL UNDER REVOLUTIONARY GOVERNMENT
1775	1776	CORNELIUS HARNETT

		STATE GOVERNORS
1776	1780	RICHARD CASWELL
1780	1781	ABNER NASH
1781	1782	THOMAS BURKE
1782	1784	ALEXANDER MARTIN
1784	1787	RICHARD CASWELL
1787	1789	SAMUEL JOHNSTON

(a)	*1st Gov of the colony established on the Ashley River*
(b)	*Chosen by the Council*
(c)	*President of the Council*

Chapter 13

New York

A.   DUTCH ORIGINS

In the late 16th century, the Dutch contested Spanish control of European trade and entered a period of economic expansion. Amsterdam was the world financial center and the Dutch fleet considered as the greatest in the world.

Henry Hudson, an Englishman sailing for the Dutch, made four voyages from 1607-1611 in his ship, "Half-Moon", to explore the New York region and the river named after him. Due to his voyages the Dutch were the first to settle the area even though it was limited to the Hudson river valley. They created New Netherland and New Amsterdam (New York) and multiple trading posts, such as Fort Orange (Albany), north along the Hudson river.

In 1609, two years after Jamestown was settled, the Dutch East India Company (DEIC) hired Hudson to discover the rumored Northwest passage which would allow a ship to cross the entirety of the North American continent and, from there, Asia. After exploring for awhile he returned to Europe and claimed the entire Hudson river valley for the Dutch. On his last voyage, he disappeared and was last seen in the area of James Bay on 6/22/1611.

After a few unsuccessful colonization efforts, the Dutch Parliament chartered the "Dutch West India Company" (DWIC), a national joint-stock company which would organize and oversee all Dutch ventures in the New World. ***They sponsored 30 families who arrived in North***

America in 1624 and established a settlement on present-day Manhattan Island. Just like the Jamestown settlers, they didn't take much interest in agriculture and focused more on the lucrative fur-trade. In 1626, Director General Peter Minuit arrived in Manhattan with the task assigned by the DWIC to administer the struggling colony. Minuit purchased Manhattan Island from the Indians for 60 "guilders" (about $24) and formally established New Amsterdam plus consolidated the fort at Fort Orange (Albany). Historians claim the Indians did not own the island of Manhattan to sell it to the Dutch.

The original stockade was built at today's "Wall Street". The villages of "Haarlem & Breukelen" would become New York City boroughs and early Dutch towns called "bouweries" provided the name for a section of the city to be known as "the Bowery".

To support Dutch control of the area, the DWIC created the "patroon system" (landowner) which granted large tracts of land and ownership rights to individuals who could finance the settlement of 50 adults. Land ownership was denied to common workers who then became tenant farmers. The result of this system was the concentration of large blocks of land and political power in the hands of the few. The patroon system lived on in New York until the early 19th century and ***it derived from the 1629 "Charter of Freedoms and Exemptions" which stated that any company member who in four years transported 50 families to American at their own expense would be entitled to an extensive tract of land to do with as he pleased.***

K. Van Rensselaer, a wealthy jeweler and company stockholder, believed the colony could become prosperous thru agriculture and serve as a supply and repair station for ships going to and from the West Indies. Company members who profited from re-fittting these ships in Holland opposed the plan but eventually it proved more economic to approve the plan. The benefit of their plan shifted the burden of colonization from the company stockholders to individuals.

The colony grew slowly because settlers were moving north along the Hudson river so that by 1633 there were multiple trading posts beyond New Amsterdam scattered along the Connecticut, Hudson, and Delaware rivers all lying in disputed territories. Also, Holland was a wealthy country where many Dutch didn't feel a need to emigrate to risk everything in the New World. But, even the slow growth produced friction with the English settlers and the Indians. The Dutch tried to establish a settlement in the Connecticut river valley but ran into opposition from the English settlers so they recalled the expedition and left the area.

In the area near Fort Orange their fur-trading success depended on friendly relations with the Iroquois Confederacy. But, in other areas during the 1630's and 1640's, the Dutch were generally hostile to the Indians and made the situation worse by expanding into Indian hunting grounds. Up to this time, the Indians and Dutch were friendly.

B.   PETER STUYVESANT

The combination of slow colonial growth, Indian problems, and the company facing bankruptcy caused the Company directors to seek someone else to provide leadership and improve the situation. In 1647, they selected Peter Stuyvesant who had previously managed company affairs in Curacao. The task was viewed as difficult because of a diversified population with Puritans on Long Island and infiltrating Swedes along the Delaware river. The 400 people in New Amsterdam spoke 18 different languages and practiced multiple religions, all of which led to multiple political factions and many disputes.

He decided to focus attention on the small settlements along the Hudson river between Fort Orange and New Amsterdam (New York). By 1652, about 60-70 settlers had moved south to present-day Kingston, which they named "Wiltwyck". They farmed the area with the Esopus Indians who were the original settlers in the area. Eventually there was conflict between them. In 1657, Stuyvesant sent troops into the area to defeat the Indians and protect the citizens by building a fort and houses within it, where they lived until 1664 when the English captured the area from the Dutch.

Wiltwyck grew to become the 2nd largest settlement north of New Amsterdam. It became profitable and grew to 1,500 citizens with a very diverse population with only 50% being of Dutch origin. The population grew from 2,000 in 1655 to almost 9,000 in 1664. Indian problems subsided and stable families were slowly replacing single adventurers who were interested only in quick profits. New Netherland produced great wealth for the Dutch and foreign nations began to envy the riches flowing from the Hudson river valley.

By 1649 the citizens had complained to the company about the lack of self-government, lack of schools, and the failure of trade. The first Anglo-Dutch War of 1652 would also contribute to the problems in the colony. In 1653 a convention was called to decide on a course of action if they were attacked. The Puritans from Long Island took over the meeting and demanded self-government. Stuyvesant ignored their requests because the Dutch didn't believe in self-government of their overseas colonies.

In 1654, Lutheran settlers asked the colonial government for permission to hire their own Ministers. Stuyvesant rejected their request saying that his oath forbade any form of worship except that of the established Dutch Reformed Church. The company eventually agreed and a few years later allowed slightly more freedom of worship.

In 1655 Governor Stuyvesant attacked Swedish outposts along the Delaware river at Wilmington, Delaware, named "Christina" for their Queen. The Swedish outposts were cutting into the Dutch fur-trade which caused Stuyvesant to attack.

By the time of the 2nd Anglo-Dutch War in 1664, New Netherlands had less than 8,000 settlers. Stuyvesant's 17 year rule was not prosperous or peaceful. Future events would prove how unpopular he was, such as when the British arrived to take New Netherland from the Dutch and the local citizens failed to support a Stuyvesant resistance to the English.

C. NEW NETHERLAND BECOMES ENGLISH

The Dutch lost New Netherland to the English during the 2nd Anglo-Dutch War in 1664 only a few years after the establishment of Wiltwyck. There had been conflict between them along the West Coast of Africa over rights to slavery, ivory, and gold. There was also a conflict for Naval superiority between the 2 nations and by 1664 both were preparing for another war. ***King Charles II granted his brother, James, the Duke of York, vast lands which included all of New Netherland. James then sent a fleet to New Amsterdam to force the surrender of Peter Stuyvesant in September, 1664, thus ending the Dutch direct involvement in America*** although there remained significant symbols of Dutch influence throughout the New York territory.

Aware that he had more land to govern than he expected, James gave away some of those lands. ***To his friends, Lord John Berkeley and Sir George Carteret, he ceded lands between the Hudson and Delaware rivers and called it "Nova Caesaria", for present-day New Jersey. He then gave to William Penn the "3 Lower Counties" as Delaware was called at the time.***

New Amsterdam was renamed New York in honor of James, Duke of York. The English justified their claim to the area based not on Hudson's travels, as an Englishman sailing for the Dutch, but on the initial discovery of the continent by Cabot in 1497 probably around the Labrador region. ***At the same time, the Swedes along the Delaware river and Bay also surrendered to the English. Colonel Nichols, who commanded the attacking force, assumed the government for 3 years. His administration was moderate but he did not allow a representative government and exercised both the legislative and executive power by himself.***

When Nichols became Governor, he made minimal changes in the government except to adopt English titles for the public officers. To understand this, we should know that ***the charter for New York, true to the Stuart philosophy of government, made the Duke of York absolute master and made no provision for the people to take any part in their own government. He did, however, frame a set of laws known as "Duke's Laws",_which were intended only for the English settlers but later_extended to all of the citizens of the colony.***

These laws (1665) defined 11 capital crimes, provided for trial by jury, religious toleration, and every town was required to build a church and provide for its support. The Long Island Puritans opposed the laws because they were imposed on them from above and included taxation without their consent.

Nichols was replaced by Governor Lovelace in 1667 who followed a similar government, allowing no representation. During his administration in 1672, war was declared by England, again, against Holland who had sent a fleet to attempt to recapture the colony. Lovelace was absent at the time, 8/9/1672, and the city surrendered to the Dutch. Peace was restored in February, 1673, and by November the area was restored again to England as were New Jersey and Delaware which had temporarily submitted to Dutch rule.

To remove all controversy respecting his title to the lands granted him while they were in possession of the Dutch, the Duke of York took out a new patent, and appointed Sir Edmund Andros as Governor in October, 1674. His administration was arbitrary and severe, also opposing a form of representative government.

There was no popular government called for in this plan which did not become permanent. The English settlers still desired some form of representation until 1681. The people were close to open rebellion unless their demands for an assembly were granted. So, Andros promised an Assembly in 1682 and the first one was elected in 1683 while Thomas Dongan was Governor.

In 1683, Colonel Thomas Dongan, a Catholic, was appointed Governor to replace Andros. His instructions were to call an Assembly to consist of a Council of 10 plus 18 Representatives, elected by the freeholders. *The Assembly then adopted the "Charter of Liberties" on 10/30/1683 which declared that representatives of the people were to coordinate with the Governor and Council and that no taxes could be levied without their consent. It also provided that all laws were to be subject to the Duke of York's approval.*

But, when the Duke was crowned as *King James II he changed his position and refused to confirm the privileges which had been promised to them while he was the Duke. He permitted no Assembly to convene, prohibited printing presses, and the most important political offices were given to Catholics. New York now became a Royal colony and the new King refused to approve the Charter of Liberties, abolished the New York Assembly, and in 1687 sent Edmund Andros to govern the colony as part of the new "Dominion of New England".* He then replaced Dongan with Andros. With a staff of seven, Andros was expected to govern nine colonies as a conquered province but when William and Mary replaced King James II, Andros was replaced.

Such was the situation in New York in 1689 when news of accession of William and Mary to the throne arrived in New York. The good news caused the arrest and imprisonment of Andros in Boston. The people of New York also rebelled against Andros. Jacob Leisler and 49 others seized the fort at New York city and held it for William and Mary. They were opposed by Lt. Governor Francis Nicholson who was viewed as trying to hold the colony for France and the hated-Catholics.

By March, 1691, after considerable fighting between the forces of Leisler and Nicholson, the Crown sent Colonel Sloughter to take command of the situation. *He became Governor, convened an Assembly which formed a Constitution which confirmed trials by jury, freedom from taxation without consent of the Assembly, and toleration to all Christians except Catholics.*

An event of great significance did occur in New York in 1735, known as the *"Zenger Case"*. Governor Cosby had entered a suit before the Supreme Court of New York to obtain a sum of money and had lost. He then removed the judge which offended the public. Peter Zenger was the publisher of a newspaper, "The New York Weekly Journal", who attacked the Governor through his columns, thus enraging the Governor who ordered the paper burned and the editor arrested for libel.

At the trial, Zenger was defended by Alexander Hamilton, of later fame. The justice of the cause and the eloquence of Hamilton influenced the jury and produced a victory for the editor, Zenger. This *was the first important victory for the liberty of the press in America.*

The colony of New York grew steadily to the time of the American Revolution. By 1750, the population was probably 80,000 and this number was more than doubled by the opening years of the Revolution. New York city had grown to a population of 12,000 in 1750. The city became the political, social, and business center of the province.

For the next 50 years the Governors of New York were more attached to the interests of the Crown and their own self-survival than to pursue policies for the welfare of their colony. As a result, there were frequent conflicts between them and their colonial assemblies which disturbed the general peace and retarded the prosperity of the colony.

D. KEY DATES AND SIGNIFICANT EVENTS

1607 – 1611	Four voyages of Henry Hudson sailing for the Dutch explores the New York region and Hudson river valley.
1621	Dutch West India Company established, focused primarily on the fur trade
1624	West India Company sponsors 30 families to settle on Manhattan Island (New Amsterdam). Focus on fur trade.
1626	New Amsterdam settled at mouth of Hudson River
1626	Peter Minuit purchases Manhattan from the Indians for equivalent $24 and formally establishes New Amsterdam.
1629	Dutch create "Patroon system" resulting from the "Charter of Freedoms and Exemptions"
1633	Multiple trading posts beyond New Amsterdam along 3 rivers, Connecticut, Hudson, and Delaware.
1647	Peter Stuyvesant to manage New Amsterdam colony with 400 settlers speaking 18 different languages and practicing multiple religions.
1652	1st Anglo-Dutch War
1653	New York City incorporated as New Amsterdam
1653	Colony calls Convention to decide course of action if attacked by the English
1654	Lutheran settlers ask permission to hire their own Ministers. Stuyvesant refuses. Only Dutch Reformed Church permitted.

	1655	Governor Stuyvesant attacks Swedish outposts along Delaware river at Wilmington, Delaware, named "Christina" for the Swedish Queen.
	1657	Stuyvesant sends soldiers to protect settlers from Indians by building a Fort.
	1664	2nd Anglo-Dutch War
Sep	1664	England captures New Netherland from the Dutch, only has 8,000 settlers. Stuyvesant rule not popular or successful. New Amsterdam renamed New York.
3/1	1665	"Duke's Laws" defined 11 capital crimes and provided for trial by jury and religious toleration
8/1	1673	3rd Anglo-Dutch War. Dutch temporarily recapture New York but it and New Jersey are returned to England per the Westminster Treaty of 1674.
10/30	1683	1st New York Assembly adopts "Charter of Liberties" which creates Representative Government and no taxes without consent. Laws subject to Duke of York approval. But, when Duke of York becomes King James II he refuses to confirm. New York becomes Royal colony. Assembly abolished. Edmund Andros appointed as Governor of new "Dominion of New England".
	1689	William & Mary assume English throne. Andros arrested and imprisoned. Jacob Leisler and supporters seize fort at New York city and hold it for William & Mary.
March	1691	Crown sends Colonel Sloughter to become Governor, convene Assembly, form a Constitution confirming trials by jury, freedom from taxation without consent, ***toleration of all Christian denominations except Catholicism.***
	1735	Zenger Case establishes freedom of the press. Zenger defended by Alexander Hamilton
	1750	New York colony population 80,000 in 1750. New York city population 12,000 in 1750.

345

E.   ATTACHMENTS;

Attachment 13a	Map of the New Sweden, New Netherland, and Connecticut settlements in 1623
Attachment 13b	Map of New Sweden during the years of 1638–1655
Attachment 13c	Map of the lower Hudson river valley settlements in 1779
Attachment 13d	Map of the Hudson river valley settlements in 1780
Attachment 13e	List of New York Governors

F.   REVIEW QUESTIONS

(Multiple Choice)

1. Which country was the world financial leader in the late 16th
    century?
    a. England
    b. France
    c. Holland
    d. Spain

2. Which commercial company hired Henry Hudson to explore
    the New York region?
    a. British Tea Company
    b. French Protectorate
    c. Dutch East India Company
    d. British West Indian Company

3. In which year did the first Dutch settlers locate in present-day
    New York city?
    a. 1609
    b. 1624
    c. 1626
    d. 1629

4. Fort Orange was the Dutch name for which present-day city?
    a. Buffalo
    b. New York
    c. Kingston
    d. Albany

5. In which year did Peter Stuyvesant become the leader of the New York colony?
   a. 1633
   b. 1647
   c. 1657
   d. 1664

6. Wiltwyck was the Dutch name for which present-day New York city?
   a. Kingston
   b. Albany
   c. New York
   d. Long Island

7. How many Anglo-Dutch Wars were fought in the colonial New York area?
   a. 1
   b. 2
   c. 3
   d. 4

8. In which year did England capture New Netherlands?
   a. 1647
   b. 1664
   c. 1665
   d. 1683

(TRUE OR FALSE)

9. In the late 16th century the Dutch contested England for control of European trade.
   a. TRUE
   b. FALSE

10. The "Patroon System" was used by the English to distribute land to the nobility.
    a. TRUE
    b. FALSE

11. The Connecticut, Hudson, and Delaware rivers were important to the development of Dutch settlements in the New York region.
    a. TRUE
    b. FALSE

12. New Netherland (New York) became English in 1663.
    a. TRUE
    b. FALSE

13. The Dutch recaptured New York from the English in 1672.
    a. TRUE
    b. FALSE

14. The Peter Zenger case dealt with the issue of religious freedom.
    a. TRUE
    b. FALSE

CHAPTER 13 SUMMARY

New York Colony

1. The Dutch are the first explorers and settlers of the New York region.

2. Henry Hudson, an Englishman sailing for the Dutch, explores the New York region and Hudson River valley during the years 1607-1611. He is seeking the northwest passage to Asia/India.

3. The Dutch West India Company (DWIC) is created to manage Dutch explorations of the New World. They sponsor the first group of 30 settlers in 1624 who occupy Manhattan Island.

4. In 1626, Peter Minuit, the new Governor, buys Manhattan Island from the Indians, who didn't own it, for $24 (equivalent). He formally establishes New Amsterdam (New York).

5. By 1633 there are multiple trading posts along the Connecticut, Hudson, and Delaware rivers..

6. Peter Stuyvesant is appointed to manage the colony in 1647.

7. Wiltwyck (Kingston) is settled in 1652 and becomes the 2nd largest settlement north of New Amsterdam

8. 3 ANGLO-DUTCH WARS:

   • 1652

   • 1664 England captures New Amsterdam/New Netherland from the Dutch.

- 1672-1673 Dutch recapture colony but return to England per the Treaty of Westminster.

9. In 1683 there is a new Governor, Thomas Dongan. The Assembly adopts a "Charter of Liberties". It is not approved by the Duke of York when he becomes King James II. He makes New York a Royal Colony, dissolves the Assembly, and sends Edmund Andros to serve as Governor as part of the "Dominion of New England". Andros is eventually replaced with the accession of William & Mary to the English Throne in 1689.

10. A colony-wide rebellion is settled in March, 1691, with a new Governor, Assembly, and Constitution which provides for trials by jury, freedom from taxation except by consent, and ***toleration for all Christian denominations except Roman Catholicism.***

13a

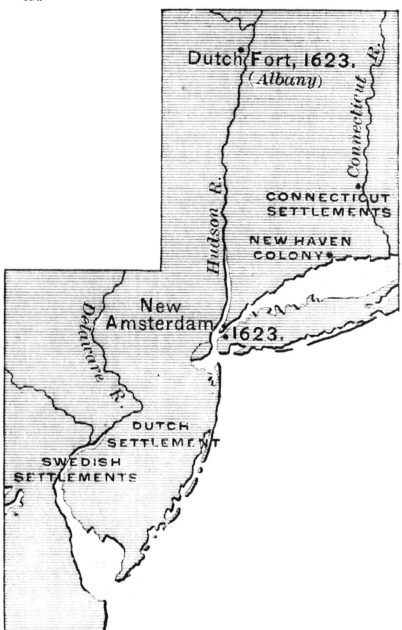

New Sweden
Edward Eggleston, The Household History of the United States and Its People
(New York, NY: D. Appleton and Company, 1898)
Downloaded from *Maps ETC*, on the web at http://etc.usf.edu/maps   [map #01189]

13b

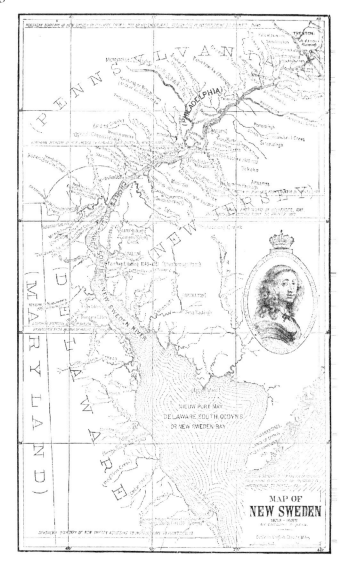

Map of New Sweden, 1638-1655

13c

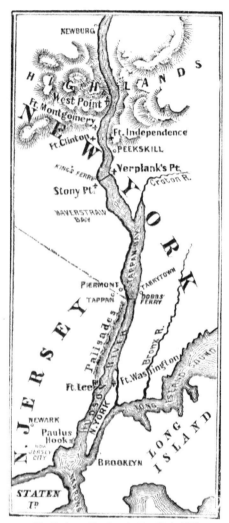

The Hudson - Newburg to New York, 1779

13d

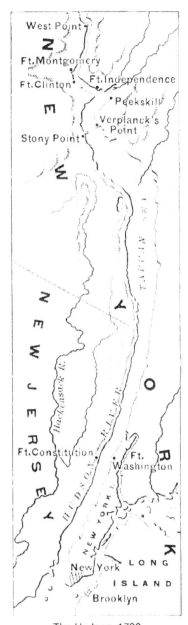

The Hudson, 1780
Edward Eggleston, The Household History of the United States and Its People
(New York, NY: D. Appleton and Company, 1898)
Downloaded from *Maps ETC*, on the web at http://etc.usf.edu/maps   [map #01225]

13e

NEW YORK GOVERNORS		
DATES		NAME AND TITLE
CHIEF MAGISTRATES OF NEW NETHERLANDS		
1623	X	ADRIAEN JORIS
1624	1625	CORNELIUS JACOBSEN MAY
1625	1626	WILLEM VERHULST
1626	1632	PETER MINUIT
1632	1633	THE COUNCIL
1633	1638	WOUTER VAN TWILLER
1638	1647	WILLEM KIEFT
1647	1664	PETER STUYVESANT
CAPTURED BY ENGLAND 1664		
1664	1667	RICHARD NICOLLS
1667	1673	FRANCIS LOVELACE
RECAPTURED BY THE DUTCH 1673		
1673		ANTHONY COLVE

13e (2nd part)

		RECAPTURED BY THE ENGLISH 1674
1674	1682	EDMUND ANDROS
1682	1687	THOMAS DONGAN
1687	1688	SIR EDMUND ANDROS
1688	1689	LT GOV FRANCIS NICHOLSON
1689	1691	JACOB LEISLER
1691		HENRY SLOUGHTER
1691	1692	ACTING GOV RICHARD INGOLDESBY
1692	1698	BENJAMIN FLETCHER
1698	1699	RICHARD COOTE, EARL OF BELLOMONT
1699	1700	LT GOV JOHN NANFAN
1700	1701	RICHARD COOTE, EARL OF BELLOMONT
1701	1702	LT GOV JOHN NANFAN
1702	1708	EDWARD HYDE, VISCOUNT CORNBURY
1708	1709	JOHN LOVELACE, BARON LOVELACE OF HURLEY
1709	1710	*PERIOD OF TRANSITION AWAITING ROYAL GOVERNOR*
1710	1719	ROBERT HUNTER
1719	1720	PETER SCHUYLER *(a)*
1720	1728	WILLIAM BURNET
1728	1731	JOHN MONTGOMERIE
1731	1732	RIP VAN DAM *(a)*
1732	1736	WILLIAM COSBY
1736	1743	LT GOV GEORGE CLARKE
1743	1753	GEORGE CLINTON
1753	1755	LT GOV JAMES DE LANCEY
1755	1757	SIR CHARLES HARDY
1757	1760	LT GOV JAMES DE LANCEY
1760	1761	LT GOV CADWALLADER COLDEN

13e (3rd part)

1761		ROBERT MONCKTON
1761	1762	LT GOV CADWALLADER COLDEN
1762	1763	ROBERT MONCKTON
1763	1765	LT GOV CADWALLADER COLDEN
1765	1769	SIR HENRY MOORE
1769	1770	LT GOV CADWALLADER COLDEN
1770	1771	JOHN MURRAY, EARL OF DUNMORE
1771	1774	WILLIAM TRYON
1774	1775	LT GOV CADWALLADER COLDEN
1775		WILLIAM TRYON
1776	1795	GEORGE CLINTON

(a)President of the Council

Chapter 14

New Jersey

A.   BACKGROUND

The earliest European settlement efforts of New Jersey were primarily a contest between the Dutch and Swedes prior to 1664 at which time England became involved by its capture of New Netherland from the Dutch..

1. **DUTCH EFFORTS**

   Early New Jersey was an extension of the Dutch influence from New Netherland. The Dutch West India Company (DWIC) used "patroonships", as we learned from our study of the New York colony, to encourage settlement which eventually created many small colonies at the sites of present-day Hoboken, Jersey City, and Gloucester City. The Swedes and Finn's of New Sweden, who were predominant in the Delaware river valley after 1638, were annexed by the New Netherland colony in 1655 when the Dutch evicted the Swedes.

   The first Dutch settlement was probably in 1620 at Bergen, a village just a few miles west of New York City. *In 1623, Fort Nassau just 5 miles from present-day Camden, was built but then quickly deserted. Pavonia, present-day Jersey City, was founded in 1630 but it was the settlement of Elizabethtown in 1664 which is considered the first permanent white settlement in New Jersey and also marks the beginning of the colonization era in New Jersey.*

2. **SWEDISH EFFORTS**

   Sweden had experienced significant prosperity under King Gustavus II at about the same time as the Dutch began taking an interest in the New World. *Shortly after the Dutch founded Pavonia, the Swedes settled New Sweden near present-day Salem, New Jersey, in an attempt to dispute Dutch control of the Delaware river valley and the fur-trade. The Dutch, led by Peter Stuyvesant, captured New Jersey in 1655 ending Sweden's claim to New Jersey.*

3. **ENGLISH EFFORTS**

   In 1664, King Charles II issued the "Grant of New Netherland" to the Duke of York, his brother James, and sent a military force to capture New Netherland from the Dutch, led by Colonel Richard Nicolls who was then named the first Governor of the new territory now named "New York".

   Nicolls granted patents to emigrants from Long Island and New England who settled at Elizabethtown. However, at the same time, *the Duke of York gave much of the same territory to two of his supporters, Lord John Berkeley and Sir George Carteret.* They offered, as inducements, land ownership plus full religious toleration.

   Settlements from Nicoll's grants began at Newark, Middleton, and Shrewsbury. The Duke's tract of land was named "New Jersey" after Carteret. The new Proprietors formed a Constitution and Philip Carteret, the cousin of Sir George, was sent from England as Governor. Emigrants came to the area which he named Elizabethtown, after the wife of Sir George. In spite of some unrest, by 5/26/1668, the first Legislative Assembly met at Elizabethtown and was largely composed of New England Puritans.

   Phillip Carteret quickly angered many of the settlers with the following demands in 1670;

   a. 1/7 of all land within any settlement was to be reserved for the Proprietors

   b. The payment of "quit-rents" (fixed rent payable to the Proprietors)

c. To take control of town affairs and meetings

d. The people had one year to get their land patented by the Governor or it would be confiscated and sold by the Proprietors

There was also anger over the origin of land-titles which had been gained from multiple sources, such as the Indians, Dutch landowners, Nicolls, and the new Proprietors. Open insurrection was imminent but the coming of the second son of Sir George Carteret, James, as the new Governor, made things worse. He was dishonest, greedy, and positioned himself as the leader of the dissidents who were opposing his cousin, Philip Carteret, the current Governor. James and his supporters called an Assembly at Elizabethtown in the spring of 1672 and formally deposed Philip Carteret and elected James as their Governor. Philip sailed for England to gather support and while he was away the settlers began to see James as a troublesome incompetent and began to support Philip's deputy, Captain Berry in May, 1673. Philip returned as Governor in 1674 and again won the support of the people.

In 1674, Berkeley sold his share to two Quakers, John Fenwick and Edward Byllinge. They immediately argued over their holdings and referred the matter to William Penn for resolution, which turned out to be acceptable to both.

B. NEW JERSEY PROVINCE DIVIDED INTO EAST JERSEY AND WEST JERSEY

On 7/1/1676, the "Quintipartite Deed" was signed by Carteret on one side with Penn and his two friends on the other side. The agreement divided the Province into East and West Jersey, per Attachment 14a;

- East Jersey became the property of Sir George Carteret

- West Jersey became the property of Penn and his Quaker friends and was divided into 100 parts, with 10 parts set aside for Fenwick to make the first settlement at Salem, on the Delaware river.

Meanwhile, a large number of Quakers from England arrived and settled near the Raritan river. Edmund Andros, acting under the authority of Richard Nicolls, required the settlers to acknowledge his authority as the representative of the Duke of York, which they refused because the territory had passed out of his possession. The matter was referred to an arbitrator who sided with the colonists.

The first popular assembly in west Jersey met at Salem on 11/3/1681 and adopted a code of laws for their government. Meanwhile, Carteret had died in late 1679 so William Penn and some of his supporters in 1682 bought East Jersey from the Carteret heirs and appointed Robert Barclay as Governor, a young Scotch Quaker. Quakers from England, Scotland, and Long Island flowed into East Jersey but they had to endure the tyranny of Andros until King James II was driven from his Throne.

For several years there was no official government, which caused many problems. The situation was further complicated by New Jersey's twin capitals, Perth Amboy in the East and Burlington in the West.

The Quaker leadership was no more popular than the original Proprietors, Carteret and Berkeley. Significant unrest led to rioting which led to the eventual surrender of the Quaker charters to Queen Anne in 1702 making the province a Royal colony. Sir Edward Hyde, Lord Cornbury, Governor of New York, ruled the Province as a dependency of New York until 1738 when it became an independent colony. He served both colonies until public protests resulted in the appointment of a separate official for New Jersey.

Although the most important political issue had been resolved, the 1740's were years of great unrest with the religious, economic, and ethnic issues combining with new immigration of the Dutch, Germans, Scots-Irish, Welsh, Swedes, and French adding to produce more friction.

In 1738 New Jersey became an Independent Royal colony with Lewis Morris as the first Governor of the free colony. William Franklin, son of Ben, was the last of the Royal Governors of New Jersey. *A conditional State Constitution was adopted in the Provincial Congress at Burlington on 7/2/1776 and a State Government was created with William Livingston as Governor.*

After the new Federal Constitution was ratified in December, 1787, the New Jersey State Capital was established at Trenton in 1790.

C.   EARLY INDIAN CONTACTS

The earliest settlers to New Jersey met a peaceful tribe of Indians known as the "Lenni-Lenape Tribe". They were part of the Algonquin nation and linguistic group, often referred to as the "Delaware Indians". The Indian name for New Jersey was "Scheyichbi" which meant "Long-Land Water". There were 3 branches;

- Minsi   Northern Tribe

- Unami   Central Tribe

- Unitachtigo   Southern Tribe

D. KEY DATES AND SIGNIFICANT EVENTS

	1497	John Cabot, sailing for England, explored the northeast coast
	1524	Giovanni Verrazano, sailing for France, possibly explored the New Jersey shore
	1609	Henry Hudson, sailing for the Dutch, explored the New York/New Jersey area and the Hudson River.
	1620	First Dutch settlement at Bergen
	1623	Captain Cornelius Mey built Fort Nassau near Gloucester City.
	1630	Michael Pauw receives first Dutch land-grant on west bank of Hudson river, present-day Jersey City, which they name "Pavonia".
	1638	New Sweden settled by Peter Minuit who builds Fort Christina (Wilmington, Delaware) along the Delaware river.
	1643	Colonel Johan Printz became Governor of New Sweden to 1653
	1643	Fort Elfsborg (Sussex County) was constructed by settlers of New Sweden
2/25	1643	Pavonia Massacre as part of William Kieft's War
	1647	Peter Stuyvesant became Director General of New Netherland
	1652	1st Anglo-Dutch War
	1655	Dutch, led by Peter Stuyvesant, force Swedes to give up their Forts in south Jersey
	1655	Second destruction of Pavonia by Indians
3/12	1664	King Charles II issues "Grant of New Netherland" to brother James, Duke of York. Land includes present-day New York and New Jersey.
6/23	1664	Duke of York grants most of the same lands to friends Lord John Berkeley and Sir George Carteret.

8/18	1664	England capture New Netherland from Dutch. Colonel Richard Nicolls named Governor of the Duke of York's territories. New Amsterdam renamed New York
12/1	1664	Governor Nicolls grants lands for Elizabethtown.
4/8	1665	Governor Nicolls grants lands for Middletown and Shrewsbury settlements which probably marks the date of the colonization period in New Jersey. Duplicate grants from Duke of York and Nicolls leads to land-grant confusion and unrest.
Aug	1665	The Proprietors introduce a Constitution and Philip Carteret sent as Governor
7/11	1666	Newark tract of land purchased by Robert Treat; settlers had landed 5/17/1666.
5/26	1668	First Assembly meeting held at Elizabethtown
8/1	1673	Dutch recapture New Netherland
2/9	1674	Westminster Treaty returns Dutch-held New York and New Jersey to England
3/18	1674	Edward Byllinge and John Fenwick, Quakers, purchase West Jersey from Lord Berkeley
7/1	1674	Edmund Andros commissioned Governor of New York by Duke of York, James
Nov	1675	John Fenwick establishes Quaker colony at Salem in West Jersey
7/1	1676	Quintipartite Deed divides colony into East and West Jersey
3/3	1677	West Jersey's "Concessions and Agreements" drafted by Edward Byllinge sets up government and fundamental laws of the colony.
Jan	1680	Sir George Carteret dies
Nov	1680	Governor Andros relieved of his duties governing East and West Jersey

11/3	1681	First popular Assembly in West Jersey meets at Salem
3/14	1682	Gov Philip Carteret dies and his estate is sold to 24 Proprietors including William Penn
Sep	1682	Scottish Quaker elected by Proprietors as Governor of East Jersey
	1686	Perth Amboy becomes capital of East Jersey
Sep	1687	Daniel Coxe assumes Governorship of West Jersey
	1688 – 1689	New Jersey and New York temporarily annexed to the Dominion of New England under Governor Andros in Boston
4/15	1702	East and West Jersey Proprietorships end. Queen Anne takes control making New Jersey a Royal colony; ruled by Governor of New York, Lord Cornbury.
	1738	New Jersey becomes separate Royal colony from New York. Lewis Morris first Royal Governor
	1763	William Franklin, son of Benjamin, is New Jersey's last Royal Governor
	1789	New Jersey becomes the first State to ratify the Bill of Rights
11/25	1790	Trenton selected as State Capital

(Attachment 14b List of New Jersey and New York Governors.)

E . REVIEW QUESTIONS

(Multiple Choice)

1. Which nation did not attempt to explore and/or settle New
   Jersey?
   a. England
   b. France
   c. Spain
   d. Holland

2. Which was the first permanent white settlement in New
   Jersey?
   a. Bergen
   b. Fort Nassau
   c. Pavonia
   d. Elizabethtown

3. The Swedes were forced out of New Jersey by which
   country?
   a. England
   b. Holland
   c. France
   d. All of the above

4. Which English King made the first charter/grant for
   settlement?
   a. Charles I
   b. James II
   c. Charles II
   d.. William & Mary

5. In what year did the British capture New Netherlands from the Dutch?
   a. 1638
   b. 1664
   c. 1676
   d. 1682

6. Who was the first English Governor of the new English territory after capture from the Dutch?
   a. Edmund Andros
   b. Richard Nicolls
   c. Lord Cornbury
   d. None of the above

7. The Dutch settlement of Pavonia is known by which name today?
   a. Jersey City
   b. Newark
   c. Camden
   d. Salem

8. In what year did the New Jersey province officially separate into East and West Jersey?
   a. 1664
   b. 1676
   c. 1680
   d. None of the above

9. In what town did the first popular Assembly meet in West Jersey?

    a. Salem

    b. Nassau

    c. Newark

    d. Jersey City

10. Which town was the capital of East Jersey?

    a. Perth Amboy

    b. Burlington

    c. Jersey City

    d. Newark

(True or False)

11. 1738 was the year that New Jersey became an independent colony from New York.

    a. TRUE

    b. FALSE

12. The Proprietors gave up their Charters to King Charles II.

    a. TRUE

    b. FALSE

13. Richard Nicolls and the Duke of York issued duplicate charters/ land grants to basically the same territory.

    a. TRUE

    b. FALSE

14. The Dutch gave up their interest in New Jersey in 1655.

    a. TRUE

    b. FALSE

15. The settlement of Elizabethtown was named after the wife of Philip Carteret.
    a. TRUE
    b. FALSE

16. The Swedes were evicted from New Jersey by the Dutch.
    a. TRUE
    b. FALSE

CHAPTER 14 SUMMARY

New Jersey

1. The earliest explorations and settlements were made by the Dutch, Swedes, and English;

a. Bergen	1620	Dutch
b. Fort Nassau	1623	Dutch
c. Pavonia (Jersey City)	1630	Dutch
d. Fort Christina (Wilmington, Delaware)	1638	Swedes
e. Fort Elfsborg (Sussex County)	1643	Swedes
f. Elizabethtown	1665	English

2. In 1655, the Dutch, led by Peter Stuyvesant, evict the Swedes from New Jersey.

3. In 1664, England captures New Netherlands from the Dutch and renames it New York.

4. In 1664, King Charles II appoints Richard Nicolls as the first English Governor who grants land for settlement. This leads to the Elizabethtown settlement.

5. The Duke of York awards a Grant to two Proprietors, Lord John Berkeley and Sir George Carteret to settle in the same general area. This leads to confusion with the Nicolls land-grants.

6. In 1665, the Proprietors introduce a Constitution and send Philip Carteret as Governor. His policies quickly create unrest and rebellion which leads to the first Assembly in 1668 at Elizabethtown.

7. In 1676, the "Quintipartite Deed" creates two separate colonies, East and West Jersey.

8. In 1681, the first popular Assembly is held in Salem, West Jersey.

9. Major unrest leads to the Proprietors giving up their Charters to Queen Anne in 1702. She appoints New York Governor Lord Cornbury to rule both colonies. New Jersey now becomes a Royal Colony.

10. In 1738, New Jersey becomes a separate colony from New York with its own Governor, Lewis Morris.

11. In 1789, New Jersey becomes the first State to ratify the Federal Bill of Rights.

12. In 1790, Trenton is selected as the State Captial.

14a

The Two Jerseys, 1702
Edward Eggleston, The Household History of the United States and Its People
(New York, NY: D. Appleton and Company, 1898)
Downloaded from *Maps ETC*, on the web at http://etc.usf.edu/maps   [map #01192]

373

NEW JERSEY GOVERNORS

ATTACH 14b

NEW JERSEY & NEW YORK GOVERNORS

DATES		NAME AND TITLE
E A S T J E R S E Y		
1677	1682	PHILIP CARTERET
1682	1690	ROBERT BARCLAY (a)
1682	1683	DEPUTY GOV THOMAS RUDYARD
1683	1686	DEPUTY GOV GAWEN LAWRIE
1686	1687	DEPUTY GOV LORD NEIL CAMPBELL
1687	1688	DEPUTY GOV ANDREW HAMILTON
1688	1689	SIR EDMUND ANDROS
1690		JOHN TATHAM (b)
1691		JOSEPH DUDLEY (b)
W E S T J E R S E Y		
1676	1679	BOARD OF COMMISSIONERS
1679	1684	DEPUTY GOV SAMUEL JENNINGS
1684	1685	THOMAS OLLIVE
1685	1687	JOHN SKENE
1687	1690	DANIEL COXE
1691		WEST JERSEY SOCIETY OF PROPRIETORS
N E W J E R S E Y		
1692	1697	ANDREW HAMILTON
1697	1699	JEREMIAH BASSE
1699	1702	ANDREW HAMILTON
GOVERNOR OF NEW YORK & NEW JERSEY		
1702	1708	EDWARD HYDE, VISCOUNT CORNBURY
1708	1709	JOHN LOVELACE, BARON LOVELACE OF HURLEY
1709	1710	LT GOV RICHARD INGOLDESBY
1710	1720	ROBERT HUNTER
1720	1728	WILLIAM BURNET
1728	1731	JOHN MONTGOMERIE
1731	1732	LEWIS MORRIS (c)
1732	1736	WILLIAM COSBY
1736	1738	JOHN HAMILTON (c)
1738	1746	LEWIS MORRIS
1746	1747	JOHN READING (c)
1747	1757	JONATHAN BELCHER
1757	1758	JOHN READING (c)
1758	1760	SIR FRANCIS BERNARD
1760	1761	THOMAS BOONE
1761	1763	JOSIAH HARDY
1763	1776	WILLIAM FRANKLIN
1776	1790	WILLIAM LIVINGSTON

(a) Proprietary Governor in England
(b) Proprietary Governor rejected by Province
(c) President of the Council

Chapter 15

Pennsylvania

A.   EARLY HISTORY

The early history of Pennsylvania is similar to New York and New Jersey in that the Dutch and Swedes were the most active until 1664 when the English captured New Netherland from the Dutch. The Dutch had evicted the Swedes from the region in 1655 and then the English evicted them.

B.   GEORGE FOX AND THE QUAKERS

George Fox was the originator of the goal of founding a separate colony as a refuge for persecuted Quakers, not William Penn. Fox was a man of intense religious beliefs and very persuasive. He began preaching "the inner light" at age 20, in 1644, the same year that William Penn was born. Fox was a shoemaker from Leicestershire, England.

Fox believed that he had been called upon by God to preach the Gospel of Jesus, which he did to all would listen. In 1650, he was brought before a local judge and took the opportunity to admonish the judge to repent and "tremble and quake" before the word of the Lord, thus the term, "Quaker".

The Quakers refused to recognize all social ranks or pay taxes to finance wars and, as a result, they were faced with much opposition for their views. An Act of Parliament branded them as a "mischievous and dangerous people". Eventually, fear of persecution in England drove many of them to emigrate to the New World. In some parts of the New World, their reception wasn't much better, especially in Massachusetts. They realized it would be better to locate a separate site for their own colony.

C. WILLIAM PENN (10/14/1644 - 7/30/1718)

His father was Admiral William Penn who was a supporter of Oliver Cromwell and was rewarded with Irish estates. By the time of the Restoration (1660), William had enrolled at Oxford only to be expelled two years later and then to return in 1664 to study law. His father was a close friend of King Charles II and even loaned him money.

William was briefly exposed to Quakerism and quickly converted to it in spite of objections from his father. He was jailed for nine months in 1668 with nine other Quakers where his political and social beliefs were developed. His political beliefs strongly favored Parliament and opposed attempts by King Charles II to increase Royal authority. In 1676, he traveled through Europe with George Fox, the founder of the Quaker movement in 1647. During these travels, Penn believed there were many Quakers who would be interested in a separate colony of their own. His and Fox's motive was to locate a refuge for persecuted Quakers of Europe, to be called the "Holy Experiment".

On 3/4/1681, Penn received a grant from King Charles II in return for cancelling a debt owed to his father by the King. *In the charter there was no mention of a "Holy Experiment". Its stated purpose was to enlarge the English Empire, trade, commerce, and convert the Indians. The Charter made him the Proprietor of an immense tract of land, roughly south of New York and north of Maryland. He was required to obtain the consent of the settlers when making laws and only a provincial assembly could raise taxes.*

Several limitations in the Charter that had not existed in earlier Proprietary grants indicated a gradual tightening of colonial policy by the Crown. The colony was ordered by the Crown to pay strict attention to the Navigation Acts of England. The Proprietor had to admit all Royal Officers to collect duties and the province was required to send, within five years, transcripts of all laws passed for review and approval by the Crown. He was also required to appoint an Agent in London available at all times to represent the colony. He was denied the authority to wage war but could approve a militia for self-defense.

He chose to name the colony "New Wales" to honor his ancestors but the Welsh Secretary of State opposed it. He then suggested "Sylvania", meaning "woods", because of the wooded countryside. The secretary who drew up the document then added his name, Penn, to that of Sylvania, thus, "Pennsylvania".

This land grant encroached on the territory of Lord Baltimore in Maryland and some parts of Connecticut, thus producing friction between the colonies which were not completely settled until the next century. The King compounded the original problem by also granting to him land to the south, known as "the territories", to become the entire state of Delaware.

Penn realized that he would need access to the seacoast and coveted the Delaware territories for that purpose. However, Delaware had been claimed by Lord Baltimore as part of Maryland and had been a matter of dispute between him and the Duke of York, the future King James II. The Duke, for the sake of peace, offered to buy the territory from Baltimore, who refused to sell. Penn then assured the Duke that Lord Baltimore's claim was illegal, so, *in 1682, the Duke of York deeded to Penn his claim to the three lower counties of Newcastle, Kent, and Sussex, the current state of Delaware.*

In April, 1681, Penn made his cousin William Markham deputy-governor of the province and sent him to take control of the proposed colony. He left with three shiploads of emigrants and a letter to the Swedes in which he declared that they would be governed by laws of their own making and would live free of persecution. Philadelphia was then founded by Markham in late spring 1681.

In England, Penn drew up the *"First Frame of Government", his proposed Constitution for Pennsylvania.* In November, 1682, Penn followed in the ship, "Welcome", with 100 settlers of which about 1/3 died of smallpox on the voyage. They landed at Newcastle and were well received by the Swedes, English, Huguenot, and German settlers already there. He moved to Chester, Pennsylvania, where he summoned a General Assembly on 12/4/1682. *The first assembly united the Delaware counties with Pennsylvania and on 12/7/1682 adopted the "Great Law", a humanitarian code which became the fundamental basis of Pennsylvania law which guaranteed liberty of conscience. The 2nd Assembly, in 1683, amended Penn's "First Frame" and created the "2nd Frame".* By the time of Penn's return to England in 1684, the foundation of the Quaker province had been established.

By the end of the second year, 1684, there were 2,500 settlers. The quick growth of the colony, greater than any of the other colonies, was due to a great climate, fruitful soil, and the positive impact of religious toleration which characterized its laws and administration.

Markham was able to secure a treaty with the Indians, after Penn had made the initial peace effort. A few weeks after Penn's arrival he and Markham met with a delegation of the various Indian tribes to ratify the peace treaty. The spot selected was beneath a large elm tree, at "Shaxamaxon", since then to be known as Kensington, a northeast suburb of Philadelphia, where Penn pledged that the settlers and Indians would become "as one body". As a result, not a drop of Quaker blood was ever shed by an Indian. This is remarkable since at the very time there were many Indian battles in New England, not that far away.

Another reason why there were so few Indian problems is because the Penn government chose not to grant or settle any part of it without first buying the claims of the Indians who lived there. In this manner, all of Pennsylvania except the northwestern third was purchased by 1768. The Commonwealth bought the Six- Nations' claims to the remainder of the land in 1784 and 1789, and the claims of the Delawares and Wyandot tribes in 1785.

In 1684, Penn returned to England, leaving the administration of the government in the care of five commissioners. Soon after, King James II gave up his throne but since Penn had such great affection for the King, he continued to administer the colonial government in his name, which angered the successor, King William. The King's friends caused Penn to be imprisoned and from 1692-1694 control of the colony was taken from him and given to the current Governor Fletcher of

New York. After the charges against Penn were dropped he was able to return to his position where he appointed William Markham to be his deputy-governor.

In 1699, Penn made a second visit to Pennsylvania where he found some discontent toward the government. *He prepared a new charter, "The Charter of Privileges", which was offered on 11/7/1701 and accepted by the people of Pennsylvania on the same day but the "territories" of Delaware declined, who were then offered a distinct assembly under their current Governor. Their Assembly was first convened in 1703 and the 1701 Charter remained in effect until 1776.*

Penn then returned again to England, leaving the government in the hands of his deputy-governor, Markham. Discontent again arose even though the colony continued to grow and maintain friendly relations with the Indians.

Penn died in England in 1718 and left his interest in Pennsylvania and Delaware to his surviving sons, John, Thomas, and Richard who continued his policies in their management of the government until the American Revolution.

At the beginning of the Revolutionary War, the people formed a new Constitution by which the Proprietor was excluded from all participation in the government.

D.   IMMIGRATION

The English Quakers were the dominant element although many English settlers were Anglican. The English settled heavily in the southeastern counties, which soon lost its' frontier characteristics and became the center of a thriving agricultural and commercial society. Philadelphia became the metropolis of the British colonies and a center of intellectual and commercial life.

Thousands of Germans were also attracted to the colony and, by the time of the Revolution, comprised 1/3 of the population. The volume of German immigration increased after 1727, coming largely from the Rhineland. The Pennsylvania Germans settled mostly in the interior counties of Northampton, Berks, Lancaster, and Lehigh. Their skill and work-ethic transformed this region into a rich farming country, contributing greatly to the expanding prosperity of the province.

The Scotch-Irish migrated from 1717 until the Revolution in a series of waves caused by hardships in Ireland. They were primarily frontiersmen, pushing first into the Cumberland valley region and then farther into central and western Pennsylvania. They, with immigrants from old Scotland, numbered about 1/4 of the population by 1776.

Despite Quaker opposition to slavery, about 4,000 slaves were brought to Pennsylvania by 1730, most of them owned by English, Welsh, and Scotch-Irish colonists. The census of 1790 showed that the number of African-Americans had increased to about 10,000 of whom about 6,300 had received their freedom. The Pennsylvania "Gradual Abolition Act" of 1780 was the first emancipation statute in the United States.

Many Quakers were Irish and Welsh, and they settled in the area immediately outside of Philadelphia. French Huguenot and Jewish settlers, together with Dutch, Swedes, and other groups, contributed in smaller numbers to the development of colonial Pennsylvania. The mixture of various national groups in the Quaker province helped create its broad-mined toleration and cosmopolitan outlook.

E.   AGRICULTURE

From its beginnings, Pennsylvania ranked as a leading agricultural area and produced surpluses for export, adding to its wealth. By the 1750's an exceptionally prosperous farming area had developed in southeastern Pennsylvania. Wheat and corn were the leading crops, though rye, hemp, and flax were also important.

F.   MANUFACTURING

The abundant natural resources made for early development of industries. Arts and crafts plus home manufactures grew rapidly. Sawmills and gristmills were usually the first to appear, using the power of the numerous streams. Textile products were spun and woven mainly in the home, though factory production was not unknown. Shipbuilding became important on the Delaware River. The province gained early importance in iron manufacture, producing pig iron as well as finished products. Printing, publishing, and the related industry of papermaking were significant industries.

G.   COMMERCE AND TRANSPORTATION

The rivers were important as early arteries of commerce and were soon supplemented by roads in the southeastern area. Stagecoach lines by 1776 reached from Philadelphia into the south-central region. Fur trade with the Indians was important in the colonial period. Later, the transport and sale of farm products to Philadelphia and Baltimore, by water and road, formed an important business. Philadelphia became one of the most important centers in the colonies for the conduct of foreign trade and the commercial metropolis of an expanding frontier. By 1776, the province's imports and exports were worth several million dollars.

H.   RELIGION

Quakers held their first meeting at Upland (present-day Chester) in 1675, and came to Pennsylvania in great numbers after Penn received his Charter. Most numerous in the southeastern counties, the Quakers gradually declined in number but retained considerable influence. The Pennsylvania Germans belonged primarily to the Lutheran and Reformed churches *but there were also several smaller sects:*

1.   Mennonites, Amish, German Baptist Brethren (Dunkers), Schwenkfelders, and Moravians

2.   The Lutheran Church was established by the Swedes on Tinicum Island in 1643. It began its growth to become the largest of the Protestant denominations in Pennsylvania upon the arrival of Henry Muhlenberg in 1742.

3.   The Reformed Church owed its expansion to Michael Schlatter who arrived in 1746

4. The Moravians did missionary work among the Indians

5. The Church of England held services in Philadelphia as early as 1695

6. The first Catholic Parish was organized in Philadelphia in 1720 and the first Chapel erected in 1733. Pennsylvania had the 2nd largest Catholic population among the colonies.

7. The Scotch brought Presbyterianism and its first congregation was organized in Philadelphia in 1698. Scotch-Irish immigrants swelled its numbers.

8. Methodism began late in the colonial period. St. George's Church built in Philadelphia in 1769 is the oldest Methodist building in America.

9. There was a significant Jewish population in colonial Pennsylvania . Its Mikveh Israel Congregation was established in Philadelphia in 1740.

I.   POLITICS

There was considerable political conflict during the Provincial era. There was a natural conflict between the Proprietary elements in the government and the democratic elements begun under Penn which grew stronger under his successors. As a result of the English "Glorious Revolution" of 1688 which replaced King James II with William and Mary on the Throne, Penn was deprived of his province from 1692-1694. A popular party led by David Lloyd demanded greater powers for the Assembly and, in 1696, William Markham's "Frame of Government" granted some of those concessions. In December, 1699, Penn again visited Pennsylvania and, just before his return to England in 1701, agreed with the Assembly on a *revised Constitution, known as "The Charter of Privileges", which remained in effect until 1776. This gave the Assembly full legislative powers and permitted the three Delaware counties to have a separate legislature.*

J.   PENNSYLVANIA BY 1776

By 1776, the Province had become the 3rd largest English colony in America, though one of the latest to be founded. Philadelphia had become the largest English-speaking city in the world other than London, England. There were originally only three counties, Philadelphia, Chester, and Bucks. By 1773 there were 11. Westmoreland County was the last new county created before the Revolution and was the first located entirely west of the Allegheny Mountains.

The American Revolution had urban origins and Philadelphia was a center of the dissension. Groups of artisans and mechanics, many loyal to Benjamin Franklin, formed grassroots leadership. Philadelphia was a center of resistance to the Stamp Act (1765) and moved quickly to support Boston in opposition to the Intolerable Acts in 1774.

K.   PENNSYLVANIA POPULATION TRENDS

YEAR	POPULATION		
1680	400		
1720	30,000		
1730	45,000	Philadelphia	12,000
1740	55,000		
1750	120,000	Philadelphia	18,000
1760	200,000		
1770	300,000		
1790	440,000	Philadelphia	45,000
1800	600,000		

L.   KEY DATES AND SIGNIFICANT EVENTS

Although William Penn was granted all of the land in Pennsylvania by the King, he and his heirs chose not to grant or settle any part of it without first buying the claims of Indians who lived there. In this manner, all but the northwestern third of the province was purchased by 1768. The Commonwealth bought the Six- Nations claims to the remainder of the land in 1784 and 1789, and the claims of the Delawares and Wyandots in 1785. The defeat of the French and Indian War alliance by 1763, the withdrawal of the French, the defeat of Chief Pontiac's Indian alliance in 1764, and the failure of all attempts by Indians and Colonists to live side by side led the Indians to migrate westward, gradually leaving Pennsylvania.

	Early 1600's	Dutch & Swedes arrive
	1616	Dutch Captain Cornelius Hendrickson is the first to sail the Delaware River
	1630	A failed Dutch settlement in the lower Delaware River valley
	1638	New Sweden established at Wilmington, Delaware, both sides of the river claimed for Sweden
	1643	Another Swedish settlement "upland" at Tinicum Island, present-day Chester, Pennsylvania
	1647	Quaker religion established in England by George Fox
	1655	New Sweden is conquered, peacefully, by the Dutch
	1656	Quaker persecution in New England begins
	1664	New Amsterdam captured from the Dutch by England
	1667	William Penn becomes a Quaker in England
3/4	1681	King Charles II gives charter to William Penn Jr. of land ranging roughly from south of New York to north of Maryland.
May	1681	Penn sends cousin William Markham to take possession of the province. Founding of Philadelphia.
	1682	Duke of York deeds to William Penn his claim to the 3 lower counties of current Delaware
Nov	1682	Penn arrives at Newcastle on the ship "Welcome" with 100 settlers

12/4	1682	Penn summons a General Assembly which united the new Delaware counties with Pennsylvania
12/7	1682	First Assembly creates the "1st Frame of Government" which creates the "Great Law" guaranteeing liberty of conscience.
	1683	Second Assembly creates the "2nd Frame of Government"
	1684	Penn returns to England leaving the administration of the colony to 5 commissioners
	1692	Penn imprisoned in England when William & Mary assume the Throne, replacing King James II.
	1694	Penn freed from prison and appoints William Markham as Deputy-Governor of the colony.
	1699	Penn makes 2nd visit to Pennsylvania and finds discontent. Creates new "Charter of Privileges" which are proposed and accepted 11/7/1701.
11/7	1701	New Constitution adopted, Delaware "territories" oppose, allowed their own Charter, Governor, and Assembly.
	1765	First Congress of American Colonies meets at Philadelphia
	1774	First Continental Congress meets in Philadelphia
	1775	A Provincial Congress meets in Philadelphia

(Attachment 15a. List of Pennsylvania and Delaware Governors)

M. REVIEW QUESTIONS

(Multiple Choice)

1. Who was the first explorer of the Delaware River?
    a. Dutch Captain Cornelius Hendrickson
    b. Henry Hudson
    c. John Cabot
    d. Samuel de Champlain

2. In which year did Sweden establish a settlement near Wilmington, Delaware?
    a. 1616
    b. 1630
    c. 1638
    d. 1643

3. In what year did the Dutch evict the Swedes from the Pennsylvania, New Jersey, New York region?
    a. 1647
    b. 1651
    c. 1655
    d. 1664

4. In what year did King Charles II give the land-grant to William Penn in settlement for a claim of his father's?
    a. 1674
    b. 1681
    c. 1682
    d. None of the above

5. In what year did George Fox create the Quaker religion?
   a. 1633
   b. 1647
   c. 1660
   d. 1664

6. What was the primary motivation for the creation of the Pennsylvania colony?
   a. Economic opportunity
   b. Religious freedom from persecution
   c. Fur trade
   d. All of the above

7. In what year was the "Great Law" of Pennsylvania created which became the fundamental basis of colonial law?
   a. 1681
   b. 1682
   c. 1683
   d. None of the above

8. In which year was the first Roman Catholic Parish created in Pennsylvania ?
   a. 1685
   b. 1700
   c. 1720
   d. 1733

(True or False)

9. By 1776, the Pennsylvania Province had become the 3rd largest English colony in America.
   a. TRUE
   b. FALSE

10. Quakers held their first meeting at Upland (present-day Chester, Pennsylvania) in 1678.
    a. TRUE
    b. FALSE

11. William Penn's father, Admiral Penn, was an early supporter of William Cromwell in England.
    a. TRUE
    b. FALSE

12. In the 1681 Charter grant to Penn, one of the requirements was that the colony must pay close attention to the British Navigation Acts.
    a. TRUE
    b. FALSE

13. The name of the ship Penn arrived on in Newcastle in 1682 was "The Dover".
    a. TRUE
    b. FALSE

14. The Quakers and Indians had a peaceful relationship under William Penn.
    a. TRUE
    b. FALSE

15. Under the dual Monarchs of William & Mary, Penn was jailed in England in 1692.
    a. TRUE
    b. FALSE

CHAPTER 15 SUMMARY

Pennsylvania

1. Pennsylvania experienced a similar exploration and settlement history with that of New York and New Jersey in that the Dutch and Swedes came first and were then followed by the British in the mid-1660's.

2. William Penn Jr was a Quaker influenced by George Fox, an English Quaker. Fox was the first to desire a separate colony in America for religious freedom for his followers.

3. In 1681,Penn received a Land-grant from King Charles II in payment of a debt to his father. The land granted to him extended roughly from south of New York to north of Maryland. The Grant was intended for the expansion of English trade and commerce and to convert the Indians but Penn sought to use it for a religious refuge for the Quakers.

4. Penn wanted to call the land "New Wales" but the Welsh Secretary of State objected. He suggested "Sylvania", meaning "woods", because of the wooded countryside and then it was suggested to add his name, "Penn", making it "Pennsylvania".

5. In 1682, the Duke of York granted Penn the three "Lower Counties" of present-day Delaware.

6. On 12/7/1682, the first Colonial Assembly united the Delaware Counties with Pennsylvania and adopted the "Great Law" which

became the fundamental basis of colonial law which guaranteed liberty of conscience.

7. In 1684, Penn returned to England and left the administration of the colony to five commissioners. Soon after, King James II was replaced on the Throne by William & Mary (Glorious Revolution) who imprisoned Penn from 1692-1694.

8. In 1669, Penn returned to Pennsylvania to find discontent toward the government. He prepared a new Charter, "The Charter of Privileges", which was accepted and adopted on 11/7/1701. But, the "Delaware Counties" opposed and they were eventually allowed their own charter, governor, and assembly which was convened in 1703 and remained until 1776.

9. By 1776, Pennsylvania was the 3rd largest English colony in America.

10. The Pennsylvania population grew from 400 in 1680 to 440,000 in 1790, with the Philadelphia population of 45,000.

PENNSYLVANIA GOVERNORS		
DATES		**NAME AND TITLE**
PENNSYLVANIA & DELAWARE		
1681	1682	DEPUTY GOV WILLIAM MARKHAM
1682	1684	WILLIAM PENN
1684	1688	THE COUNCIL, THOMAS LLOYD *(a)*
1688	1690	DEPUTY GOV JOHN BLACKWELL
1690	1691	THE COUNCIL, THOMAS LLOYD *(a)*
1691	1693	DEPUTY GOV THOMAS LLOYD
1693	1694	ROYAL GOV BENJAMIN FLETCHER
1694	1699	LT GOV WILLIAM MARKHAM
1699	1701	WILLIAM PENN
1701	1703	DEPUTY GOV ANDREW HAMILTON
1703	1704	THE COUNCIL, EDWARD SHIPPEN *(a)*
1704	1709	DEPUTY GOV JOHN EVANS
1709	1717	DEPUTY GOV CHARLES GOOKIN
1717	1726	DEPUTY GOV SIR WILLIAM KEITH
1726	1736	DEPUTY GOV PATRICK GORDON
1736	1738	THE COUNCIL, JAMES LOGAN (a)
1738	1747	DEPUTY GOV GEORGE THOMAS
1747	1748	THE COUNCIL, ANTHONY PALMER *(a)*
1748	1754	DEPUTY GOV JAMES HAMILTON
1754	1756	DEPUTY GOV ROBERT HUNTER MORRIS
1756	1759	DEPUTY GOV WILLIAM DENNY
1759	1763	DEPUTY GOV JAMES HAMILTON
1763	1771	DEPUTY GOV JOHN PENN
1771	1776	LT GOV RICHARD PENN
PRESIDENTS OF THE SUPREME EXECUTIVE COUNCIL		
1777	1778	THOMAS WHARTON JR
1778	1781	JOSEPH READ
1781	1782	WILLIAM MOORE
1782	1785	JOHN DICKINSON
1785	1788	BENJAMIN FRANKLIN
(a)	*President of the Council*	

Chapter 16

Delaware

A.   EARLY EXPLORATIONS

The earliest explorations of the Delaware coast were those of the Spanish and Portuguese around 1526. Henry Hudson discovered the Delaware river and Bay for the Dutch in 1609 and Captain Samuel Argall of Virginia also explored and named the Bay for his Governor, Lord De La Warr. The region was also explored by Cornelius Henricksen on-board the ship, "Onrust", meaning, "Restless". He is regarded by many as the first "civilized man" to set foot on Delaware soil. In his journal, he records that he traded with the Indians for skins of various kinds, sables, otter, mink, bear robes, etc.

In 1638, the Delaware valley was settled by Swedes, Finns, Dutch, and Walloons and became the colony of New Sweden. The importance of Delaware was due more to where it was located than anything about its resources, climate, or soil. It lies along a great river and Bay and its importance consisted of its command of these and of the great fertile valley drained by them. You can see its importance by considering its *multiple settlers;*

- First claimed by the Dutch by right of the discovery by Henry Hudson

- Next came the Swedes who made the first permanent settlement at Wilmington

- Then the English captured the territory by virtue of its capture of New Netherlands and its possessions

- It was also claimed by Lord Baltimore as part of Maryland

- It then became the property of the Duke of York

- William Penn became the Proprietor by virtue of it being sold to him by the Duke of York

- Only after the American Revolution did the inhabitants of Delaware become the owners

B. DUTCH SETTLEMENT ACTIVITY

A group of Dutchmen formed a trading company led by Captain David Pietersen de Vries for the purpose of gaining wealth from the New World. An expedition of 30 sailed from the town of Hoorn, Holland, led by Captain Peter Heyes in the ship, "De Walvis" (The Whale). *Their settlement was named Zwaanendael, meaning "valley of the Swans", and was located in 1631 near Lewes, Delaware.* When he arrived in the New World in 1632 to visit the colony Captain de Vries found that the settlers had been killed and their buildings burned by the local Indians. Their settlement is commemorated by a Museum today in Lewes.

C. SWEDISH INFLUENCE

It was the goal of the Swedish King, Gustavus Adolphus, to colonize the western bank of the Delaware River to invite colonists from all of Europe and to exclude slavery and make a home for all oppressed Christians. He incorporated a company in 1627 and pronounced the venture as the "jewel of his kingdom". However, his country was involved in the "30 Years War" in Germany at the same time and during the Battle of Lutzen, in 1632, he was killed. This put a temporary hold on Swedish colonization.

However, the Executor and Chief Minister of the dead King, a man named Oxenstiern, renewed the patent of the company and gained the services of Peter Minuit, the former Governor of New Amsterdam, to lead his desired new colony in the New World.

No further attempts at colonization were made in Delaware until 1638 when the Swedes established the first permanent settlement at Fort Christina near present-day Wilmington, Delaware. It was named "New Sweden". The expedition was led by Peter Minuit in two ships, "Kalmar Nyckel" and the "Vogel Grip" which landed on 3/29/1638 on the Christina river, so named after their young Queen of Sweden, Christina. Minuit had purchased the area from the Minquas Indians.

Trouble soon developed with the Dutch who had earlier claimed the Delaware valley as part of New Netherland and their Governor Kieft protested the settlement but the Swedes were a powerful country at this time so the Dutch held off taking any action for awhile. In 1651, the Dutch built Fort Casmir at the site of present-day Newcastle, Delaware, thus controlling the Delaware Bay.

In 1642, a charter and Governor were appointed, Johan Printz, who ruled the colony under Swedish law for 10 years, from 1643-1653. He was succeeded by Johan Rising who, upon his arrival in 1654, seized the Dutch post, Fort Casmir, which the Governor, Peter Stuyvesant, of the Colony of New Netherland had built in 1651, on the site of the present town of Newcastle.

Rising governed the Swedish colony from Fort Christina until autumn 1655 when Peter Stuyvesant arrived from New Amsterdam with a Dutch fleet, captured the Swedish forts, and established the authority of the Colony of New Netherlands throughout the area formerly ruled by the colony of New Sweden. ***This marked the end of the Swedish rule in Delaware*** although the cultural, social, and religious influence of the Swedes has had a lasting effect upon the cultural life of the people in the area.

Old Swedes Church (Holy Trinity) built by the Swedes at Wilmington in 1698 was supplied by the Mother Church with missionaries until after the Revolution. It is one of the oldest Protestant Churches in North America. Fort Christina in Wilmington commemorates the memory of these first settlers.

D.   DUTCH RULE

Following the seizure of the Colony of New Sweden, the Dutch restored the name of Fort Casmir and made it the principal settlement of the Zuyd/South river (Delaware river). The area within the fort wasn't large enough to accommodate all of the settlers so a new town, named New Amstel (present-day Newcastle) was laid out in 1657. *By 1663 all of Delaware territory was under the control of New Netherland.*

E.   ENGLISH PRESENCE

After years of changing control by the Dutch, Swedes, and the English, *Delaware came under permanent English rule in 1674. It was part of the Duke of York's colonial lands and was managed as a Proprietary colony. It became known as the "The three Lower Counties of Delaware". Also in 1664 the English captured New Netherland from the Dutch thus eliminating the Dutch presence in the area. So, Delaware became a part of the New York colony until it was then transferred to Pennsylvania by virtue of the Crown's grant to William Penn.*

F.   WILLIAM PENN

In 1681, the Province of Pennsylvania was granted to William Penn by King Charles II which was quickly followed by the arrival of Penn's agents on the Delaware River. They reported to the Proprietor that the new province would be landlocked if the colonies on either side of the Delaware River or Bay were hostile. As a result, *Penn petitioned the Crown for the land on the west side of the Delaware River and Bay below his province. In March, 1682, the Duke of York granted deeds and leases to the land in the Counties of New Castle, St. Jones (Kent), and Deale (Sussex).*

When Penn arrived in Pennsylvania on 10/27/1682, he controlled 2 different colonies. He could not join them together because he had received each one under different terms .He took possession as Proprietor, from the Duke of York's agents, of the "three lower counties" as they were called at the time. The colonists then took an oath of allegiance to the new Proprietor and the first general assembly was held in the colony. The assembly included delegates from both Pennsylvania and Delaware and it was the first time Delawareans took part in representative government.

The following year, 1683, the "three lower counties" were annexed to the Province of Pennsylvania as territories with full privileges under Penn's famous "Frame of Government". In the same year the counties of St. Jones and Deale were renamed Kent and Sussex counties respectively.

For the rest of the colonial period, Delaware had its own legislature but shared a Governor with Pennsylvania, however, the Governor of Pennsylvania rarely visited Delaware and did not play a significant role in its government.

Penn hoped the Assembly, with members from both colonies, would continue permanently but tensions between them began almost immediately. *After more than 20 years of conflict, Delaware finally elected its own one-house Assembly in 1704.*

In 1776, at the time of the Declaration of Independence, Delaware not only declared itself free from the British Empire but also established a State Government entirely separate from Pennsylvania.

With the coming of the Revolutionary War almost 4,000 men enlisted for service from Delaware. The colonial wars had developed a militia which eventually supplied many capable officers and troops who fought in the war. The only military engagement fought on Delaware soil was at the battle of Cooch's Bridge, near Newark, on September 3, 1777.

John Dickinson of Delaware presided over the Annapolis Convention in 1786 which called for the Federal Constitutional Convention which met in Philadelphia the next year. When the new Constitution was submitted to the states for ratification, Delaware was the first of the 13 original states to ratify it. That unanimous ratification took place in a convention at Dover on 12/7/1787.

G. KEY DATES AND SIGNIFICANT EVENTS

	1526	Portugal exlores area
	1609	Henry Hudson explores and claims the area for the Dutch
	1610	Captain Samuel Argall of Virginia names the Bay for his Virginia Governor, Lord De La Warr.
	1615	Territory explored by Dutchman Cornelius Henricksen
	1631	First Dutch settlement near present-day Lewes, named "Zwaanendael", meaning "valley of swans". Last less than one year.
3/29	1638	Swedes settle Fort Christina at Wilmington, named "New Sweden". Expedition led by Peter Minuit.
	1651	Dutch build Fort Casmir near present-day New Castle
	1654	New Swedish Governor, Johan Rising, seizes Dutch Fort Casmir
	1655	Peter Stuyvesant, Governor of New Netherlands, captures Swedish forts and ends its influence in the area.
	1657	New Castle developed by the Dutch
	1663	Almost all of Delaware territory under control of New Netherlands (Dutch)
	1664	English capture New Netherland and its possessions
	1674	The " Three Lower Counties of Delaware" owned by the Duke of York come under English control
	1681	Province of Pennsylvania granted to William Penn by King Charles II
10/27	1682	Duke of York granted the "Three Lower Counties" to Penn and the First General Assembly is held in the colony.

397

1683   "Three Lower Counties" annexed to Pennsylvania as territories with full government privileges under Penn's "Frame of Government"

1683   Counties of St. Jones and Deale renamed Kent and Sussex, respectively.

1704   Delaware given its own Assembly

12/7   1787   Delaware becomes the first state to ratify the U.S. Constitution

(Attachment 16a List of Delaware and Pennsylvania Governors)

H.   REVIEW QUESTIONS

(Multiple Choice)

1. Which two countries were the first to explore the Delaware coast?
    a.   France and Spain
    b.   England and Holland
    c.   England and Sweden
    d.   Spain and Portugal

2. What was the primary importance of the Delaware River and Bay?
    a.   Controls a major waterway into the interior of America
    b.   Access to tremendous sources of gold and silver
    c.   Key to fishing rights
    d.   Great potential source for the fur trade

3. In which year was the first major settlement attempt made?
    a.   1621
    b.   1631
    c.   1638
    d.   None of the above

4. What was the name of the first Dutch settlement in Delaware?
    a.   De Walvis
    b.   Onrust
    c.   Zwaanendael
    d.   New Sweden

5. How many countries and/or entities claimed an interest in Delaware?
   a. 3
   b. 4
   c. 6
   d. 7

6. In what year was the first permanent settlement in Delaware?
   a. 1631
   b. 1638
   c. 1651
   d. None of the above

7. What was the name of the Fort built by the Dutch in 1651?
   a. Zwaanendael
   b. Casmir
   c. Christina
   d. New Amstel

8. In what year did Governor Peter Stuyvesant capture the Swedish settlements in Delaware?
   a. 1642
   b. 1651
   c. 1655
   d. 1664

(True or False)

9. Johan Rising was Governor of New Sweden from 1643-1653.
   a. TRUE
   b. FALSE

10. The settlement of New Amstel is known today as New Castle.
    a. TRUE
    b. FALSE

11. By 1670 all of Delaware territory was under the control of New Netherland.
    a. TRUE
    b. FALSE

12. Delaware became a part of the New York colony until it was transferred to Pennsylvania by virtue of the Crown's grant to William Penn.
    a. TRUE
    b. FALSE

13. In 1683 the 3 lower counties of Delaware were annexed to New Jersey.
    a. TRUE
    b. FALSE

14. The Delaware counties of St. Jones and Deale were renamed Kent and Sussex, respectively.
    a. TRUE
    b. FALSE

15. The only military engagement of the American Revolution fought on Delaware soil was near Newark on 9/3/1777.
    a. TRUE
    b. FALSE

CHAPTER 16 SUMMARY

Delaware

1. The earliest explorations of the Delaware coast were made by the Spanish and Portuguese in 1526

2. There were subsequent explorations by;
   a. Henry Hudson   Dutch   1609
   b. Captain Samuel Argall   Virginia   1610
   c. Cornelius Hendricksen   Dutch   1615-1616

3. The first settlement attempt was made by the Dutch in 1631 at "Zwaanendael", meaning, "Valley of Swans, near present-day Lewes, Delaware, which lasted less than one year..

4. The first permanent settlement made by the Swedes was at Fort Christina, near present-day Wilmington, Delaware. It became known as "New Sweden".

5. In 1642, the Swedes appoint a Governor, Johan Printz, who rules the colony from 1643-1653.

6. In 1651, the Swedes build Fort Casmir at the Site of present-day Newcastle, giving them control of the Delaware Bay and river.

7. In 1654, new Swedish Governor Johan Rising captures the Dutch Fort Casmir.

8. In 1655, the New Netherlands Dutch Governor Stuyvesant re-captured all of the Swedish forts and settlements. This permanently ends the Swedish influence in Delaware.

9. In 1664, England recaptures New Netherlands and all of its possessions, including Delaware.

10. In March, 1682, the Duke of York grants the "Three Lower Counties" of Delaware to William Penn.

11. From 1682 until the end of the colonial period there is a conflict between Penn and Lord Baltimore of Maryland over the exact territory controlled by Penn along the lower Delaware river.

12. In 1683, the "Three Lower Counties" are annexed to the Province of Pennsylvania as territories with full governmental powers under Penn's "Frame of Government".

13. For the remainder of the colonial period, Delaware has its own Legislature but shares a governor with Pennsylvania.

14. In 1704, Delaware elects its own one-house Assembly.

15. In 1787, Delaware becomes the first State to ratify the U.S. Constitution.

16a

DELAWARE GOVERNORS		
DATES		NAME AND TITLE
PENNSYLVANIA & DELAWARE		
1681	1682	DEPUTY GOV WILLIAM MARKHAM
1682	1684	WILLIAM PENN
1684	1688	THE COUNCIL, THOMAS LLOYD *(a)*
1688	1690	DEPUTY GOV JOHN BLACKWELL
1690	1691	THE COUNCIL, THOMAS LLOYD *(a)*
1691	1693	DEPUTY GOV THOMAS LLOYD
1693	1694	ROYAL GOV BENJAMIN FLETCHER
1694	1699	LT GOV WILLIAM MARKHAM
1699	1701	WILLIAM PENN
1701	1703	DEPUTY GOV ANDREW HAMILTON
1703	1704	THE COUNCIL, EDWARD SHIPPEN *(a)*
1704	1709	DEPUTY GOV JOHN EVANS
1709	1717	DEPUTY GOV CHARLES GOOKIN
1717	1726	DEPUTY GOV SIR WILLIAM KEITH
1726	1736	DEPUTY GOV PATRICK GORDON
1736	1738	THE COUNCIL, JAMES LOGAN *(a)*
1738	1747	DEPUTY GOV GEORGE THOMAS
1747	1748	THE COUNCIL, ANTHONY PALMER *(a)*
1748	1754	DEPUTY GOV JAMES HAMILTON
1754	1756	DEPUTY GOV ROBERT HUNTER MORRIS
1756	1759	DEPUTY GOV WILLIAM DENNY
1759	1763	DEPUTY GOV JAMES HAMILTON
1763	1771	DEPUTY GOV JOHN PENN
1771	1776	LT GOV RICHARD PENN
GOVERNORS OF DELAWARE		
1777	1778	THOMAS MC KEAN
1778	1781	CAESAR RODNEY
1781	1783	JOHN DICKINSON
1783	1786	NICHOLAS VAN DYKE
1786	1789	THOMAS COLLINS
(a)	*President of the Council*	

Chapter 17

Georgia

A. JAMES OGLETHORPE (12/22/1696-6/30/1785)

Georgia was the last American colony founded over 100 years after the first of the other twelve colonies. It was founded by James Oglethorpe, a prison reformer in England who was a member of Parliament concerned about the poor prison conditions of the debtor prisons in England and was seeking a location where they would live in better conditions.

B. CHARTER OF 6/9/1732 (The Trustees for Establishing the Colony of Georgia)

King George II granted a Charter to a board of 21 trustees for the land between the Savannah and Altamaha rivers. They were vested with legislative powers for the government of the colony for 21 years, at which time a permanent government was to be established by the King or his successors in accordance with British law and practice.

In the charter, the liberties of Englishmen were guaranteed to the colonies including freedom of religion to all except Catholics. The colony of Georgia was named for King George II who had granted the charter.

The territory of Georgia was originally included in the Carolina grant to Lord Clarendon and his associates but it was a region which was wild with many Indian tribes at the time the Proprietors surrendered their interest in it to the Crown in 1729.

The purpose of the colony was not just an opportunity for the inmates to begin a new life but to also provide a refuge for persecuted Protestants and a military presence between the other colonies and Spanish Florida.

C.   SETTLEMENT ACTIVITIES

James Oglethorpe was selected to be the Governor of the colony and left England for America on 11/6/1732 with 120 settlers on the ship, "Anne". He landed in Savannah on 2/1/1733. The land was inhabited by Indians, primarily the Creek and Cherokee tribes. On Yamacraw Bluff *they founded the first city on 2/12/1733 and named it after the Indian word for river, "Savannah".*

Once the settlers completed building a fort the next objective for Oglethorpe was to establish friendly relations with the Indians. He met with 50 Chiefs in May, 1733, and presented them with gifts hoping to extract land rights. He was assisted by an Indian woman named Mary Musgrove who had lived with both the Indians and English and knew both very well. She served as an interpreter.

She was befriended by Thomas Bosomworth who was the Chaplain of the colony. He proved to be a deceitful man who misled Mary who eventually warned the Indians that the white men were evil and planning on taking their lands. She became known as "Queen Mary" to the Indians. After a brief attempt to attack the settlers at Savannah, a man known as Noble Jones saved the day by persuading the Indians to lay down their arms and have a meeting. After some tension, Mary and Bosomworth were made to confess their sins and promise to not begin any further trouble in the future.

A Treaty was signed by which all unoccupied lands within defined boundaries were assigned to the English.

Georgia became a haven for those Protestants fleeing religious persecution in Europe. In 1734, the first religious immigrants arrived in Savannah. The Salzburgers, a devout Protestant sect, were led by Oglethorpe up the mouth of the Savannah where they founded the town of Ebenezer. Others came soon, such as John Wesley, the founder of Methodism who came as a Missionary, and also a large group of Scottish Highlanders. Within three years from the first settlement 1,400 planters had arrived.

Georgia was different from the other 12 colonies in that it received money from Parliament to get it started. It was the only colony which prohibited slavery from the very beginning and also the import of alcohol. *The settlers were to have no control of their own government as it was to be entirely ruled by the trustees.*

D.   THE WAR OF JENKINS EAR (1739-1743)

Because of their location as the southernmost colony which bordered Spanish Florida, Savannah was fortified to defend from attacks by the Spanish and local Indians. In 1739, the colonists were involved in one of the wars caused by colonial rivalries in the New World. The Spanish had excluded English traders from their American colonies which led to smuggling and resentment. In 1738, Captain Robert Jenkins appeared before Parliament with his ear having been cut off by the Spanish when his ship was boarded in 1731.

The "War of Jenkins Ear" was declared in 1739 although the conflict was soon absorbed by the "War of the Austrian Succession" of 1740-1748, and by 1743 the hostilities in America became part of the "King George's War" of 1744-1748. There were also English attacks on Spanish colonies in the Caribe in 1739/1740 and attacks on St. Augustine, then in Spanish control, in 1740 and 1743 while the Spanish attacked Georgia in 1743.

E.   COLONIAL DEVELOPMENT

The colonists were not happy with the governmental restrictions placed on the colony. After twelve years as Governor, Oglethorpe returned to England bearing their grievances. They wanted permission to have alcohol and slaves, to participate in their own government, and demanded land reform. They were successful. Alcohol was permitted because it was believed that its importation would improve its trade.

There remained strong opposition to slavery, particularly from the religious immigrants, but they were in the minority and in 1749 Georgia became a slave colony.

Georgia was not a prosperous colony under the trustee system. By 1749, just 16 years into the trustee system, the colony exported goods for the first time. In 1752 the trustees returned the colony to the Crown, unwilling to continue for the entire 21 year period stated in the charter. ***Freemen were given the right to vote unless they were Catholics. The people elected the Assembly and the Governor was appointed by the Crown.***

Georgia began to grow rapidly after becoming a Royal colony in 1752 and, by the time of the American Revolution, numbered close to 50,000 population, about half of whom were slaves. It was the least populated of the colonies and mostly wilderness.

There were some rich planters but most were small farmers. There were no schools, very little town life with Savannah the only town of some importance. The roads were mere Indian trails and the settlers saw very little of one another.

The initial slow growth of the colony was due to:

- English debtors did not migrate in expected numbers

- Land holders were restricted to 500 acres as a defense measure

- Negro slaves were forbidden thus preventing the growth of a plantation economy

- Constant conflicts with Spanish Florida deterred timid settlers

F.   KEY DATES AND SIGNIFICANT EVENTS

	1540	Hernando de Soto was the first European to explore Georgia. The French made a brief appearance but were quickly chased away by the Spanish.
	1566	The Spanish establish a fort on St. Catherine Island south of Savannah, the first of a series of forts along the coast. This region known to Spanish as "Guale".
	1633	England reasserted its earlier claim to the area when King Charles II granted the rights in Carolina to 8 Proprietors.
	1680	England chase Spanish away from St. Catherine Island
	1721	Fort King George established near mouth of Altamaha River
	1730	Oglethorpe and Egmont develop plan for new colony of Georgia
6/9	1732	Georgia Society receives Royal Charter from King George II
	1733	Oglethorpe leads 120 settlers to found Savannah
	1734	Salzburgers (German Protestants) arrive and settle at Ebenezer
	1734	Treaty of 1734 between Oglethorpe and the Creek Indians
	1735	Arrival of Highland Scots and settlement at Darien
	1739	War of Jenkins Ear between English and Spanish
	1740	Oglelthorpe invades Florida with force of Georgia and South Carolina settlers and Indians. Captures St. Augustine.
	1742	Spanish invade Georgia
7/22	1743	Oglethorpe leaves Georgia and never returns
	1752	Colony returned to King and it becomes a Royal Colony

1754   John Reynolds becomes first Royal Governor of Georgia

1758   Henry Ellis becomes 2nd Royal Governor of Georgia

1788   Georgia becomes 4th state in the Union

G.   REVIEW QUESTIONS

(Multiple Choice)

1. The name "Oglethorpe" is associated with the founding of which colony?
    a.   Maryland
    a.   North Carolina
    b.   New York
    c.   Georgia

2. Georgia was the last American colony founded almost how many years after the other 12 original English colonies?
    a.   15
    b.   25
    c.   50
    d.   100

3. The Georgia Charter was authorized for how many years?
    a.   10
    b.   15
    c.   20
    d.   None of the above

4. The purpose of the colony was for:
    a.   Refuge for criminals to begin a new life
    b.   Persecuted Protestants
    c.   Military buffer between other colonies to the north and Spanish Florida to the south
    d.   All of the above

5. James Oglethorpe arrived in America with 35 families in which year?
   a. 1732
   b. 1733
   c. 1734
   d. None of the above

6. How was Georgia different from the other 12 English colonies?
   a. It received money from Parliament to get started
   b. Was the only colony which prohibited slavery from the very beginning and also the import of alcohol
   c. Settlers were to have no self-government, it was to be entirely ruled by the trustees
   d. All of the above
   e. (a) & (b)

7. How many years did it take before Georgia was able to export goods for the first time?
   a. 10
   b. 13
   c. 16
   d. 19
   e. 22

8. In which year did Georgia become a Royal Colony?
   a. 1733
   b. 1742
   c. 1749
   d. 1752

(True or False)

9. The territory of Georgia was originally included in the Carolina grant.
   a. TRUE
   b. FALSE

10. The War of Jenkins Ear was between England and Holland.
    a. TRUE
    b. FALSE

11. Georgia became a slave colony in 1749.
    a. TRUE
    b. FALSE

12. Georgia grew faster or slower after becoming a Royal colony.
    a. FASTER
    b. SLOWER

13. By the time of the American Revolution about half of the population of Georgia were slaves.
    a. TRUE
    b. FALSE

14. Atlanta was the only town of commercial importance.
    a. TRUE
    b. FALSE

15. Savannah was the first permanent settlement.
    a. TRUE
    b. FALSE

(Attachment 17a List of Georgia Governors)

CHAPTER 17 SUMMARY

Georgia

1. The Georgia colony was founded by James Oglethorpe who was a prison reformer and member of Parliament concerned about poor debtor-prison conditions.

2. Oglethorpe seeks a colony to provide for;
   a. A safe-haven for debtors.
   b. A refuge for persecuted Protestants.
   c. A military buffer against Spanish Florida.

3. The Charter of 6/9/1732;
   a. Granted by King George II.
   b. Provided for a Board of 21 Trustees for 21 years.
   c. Guaranteed the liberties of Englishmen including the freedom of religion to **all except Roman Catholics.**
   d. Named for King George II who granted the Charter.

4. Oglethorpe lands at Savannah on 2/1/1733 with 120 settlers on the ship, "Anne".

5. Signs a Peace Treaty with the Creek Indians in 1734.

6. The War of Jenkins Ear between England and Spain in 1739.

7. In 1749, Georgia becomes a Slave colony.

8. In 1752, Georgia becomes a Royal colony.

9. The growth of the colony was slow because of;
   a. English debtors did not migrate in expected numbers.

b. Land holders were restricted to 500 acres as a defense measure.

c. Negro slaves were forbidden which prevented the growth of a plantation economy.

d. Constant conflicts with Spanish Florida deterred timid settlers.

10. In 1788, Georgia became the 4th State of the Union.

17a

GEORGIA GOVERNORS		
DATES		**NAME AND TITLE**
1732	1743	JAMES OGLETHRORPE
1743	1751	ACTING GOV WILLIAM STEPHENS
1751	1754	ACTING GOV HENRY PARKER
1754	1757	JOHN REYNOLDS
1758	1760	HENRY ELLIS
1760	1776	SIR JAMES WRIGHT
1776	1777	PRES ARCHIBALD BULLOCK *
1777	1778	JOHN TREUTLEN
1778	1779	JOHN WEREAT
1779	1780	GEORGE WALTON
1780	1781	RICHARD HOWLEY
1781	1782	NATHAN BROWNSON
1782	1783	JOHN MARTIN
1783	1784	LYMAN HALL
1784	1785	JOHN HOUSTOUN
1785	1786	SAMUEL ELBERT
1786	1787	EDWARD TELFAIR
1787	1788	GEORGE MATHEWS

Chapter 18

Regional Colonial History

A. NEW ENGLAND

Settlement of New England was slow in the coastal areas and lower Connecticut river valley primarily due to the Pequot War in 1637. The New England frontier was somewhat peaceful for the next 38 years until King Philip's War which primarily impacted Rhode Island but also, to a lesser extent, the other parts of New England. Due to a number of recurring threats to the peace and security of the New England frontier, the various colonies flirted with the idea of mutual defense or governmental organizations, such as:

1. **THE NEW ENGLAND CONFEDERATION ("United Colonies of New England" 1643 to 1684)**

   As a result of the Pequot War of 1637, New England settlements were receptive to plans for strengthening colonial defenses against the threat of Indian attacks, the French fur-trade influence in the northeast and northwest, the Dutch in the southeast and west, and the English government efforts to solidify its control over New England affairs. The Dutch opposed colonial expansion into their areas of interest, such as, Albany, Hartford, New Haven, and the Delaware river region. They had also tried to establish a trading post on Long Island and along the southern boundary of Connecticut where Puritan settlements lay within 40 miles of New Amsterdam (Manhattan). The colonists were also fearful of French efforts to Catholicize the Indians.

Massachusetts was the first colony to propose a Union of New England settlements in 1637 during the Pequot War but it was rejected because the Connecticut river towns feared eventual domination by the Massachusetts colony because of its size and influence. They now favored such a union if each settlement or colony had an equal vote to protect them against Massachusetts domination.

Massachusetts accepted in May, 1643, and signed the Constitution of the United Colonies of New England along with the river towns of Connecticut in addition to the colonies of Plymouth and New Haven. Maine settlements were not included because Massachusetts hoped to acquire them anyway. Rhode Island requested membership but was rejected.

The organization was to be composed of two delegates from each of the four member colonies with six of the eight votes required to adopt any measure. Regular annual meetings were to be held but additional conferences could be called in emergencies. The commissioners/delegates were required to be church members and could determine matters of war and peace, division of spoils, reception of new members, manage Indian affairs, and make laws for the general good.

Although their primary interest was in self-defense against the Indians, they did get involved in the various conflicts between England and the Dutch. In 1650, the Confederation participated in the "Treaty of Hartford" which basically established a boundary between the English and Dutch interests in New England. Holland accepted the settlement but England did not and reminded the Dutch that they had no rights in America and also informed the Confederation that they had no right to negotiate with foreign nations.

The Confederation was the first American experiment in Federalism. It was not intended as a central government for those colonies because each retained its own governing institutions.

(Attachment 18a represents a Map of New England colonies from 1620 to 1636.)

The powers of the Confederation were:

a. Assess member colonies defense costs and assign dues based on the number of males aged 16-60 residing in each colony.

b. Require member colonies to participate in the return of fugitives from justice and runaway slaves. This latter requirement anticipated the fugitive slave laws of later times.

The Massachusetts Bay Colony was not happy giving up so much of its power and influence and vowed to ignore any decision not in its favor. They refused to participate in the New England alliance with England in their wars against the Dutch in the 1650's. The Confederation influence declined from this point forward except for a brief interval during the King Philip's War of 1675-6.

King Charles II revoked the Massachusetts charter in 1684 as a result of colonial insubordination over the trade, tariff, and navigation laws. This led to the collapse of the Confederation. In 1686, the "Dominion of New England" was imposed by the Crown, which proved to be a very unpopular merger of New York and New Jersey with the New England colonies.

Later, just prior to the last of the French-Indian Wars, in 1754, the seven colonies would give consideration to Ben Franklin's *"Albany Plan of Union", a proposal for a federated colonial government.*

2. **ENGLAND ATTEMPTS TO TIGHTEN IMPERIAL CONTROL**

A special committee of the Privy Council, the Lords of Trade and Plantations, had been created in 1675 to enforce the "Acts of Trade" and unify the administration of the Empire. The Lords of Trade studied all the colonies with an eye to strengthening royal control over their affairs but those in New England received the most attention. They saw smuggling as the biggest problem in New England. *In 1676 the Lords of Trade ordered Massachusetts to send an agent to England within 6 months to answer charges.* Meanwhile, the Lords dispatched their own investigator to study and report on the situation in Massachusetts. They chose Edward Randolph.

EDWARD RANDOLPH

Randolph arrived in Massachusetts during the summer of 1676 as the colony recovered from King Philip's War. *His reports back to England denounced everything about Massachusetts.* New England laws suited only New England and opposed English statutes with many differing with English practice, such as; no oaths of allegiance to the King, Ministers ordained by the people or Magistrates performed marriage ceremonies and ignored royal orders. The Church of England did not exist within the Massachusetts boundaries.

Randolph returned to England after 6 months investigation. He gave a list of 24 "Assumed powers" not in the Massachusetts charter. He thought Massachusetts was ready for Royal Government, tired of the powerful oligarchy of Orthodox Puritans. He also suggested that the troops sent to Virginia to quell Bacon's Rebellion might be better used to secure Massachusetts obedience.

The Lords of Trade demanded an explanation from Massachusetts who RESPONDED THAT ENGLISH LAW DID NOT APPLY TO THEM BECAUSE THEY WERE NOT REPRESENTED IN PARLIAMENT. The Lords of Trade in 1679 demanded that Massachusetts withdraw all officers from New Hampshire thus making that colony a Royal dependency. During the first year Randolph seized 10 ships for illegal entry but the courts found against the Crown in every case. The Law allowed customs commissioners in America to enforce only the "Plantation Duty Act" of 1673. The responsibility to enforce the Navigation Acts of 1660 & 1663 belonged to colonial governors. In 1681, the King gave Randolph the authority to enforce all of the Navigation Acts.

3. **THE CROWN TAKES OVER**

In 1677, the New England colonies barely had begun recovering from King Philip's War even though there remained some fighting on the Maine frontier. *The Lords of Trade informed*

Massachusetts Bay that they must accept Royal officials to enforce obedience to the Acts of Trade.

Massachusetts continued to resist. The Oligarchy of Orthodox Puritans that still controlled Massachusetts affairs sent agents to London to discuss matters with the Lords of Trade but with firm *orders not to compromise on issues the colony regarded as their own business, such as suffrage and religious liberty. Shortly thereafter the Board recommended that proceedings be started to revoke the Bay Colony charter. The "Court of Chancery" in 1684 declared the charter vacated and Massachusetts became a Royal colony.*

Revocation of the Charter completed the first phase of the administration plan to manage the colonies. Next, writs were filed against Connecticut and Rhode Island. *Once they were Royal dependencies all of New England would be united under a single Royal governor.* The original plan had called for two or three administrative units for the 11 colonies but the Lords of Trade realized it would take time to revoke the charters of the Proprietaries especially when England faced such formidable opponents as Penn and Lord Baltimore.

Meanwhile, New England would serve as the testing ground because the need for strong central government was greatest where the King's authority was most defied and there was the menace of the French and Indians, thus the need for self-defense.

4. **THE DOMINION OF NEW ENGLAND 5/25/1686 to 4/1689**

Governor Dongan of New York showed interest in a *mutual defense organization* because of fear of the French to the north. *Plans were made to include New York and New Jersey in the Dominion of New England, as it would be called.* It would cover an area from Nova Scotia to the Delaware River and would embrace over half the settlers on the American continent. The death of King Charles II in 1685 delayed inception of the

Dominion until his brother, the Duke of York, (King James II) gave Royal assent to the plan. *In the interim, the Lords of Trade arranged for a "Provisional government" which would include Massachusetts, Maine, New Hampshire, and the Narragansett territory.* Joseph Dudley, then acting Governor of New York, became President because there was no Representative Assembly. He ruled with a Council of 17 with all but two being New Englanders. All were moderates who had favored the Crown taking over the Dominion. *With the Provisional Government taking power the Massachusetts government would no longer be ruled by the Orthodox Puritan Oligarchy which had ruled from the beginning.*

5. **INTERIM PROVISIONAL GOVERNMENT (5/25/1686 - 12/31/1686)**

    President Dudley and the Council took office 5/25/1686. Dudley opposed Randolph's call for special status for the Church of England. Trade and financial problems confronted the new government, huge debt from King Philip's War included. The Council had no authority to pass new revenue measures so the Provisional government could do little during its seven months of existence to solve their problems. The omission of Connecticut and Rhode Island allowed them to become smuggling centers. Dudley sought less to enforce the Navigation Laws than to appear to enforce them. *Randolph strongly opposed the Provisional government. During Dudley's tenure England had developed a Constitution for the Dominion. It provided for freedom of worship but favored the Church of England. King James II omitted a provision for a representative assembly.* His brother's troubles with popular government and his own preference for France's autocracy had reinforced a conviction that representative government only caused problems. The Constitution also included a provision which would upset New England, that all land henceforth granted would be held in the King's name with a quitrent levied on every 100 acres. This would add revenue and also tie the settlers closer to the Crown. The Lords of Trade did not consider the provision oppressive and sought only to make the land laws more like those of England.

6. **SIR EDMUND ANDROS**

Rhode Island and Connecticut were annexed to the Dominion in 1687 as were New York and New Jersey in 1688 plus the Plymouth Colony.

On 12/20/1686, Sir Edmund Andros arrived in Boston as the new Governor of the Dominion of New England. He inherited many problems. He ruled over an area which exceeded that of England and even though he had the power of a King *he lacked popular support of the people*. He lacked a government bureaucracy and was forced to militarily defend this large territory without an army of forts from French and Indian attacks. At the same time he had to reform a society whose customs were fixed by a half-century of experience in a new world. All of this had to be done by an outsider. He was also disliked, not only for being an outsider but because, as Governor of New York, he refused to come to the aid of New England during King Philip's War. He also offended his religious supporters by asking for a hall in which to hold an Anglican service. This request opened up some previous religious issues.

He had power to make laws, levy taxes, and administer justice limited only by the consent of his council. Representation on the Council was more equitable than under the Confederation of New England; Massachusetts held seven votes, New Hampshire one vote, Maine two votes, Plymouth six votes, Narragansett one vote, Rhode Island seven votes, Connecticut two votes, New York eight votes, and New Jersey no votes.

The Council met quarterly in its legislative capacity. Its primary task was that of raising revenue which they did by passing a bill levying a heavy tax on imported rum, wine, and brandy which was heavily supported by landowners eager to shift the tax burden from land to trade. Andros also agreed with this view but also placed a direct tax on landowners that could not be passed on to the consumer. The Land Tax presented the first test of the Andros power and it created dissension everywhere.

Several of the key opponents were brought to trial, jailed, and heavily fined. *People continued to oppose a tax levied without their consent* but gradually realized that their rates were lower under Andros than before. Another task for Andros was to develop a judicial system. He set rates on legal fees similar to those in other colonies where English customs prevailed but because they exceeded the old rates, Puritans saw them as excessive. Andros ordered all Writs in the King's name. He tried to make New England more like England.

The merchants who opposed the rule of Puritans and favored making Massachusetts a Royal colony now had mixed feelings about Andros. His enforcement of the Navigation Acts stifled trade, his use of the Vice-Admiralty rather than common-law courts to try violations of the acts filled them with fury. The land problem mostly angered New England. Andros also wanted the land policy like that of England with the land held in the King's name.

By 1688 he questioned the validity of all New England land titles. If landowners wanted secure titles they had to obtain new patents from the King's men, in the King's name, with a quitrent. *This was opposed by all of Massachusetts* but not as badly in Connecticut and Plymouth where greater care had been taken in granting land titles. *Massachusetts Orthodox Puritans objected because innovations limited their independence, taxed them without their consent, and required recognition of the Crown as the ultimate power.*

Governor Andros tried to improve defenses against the French and Indians. By late 1688, the Dominion defenses were better. The overthrow of Governor Andros in 1688 with the coming of the Glorious Revolution destroyed his military accomplishments. England lost the only effective defense system she ever had in America.

The Dominion of New England lasted from 12/1686 until 4/1689. Its' purpose had been to reconstruct New England society but failed.

Andros did a relatively good job but didn't have the appropriate tools to get it done. The Navigation Acts were being enforced by the end of his 2nd year in office, Vice-Admiralty Courts were handing out convictions against offending merchants, local government power had been weakened, centralized government strengthened , and colonial militia's had been brought under unified control of a Royal commander. Land taxes had been lowered. The costs of government administration came from current income.

In August, 1688, Indians raided the towns of Northfield, Massachusetts, and Penobscot, Maine. Governor Andros sent troops. Rumors spread that Andros was a "Papist" at heart and planned to turn New England over to France if King James II was forced from the Throne. When news of William & Mary's accession to the throne reached New England the people decided that Andros must be removed so he can't complete his plan. Andros was jailed, escaped, and recaptured along with Randolph and other Dominion officials. The rebels blamed the loss of the Massachusetts charter on Randolph and Andros. They remained in jail until 2/1690 when English authorities ordered them freed and returned to England.

7. **THE EFFECT OF THE GLORIOUS REVOLUTION OF 1688**

In November, 1688, William of Orange and Mary assumed the Throne as successors to King James II. Few of the gains that made the Glorious Revolution memorable in English history were passed on to the colonies. In January, 1689, William issued orders that all colonial officers, *except Catholics*, were to remain at their government posts.

A few months later, William dragged the colonists into King William's War with France which unleashed the Indians upon New York and all of New England. When the War ended the King implemented severe government measures and taxes. It needed revenue to fight the war but the people refused to pay the taxes and began to wish for the return of the Royal Governor.

Opponents established a "Council of Safety" with Simon Bradstreet as President. On 5/24/1690, the Council summoned a convention which voted to re-establish the government as it had existed under the Charter. Two days later William & Mary issued a Proclamation approving the new regime.

Although most of the opposition centered in Boston, neither Connecticut or Rhode Island surrendered their Charters when ordered by Andros. When Andros was removed, both colonies proceeded to govern themselves as they had before the Dominion.

The Glorious Revolution had religious significance for the colonies as well. Up to 1688 the Anglican Church flourished on a colony-wide basis only in Virginia. After 1689 every Royal Governor would be instructed to promote and safeguard the English Church. Politically, the shift of Constitutional power from the Crown to Parliament would take time to be understood. A subtle change in the Crown attitude toward the colonies proved easier to observe. The arbitrary nature of Royal administration failed, never again was there an attempt to rule without a colonial legislature. ***The experiment in centralization was never repeated.***

In summary, the effects of the Glorious Revolution on New England were:
a. Established the supremacy of the English Parliament over the King/Monarchy;
b. The immediate result in the colonies was the collapse of the Dominion of New England;
c. Massachusetts, Plymouth, Maine, and New Hampshire were made Royal colonies in 1691;

d. Rhode Island and Connecticut were allowed to retain their Corporate Charters;

e. In New York there was a revolt against Governor Andros led by Jacob Leisler which ended with New York becoming a Royal Colony and New Jersey in 1702 and the Carolina's in 1729;

f. Pennsylvania and Maryland were eventually restored to their Proprietors;

g. By 1754 all were Royal colonies except Maryland, Pennsylvania, which included Delaware, which were Proprietary, and Connecticut and Rhode Island which were Chartered.

8. **VERMONT**

It was discovered and claimed for France by Samuel de Champlain on 7/30/1609 when he came upon present-day Lake Champlain and named the mountains "Les Verts Monts" (The Green Mountains). The French influence is reflected in many of their place names, such as Montpelier, Calais, and Lake Champlain.

Native Americans, primarily from the Abenaki tribe, lived in Vermont for years. After Champlain discovered the area the French established military outposts primarily for their fur-trade. *The Lake Champlain area became a major thoroughfare between French and Indian settlements in the north and the English settlements to the south, primarily along the Hudson River.*

As the English moved north, the first settlements were made at Fort St. Anne, on Isle La Motte, in the middle of Lake Champlain near the present-day Canadian border. Fort Drummer, near present-day Brattleboro, was established in 1724 by Massachusetts colonists and became the first permanent European settlement in Vermont. By the time of the American Revolution, more colonists had migrated to Vermont, coming from Massachusetts, Connecticut, New Hampshire, and New York, as those colonies had extended their boundaries into the Vermont territory.

With multiple claims to the same territory there was considerable confusion. In the years prior to the American Revolution, several acts of rebellion occurred, not against the English, but against the province of New York. Vermont's famous "Green Mountain Boys", a group of colonists from New Hampshire organized by Ethan Allen in 1770-1771, were among those harassing and attacking Vermont settlers with land titles issued from New York. These disputes were set aside once the Revolutionary War began and efforts were then directed against British outposts. *Vermont never existed as a chartered colony but belonged to New York until it was admitted to the Union as the 14th state in 1791.*

Vermont timeline:

1535   French explorer Jacque Cartier was the first European to explore current Vermont

1609   Samuel de Champlain discovers Lake Champlain

1666   Fort St. Anne is constructed on Isle Lal Motte, site of the first white settlement and first Catholic Mass

1690   A small British fort is constructed at Chimney Point

1724   The British build Fort Dummer at Dummerston

1731   The French build a Fort and settlement at Chimney Point under Seigneur Gilles Hocquart

1749   Governor Benning Wentworth makes the first New Hampshire grant for the town of Bennington

1760   The Crown Point military road from Springfield, Vermont, to Chimney Point is completed East-West across Vermont.

1761   Governor Wentworth resumes the New Hampshire grants

1770   The Green Mountain Boys are organized to protect the New Hampshire grants

1775   Ethan Allen captures Fort Ticonderoga

1776   Construction of the American Fort Independence at Orwell

1777   Vermont declares itself a Republic and adopts its 1st Constitution with universal suffrage, public schools, and abolishes slavery.

1780   The last Indian raid is led by the British in Royalton

1791   Vermont becomes the 14th state with a population of 85,341.

9. **MAINE**

The History of Maine, although never a separate original English colony, is covered in the Massachusetts chapter.

B.   THE MIDDLE AND SOUTHERN COLONIES

1. **BACKGROUND**

The history and development of the middle colonies occurs in two phases;

   a. Sporadic early explorations by Dutch, French, Swedish, and English in the early 17th century,

   b. Serious English settlement efforts after the Restoration of the Stuarts, with King Charles II, in 1660.

The middle colonies were considered the "bread colonies" because they produced grain, wheat, corn, livestock, vegetables, and fruits. Fertile land plus a favorable climate encouraged family-sized farms which produced surplus grains for export to other colonies and England. Long, navigable rivers such as the Hudson, Susquehanna, and Delaware promoted fur-trade with the Indians. Good harbors like New York and Philadelphia stimulated trade with other colonies as well as England and Europe.

2. **PROPRIETARY GOVERNMENTS**

During the Restoration period, England returned to its oldest method for settling the New World, the Proprietary Colony. King Charles II adopted the technique reluctantly although the

Proprietor did receive its authority directly from the Crown, thus the King could still maintain overall control of the Empire.

In 1663, King Charles II started England on the second and final wave of colonization, this time dominated by Proprietors, not Companies. This method was used in 12 of the 13 original colonies.

How did it work? Proprietors granted land to individuals in return for a "quit-rent" which were difficult to collect, so most of the land came to be owned by "fee simple". Land was first acquired as headrights instead of by outright purchase which became the rule in the 18th century. Indentured servants or redemptioners served as the most important source of labor. Farms were usually small.

"Redemptioners" were another class of bound servants distinguished from indentured servants. These "free-willers" came voluntarily and with families, usually had some savings, and made a more respectable contribution to society. Both kinds of servants were released at the end of their contract and were usually given 50 acres of land, clothing, and tools.

After 1750, Pennsylvania became the leader in iron production with abundant ore and wood for smelting. Flour milling also became an important industry in Pennsylvania and New York so these colonies exported large quantities of flour but all colonies produced flour for local consumption.

3. **IMPACT OF THE GLORIOUS REVOLUTION ON THE MIDDLE & SOUTHERN COLONIES**

In New York, the impact was difficult to assess because of the many factions and considerable infighting among them. When Lieutenant Governor Francis Nicholson, a Catholic who ruled both New York and New Jersey at the time, was hesitant to announce the accession to the Throne of William and Mary, some suspected that he was planning on turning the colony over to the Pope. One person, in particular, Jacob Leisler, a German immigrant, took advantage of the situation to create turmoil which led to considerable political upheaval in the colony, not directly due to the Glorious Revolution, however.

In the Carolina's the news of the Glorious Revolution was met without any significant problems. As in New York, at the time South Carolina was in the midst of political turmoil due to dissatisfaction over high quit-rents, to the inappropriateness of the Fundamental Constitution, to the lack of the right to initiate legislation and to Governor Colleton's arbitrary rule. But, the opposition lacked a strong leader to use the Glorious Revolution as an excuse to stage a revolution of its own. The Carolinian's grumbled but endured their grievances even when Governor Colleton dissolved the Parliament and ruled by Executive decree.

The colony of Georgia was founded after the Glorious Revolution so there is no impact to discuss.

C.   GLOSSARY

1. **"Fee simple"** means the absolute ownership of land and the owner can do whatever he/she wishes with the land. Stated another way, it gives absolute title to the land and free of any other claims against the title.

(Attachment 18b represents a Map of the Middle Colonies from 1620)

(Attachment 18c represents a Map of the Southern Colonies, unknown date)

18a

New England Colonies, 1620-1636
Robert Hall, Harriet Smither, and Clarence Ousley. A History of the United States (Dallas, TX: The Southern Publishing Company, 1920)
Downloaded from *Maps ETC*, on the web at http://etc.usf.edu/maps   [map #05273]

18b

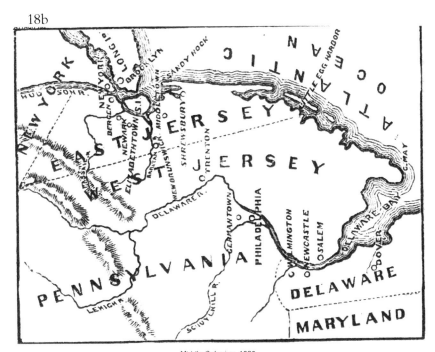

Middle Colonies, 1620

18c

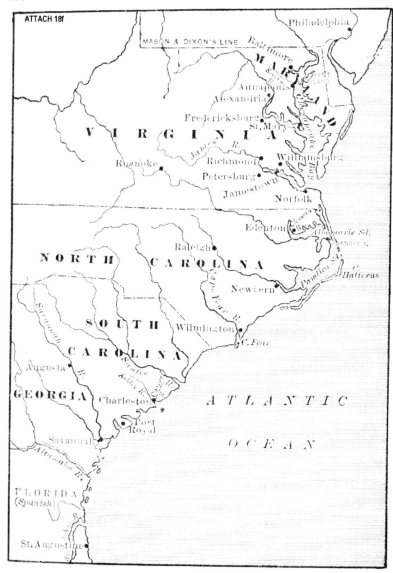

The Southern Colonies

Chapter 19

Indian Relations and Imperial Wars

A.   INDIAN RELATIONS

There are questions among historians as to the origins of the American Indians but my intent is to rather examine the relationship between the early colonists and the Indians who sometimes were friendly and sometimes very hostile.

1. **BACKGROUND**

Some of the most advanced tribes in North America at the period of European discovery were those of the Northwest Coast, extending from Alaska to Oregon. Their economy was based on salmon and other fish, which they learned to preserve by smoking, so that everyone had plenty to eat at all times. They wove baskets so tight that water and food could be boiled in them by using hot stones, they built great dugout canoes, and ornamented their dwellings with carved trees, or "totem poles", which told every passerby who you were and from whom you were descended.

There is even less known of the Indian history east of the Rocky Mountains because they moved around so much. These Indians recorded themselves by building gigantic earthen mounds, often built in shapes of serpents and birds. The Cahokia Mound at East St. Louis, Missouri, is one hundred feet high and covers 16 acres. Within these mounds the Indians buried their dead almost as elaborately as did the ancient Egyptians and the contents of their tombs tell us how they lived.

At the time the first Europeans arrived, the Indians of the Great Plains between the Rocky Mountains and the forested areas bordering on the Mississippi River lived partly by corn culture but more by hunting the buffalo.

2. **VARIOUS INDIAN TRIBES AND NATIONS**
   The first Language Group, the Algonquins, included the:

   • Abenaki of Maine and Nova Scotia

   • All tribes of southern New England including the Pequot and Mohegan tribes

   • Delaware and Powhatan of the middle states and Virginia

   • Sauk and Fox tribes

   • Kickapoo, Pottawatomi, and Blackfoot tribes of the middle west

These tribes cultivated beans, pumpkins, tobacco, and maize which, on many occasions, saved the English colonists from starvation. This was the largest language group east of the Mississippi river and controlled most of Canada, the Ohio river valley, all of New England, and were scattered southward through eastern Pennsylvania, New Jersey, Maryland, and Virginia.

They greeted the early settlers at Jamestown, Plymouth, Boston, and the French wherever they went in Canada. They were semi-nomadic, lived in bark-covered huts, and were noted for their enterprise and the birch bark canoe, which they invented. They were excellent fishermen and hunters of deer and moose for their meat and beaver for their furs.

These tribes produced some great and noble leaders, such as; Powhatan, Massasoit, King Philip, Tammany, Pontiac, Tecumseh, and Keokuk. The Algonquin were receptive to Christianity and assimilated European culture better than most Indians, although some of the previously mentioned Chiefs eventually attempted to unite their people against the English and perished in the attempt.

The Pequot and Mohegans probably lived in present-day southeast Connecticut for several hundred years before the arrival of the Europeans. Just before the Pequot War in 1637, the Mohegans were led by a Chief named Uncas who split from the Pequots and aligned with the English. At this time, the Pequot strength was concentrated along the Pequot, now the Thames, and Mystic rivers in southeastern Connecticut. Their only serious rival was the Narragansett tribe.

If the Mohegans are included, the Pequot probably numbered about 6,000 in 1620. Less than half survived the Pequot War with the remainder placed under the Mohegan who treated them so badly that, by 1655, the English were forced to remove them. Two reservations were created for them in 1666 and 1683. By 1762, there were only 140 Pequot and the decline continued until there were only 66 in the 1910 census. At the present-time, the State of Connecticut recognizes just 2 Pequot tribes.

a. *The 2nd Language Group was the "Five Nations of the Iroquois Confederacy", consisting of the:*

- Mohawk, Cayuga, Oneida, Onandaga, and Seneca tribes (The Tuscarora and southern Cherokee joined later)

They had a reputation as being among the toughest fighters in North America which was necessary to defend against the Algonquin tribes. In 1600, when first seen by the Europeans, they occupied the territory from Lake Champlain to the Genesee river and from the Adirondack Mountains to central Pennsylvania. The Iroquois survived the arrival of the Europeans and even extended their dominion by uniting or being allied with the English and Dutch. Among their greatest leaders were Henrick, Cornplanter, Red Jacket, Brant, and Logan.

They were the 2nd largest language group which had moved up from the south and cut the Algonquin nation in half. They were centered in New York, northern Ohio, and western Pennsylvania. Their Confederacy was probably formed sometime in the 15th century and were very aggressive, usually at war with someone.

They could field large armies of 500–1,000 warriors per battle. Quite often their Indian disputes would involve the French, who backed the Algonquin, and the English, who backed the Iroquois.

The Tuscarora moved north in 1720 and became the Sixth Nation of the Iroquois Confederacy along with the southern Cherokee who were also of Iroquois origin. The Cherokee produced one of the greatest of American Indians, Sequoya, who invented an alphabet for his people which greatly advanced their culture.

b. *The 3rd Language Group was the Muskogean, which included the:*

- Chickasaw, Choctaw, Creek, Natchez, and Seminole tribes

They were centered in the deep south, from Georgia into northern Florida, Tennessee, Alabama, and Mississippi. They were considered by colonial Europeans as the "elite" of the North American Indians. They were planters of maize and expert potters, weavers, and curers of deerskin for clothing. They quickly learned from the Europeans how to plant orchards and keep cattle. They were courted by the French along the Mississippi river, the Spanish in Florida, and the English along the Atlantic coast.

c. *The 4th Language Group was the Sioux:*

They were centered mostly west of the Mississippi river valley, except for the Catawba, who were centered in the Piedmont region of the Carolina's.

There really isn't much known about the many different Indian languages of the Algonquins, Iroquois, and Muskogean tribes. The Algonquin dialects were spoken as far north as Hudson Bay, west to the Rockies, and south to the Carolina's, but there was no mutual knowledge or connection between the widely separated tribes who spoke them.

3. **OVERVIEW**

The coming of the white man devastated the Indian's way of life. The French regarded the Indians with genuine respect but only a few of the English treated them with respect and most Englishmen were dishonest and patronizing in their relationships with the Indians. The most prevailing attitude of the English was that the Indians were barbaric and must be made to adapt to the superior white culture, become Christian, live in houses, and work hard. The English never expected that the Indians would reject their attempts to "civilize them".

By 1619, at least 50 missionaries had been sent to the colonies to spread the Gospel among them and within a few years most had been killed by the Indians. Eventually the English became more realistic and gave up their attempt to civilize them but planned to destroy them as competitors for land and resources.

While the American colonist changed his opinion of the Indians, the English at home continued to view him as a "noble savage", innocent and dignified, pure and strong, needing only Christianity to make him a perfect man. The colonists' changing view puzzled and distressed the English at home. As they failed to see how the American experience had changed the settlers' image of the Indian, they also failed to see other changes the New World was shaping on the ideas and habits carried across the Ocean.

The land, the Indians, and the distance from England had worked together to slowly dilute the attitudes the settlers brought with them. Within a generation, a society had arisen around the shores of the Chesapeake and Massachusetts Bays which was much different from the England they had left behind.

4. **THE PEQUOT WAR (1636-1638)** (*Attachment 19a represents a Map of the location of the Pequot War.*)

Other than a few incidents in other colonies and locations, there was no general Indian uprising until the Pequot War in 1636 in New England. The Puritans arrived in New England expecting to make the Indians over in their own image. When the Indians resisted, the Puritans adopted a "get-tough" attitude, with the exception of a few colonists like Roger Williams who treated them with genuine respect.

The Pequot War was the result of many conflicts between the colonists and Indians over property, damage to Indian crops, hunting and dishonest traders. The colonists believed they had a God-given right to settle the land and viewed the Indians as savages to be converted to their way of God. They felt superior to all Indians who were in a tough situation; they were abused by the settlers but depended on their trade and goods. Two events weakened the Pequot's prior to their war with the English and their settlers:

a. In 1631, the Tribe was divided into two factions, one was pro-Dutch and the other was pro-English. The problem had not been solved when their Chief, Wopigwooit, died, leading to a power struggle between Sassacus who was pro-Dutch and Uncas who was pro-English. The Tribe supported Sassacus but Uncas and his followers continued to oppose the pro-Dutch faction. Eventually, they formed their own tribe, the Mohegans, who became hostile to the Pequot's.

b. An outbreak of smallpox in 1633-1634 killed many Pequot's. These two events eliminated almost half of the original Pequot's.

Hostilities actually occurred on 7/20/1636 when the Pequot's killed a dishonest trader, John Oldham. Settlers demanded that the Pequot's be punished. The Massachusetts Bay colony raised a small force of 90 led by John Endicott who landed on Block Island, killed 14 Indians, and burned their village and crops. Endicott then sailed to Saybrook where he demanded tribute from the Pequot's. This was the first indication that Connecticut had that the Massachusetts Bay colony was fighting the Pequot's. At the approach of Endicott and his troops, the Pequot's fled their village which was burned down by Endicott who then left, leaving some troops at Fort Saybrook to face the angry Pequot's who attacked anyone leaving the fort. That winter the Pequot's tried to recruit supporters but were rejected by the Narragansetts and the Mohegans, who even sided with the English.

On May 26, 1637, a military force led by Captain John Mason of

Connecticut and Captain John Underhill of the Massachusetts Bay colony, attacked a Pequot village near New Haven, Connecticut, where they destroyed a village and killed over 500 Indians. The Pequot leader, Sassacus, was captured and executed by the Mohawk's who were allied with the English. Some Pequot's escaped to friendly tribes and assimilated with them but, overall, the tribe was effectively destroyed.

The Treaty of Hartford (9/21/1638)

Roger Williams helped negotiate this **Peace Treaty which settled the Pequot War.** Strangely enough, the Pequot's were not a party to the terms. The Massachusetts Bay colony, the Connecticut river colonies, the Mohegan and Narragansett tribes were included. These were the "victors" who met to divide the fruits of victory **per the following terms:**

- surviving prisoners were divided between tribes with 40% each, and the remaining 20% awarded to the tribes on Long Island who had supported the Narragansett

- the Pequot lands were given to the Connecticut river towns

- the Pequot language was outlawed as was the name "Pequot"

- any survivors would be referred to in the future as Mohegans or Narragansett

- no future Pequot towns or settlements would be allowed

NOTE: Uncas was born into the Pequot Tribe, rebelled against his father-in-law, Sassacus, and formed his own Mohegan tribe. He aided the English colonists in the Pequot War of 1637 and subsequently fought and defeated the Narragansett's in 1643. In 1661, he made war on an ally of the English, Chief Massasoit of the Wampanoag tribe. The English forced Uncas to give up his captives and plunder. With the beginning of King Philip's War in 1675, he was required to turn over his sons as hostages to the English to insure his neutrality. The character, "Uncas", was immortalized in literature in *"The Last of the Mohicans" written in 1826 by the American writer, James Fenimore Cooper.*

5. **CONTINUING INDIAN PROBLEMS.**
The Indians rose again in 1644, led by Opechancanough, now old and feeble, against the Virginians. He decided that now was the time to once and for all rid the area of settlers. The "Great Massacre" of 1622 didn't achieve the goal so, now, with England pre-occupied with their Civil War, the time seemed right to try again.

He persuaded many of the Chesapeake tribes to join him in his repeat effort. They realized from their previous failure in 1622 that another failure would mean more reprisals against them. They attacked and killed many settlers but Opechancanough was captured and killed.

Virginia responded with enough ferocity that the Indians asked for peace in 1646. By terms of a signed Peace Treaty, they became subjects of England and ceded all of the land between the York and James rivers from the fall-line to the Ocean. No Indian was allowed to enter this area except with the Governor's permission. The treaty also prohibited settlers to enter the protected Indian territory.

This well-intended attempt to give the Indians specific lands preserved for them alone failed before it went into effect because it came during a population explosion. Virginia's population doubled in the 1640's from 8,000 to 16,000 and then to 40,000 during the next decade. Expansion into Indian areas continued which caused the Indians to react, unsuccessfully again.

Once the Virginia Assembly realized that its' policy of reserving Indian lands had failed it tried again to "civilize" them. They tried using the "headright system" for the Indians which had worked so well for attracting white settlers. They offered a cow for every eight wolf-head's brought in. Eventually, this too failed. The Indians just refused to be converted to the white man's culture. As a result, friction continued between the expanding settlers and the Indian's attempt to hold on to their hunting and fishing territories.

6. **BACON'S REBELLION (1674-1676)**

   Trouble with the Indians, wherever it occurred, unsettled a whole colony and sometimes spread to other colonies. Although well-meaning men in every colony made sincere efforts to deal fairly with the Indians, it failed partly because the Indians refused to conform to the white man's culture and also because any plan for humane treatment of them conflicted with some segment of colonial interests.

   Bacon's Rebellion in Virginia, unrest in Maryland and Carolina, and King Philip's War in New England were united by a common failure to resolve the tensions between white and red men.

   Virginian's in 1675 were unhappy with many things about their life; economic, political, and social. Expansion into the back-country not only created conflict with the Indians but also between various governmental and political factions in the various colonies.

   Virginia Governor Berkeley, after the Indian Wars of 1644, tried to block expansion by erecting a line of forts between their respective lands. In 1671, he believed the "Indian problem" had been resolved and there was no fear of further conflict. But, as we learned in Chapter 5, unrest along the Virginia frontier continued until the settlers rebelled against Governor Berkeley until Bacon died and order was restored by two peace commissioners sent from England in early 1677.

7. **KING PHILIP'S WAR (1675-1676) (The Treaty of Casco Bay 4/1678)**

   Governor Berkeley of Virginia had blamed Virginia's Indian problems on New England. He believed that more than local issues had stirred up the Indians but blaming it on New England went too far. It is true that the unrest in 1675 in Virginia and New

England had a common enemy and cause, the spread of settlers into Indian lands, but his view that New England was the cause of the problems was wrong.

The War was an armed conflict between the Indians of present-day southern New England and the English colonists. It was named for the Indian leader, Metacomet, or "King Philip", as he was called by the English. ***The War had many names:***

a. First Indian War

b. Metacom's War

c. Metacomet's War

d. Metacom's Rebellion

Major Benjamin Church was the Puritan hero of the war as it was his company of Puritan rangers which finally hunted down and killed King Philip on 8/12/1676. But, the war did continue in northern New England, primarily in Maine, until the ***Treaty of Casco Bay in April, 1678***. The terms weren't much more than just assuring that all captives were to be returned without ransom and all inhabitants returning to their homes were to "enjoy their possessions unmolested".

By 1675, almost 50,000 settlers had moved into the northern colonies pushing the Indians out of their favorite hunting and fishing areas. The effects of this expansion remained within New England and the Indians' retreat was blocked by the Appalachian Mountains to the west plus the hostile Iroquois Indians as well. These obstacles localized and intensified the Indians' growing hatred which, when it burst forth, came close to consuming all of New England.

Tensions between whites and Indians had been contained for nearly 40 years. Memories of the Pequot defeat helped restrain any Indian desire for another war. Some missionary work had proved successful in converting some of the Indians to Christianity and adopting the white man's way. The un-converted Indians were not happy but not enough to start another war. However, the Puritans continued to treat them disrespectfully by forcing them to obey Puritan laws. They were punished if they hunted or fished or jailed if they stole, fined if they became drunk on alcohol sold to them by white settlers. The laws applied to them were harsh.

Metacomet, King Philip as the Puritans called him, was the son of Massasoit, the great Indian Chief who had befriended the Pilgrims. Philip lacked his father's dignity and character, was weak and deceitful, but he was the leader of the Wampanoag tribes. Plymouth colony, which in 1621 had humbly sent a peace delegation to Massasoit, now in 1671 sent soldiers to arrest his son for plotting against the colony. He was sentenced to pay a heavy fine, forced to admit that he and his people were subject to English law, and ordered to deposit his people's guns with the Plymouth Court.

It is true that Metacomet distrusted the colonists and had been negotiating with other tribes against the Plymouth colony since 1661. John Sassamon, a converted Indian ("Praying Indian") and an adviser to Metacomet, spread a false rumor to Plymouth colony officials that Metacomet was planning attacks on Plymouth colony. He was brought before a court to answer the rumors and, after the court admitted that it had no proof, it warned him that further rumors, true or not, would permit the colony to confiscate their land and guns. Soon, Sassamon was killed, supposedly by some of his supporters, angry at his betrayal.

Based on the testimony of an Indian witness, the Plymouth colony officials arrested three Wampanoags, including one of Metacomet's advisers. A jury, including some Indians, convicted the men of murder and they were hanged on 6/8/1675 at Plymouth. Some Indians believed the trial and sentence was an insult to their sovereignty. On 6/20/1675, a band of Indians, possibly without Metacomet's approval, destroyed many homes in Swansea, Massachusetts, and killed several settlers. Officials from Plymouth and Boston sent a military expedition on 6/28/1675 to destroy the Indian town at Mount Hope, present-day Bristol, Rhode Island. All of New England supported the retaliation but also believed the harshness toward Metacomet had created the conditions for the attacks.

At the time, the white population of New England was about 80,000 and lived in 110 towns with 64 located in Massachusetts. Many towns had built strong garrison houses for defense and others had stockades enclosing most of the houses. The region also included about 10,500 Indians although the Wampanoag and Pokanet of Plymouth and eastern Rhode Island by then numbered fewer than 1,000 each.

The war spread to other tribes and during the summer of 1675 many towns were attacked. The New England Confederation declared war on 9/9/1675 but on 9/18/1675 a group of colonists were ambushed and defeated while recovering crops for the winter at the "Battle of Bloody Brook" near present-day Hadley, Massachusetts. There were other Indian attacks in October including an attack on Springfield, Massachusetts, on 10/5/1675.

On 11/2/1675, Plymouth Governor Josiah Winslow led an attack against the Narragansett tribe which caused them, the most powerful and peaceful tribe in New England, to support Philip, joined soon after by the Nipmuck tribe. The war now spread from the Atlantic coast up the Connecticut river valley. By the end of summer, the Connecticut-Massachusetts frontier was in flames.

On 12/16/1675, Massachusetts again attacked the Narragansetts promising their soldiers that if they were successful, they would be rewarded with Narragansett lands. The Narragansetts lost between 200–300 men, women, and children but bickering among the colonial leaders allowed the main body to escape. The Indians kept up their attacks through the winter until by April, 1676, the village of Sudbury, only 17 miles from Boston, had become the most exposed outpost of New England. If the Indians at this time could have united behind a single leader they might have defeated the Puritans.

The situation became so dangerous for the colonies that Massachusetts and Connecticut imposed a "draft" of every male between the ages of 16-60 liable for military service. Eventually, the Indians ran out of supplies, with no allies to resupply them, the whites outnumbered the Indians 4-1, and by Spring, 1676, it was becoming obvious the Indians would lose the war. The main cause of defeat was the lack of food reserves and the necessity for food forced them to end the fighting. At the same time, Philip was shot and killed by one of the "converted" Indians. Peace treaties were signed with the tribes of southern New England but those in the north continued to raid the settlements of New Hampshire and Maine until 1678.

In proportion to the population, this war inflicted greater casualties upon the people than any other war in our history. 13 frontier villages were destroyed and six others partially burned. 10% of Massachusetts 5,000 males of military age had been captured or killed. Indian leaders had been captured and executed plus many other warriors were shipped as slaves to the West Indies.

The War killed the long-dying Confederation of New England. The conquest of New Netherland by the English in 1664 had removed one of the sources of the need for self-defense, the Dutch. With the English Restoration in 1660, the Crown's resumption of control over foreign affairs had eliminated another reason for the Confederation. Since the Confederation had failed in every emergency to produce cooperation among the colonies all of *the colonies basically adopted a policy of taking care of their own business and ignoring the needs of their neighbor colonies. As a result, New Englanders had developed a distaste for any plan of union or self-defense.*

8. **BEYOND KING PHILIP'S WAR**

By 1689, the Indians were still a menace to the colonists. By now they were being assisted by the French and Spanish. The Puritans continued to treat the Indians with disrespect by trying to impose their lifestyle on them. Toward the end of the 17th century it dawned on the authorities in London that unless something was done, the French and Indians together might push the colonists off the continent.

Official English policy began to change from remaking the native in the image of the white man to one of treating the Indians as an instrument of trade and a useful ally against the

French. Settlers were ordered to stay off Indian lands and only licensed traders were permitted to deal with the Indians. As more potential enemies arose, the colonists realized the need for English protection and some leaders even requested that the Crown take over their governments.

But, the experience of defending themselves against the Indians caused the colonists to realize that there was no time to wait for orders or aid from England. Often, when England did come to their aid, it was often inadequate, too late, or at odds with what the colonists had done or wanted to do. America's enemies caused relations between England and her colonies to change.

The settlers welcomed imperial control when it protected them from their enemies but complained when it restrained their freedom of action. Relations between Crown and Colony, which had been confused up to now, took on a shape which would remain to the end of the colonial period.

B.   THE 4 IMPERIAL WARS

All of these changes were visible in the years following the accession of William & Mary in 1689. The period between 1689 and 1713 embraced two wars which began in Europe but affected America. As far as the colonists were concerned, the French menace at their backs caused the trouble.

1.   THE FRENCH MENACE

Louis XIV came to the throne of France in 1661 and brought with him Jean Baptiste Colbert to help realize his ambition. *They made France the greatest power in Europe and, at the same time, they transformed Canada from a feeble colony into an enemy potentially capable of conquering the English Empire in America.* Colbert assumed that French strength in Europe was related to her resources overseas. The fur trade of New France would be extended to meet the costs of developing the American Empire. Colbert's mercantilism differed from England's in that the full strength of the

French Monarchy stood behind his plan whereas in England, the government needed to be pushed into developing a policy. Colbert never succeeded in making New France (Canada) a profitable enterprise for France, but when he died in 1683, New France was viewed as a threat to the well-being of British America.

King Louis XIV and Colbert built New France by sending competent leaders, such as Jean Talon, who focused his attention on the west. The French feared the English would reach the Mississippi river before the French. He persuaded Frontenac, the recently arrived Governor-General, to quickly send an expedition. Louis de Buade, Count Frontenac, was a key government official and arrived in 1672 with the goal of investigating the Mississippi river, which France believed was the passage to the "South Sea", or, Pacific Ocean as it was thought to be. As we learned in Chapter 2, Louis Joliet in May, 1673, a onetime Priest-turned fur trader, and Father Marquette, a Jesuit who had lived many years in the western country and knew many Indian dialects, also explored the area.

Fortunately, their explorations were noticed by Sieur de La Salle who explored the area and returned to France to convince the King and Colbert to invest in developing a commercial interest in North America. He made plans to build a series of forts to protect France's fur trade and other commercial interests. Most importantly, he developed good relations with the Indians. In late 1682, he explored the Mississippi river to its mouth. On 4/9/1683, he claimed the Louisiana territory for France. The King gave him ships and troops to establish a settlement at the mouth of the Mississippi. In 1685 he sailed into the Caribbean but missed the mouth of the river and landed at Matagorda Bay, Texas. The settlement had only 45 settlers by 1687 when he made a last attempt to reach Fort St. Louis on the Illinois river. On the way, he was killed, at age 43.

England and her colonies reacted to the French presence in the Iroquois territory of upper New York, the one spot France did not dominate. ***Many attempts by Jesuit Missionaries and fur traders to***

convert the Iroquois to their side failed because the French were allied with their chief enemy, the Algonquins. The furs of the Iroquois had been depleted since the early 17th century which meant, to prosper, the Iroquois must become middlemen between tribes in the west, mainly the Algonquins, and the Dutch merchants at Fort Orange who supplied them with guns and other necessities of life purchased by beaver skins alone. But, the French controlled the sources of the trade. The Iroquois attempted to cut into this trade by attacking the Hurons in 1649 and some of their allies until 1651 when the brief war ended but with the furs still flowing into French possession.

The arrival of the English in New York complicated the story after 1664. France sent 1,000 troops into upper New York in 1666 that destroyed villages and left the Iroquois weakened. But, even though the French militarily commanded the area, the English did have an advantage over the French in trade. British woolens were better than any made in France or bought anywhere in the world. English products could be delivered to the customer so cheaply as to force the French out of competition. The Iroquois had a significant advantage, then, because their beaver skins/furs would always buy two or three times as much at Albany as from any French trader. **This bargaining power gave the Iroquois a weapon more potent than their skill in battle and with that leverage, they launched an invasion of the west which initiated what came to be known as "King William's War".**

2. **THE IMPERIAL WARS IN EUROPE AND THE COLONIES**
   Beginning in the late 1600's, a series of wars swept across Europe and other parts of the world, all of which involved both England and their American colonial allies against the French and their Indian allies. The European components of those wars often dealt with issues of little or no concern to the colonists even though they were often affected directly or indirectly by the outcomes, sometimes to their detriment. In some wars they fought alongside British

regulars and made significant contributions on the battlefield only to see the fruits of those efforts bargained away by treaties made across the Ocean, without having any opportunity to participate in the negotiations.

Most of the wars dealt with "Empire" issues with the net result being that England was left in command of most of North America, north of Mexico and east of the Mississippi river.

As King Louis XIV came to power in 1661 and began to project French power and influence around the world, *the goal of the colonists was to defend against the Indians and the other colonial powers, especially France.*

In the American colonies each of these imperial wars was named for the English Monarch on the throne at the time of the war, thus:

COLONIAL WAR DATES	EUROPEAN WAR DATES
King William's War (1689-1697)	European War of the Grand Alliance or War of the League of Augsburg (1688-1697)
Queen Anne's War (1702-1713)	War of the Spanish Succession (1701-1714)
King George's War (1744-1748)	War of Jenkins Ear, or War of the Austrian Succession (1740-1748)
French & Indian War (1754-1763)	7 Years War (1756-1763)

a. King William's War (War of the Grand Alliance) 1689-1697 (War of the League of Augsburg)

This was the first of what came to be known as the "French and Indian Wars" which were a series of colonial wars between England and France lasting 3/4 of a century. War began in America in

Schenactady, New York, which was attacked on 2/9/1690 by the French and Indians. Then, the English colonial forces seized Port Royal (Nova Scotia) on 5/11/1690 although the next year the French recaptured it again. There were many attacks from both sides throughout New England over the next 6-7 years but *eventually it ended as a stalemate and settled by the Treaty of Ryswick, 1697, which also settled the European phase of the "War of the Grand Alliance".*

The European phase of the war began when King William III joined the League of Augsburg and the Netherlands, forming the "Grand Alliance", on 5/12/1689. *His purpose was to resist the French invasion of the Rhenish Palatinate on 9/25/1688. The French began this war to be in position to name the new ruler to the Spanish Throne since King Charles II was ill and expected to die soon without a legal heir.* Leopold I, the Holy Roman Emperor, was aware of the French plans and formed the "League of Augsburg" in 1686. In 1689 he expanded it to the "Grand Alliance" consisting of England, Spain, Netherlands, Brandenburg, Saxony, Bavaria, and Sweden.

b. <u>Queen Anne's War</u> (War of the Spanish Succession) 1702-1713

After the death of the Spanish Habsburg King Charles II on 11/1/1700, his last Will designated King Louis XIV's 2nd grandson, Philip Duc d'Anjou, as his successor. His closest heirs, both by marriage, were King Louis XIV of France and Emperor Leopold I. Both England and Holland made it clear that they would oppose either of them assuming the Throne so the candidates were Philip of Anjou and Archduke Charles, the second son of Leopold I. Per the Will, Philip became King Philip V and assumed the Throne. *The Archduke Charles did not give up his claim and fighting began in parts of Spain, France, and today's Belgium.*

The first military action was the French occupation of the Spanish Netherlands in March, 1701, creating war preparations in England, Holland, and Austria. *The war spread over Europe and eventually it was ended by the Treaty of Utrecht on 4/11/1713 for everyone except France and the Archduke Charles of the Holy Roman Empire.* Philip was recognized as the King of Spain but the Spanish Netherlands and most Spanish lands in Italy became part of the Holy Roman Empire. France promised that they would never unite with Spain under a single Crown. Archduke Charles attempted to continue fighting but he had no allies and *eventually, in 1714, the War ended with the Treaty of Madrid.* The outcome of the war altered the balance of power in Europe. Formerly, Spain and the Austrian Empire had been allies but now Spain became an ally of France. Fortunately for the rest of Europe, Spain was already in decline and her importance was diminished.

The War in America began in New England with raids by Indians led by the French. In August, 1703, 39 settlers were murdered at Wells, Maine. Raids continued into the autumn along a 200 mile frontier from Maine through New Hampshire and into western Massachusetts. Deerfield, Massachusetts, was raided with 38 settlers killed and 100 captives marched to Canada for ransom money. New England begged for aid from the other colonies but New York, the Pennsylvania Quakers, and Virginia refused. New England was on its own and, in 1704, some 500 New Englander's attacked Acadia (Nova Scotia) but failed to capture Port Royal and, in 1707, another expedition failed.

In 1708, London realized that the colonies would be unable to defeat the French forces of New France without its assistance. Queen Anne was urged to provide support to the colonists to defeat the French to the north and the Spanish to the south. She provided a fleet and five Regiments of troops against her enemies but the attack failed to materialize. In the fall of 1710, they began another attack and captured Port Royal in Acadia.

In 1711, they began a two-pronged attacked, overland from Albany, and a fleet of 70 ships and 12,000 troops targeting the St. Lawrence River Valley. The expedition eventually returned to Boston without having fired a shot which also caused the attack from Albany to be withdrawn. This ended the threat of invasion of Canada during the remainder of the Queen Anne's War.

The terms of the Treaty of Utrecht concerning Europe basically preserved the current balance of power. Those dealing with the New World were:

- The Iroquois, without being consulted, became English subjects

- Both England and France agreed not to interfere with the Indians within their respective jurisdictions

- Newfoundland and Acadia (Nova Scotia) became English possessions, this time for good

- France acknowledged English sovereignty over Hudson Bay plus England retained Cape Breton Island at the mouth of the St. Lawrence River, and English fishermen were allowed to dry their catches on the coast of Newfoundland

- In the West Indies, England acquired all of St. Kitts and Nevis islands

- Spain suffered most of its losses in Europe including the transference of Gibraltar to England but retained her New World possessions intact.

Hereafter, all European settlements would involve the holdings of belligerents in the New World. The Treaty settled little else.

c. <u>King George's War</u> (War of the Austrian Succession) 1744–1748

In 1740, the death of 2 European Monarchs started a war in Europe. King Frederick William I of Prussia died on 5/31/1740 and the Throne passed to his ruthless son, Frederick, to be known as "Frederick the Great". He inherited a powerful country and looked forward to asserting that power.

Archduke Charles had become King Charles VI, Emperor of Austria, but died on 10/19/1740 leaving his Throne to his daughter, Maria Theresa. Fearing that she, as Monarch, would not be able to defend Austria against other Monarchs, he developed the "Pragmatic Sanction of Prague", a convention which guaranteed the integrity of Austria and worked to persuade the other Monarchs to honor it, before he died.

Upon the death of King Charles VI, Frederick the Great refused to honor the convention, seized Silesia, and annexed it to Prussia. *This began a war which would last over 20 years. It didn't end until the "Treaty of Paris" of 1764 confirmed Prussia's ownership of Silesia. The first period of fighting from 1740-1748 was known as the "War of the Austrian Succession".* Austria and Prussia fought in Silesia and Bohemia while French armies invaded Bavaria. King George II of England vowed to send troops to support Maria Theresa but feared France would pass through his homeland of Hanover. The English force did travel to Flanders in 1742, however, and remained until 1748. *The War ended with the "Treaty of Aix-la-Chapelle" on 10/18/1748 which restored all of the conquered lands other than Silesia.*

The American version of the War, "King George's War", did not begin until 1744 when the French made an unsuccessful assault on Port Royal. In 1745, an expedition was led by William Pepperell with a British fleet under Sir Peter Warren who captured Louisburg.

Louisburg was built on a point of land on Cape Breton Island near the entrance to the St. Lawrence river. It was a powerful fortress but very costly to build and took 20 years to do so. It was the pride of the French presence in North America, considered to be an impregnable fortress but it was captured by a small naval fleet and a few thousand soldiers, primarily New England farmers and fishermen.

The leader of the Louisburg expedition was William Shirley, Governor of Massachusetts, with William Pepperell of Maine designated as its Commander. New England provided the men, Pennsylvania provided some provisions, and New York a small amount of artillery. On 5/1/1745, a fleet of 100 vessels attacked

Louisburg, landed its troops, and began a siege of 6 weeks. On 6/16/1745, the Fort surrendered to England.

The French King was upset at the news and made plans to recapture the Fort but the expedition never materialized. The next year, 1747, the King sent another fleet but it was captured by the British.

Per the terms of the Treaty of Aix-la-Chapelle, Louisburg was to be returned to the French. *The colonists, who had provided considerable resources to the war, were upset at this decision being made without their consent or knowledge. This led many colonists to believe that American affairs must be managed in America and not by diplomats across the Ocean who had minimal interest in the welfare and future of the New World.*

The results of this war, which basically maintained the current world balance of power, led, indirectly, to the next, and final, French and Indian War in the colonies.

d. The Final French & Indian War (1754-1763) (The 7 Year's War)

As the colonists and British officials began to fear the beginning of a war with the French, the English Board of Trade called for a Congress of the New England colonies to meet in Albany, New York, from 6/19 to 7/11/1754. 23 delegates were invited from seven of the 13 colonies, (Connecticut, Rhode Island, New York, Maryland, Massachusetts, Pennsylvania, and New Hampshire).

e. *They were to deal with two issues:*

1. *The Albany Plan of Union;*

   It was drafted by Ben Franklin and Thomas Hutchinson with the *purpose of forming a single colonial government.* That government would manage defense and Indian affairs, pass laws, and raise taxes. The Chief Executive was to be a "President-General" appointed and supported by the Crown. There would be a Grand Council consisting of Representatives appointed by each Colonial assembly. *The plan was an attempt to stop the French from taking control of the Ohio river valley because, if they possessed it, it would link the French territories of Louisiana and Canada together and block the growth of the English colonies.*

2. The 2nd issue was the ***Iroquois Indian Confederation complaints against the Colonists.*** A delegation of 150 Indians from the Confederation presented their grievances to the Congress, ***which were;***

    • Land speculators were stealing their lands

    • Illegal English-French trade was bypassing them, thus preventing them from acting as middlemen for profit

    • The colonials were trading directly with other Indians supposedly under the rule of the Iroquois.

The Congress had to satisfy the Iroquois because they were needed as allies in the war against the French.

The Congress was successful because the Iroquois Confederacy allied with the English during the French-Indian War of 1754. However, the Albany Plan of Union failed because of opposition from both the King and the colonists. Both thought it granted too much central power. It was a far-sighted plan because it included solutions used by the colonies in their Articles of Confederation after Independence was declared in 1776. The British also resisted it because they feared that it might serve as a precedent for independence.

f. *The Beginnings of the War (1754-1763)*

The basic cause was the rivalry over the upper Ohio river valley, beginning in 1748 when a group of Virginian's interested in western lands formed the "Ohio Company" at the same time as the French were building two Forts. Virginia Governor Dinwiddie sent George Washington to protest the French action. The contested site was at the junction of the Monongahela and Allegheny rivers where they join to form the Ohio river, ***at present-day Pittsburgh.*** The British attempted to build a fort but were expelled by the French who did succeed in building Fort Duquesne in 1754.

Dinwiddie again sent Colonel Washington who defeated a small French force but had to withdraw and build a Fort nearby, **Fort Necessity**, where he held his ground until forced to surrender in July, 1754. *So, the war actually began in the colonies before it began in Europe as their "7 Years War" was fought from 1756-1763. This war would prove to be the most important and consequential of the four "Imperial Wars" because of the significance of the results and because it led to the British policies requiring the colonists to share in the cost of the war and rebuilding their national finances.* THOSE POLICIES CAUSED THE COLONISTS TO BEGIN THE RESISTANCE MOVEMEMNT.

As far as the war was concerned, the English planned to capture the French forts in the west, not just at Duquesne, but at Fort Frontenac (Kingston, Ontario), Fort Niagara, and the posts at Fort Ticonderoga and Crown Point, New York and Vermont. They also planned to capture Louisburg and the French cities on the St. Lawrence river, Montreal and Quebec. At first, they failed. The expedition led by General Braddock against Fort Duquesne in 1755 failed as did the attempt to blockade Canada and capture the other posts.

After 1757, when the British Ministry of William Pitt was reconstituted, Pitt was able to supervise the War in the colonies which proved more successful. Lord Amherst in 1758 captured Louisburg and in the same year General Forbes captured Fort Duquesne, which became Fort Pitt. The French General, Montcalm, in 1758 defeated attacks by James Abercromby against Fort Ticonderoga which was eventually captured in 1759 by General Amherst. The British were also able to maintain the loyalty of the Iroquois Tribe in the west mostly through the efforts of Sir William Johnson and the Militia known as "Rogers Rangers".

The final battles of the war were fought in the St. Lawrence River Valley with French General Montcalm against General Wolfe of England. In 1759 the English captured the fortress and city of Quebec at the "Plains of Abraham" where both Generals were killed. The next year, 1760, the English captured Montreal which basically ended the war. ***The "Treaty of Paris" of 1763 was signed on 2/10/1763 which ended French control of Canada which was ceded to England.***

At the end of the fighting, there was still one more problem, that of ***"Pontiac's Rebellion",*** where the Indians refused to accept the defeat of the French in the Ohio valley. Once Pontiac was defeated there was relative calm on the frontier.

C.   SIGNIFICANCE OF THE LAST FRENCH-INDIAN WAR

Some of the major consequences of this war were:

1. The colonists gained considerable military experience while assisting the British in the fight against the French and their Indian allies.

2. The colonists believed that they no longer had to fear the French

3. The colonists felt more self-sufficient and self-confident of their ability to defend themselves

4. The colonists gained a stronger sense of their own importance and worth

5. The colonists did recognize a need for greater cooperation with other colonies

6. During the war the English allowed the colonists greater self-government which they would seek in the future.

The most significant consequence of this war was in the steps England would have to take to resolve their financial debt resulting from the war and the impact of those steps on their relations with the colonists. As we will see, the seeds of the American Revolution were contained in many of the direct and indirect results of this final French and Indian War.

D.   GLOSSARY

1. **"Smoking" of fish and meat**   Method to preserve food

(Attachment 19b Map of Lake Champlain and Mohawk Frontier 1609-1763)

For further information about the French-Indian Wars, see "The Crucible of War" by Fred Anderson listed in the Bibliography

E.   KEY DATES AND SIGNIFICANT EVENTS

	1631	Pequot Tribe divides into pro-English and pro-Dutch factions
	1634	Smallpox epidemic kills many Pequots
	1637	Pequot War
	1638	Peace Treaty of Hartford ends Pequot War
	1644	Indian problems in the middle colonies with Opechancanough
	1646	Indian attacks in Virginia fail and they sue for peace, cede their land between the York and James Rivers
	1661	King Louis XIV of France assumes Throne. Plan to build up New France and compete with England in North America
	1673	Father Marquette and Louis Joliet explore Mississippi river valley for France
	1675-1676	King Philip's War
	1676	Bacon's rebellion
	1678	Treaty of Casco Bay ends King Philip's War
	1689	William & Mary assume Throne of England
	1689-1697	King William's War (European War of the Grand Alliance, or, War of the League of Augsburg
	1697	Treaty of Ryswick ends War of the League of Augsburg in Europe
	1702-1713	Queen Anne's War (War of the Spanish Succession)
4/11	1713	Treaty of Utrecht ends War of the Spanish Succession
	1720	Tuscarora tribe becomes Sixth Nation of the Iroquois Confederacy
	1744-1748	King George's War (War of Jenkins Ear, or, War of the Austrian Succession)

10/18	1748	Treaty of Aix-le-Chaelle ends the War of the Austrian Succession
	1754–1763	Final French-Indian War
6/19	1754	Albany Plan of Union discussed
	1758	English General Forbes captures French Fort Duquesne, becomes Fort Pitt
	1759	English capture Fort Ticonderoga from French
	1759	English capture Quebec from France at the "Plains of Abraham"
	1760	English capture Montreal, ends War
2/10	1763	Treaty of Paris ends French/Indian War . Ends French control of Canada

F.   REVIEW QUESTIONS

(Multiple Choice)

1. The major Indian tribes and language groups were:
    a.   Algonquins
    b.   Iroquois
    c.   Muskogean
    d.   Sioux
    e.   All of the above

2. Which of the following Indian tribes did NOT belong to the Iroquois Confederacy?
    a.   Cayuga
    b.   Powhatan
    c.   Seneca
    d.   Creek

3. The Pequot War was fought in which region of America?
    a.   Middle colonies
    b.   Southern colonies
    c.   New England
    d.   All of the above

4. Bacon's Rebellion was fought because of:
    a.   failure of government to protect settlers against the Indians
    b.   high taxes
    c.   corruption of government officials
    d.   competition over the fur-trade

5. In which colony did most of the fighting occur?
    a. Maryland
    b. Virginia
    c. North Carolina
    d. None of the above

6. King Philip's War was fought because of:
    a. border problems between New England colonies
    b. tensions between Indians and settlers
    c. competition between Indian tribes
    d. all of the above

7. Which of the following wars was NOT considered one of the Indian/Imperial Wars fought in the colonies?
    a. King William's War
    b. Queen Anne's War
    c. King Philip's War
    d. King George's War
    e. French/Indian War

8. Which Treaty ended the War of the Austrian Succession?
    a. Treaty of Ryswick
    b. Treaty of Utrecht
    c. Treaty of Aix-le-Chapelle
    d. Treaty of Paris

9. What was the major cause of the French/Indian War in the colonies?
    a. Competition over trade
    b. Land expansion into the western lands
    c. Fur trade
    d. All of the above

10. The largest Indian language group east of the Mississippi river was the Algonquin tribe.
    a. TRUE
    b. FALSE

11. The Pequot Indian tribe was NOT a part of the Algonquin tribe.
    a. TRUE
    b. FALSE

12. Indian Chief Sequoya was a Cherokee.
    a. TRUE
    b. FALSE

13. The Pequot War was caused primarily by the intolerant attitude of the Puritans toward the Indians.
    a. TRUE
    b. FALSE

14. The Indian leader, Metacomet, was known by the colonists as "King William".
    a. TRUE
    b. FALSE

15. There were 5 major Indian/Imperial wars in the colonies; King William's War, Queen Anne's War, King George's War, King Philip's War, and the French/Indian War.
    a. TRUE
    b. FALSE

CHAPTER 19 SUMMARY

INDIAN RELATIONS AND IMPERIAL WARS

1. For years there were problems on the frontier between the native Indians and settlers who were occupying their lands

2. Added to that conflict was the competition and rivalry between the major European nations who were trying to gain influence in North America, such as the British, French, Spanish, and Dutch.

3. These nations were also in conflict in Europe. Many of those conflicts spread to America. The Indians took sides with the Iroquois generally supporting the British while many other tribes supported the French.

4. Even though there were Indian attacks and uprisings throughout the colonial settlement period, roughly most of the 1600's, it wasn't until the first of the "Imperial Wars" where all of these factors combined to keep the colonies in turmoil for almost 100 years.
   a. KING WILLIAM'S WAR 1689-1697
   EUROPEAN WAR OF GRAND ALLIANCE 1688-1697
   WAR OF THE LEAGUE OF AUGSBURG
   b. QUEEN ANNE'S WAR 1702-1713
   WAR OF THE SPANISH SUCCESSION 1701-1714
   c. KING GEORGE'S WAR 1744-1748

WAR OF JENKINS EAR 1740-1748
WAR OF THE AUSTRIAN SUCCESSION
d. FRENCH & INDIAN WAR 1754-1763
7 YEARS WAR 1756-1763

5. *How did the "European Wars" spread to the colonies? The competition for power, trade, and commerce caused the European nations to fight some of those battles in America and Canada.* The English and French fought over Nova Scotia, during "Queen Anne's War" the French aroused the Indians in New England and the Spanish did the same in Florida. The British and French also fought over the new Northwest territories, in the Ohio river valley, and western Pennsylvania, which impacted their fur-trade rivalry.

6. *Some of the significant results of the last French-Indian War (1754-1763) were;*
   a. England ended France's power and influence in Canada and North America.
   b. The colonists learned that they could defend themselves
   c. The colonists also learned that they needed each other and became more receptive to the ideal of colonial unity.
   d. The British Treasury was depleted by these wars and needed to develop a colonial policy to require the colonists to contribute more to their own defense. *It was those policies which the colonists most resisted and which led to the Revolutionary War.*

19a

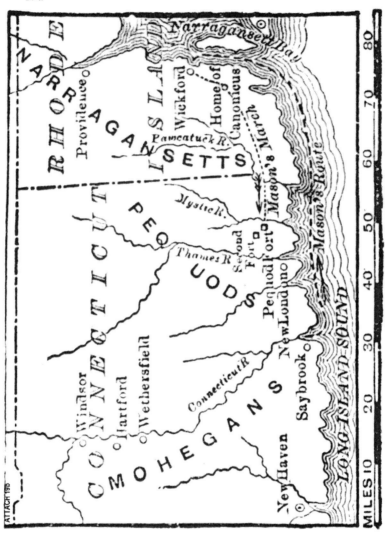

19b

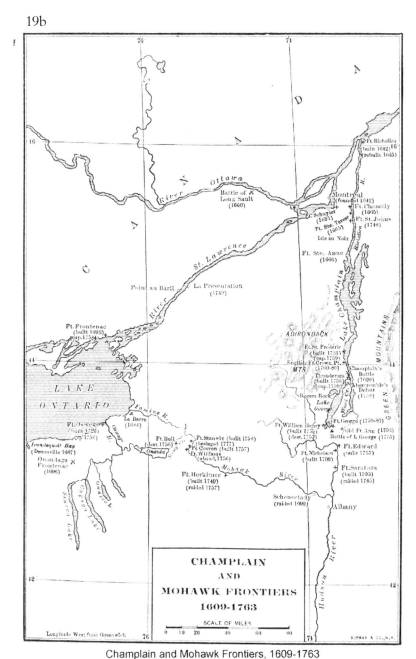

Champlain and Mohawk Frontiers, 1609-1763

Chapter 20

Early Efforts at Self-Government & Colonial Unity.

As we are learning, America didn't suddenly become Independent on 7/4/1776. For almost 170 years the colonists had gradually assumed various types and levels of independence which led to their Declaration of 1776.

In this chapter, we will identify those English and American "roots" of Independence from the earliest colonization charters through 1700, well before the colonists began considering the idea of independence from England.

A.   ENGLISH ROOTS OF AMERICAN DEMOCRACY

EVENT	DATE	CHAPTER
1. Magna Carta	1215	4
2. Model Parliament	1295	4
3. Petition of Right	1628	4
4. Structure of English Government:		4

    a. Executive

    b. House of Common

    c. House of Lords

These foundations of English liberty were passed along to the colonists, either by way of their own personal emigration to the colonies, or the ideas expressed in these documents which were implemented by various government officials in the colonies. *No matter how, the ideas and principles contained in these documents made their way into colonial life.*

B.   ENGLISH COLONIAL CHARTERS IN THE 1600's

1. *Many of the political institutions of England were transmitted to America through the Colonial Charters.* The privileges of self-government granted by colonial charters combined with governmental neglect by England allowed the colonials to experience a relatively large degree of freedom. *In some of the charters, there were provisions for a Governor, Council, and Assembly elected by voters. In some charters, the governor and both houses of the Legislature were elected by the voters.*

2. The legal rights of the colonists were protected by colonial judges who followed English Common Law.

C.　COLONIAL GOVERNMENT; The following source documents explain the foundations of the American government;

1. **VIRGINIA**	MO	DATE	YEAR	CHAPTER
First Charter for the Virginia Colony	4	10	1606	5
Second Charter for the Virginia Colony	5	23	1609	5
Third Charter for the Virginia Colony	3	12	1612	5
The Great Charter of 1618	11	18	1618	5
Virginia House of Burgesses	7	30	1619	5

2. **PLYMOUTH/MASSACHUSETTS BAY**	MO/	DATE/	YR	CHAPTER
Mayflower Compact	11	20	1620	6
Cambridge Agreement	8	26	1629	6
General Fundamentals of Plymouth Colony★	11	15	1636	6
Body of Liberties	12	10	1641	6
New England Confederation	5	29	1643	6 & 9
(United Colonies of New England)				
Dominion of New England	May		1686	18

3. **MARYLAND**	MO/	DATE/	YR	CHAPTER
Lord Baltimore Charter	6	20	1632	7
Representative Government formed			1639	7
Toleration Act	4	21	1649	7

4. **RHODE ISLAND**	MO/	DATE/	YR	CHAPTER
First General Assembly	5	19	1647	8

5. **CONNECTICUT**	MO/	DATE/	YR	CHAPTER
Fundamental Orders	1	14	1639	9
New England Confederation	5	19	1643	9 & 6
(United Colonies of New England)				
Ludlow Code of Laws	May		1650	9

6. **NORTH & SOUTH CAROLINA**	MO/	DATE/	YR	CHAPTER
Charter of 1663	3	24	1663	11

7. **NEW YORK**	MO/	DATE/	YR	CHAPTER
Duke's Laws	3	1	1665	13
Charter of Liberties	10	30	1683	13

8. **NEW JERSEY**		MO/	DATE/	YR	CHAPTER
First Legislative Assembly	5	26	1668		14
First Popular Assembly in West Jersey		11	3	1681	14

9. **PENNSYLVANIA**	MO/	DATE/	YR	CHAPTER
King Charles II Charter to William Penn	3	4	1681	15
Penn's "Great Law" adopted	12	7	1682	15
Penn Charter of Privileges	11	7	1701	15

★Also known as the "Declaration of Rights

Chapter 21

The Critical 13 Years from 1763 to 1776

A. BACKGROUND

Historians begin their accounts of the road to Revolution in 1763. The colonists had many grievances against Britain prior to that date but the signing of the Peace of Paris on 2/10/1763 ended the last of the French-Indian Wars. Rather than resolve all of the previous problems, it created some new ones.

It had taken decades of experience in the 17th century for Britain to mold the old colonial system that had governed a strip of land stretching some 1000 miles along the Atlantic coast. Now, England must erect a new system to deal with a much larger empire but there was a question whether England had the finances to achieve the goal. *(Attachment 21a represents a Map of the British possessions in North America in 1765.)*

The British subjects in the colonies were then the freest people in the world. *They argued and fought not to obtain freedom but to confirm their existing freedom.*

Prior to 1775, there was no colonial nationalism or separatist feeling that they were entitled to be a separate and independent nation. On the contrary, they were not only content but proud to be a part of the British Empire but they did feel very strongly that they were entitled to all of the Constitutional rights of Englishmen in England. It took the Radical leaders 10 years after the Stamp Act to reach the decision that Parliament had no rightful jurisdiction over the colonies.

There is no clear evidence that the American Revolution was

inevitable and that the 13 colonies were too big and self-sufficient to continue as colonies. Many interventions of the English government in colonial administration had been to protect minority groups against majorities, or small colonies against big ones, such as, Quakers and Anglicans in New England against the dominant Puritans, Delaware against Maryland, New Hampshire and Rhode Island against Massachusetts Bay.

By 1763 there appeared to be movement toward a compromise between imperial control and colonial self-government, between the principle of authority and that of liberty. King and Parliament had control of foreign affairs, war and peace, and overseas trade. Parliament tried to direct all colonial trade into channels deemed profitable to all. *In almost every other respect, the colonists were relatively free with their assemblies having the exclusive right to tax their citizens, to appoint officials, and fix their salaries, and to control their own schools and churches.*

So, overall, the colonists were fairly well satisfied with their situation in 1763 but not with the Government of King George III, as we shall see. *Eventual resistance to English rule can be summed up in 5 phases;*

- Up to 1764 there were simmering resentments which had not yet broken out into the open

- From 1764-1766 there was the implementation of the Grenville Plan with resistance focusing on the Stamp Act

- From 1767-1770 there was the implementation of the Townshend Acts which produced a colonial boycott and other forms of protest

- From 1770-1773 there was a "Period of Calm" after the repeal of the Townshend Acts

- From 1773-1776 tensions significantly inceased with the passage of the Tea Act and the colonial reaction against it.

B.   BRITISH IMPERIAL SYSTEM IN 1763

The casual administrative system by which England ruled the colonies had not changed in 1763, owing to the failure of the Albany Plan of Union. Although no general opposition to its rule had been voiced by the colonies yet, there were some things which made the colonists restless. They objected to the Governor's instructions from the Crown being considered mandatory. They also did not like the Admiralty Courts which gave verdicts without a local jury and they particularly disliked the tenure of judges.

Successive Ministries of King George III tried to resolve multiple problems at the same time. The British Government approached these problems without a clear plan. For example, Governor Bernard of Massachusetts, in letters to leading English politicians suggested that to reform the Empire, England should reform colonial governments first, then strengthen her Royal Governors and judges by paying their salaries, confer titles of nobility on leading colonials, and admit some colonial representatives to the English House of Commons. *(Attachment 21b provides a chronology of the British Prime Ministers and their Secretaries of State during the pre-Revolutionary Period.)*

George Grenville in 1763 was placed in charge of a government deeply in debt and in need of new approaches for financing the expanded administration. He had to do this while his people in England were demanding to be relieved of at least a part of their wartime tax burden. Neither the Colonists or the people and government of England seemed able to comprehend the enormity of the task ahead of them.

When the British government looked at the task ahead, they saw the following

1. Financial problems. How to pay their debt and secure new sources of revenue.

2. How to deal with settlers moving across the Appalachian Mountains into new territories previously inhabited solely by the Indians.

3. How to make and keep peace with the Indians, some of whom who did not accept the defeat of the French, such as "Pontiac's Rebellion".

Pontiac's Rebellion.

It turned out, in the spring of 1763, an Ottawa Indian Chief named "Pontiac", upon learning of the Treaty of Paris and the ceding of Canada to the English, who he hated, decided to free his people from their new masters. He launched a series of attacks in the Ohio valley. His attacks brought support from other Indian tribes, such as the Delaware's, who also began attacks in the area. Then, the Seneca tribe joined in the attacks. General Amherst, the top British Army commander in America, opposed their attacks.

Finally, Pontiac was told by the French that he must make peace because France could no longer protect his tribe. In July, 1766, peace was finally concluded. After much discussion, the British government extended the boundaries further west, with Indian approval, and by 1770 England thought it had done its best to tame the western frontier.

So, there was a 13 year period of time between the Treaty of Paris in 1763, which ended the last of the four French-Indian Imperial Wars and the Declaration of Independence. The events of those 13 years did not totally cause the beginning of the war but it was during that period that both England and the colonies were facing the unknown plus their previous attitudes and positions gradually hardened, thus producing further obstacles for compromise.

A quick revue of what we have already learned is in order to set the stage:

1. America did not discover the concept of "self-government". We can go back to the English Magna Carta for the first example of limitations on the authority of the King. Years later, in

1620, before they even landed at Plymouth, the Pilgrims signed the "Mayflower Compact" which established their own self-government once ashore. In the previous chapter we identified a number of British and American concepts which paved the way for colonial independence long before 7/4/1776. So, independence didn't "just happen", the colonists lived under an evolving system of self-government from Jamestown and Plymouth right up to the moment of the signing of the Declaration of Independence.

2. The colonies were first conceived of and administered in the minds of English explorers, merchants, and rulers. The charters initially granted by the Monarchy established guiding principles of management for the Proprietors, their appointed Governors, then the Governor's Councils, and subsequently the Representative Assemblies. The evolution of government over the years was a key factor in the development of the colonies which led them to believe, in 1776, that they had acquired enough experience with self-government to strike out on their own.

3. ***A very difficult and serious question was never satisfactorily answered on either side of the Ocean. What were the rights of those who emigrated from England to the New World?*** Upon arriving in the New World they were basically taken care of by the English government or their representatives. The British army protected them against the French, Spanish, Indians, etc, at great cost to the British Empire. Didn't the colonists owe a debt of gratitude to the English government and, as long as they accepted that assistance, weren't they still bound to the laws and customs of the Mother Country? It almost seems as if the colonists were selfish in that they accepted the assistance of the English until they were asked/required by the English government to help pay the costs of administering the English colonies, then they rebelled and claimed that "their rights were being infringed upon". Weren't their rights being infringed

upon over the previous 150+ years? Why didn't they object then? Why did they object, and rebel, only when they were asked to help pay for their own protection?

4. *__Another serious constitutional and/or legal issue was that of representation. Throughout the colonial resistance period we will hear the colonists complain of "taxation without representation".__* To counter that complaint, the British were quick to point out that the colonists had the same sort of "virtual representation" in Parliament as many English citizens. There were effective arguments on both sides of this issue but *what matters most is that the colonists BELIEVED that they were not represented and it served as a strong motivation for their actions.*

These are some of the questions and points to keep in mind as we explore those 13 critical years when the English role of managing the colonies clashed with the colonists' position of wanting to maintain the current level of self-government they had achieved by 1776.

C.   BRITISH ATTEMPTS TO CONSOLIDATE THEIR NEW EMPIRE

After the last of the four French-Indian wars which ended with the Treaty of Paris in 1763, Britain was the premier colonial power in North America. The Treaty of Paris had doubled the English territories in North America and eliminated the French as a future threat to England and her North American colonies. While British power seemed more secure than ever, *there were signs of future trouble in the colonies. The main problem had to do with the massive debt accumulated by the English government while fighting the most recent French-Indian war and now they were looking for ways to pay off that debt.*

One way in which to help the debt problem was to require the colonists to help pay it off, since it was accumulated protecting them. King George III and his Prime Minister, George Grenville, maintained that the colonists had benefited the most from the war and had paid very little in comparison to citizens living in England. To address this disparity **Parliament passed a series of Legislative Acts designed to secure the revenue from the colonies in addition to doing a better job of enforcing the Navigation Laws. Some of those laws which upset the colonists were:**

1. **Law Enforcement**

   The Law enforcement problem was the first to be addressed. **William Pitt, the Earl of Chatham, had ordered, in 1760, the Sugar Act of 1733 to be strictly enforced.** In order to enforce this unpopular law, the Royal customs collectors at Boston applied to the Superior Court of the colony for **"writs of assistance"**, which were general warrants allowing an officer to enter any premises at any time in search of smuggled goods. As such, these "writs" seemed contrary to the traditional rights of Englishmen. **James Otis, a Boston lawyer, argued against the Writs in 1761. He made an argument which became a basic doctrine in American law, that an act against the Constitution is void and an act against "natural equity" is also void.**

2. **The Revenue Act (4/5/1764) (Revised Sugar and Molasses Act of 1733)**

   This was the first attempt by the government of King George III to raise revenues toward defense and stop leaks in the Acts of Trade and Navigation. It was passed by Parliament to counter the smuggling of foreign sugar and to establish a British monopoly in the American sugar market. The act allowed Royal officials to seize colonial cargo with little or no legal cause. Unlike previous acts, which had regulated trade to boost the entire British Imperial economy, the Sugar Act was designed to benefit England at the expense of the American colonists. **The major criticism of the Act was that it was aimed not to regulate the economy of the British Empire but to raise revenue for the British government. This distinction became important as the colonists determined which actions of the British government warranted resistance.**

News of the Sugar Act/Revenue Act reached Boston in early May. Instructions from the Boston town meeting to its legislative representatives made it clear that Boston objected mainly because it may be preparatory to new taxations. The Legislature did not go on record with a clear-cut objection to the principle that Parliament had the right to levy a revenue measure on the colony although they did make some points about "internal and external taxes". Some other State legislatures did take stronger positions such as denying that Parliament had any right whatsoever to levy taxes on the colonists.

3. **The Currency Act (9/11/1764)**
   The effect of this Act was to withdraw paper currencies from circulation. This was not done to restrict economic growth as much as to take out currency that was thought to be unsound, but it did severely reduce the circulating money during the difficult postwar period and further indicated that such matters were subject to British control.

4. **The Stamp Act (3/22/1765)**
   This was a direct internal tax imposed on the colonies by Parliament, in fact, the first tax of any sort other than customs duties. The Act was also designed to force the colonies to help pay off the national war debt. It was proposed and moved through the Parliament by Prime Minister George Grenville. It required the colonists to buy special watermarked paper for newspapers, playing cards, and legal documents such as Wills and marriage licenses. Violators faced trials without juries in Nova Scotia Vice Admiralty courts where guilt was presumed until innocence was proven.
   The colonists clearly could see that the purpose of the Act was to raise revenue from the colonists and it produced a severe reaction in the colonies on the grounds that it was "taxation without representation". Their position was that they did not elect any members of Parliament and, therefore, should be able to determine their own taxes independent of Parliament.

Prime Minister Grenville and his supporters claimed that the colonists were obliged to pay Parliamentary taxes because they shared the same status as many British males who did not have enough property to be granted the vote or who lived in certain large cities that had no seats in Parliament. This was the basis of the term, *"Virtual Representation"*. The British also argued that members of Parliament not only represented their specific geographical constituencies but they also considered the well-being of all British subjects when deliberating on legislation.

The Stamp Act produced the first colonial resistance to British rule. On 5/30/1765, the Virginia House of Burgesses passed the "Virginia Resolves", aided by a fiery speech by Patrick Henry, which denied Parliament's right to tax the colonies under the Stamp Act. By the end of the year, eight other colonial legislatures had adopted similar positions. *As dissent spread through the colonies it quickly became more organized.* Groups of colonists, calling themselves *"The Sons of Liberty", formed throughout the colonies to generate more dissent,* often burning stamps and threatening British officials. Merchants in New York began a boycott of British goods with merchants in other cities soon joining their efforts.

Representatives of nine colonial assemblies met in New York city at the "Stamp Act Congress" from October 7-25 where they proposed a petition asking Parliament to repeal the Stamp Act on the grounds that it violated the principle of "no taxation without representation". The Congress argued that Parliament could not tax anyone outside of Great Britain and could not deny anyone a fair trial. The Stamp Act Congress was the first spontaneous movement toward colonial union that came from the colonists themselves. The colonial delegations agreed that there could be no taxation without representation. Their specific resolutions were;
a. They accepted Parliament's right to make law for the colonies but rejected its right to tax them

b. They rejected the idea of representation in Parliament, either "virtually" or actually

c. They discarded the "illogical" distinction between "internal and external taxes".

5. **Repeal of the Stamp Act and passage of the Declaratory Act (3/18/1766)**

Due to strong pressure from the colonies and with their economy slumping because of the colonial boycott of British goods, *Parliament repealed the Stamp Act in March, 1766.* But, at the same time *they passed the "Declaratory Act".* The King had removed Grenville from office in August, 1765, three months after passage of the Stamp Act and before the colonial reaction to the Act had become known in London.

King George III replaced Grenville with the Marquis of Rockingham to form a new government. *Rockingham and his supporters believed that Parliament had the right to tax the colonies but the Stamp Act had been inexpedient. He could see that the colonial rejection of the Act made it clear that the Act would have to be repealed but it must be done in a manner that did not appear that Parliament was backing down because of colonial opposition. On 3/18/1766, Parliament repealed the Stamp Act but it also passed the "Declaratory Act" which stated that Parliament had the authority to make laws for the American colonies in all cases.*

News of the repeal reached the colonies in March, 1766, causing the colonists to rejoice. *John Adams warned that the new Declaratory Act ("Dissertation on the Canon and Feudal Law") would allow Parliament to try again to tax the colonists. He was right, it happened again in 1767 when Parliament and Charles Townshend passed his "Townshend Duties".* Adams believed, and many colonists came to believe, that Parliament was in the process of developing a long-term plan to reduce the colonies to a subservient position.

6. **Impact of the Repeal and the Declaratory Act on England and the Colonies**

   The crisis had produced a change in the minds of both the British and the colonists. Previous to 1765, Parliament had been indifferent to and ignorant of American affairs. The indifference had changed to open anti-American feeling in England, convinced that the colonists would not be happy until they achieved total independence. This conviction became an obsession with many British leaders a decade before Americans gave it serious thought.

   The true significance for America of the Stamp Act and the Revenue Act resided in the minds of the colonists who now *began to raise questions about their relationship with England never before considered.* They now began to suspect the motives of every action taken by Britain toward the colonies. Soon, this suspicion toward the motives of Britain crept into every segment of colonial society, religion, trade, and literature, *causing widespread opposition and a growing sense of unity.*

   Historians agree that England had provoked the crisis although its requests for the colonists to share the financial burden seemed reasonable. Could the crisis have been avoided? Some suggest that it wasn't the policy which was offensive as much as the high-handed and arrogant manner in which England tried to achieve their goals.

   In the spring of 1766, the British said that Parliament had the right to tax the colonists and the colonists said they didn't. This was the impasse, plus others to come, which led to the Revolution.

7. **Revised Revenue Act (June 1766)**

   In early June, 1766, the Rockingham Ministry passed a conciliatory measure. It revised the Revenue Act of 1764 by reducing the duties on molasses. It would now cost no more, and in many cases even less, to bring molasses in legally than it had been previously to bribe customs officials. By the end of June, England had been forced to impose a new set of taxes at home to deal with their economic problems. Those new taxes in England spelled the end for the Rockingham Ministry. The King requested that a new Ministry be formed, to be led by the Duke of Grafton as the First Lord of the Treasury and Earl William Shelburne and Henry Seymour Conway as Secretaries of State. The King made the Pitt-Grafton Ministry the new government and **Charles Townshend** became the new Chancellor of the Exchequer whose responsibility was to balance the budget.

8. **The Townshend Duties (Revenue Act of 6/29/1767)**
   During the general jubilation following the repeal of the Stamp Act, *no serious effort was made by the British government to find out what, if anything, could be done to raise defense funds through colonial assemblies.* No Royal commission was sent to the colonies to study the issue and even the colonial agents in London were not consulted in how the colonies could help. *Instead, Parliament made a new attempt to tax the colonies which, in effect, implemented a new plan of imperial reorganization without consulting them.*

   English politics at this time is difficult to understand because the "Whig Party", dominant through most of the century, had broken into factions. The faction most concerned about colonial affairs were known as the "Old Whigs" because they represented the genuine Whig principles of the Glorious Revolution of 1688. Some of the key members of this faction were the Marquess of Rockingham, the Earl of Dartmouth, the Duke of Richmond, General Conway, Edmund Burke, and Lord Camden, the Chief Justice.

   After Rockingham resigned, the colonists expected support from the Pitt-Grafton Ministry, especially because Pitt was seen as a supporter. However, before Pitt assumed the role of Prime Minister he became ill and **Grafton assumed the position. His Lord Treasurer, Townshend, gave a speech on 5/8/1767 where he boasted that he was not afraid to tax the colonists.**

The Townshend Duties were passed on 6/29/1767, based on an unfortunate distinction made by Benjamin Franklin and other colonial spokesmen that external taxes (customs duties) which had always been levied on goods entering the colonies, were Constitutional while internal taxes, like the Stamp Act, were not. Parliament took advantage of this opening and levied duties on certain English manufactures like glass, paint, paper, and on the East India Company's tea. The profits from these taxes were to be used to pay the salaries of the Royal governors in the colonies. In practice, however, the Townshend Duties yielded little income for the British. The taxes on tea brought in the only significant revenue.

Other parts of the Townshend Acts were;

a. To reorganize the colonial customs service to improve enforcement and end smuggling

b. To enforce the Navigation Acts, the Sugar Act of 1764, and the new Duties

c. To suspend the New York Assembly until they obeyed the Mutiny Act of 1765.

Even though the Act failed to generate much revenue, ***it did succeed in creating considerable colonial dissent which had somewhat subsided since the Stamp Act. Protest against these taxes first took the form of intellectual and legal dissent and soon erupted in violence. Even Lord Grenville spoke out against the measure in Parliament.***

News of the passage of the Townshend Acts arrived in the colonies in September, 1767. At first, reaction was moderate. ***Colonial dissent received a boost when John Dickinson on 12/2/1767 published the first of 12 "Letters from a Pennsylvania Farmer to the Inhabitants of the British Colonies".*** He used precedents from English law rather than abstract principles to argue against the right of Parliament to tax the colonies in any form. His tone was moderate and disclaimed the idea that the colonies contemplated independence ***but made clear that the colonists could not be free, secure, or happy if others can legislate for them without their consent.***

485

On 2/11/1768, John Adams and James Otis drafted, and the Massachusetts assembly approved, the "Circular Letter" to the other colonial assemblies calling their attention to the Acts. It was very moderate and conciliatory but the Grafton Ministry decided to use the occasion for a showdown with the Massachusetts colony.

Townshend died in September, 1767, replaced by **Lord North who was a strong advocate of the authority of Parliament** . In January, 1768, the King created a third Secretary of State for Colonial Affairs, and named Lord Hillsborough to the position. **Hillsborough thought both the Massachusetts Circular Letter and Dickinson's Letters were "extreme".** Without consulting the other members of the government, although he did meet with the King, **he ordered Governor Bernard of Massachusetts to dissolve the legislature unless it immediately rescinded the "Circular Letter". A week later, the Massachusetts Legislature voted 92-17 to refuse. Two days later Bernard dissolved the legislature which immediately created unrest throughout the colonies.**

One of the key Patriots was John Hancock, a 31 year old merchant. The new Commissioners of the Customs decided to put him out of business. He was falsely accused of smuggling Madeira wine with his sloop, "The Liberty". A Boston mob rescued him and his ship and gave the local customs officials such a hard time they sought refuge in a castle in Boston harbor. Governor Bernard requested and received protection of two Regiments of troops from Halifax. When the troops arrived and Governor Bernard refused to recall the dismissed Assembly, the Boston town meeting invited the province to elect delegates to a convention. Some towns sent delegates but most did not and those who did attend were advised to do nothing rash, which is what happened. A few mild resolutions were passed and the convention was dissolved.

Although the Grafton Ministry failed to intimidate Boston it dealt successfully with New York where two Regiments of troops arrived in 1766. The Quartering or Mutiny Act of Parliament required local authorities to provide quarters or barracks for the King's troops and furnish free supplies, including beer and rum. The New York Assembly refused to pay for those beverages but voted for all other supplies for the 1,000 troops. Lord Hillsborough said that wasn't enough and **ordered the assembly to be suspended, just like Massachusetts.** After the next election (Fall, 1769) the new Assembly voted in favor of the British request. The "Sons of Liberty" denounced their action as a betrayal and Governor Colden jailed one of the leaders, Alexander Mc Dougall, for sedition. Even after he was released in January, 1770, New York was a scene of rioting. British troops cut down a "Liberty Pole" put up by the Patriots and a fight occurred on Gordon Hill with one death.

D.   BACK-COUNTRY ISSUES

At the same time, the backcountry was in turmoil but most of the anger was directed at the colonial governments rather than against the British government. The frontier had expanded so rapidly that colonial assemblies couldn't keep pace with representation and judicial matters. There were complaints that the backcountry was under-represented or not represented at all. Backcountry discontent was most pronounced in the 1760's in the Carolina's because of differences in the background of the settlers. Thousands of settlers arrived from Pennsylvania who greatly differed from the settlers along the coast. Almost half of the population of South Carolina and 4/5 of the white population lived in the backcountry in 1776 but the provincial government was completely centralized at Charleston. In North Carolina, the separation between coastal region and backcountry was even sharper. The grievances were not lack of government but bad government, such as corruption, unequal taxation, etc. The five western counties were well represented in the Assembly in 1769 but Governor Tryon dissolved it before it could do anything about local grievances which became worse over the next two years. As we saw in Chapter 12, the "Regulator Movement" was as serious for North Carolina as Bacon's Rebellion in Virginia.

The British government didn't concern itself too much with these backcountry disputes but they were concerned about backcountry Indian problems. How far were land speculators to be allowed to encroach on Indian country? In 1768, the two recently appointed Indian Superintendents negotiated three treaties with the Indians:

Treaty of Fort Stanwix with the Iroquois

Treaty of Hard Labor (a frontier post in South Carolina) with the Cherokee

Treaty of Pensacola with the Creek nation

***These treaties set up a new frontier line somewhat west of the King's Proclamation Line of 1763* .** This new line failed to satisfy the land speculators who felt the opportunity for new lands was too good to pass up. Many new land companies were being created and grants were then requested for large tracts of land. The English government was opposed to them primarily because of the fear of angering the Indians but also of losing part of their control over colonial events.

Immediately after the last French-Indian War, Daniel Boone and other hunter-explorers moved into Kentucky where they sent back information about great forests, prairies, fertile meadows, and large herds of buffalo and deer. These and other land speculators captured the interest of the Governor of Virginia, the Earl of Dunmore, who granted Crown lands beyond the Treaty of Stanwix line to holders of land warrants issued to war veterans. This practice differed from established British western policy. The North Ministry in 1774 ordered the Governors to make no land grants except in areas already ceded by the Indians and such ceded land was to be advertised and sold by auction.

This plan was disliked by land speculators. By the time the Royal instructions reached the colonies, Virginia was at war with the Shawnee nation which had never ceded its rights to Kentucky and was angry with explorers and settlers invading their territory. Governor Dunmore sent armed volunteers to reclaim the illegally granted lands.

After one party had been ambushed by Indians on the Kentucky river in July, Dunmore sent another 1,500 militia of western Virginia led by Colonel Andrew Lewis. On 10/10/1774, they defeated Chief

Cornstalk of the Shawnee at the "Battle of Point Pleasant" at the junction of the Ohio and Kanawha rivers. Thanks to the negotiating skills of Sir William Johnson, the "Six- Nations" and the western tribes remained neutral and allowed the Shawnee to suffer their defeat. In the subsequent peace negotiations the Shawnee ceded all of their Kentucky claims to Virginia. This was known as *"Governor Dunmore's War".*

E.   THE NON-IMPORTATION MOVEMENT (1768-1770)

The New York assembly giving in to the British and the Boston convention failing to achieve anything convinced the Patriots that the only way they could make any progress against the Townshend Acts was by co-operating with merchants to enforce a boycott. Even though boycotts had not been very effective, *the recent attempts did cause many British merchants to pressure their government to repeal the duties.* Soon that dissent turned to physical attacks on corrupt customs officials. The new duties and regulations burdensome to merchants and ship owners gave them a common interest with the agitators. *A result of this alliance was the "Non-Importation Movement" of 1768-1770.* Voluntary agreements were entered into by merchants to boycott specific British or West India goods, not only those taxed but many untaxed luxuries as well, to pressure the English government. Non-Importation associations were formed in all colonies and seaports. The merchants and southern planters agreed to import no British goods or taxed tea but promote home-industries.

Non-Importation agreements were difficult to enforce, as colonial sentiment was not as unified against the Townshend Duties as they were against the Stamp Act. Rioting alarmed many men of property and the strong-arm methods by which the "Sons of Liberty" enforced "voluntary" agreements convinced some that British taxation was preferable to mob rule.

On 10/1/1768, 1700 British troops landed in Boston to successfully prevent further violence although tension flared again with the "Boston Massacre" of 3/5/1770, in which five colonists were killed. This event and the reaction to it marked the peak of colonial opposition to the Townshend Duties.

On 5/1/1769, the King's Cabinet voted to urge Parliament to repeal the Townshend Acts in their next session. It also voted to leave the tax on tea which would still maintain the principle of Parliamentary supremacy in the Declaratory Act. On 5/13/1769, Hillsborough informed the colonial Governors of the Cabinet's plans and also informed Governor Bernard of Massachusetts to permit the legislature to reconvene *which responded by unanimously repeating on 7/1/1769 their position of "no taxation without representation".* This hardened position by the Massachusetts legislature caused General Gage to change his plans to withdraw some troops from Boston. Relations between the troops and Boston colonists became worse during the fall of 1769.

F.   THE LORD NORTH MINISTRY (1/31/1770-3/13/1782)

The Duke of Grafton resigned on 1/28/1770 so King George III asked Lord North to form a new Ministry. North was the favorite choice of the King because he wanted a Prime Minister who would be loyal to him, not to the House of Commons, which was the normal process. The King was very political and set himself up as the leader of the opposition to the most influential Whig politicians and families. This explains why Burke, Pitt, Richmond, and other leading English politicians supported the colonists and encouraged them to believe that they were fighting for liberty in England as well as in America. They suspected the King of trying to set up a Royal Absolutism.

At that time, King George III felt no strong prejudice against the colonies. He had supported the repeal of the Stamp Act on 3/18/1766 and his first gesture toward the colonies in 1770 was conciliatory. With the King's support, Lord North proposed to repeal the Townshend Duties except the one on Tea because of the colonists boycott of British goods and their infractions of law and order, the tea duty needed to be maintained as an example of the supremacy of Parliament. So, all Townshend Duties on British goods were eliminated on the very day of the Boston Massacre, 3/5/1770.

In response, the colonists ended the policy of non-importation but maintained their voluntary agreements to boycott British Tea. Non-consumption kept the Tea Tax revenues far too low to pay the Royal Governors, which basically nullified the purposes of the duties in the first place. The more radical Patriots wanted to continue non-importation until Parliament was forced to repeal the Tea Duty as well. But, they were unable to keep the merchants in line so, after the news of the repeal arrived, the merchant's associations in one colony after another lifted the boycott.

G.   THE BEGINNINGS OF OPEN OPPOSITION

(Attachment 21c summarizes British actions and Colonial reactions which led to the War)

1.   THE BOSTON "MASSACRE" (3/5/1770)

There was a confrontation on 3/5/1770, the very day the Townshend Duties were repealed. The local Radicals published a weekly newspaper, "The Journal of Public Occurrences", which they circulated throughout the colonies, intended to inflame the public against the British. Eventually, violence would occur on that evening when a group of citizens confronted a British sentry at the Customs House on King (now State) street. The main guard of about 20 soldiers were called out to confront the mob of several hundred. After they had been taunted and stoned and snow-balled for half an hour, one solider fired, without orders, and then the others fired. Three men were killed, including Crispus Attucks, a negro, who was the most aggressive, and two more mortally wounded.

The Radicals exaggerated the affair to inflame the colonies by such things as "celebrating" March 5 of every year as a way of keeping the flames of dissent alive. However, news of the repeal of the Townshend Duties had a moderating influence on the citizens and even played a role in the collapse of the non-importation agreements.

The negative reaction in England was strong, even among those who generally supported their cause. *The Marquess of Rockingham, a strong supporter, suggested that the actions of the Radicals were making it more difficult for their English friends to support their cause.* Even William Pitt, their most influential supporter in England, warned them in a speech to the House of Lords that if they carried their notions of liberty too far, as he feared they were, even he, as a strong supporter, would become opposed to them. He stated, "they must become subordinate. In all laws relating to trade and navigation, especially, this is the Mother Country, they are the children, they must obey, and we prescribe."[1] *(Morrison, pg 200)*

This advice had no impact on Sam Adams and some of his more radical Patriots who continued to exaggerate the "massacre" even though the British troops were successfully defended in court by John Adams.

It proved difficult to generate resentment toward England when the colonies were enjoying the greatest prosperity within memory. Imports to New England greatly increased in spite of more efficient enforcement of the Acts of Trade and Navigation. Short harvests in Europe created a demand for colonial corn and wheat and trade in general increased up to 1773.

2. THOMAS HUTCHINSON

John Hancock, John Adams, and Ben Franklin were becoming less confrontational with Franklin especially calling upon his fellow colonials to settle down. Sam Adams could see his "cause" becoming less reachable and needed a new emotional issue to spark the citizens again. The Boston radicals focused their attention on their new Royal Governor, Thomas Hutchinson, a native-born, scholarly, middle-aged New Englander. He was viewed as a man of integrity, devoted to Whig principles, an opponent to severe British measures against the colonists, but he had a bad habit of irritating people and making bad decisions. One of those bad decisions was to move the Massachusetts Assembly to Cambridge supposedly to free it from the pressures of the Boston mobs. This irritated the Assembly members but pleased the students at Harvard who could now listen to the speeches of the great Radical orators where many of them were converted to the Radical cause.

3. **COMMITTEES OF CORRESPONDENCE**

From 1770-1772, the British government largely ignored the colonies and tensions substantially cooled down. However, in the fall of 1772, Lord North began preparations to pay Royal Governors from customs revenue rather than the current method of the colonial assemblies having that responsibility. This change would deny the local assemblies the "power of the purse" which is how they exerted their influence over the Royal Governors.

When the Assembly voted Governor Hutchinson a salary he responded that the King had already taken care of that. Shortly after that revelation, news arrived that the King had also taken responsibility for the salaries of the judges of the Superior Court of Massachusetts. *This was the spark Sam Adams was seeking.* At a town meeting, the Governor was asked if these rumors were true. He responded that it was none of their business. *The town meeting then adopted Sam Adams' plan to appoint a "Committee of Correspondence" to discuss measures in defense of colonial liberty with similar committees in other towns and colonies.* Within a year, there were 250 "Committees of Correspondence" formed throughout the colonies. These committees served the purpose of linking many colonial political leaders in resistance to the British. Toward the end of November, 1772, the Massachusetts Committee of Correspondence presented it first report, *comprised of three papers, one by Sam Adams on the rights of Massachusetts citizens, another by Joseph Warren on their grievances, and another by Dr. Benjamin Church, an open letter to all towns in Massachusetts urging them to create their own Committees of Correspondence.* The Boston town meeting approved the reports and it was widely distributed to all colonial assemblies. Within three months there were 80 additional Committees of Correspondence just within Massachusetts.

This development upset Governor Thomas Hutchinson so that when the legislature convened in January, 1773, he expressed concern about the hardening of the colonial attitude. The legislature responded and renounced all ties with Parliament. They insisted that Massachusetts's allegiance was to the King alone, not to the Parliament.

Other events led to the hardening of attitudes on both sides:
Benjamin Franklin played a role in embarrassing Governor Hutchinson to the point where his reputation was ruined and he lost almost all of his effectiveness.

The "Gaspee Incident". The ship, Gaspee, was one of the English Warships loaned to the customs service to help suppress colonial smuggling. In the spring of 1772, the ship ran aground and a band of citizens boarded and burned the ship. Hutchinson demanded punishment for the offenders and formed a commission to find those who were guilty. They met for 17 days in early 1773 but could not find anyone guilty of the crime. Even though no one was punished just the fact that the commission was created was considered an invasion of local sovereignty.

The Virginia assembly issued a circular letter urging all of the other colonies to create Committees of Correspondence. The Governor of Virginia dissolved the assembly for the year but the action came too late. By the middle of 1773, all of New England plus South Carolina had received and accepted the Virginia invitation. The foundation for a Union of the colonies had been laid.

4. THE TEA ACT (5/10/1773)

An affair which in the beginning had nothing to do with the colonies created the worst colonial reaction of all. The British East India Company, after great prosperity, was on the verge of bankruptcy. Tea glutted the British market and the company had considerable amounts of it stored in warehouses. Some thought the Crown would revoke the company's charter and take over management of the business. Parliament thought this would be a mistake.

The British East India Company suffered from the colonial boycott of British tea. In an effort to save the Company, Parliament passed the Tea Act, which eliminated import tariffs on tea entering England and allowed the company to sell directly to consumers rather than through merchants. These changes lowered the price of British tea to below that of smuggled tea, which the British hoped would end the boycott.

The Tea Act pleased Lord North. Eliminating English taxes and middlemen was intended to put the East India company at a competitive advantage in the colonies. The colonists should be happy, he reasoned, because they would receive cheaper tea than in England. The Crown would also benefit. So, Lord North was so sure the Tea Act would be well received he didn't even send instructions to the Royal Governors in the colonies regarding its enforcement.

Governor Hutchinson somewhat invited the incident because he *was determined to show toughness toward the colonists and another retreat would end British sovereignty in the colonies. He insisted that the tea ships tie up along the wharves and that their cargoes be unloaded.*

The first to complain were the colonial merchants who had benefitted from the smuggling trade, which they might now lose. While protests of the Tea Act in the form of tea boycotts and the burning of tea cargos occurred throughout the colonies, *the response in Boston was the most aggressive. Sam Adams summoned a convention of Committees of Correspondence to meet at Old South Meeting House where they sent a message to Governor Hutchinson demanding that he order the ships to return the tea to England.*

This actually would have been unlawful since the ships had already entered the customs area. When the Governor's refusal reached the convention, Adams stirred the crowd by saying, "this meeting can do nothing further to save the country".[1] *(Morrison pg 204)* Instantly, a mob disguised as Mohawk Indians went to the waterfront and dumped 342 chests of tea worth $1 million (current value) into Boston harbor. *This event came to be known as "The Boston Tea Party" of 12/16/1773 which had the calculated effect of irritating the British government into rash and unwise reactions.*

At a Cabinet meeting on 2/4/1774, Lord North was willing to overlook the incident but the King was furious, as was English public opinion. Lord North realized that his Ministry would be unpopular if it did nothing. It seemed as if the Government was being forced to take a strong stand in spite of warnings from Burke, Barre, and even General Burgoyne to proceed with caution. *Parliament then passed the "Coercive or Intolerable Acts" of 3/28/1774 which were a series of four Acts aimed at restoring order in Massachusetts and punish Boston for the "Boston Tea Party". The King wrote to Lord North that the "dye is now cast, the colonies must either submit or triumph".*

5. **THE COERCIVE ACTS (INTOLERABLE ACTS) (3/28/1774)**

The Boston Tea Party angered Parliament and King George III into passing multiple laws known as the *"Coercive or Intolerable Acts"* which included;

a. *The "Boston Port Bill" of 3/31/1774 closed Boston harbor until the East India Company was compensated for the destroyed Tea.* It also required the compensation of revenue officers for their lost duty on the tea. Lord North believed that Boston would be forced to stand alone, without supporters. News of this Act reached Boston on 5/11/1774. Even Governor Hutchinson was shocked by its' harshness.

Edmund Burke, a colonial supporter in the English government, wrote to the New York Correspondence Committee that the real purpose of this act was the necessity for "some act of power".

The Boston Committee of Correspondence met soon after the news arrived and dispatched Paul Revere to *distribute copies of the Act plus a circular letter asking all of the colonies to consider Boston's troubles their own and to revive the old "Non-Importation" and "Non-Exportation" agreements of the past. Soon there was a call for a General Congress of the Colonies to consider a united course of action.*

b. ***Virginia*** quickly responded with a ***House of Burgesses Resolution*** drafted by Richard Henry Lee, Patrick Henry, and Thomas Jefferson on ***5/24/1774*** to establish 6/1/1774 as a day of "fasting and prayer" for their colony. ***Because of this resolution, Governor Dunmore dissolved the House of Burgesses two days later, on 5/26/1774.***
Partly because of the Coercive Acts aimed at Massachusetts, primarily, and partly because of Governor Dunmore's dissolution of the Virginia House of Burgesses, George Mason and Patrick Henry met George Washington at Mt. Vernon on 7/17/1774 to discuss the growing conflict. A statement was drafted, primarily the work of George Mason, to be known as the ***"Fairfax Resolves" which declared;***

- a concise summary of American constitutional concerns on such issues as taxation, representation, judicial power, military matters, and the colonial economy

- a proposal for the creation of a "non-importation" effort to be levied against British goods

- a call for a general Congress of the Colonies to convene for the purpose of preserving the American's rights as Englishmen

- a condemnation of the practice of importing slaves as an "unnatural trade" and urged its termination

- a statement that the colonists were "descendants not of the conquered but of the conquerors.

On the following day, 7/18/1774, the Resolves were endorsed by a Fairfax County convention and were eventually proposed to the Continental Congress. These Resolves summarized the feelings of many colonists in mid-1774, ***a conviction that their Constitutional rights were being violated by British policies but no mention was made of independence or military action. The Resolves also marked a step toward inter-colonial cooperation as more colonists began to realize that an attack on one colony was an attack on all.***

After the House of Burgesses were dissolved they met in an "association" at Williamsburg and instructed their Committee of Correspondence to exchange views with similar committees in other colonies about summoning a Continental Congress. *All of the Committees were in favor and the First Continental Congress was called to meet in Philadelphia on 9/5/1774.*

c. *The "Massachusetts Government and Administration of Justice Acts" of 5/20/1774 which included the following;*

This Act protected British soldiers and government officials, involved in suppressing riots, from trial by prejudiced juries and if the Governor believed a fair trial would not be possible, the trial could be transferred to England or another colony. *It created the strongest opposition to date.* Legally, it only amended the Massachusetts Charter of 1691 but actually it imposed on the colony a new charter meant to be permanent. Its provisions allowed the Governor to appoint his Council, which had formerly been chosen for him by the General Court. The Council could still advise but lost its power to veto the Governor's decisions. The Governor could forbid all town meetings except the annual one for election of officers. He had the power to appoint for and during the pleasure of His Majesty and the right to remove at his own discretion officers of the province.

Lord Germain made clear during a debate in Parliament that this Act sought only to make the Constitution of the colonies as similar to that of England as possible. The truth is that these two laws, if enforced, would have made Massachusetts Bay a colony strongly in support of the King. These laws were troubling because of what the future might hold for other colonies.

d. *The "Quartering Act" of 6/2/1774* which revised an earlier Act which directed local authorities to find quarters for troops.

From the day these Acts were passed, the issue between England and the colonies was one of power, who would have the final say? All other questions of taxation, customs duties, or basic rights, faded into the background. *Through all stages of dissension, resistance and outright war, the dominant issue was one of power, should England or America dictate the terms of their mutual association?*

e. **On 6/22/1774, Parliament also added the "Quebec Act"** which really was directed at a different problem;

It established Roman Catholicism as Quebec's official religion, gave Quebec's Royal Governors extensive powers, and **extended Quebec's borders south to the Ohio River and west to the Mississippi river, thereby inhibiting westward expansion.** By the time the colonists learned of the "Quebec Act" they also knew the Ministry had sent a new Governor to Massachusetts, General Thomas Gage, who was to remain as the Commander-in-Chief of the British Army in the colonies. He had been in the colonies since 1755 and knew them well plus he was married to a colonial girl. The Ministry believed that if anyone could bring harmony between the colonists and British, it would be him. The Continental Congress protested this Act because it moved the southern boundary of Quebec to the Ohio river, consistent with the early claims by France to this area. It had the effect of depriving the four colonies which claimed lands north of the Ohio river the territory for four future states. **Some colonial leaders feared that the Catholic religion would be influential in the 13 English colonies.**

H. COLONIAL REACTION..."FIRST CONTINENTAL CONGRESS" (9/5/1774)

Could these opposing claims of authority and freedom ever be reconciled? Loyalty, tradition, pride of membership in a great Empire, urged the colonials to submit, but cherished principles of English liberty impelled them to take a firm stand.

Congress faced a dilemma. **The prevailing colonial attitude at this time was of reconciliation rather than independence. They believed that every path to reconciliation must be kept open. But, Congress had to do something about the Coercive Acts and to also suggest a permanent solution to the struggle between liberty and being part of an Empire.**

In England there was a similar struggle between many Old Whigs and their merchant allies against Parliament's punitive program and the "Whigs" braved the charge of treason in applauding America's final decision to act on James Otis's motto, "where liberty is, there is my country".

The colonists saw the Intolerable Acts as a British plan to starve the New England colonists while reducing their ability to organize and protest. The colonists feared that once the colonies had been subdued, Britain would impose the autocratic model of government outlined in the Quebec Act. The colonists were correct about British plans. By the summer of 1774, their plan was to coerce the colonies into submission as the King now had firm majorities in Parliament who would support him. Public opinion in England had changed, no longer were there any strong, respected groups speaking in support of the colonists.

Governor Gage sent back reports to England stating *that the colonists were moving toward independence and only a strong stance would show them that the colonies were English colonies dependent upon England, and certainly not independent states.* During 1774 both the King and Parliament were in agreement with Gage's view and following his advice.

Attitudes were also hardening in the colonies in 1774 as well. After a decade of discussion about American rights, colonial leaders had a clear idea where they stood, and every colony except Pennsylvania and North Carolina had Committees of Correspondence. *In retrospect, by the spring of 1774, the possibility of reconciliation was slim although many colonial delegates were still hopeful. By the end of July, all colonies except Georgia had selected their delegates to the Philadelphia Convention.*

The profile of the delegates arriving at the end of August, 1774, was that almost all were experienced politicians and had been involved in their colony's affairs for at least a decade. The majority were lawyers, 12 of whom had studied in England, all of the current colonial colleges were represented by alumni and none were considered as radicals who wanted to rip up everything and start all over again.

Congress assembled for its first meeting on 9/5/1774 with Peyton Randolph of Virginia chosen as Chairman. *The Virginia delegation's instructions were drafted by Thomas Jefferson who later published a*

"Summary View of the Rights of British America". Jefferson argued for the autonomy of colonial legislative authority and stated his view of the basis of colonial rights. His belief was that the colonies and other members of the British Empire were distinct states united under the King and, therefore, subject only to the King and not to Parliament. This view was shared with other delegates, like James Wilson and John Adams, which strongly influenced the Congress.

After some debate about rules and procedures it seemed clear that the delegates were empowered to do little more than consult on the current state of affairs. A long discussion followed over voting procedure. The large colonies wanted voting strength related to population but resistance from the smaller colonies and a lack of population statistics forced the decision in favor of a single vote for each colony, regardless of size. It was during this debate that Patrick Henry of Virginia stated that he was not a Virginian but an American.

Congress then formed committees to draw up a statement of American rights, to list infringements of those rights, to study trade and manufacturing regulations which affected the colonies. *On September 17, 1774, Paul Revere delivered the "Suffolk County Resolves" (Boston's County), drafted 9/9/1774 which declared;*

The Coercive Acts to be unconstitutional and void

No obedience should be paid to the Intolerable Acts

The Massachusetts Provincial Congress should collect all taxes and withhold them from the Crown until the Massachusetts government was placed on a "Constitutional foundation"

The colony should prepare itself to resist a British attack

The jailing of any patriot leader would give citizens the right to imprison every servant of the present "tyrannical and unconstitutional government".

A key turning point during the Congress came on 9/28/1774 when Joseph Galloway of Pennsylvania introduced his own plan, *The Galloway Plan of Union* for reorganizing the Empire, *as follows;*

A separate American legislature or "Grand Council" whose members would be elected by colonial assemblies

The colonies would continue to exercise authority over internal affairs

501

The Grand Council would regulate all commercial, civil, criminal, and police affairs that concerned the colonies as well as have the right to veto all Parliamentary legislation affecting the colonies.

But, the new government would be inferior to the Parliament which could initiate legislation relevant to the colonies and also inferior to the Crown which would appoint the President-General who would exercise executive authority and would hold office during the King's pleasure.

Galloway claimed that the great principle behind his plan was that no law should bind the colonies without its consent and its great virtue was that the strength of the whole English empire may be drawn together on any emergency, the interests of both countries advanced, and the rights and liberties of Americans secured. Congress debated the plan for several days and when the vote was taken the plan was defeated by the slim margin of six colonies to five. Galloway blamed the defeat on Sam Adams and the radicals.

After Congress rejected the Galloway Plan on 10/22/1774, it approved the Suffolk Resolves plus a statement that if Britain attempted to execute the latest legislative Acts by force, then all of the colonies should resist.

Meanwhile, on 10/14/1774, Congress approved the most important document of the Congress. It was called "The Declaration of Rights and Resolves" which had been worked on for over a month because of the absence of any precedents, as the colonists were following an uncharted path. *The most difficult question was how to justify this simmering rebellion? The committee finally asked John Adams to draft something which would unite them.*

Adams based his "Declaration" on the laws of nature, the principles of the English Constitution, and several of the original Charters and Compacts issued by the English government. There were ten Resolutions which made it clear that the colonists were defying Britain on the grounds that their rights as Englishmen had been violated. It demanded the right of assembly and petition, the right to be tried by their peers, the right to be free of a standing army, and the right to choose their own councils. It rejected Parliament's right to tax the colonies in any way but accepted its right to regulate their external commerce.

The Congress also accepted John Dickinson's rewrite of an address to the King originally drafted by Patrick Henry which basically blamed Parliament and its administration for the current troubles and it also advised the King that some disloyal men in his government were interposing themselves between the King and his faithful subjects.

All of these efforts forced the delegates to make clear to themselves and to England what they believed in and why they were acting as they were. *On October 20, 1774 they resolved that every colony should create an "association" of colonists who would agree not to import, consume goods from England, nor export goods to England. It was agreed that this "Non-Importation and Non-Consumption Agreement" was to be effective 12/1/1774* and be applied against England, Ireland, and the British West Indies. But, the "non-importation" part of the agreement was not supported, in fact it almost broke up the Congress. Many of the colonies asked for exceptions or delays to aid in their trade and commerce activities. Eventually, Congress accommodated the requests for exceptions but it left a northern colony bitterness toward the southern colonies who demanded these exceptions.

The aim of Congress was to put such pressure on the British government that it would redress all colonial grievances and restore the previous harmony. Some New England and Virginia delegates advocated immediate independence but the majority of delegates went home hoping that these approved resolutions together with the new appeals to the King and to the British people would avert the need for any further such meetings. If these measures failed, however, a 2nd Continental Congress would convene in Philadelphia on 5/10/1775. The last session of the Congress was held on 10/26/1774.

I.   EVENTS IN ENGLAND

At the time the news of the Continental Congress reached England, elections were being held for a new Parliament. The English government had decided to hold the election soon after the Intolerable Acts had passed though Parliament still had one year to serve. The reasoning was that it would weaken the government to halt during a war and engage in an election campaign. Four days after the results were known, the King had a large majority in the House of Commons which would give his Ministry much freedom of action for seven years. ***They also pronounced the New England colonies to be in a state of rebellion and that action may have to be taken to decide whether or not the colonists were to be subject to or free of England.***

(WHAT MIGHT HAVE BEEN IF.................?)

The government had already decided to coerce the colonies and Parliament approved that decision by endorsing the King's position when it assembled in November, 1774. A few still spoke of compromise but fewer listened. ***William Pitt, Earl of Chatham, on 1/20/1775, proposed recalling the troops from Boston and to impose no taxes for revenue purposes without the consent of the colonial assemblies but it was defeated in the House of Lords on 1/23/1775, the same month that orders were sent to the colonial governors to prevent the election of delegates to the 2nd Continental Congress.***

The Lords debate of 1/23/1775 was followed by one in the House of Commons on a petition signed by hundreds of English merchants to repeal the Coercive Acts. Edmund Burke then delivered the first of his famous speeches on reconciliation but the motion for repeal lost. ***Then, on 2/1/1775, Pitt, the Earl of Chatham, proposed a Bill in the lower House for resolving the colonial problem with England.***

It was based on preserving Parliamentary control of trade and navigation, to recognize the Continental Congress as a legal body, and to grant money for Imperial defense. It also called for the repeal of the Coercive Acts, Quebec Act, and Tea Duty. Boston would be set free, colonial judges would be appointed during good behavior, and the sanctity of colonial charters guaranteed. Even though this bill was no clean-cut Dominion solution of the imperial problem, it conceded every practical point for which Congress had contended. ***IF IT HAD BEEN PASSED, THERE WOULD HAVE BEEN NO DECLARATION OF INDEPENDENCE OR REVOLUTIONARY WAR.***

But, it was defeated with the only concession Lord North's majority would make being a resolve that if any colony promised to raise what the government considered to be a proper quota for imperial defense and assume the cost of the domestic programs, Parliament would exempt that colony from the revenue Acts. ***North's "Conciliatory Resolve" of 2/20/1775 failed to convince the colonists because it left the ultimate power over colonial taxation to Parliament and did nothing about the Coercive Acts. Pitt warned England that time was running out to avoid a complete separation.***

There was a slight sign that the North Ministry was looking for a solution because it attempted a secret negotiation in London with Ben Franklin. It involved three intermediaries who promised significant benefits to him if he could mediate a settlement. Franklin responded that unless the Coercive Acts were repealed and the army withdrawn from Boston there could be no reconciliation.

Lord North next tried another method. He proposed another bill, the "New England Restraining Act" of 3/30/1775, which had a goal of isolating New England. It would forbid the four colonies of that area to trade with any part of the world except England and Ireland. It also denied colonial fishermen access to the fishing off the coast of Newfoundland and Nova Scotia. This Act was England's way of punishing the colonies since, if the colonies did not want to trade with England, England would make sure no else traded with the colonists.

It was designed to placate merchants who opposed confrontation with the colonies that the government was attempting to compromise. At the same time, the government dispatched three Generals, William Howe, Sir Henry Clinton, and Sir John Burgoyne, to America with reinforcements. Parliament continued to act as the Ministry wished.

J.   WAR APPROACHES

The Province of Massachusetts Bay became virtually independent in October, 1774, when the Assembly was dissolved by Governor Gage and met at Concord as a ***Provincial Congress*** *under the Presidency of John Hancock. This Congress assumed the government, ignoring both Gage and his newly appointed Council.* It appointed a new Treasurer to collect taxes and a committee of Safety. Boston was full of British troops and the harbor full of English ships sent to enforce the Boston

Port Act. The Governor could not exert any authority outside of the town of Boston. All winter the Committee of Safety collected arms and ammunition, organized and drilled selected militia ("Minutemen") for instant action, set-up a system of intelligence to anticipate any British move, and prepared to resist any attempt of the Royal government to take over the interior.

The colonies were slowly and reluctantly moving toward war with every piece of news arriving from England. By the end of 1774, ten colonies had provincial Congresses mainly composed of the same men who had sat in the regular assemblies. These local congresses approved the proceedings of the Continental Congress. All colonies except Georgia and New York adopted the "association" and local committees were busy with enforcement. Soon it became apparent that non-importation was working as British exports to New York and the Chesapeake Bay fell significantly from 1774 to 1775.

As war approached, disagreement in the various colonies surfaced. New Englanders and Virginia were strongly in favor of war others still proposed conciliation. Boston remained the center of opposition to England and when General/Governor Gage arrived with 4,000 troops in mid-May, 1774. The Boston Committee of Correspondence then ordered non-cooperation.

Gage tried to be fair, he kept the military in the background, he listened to citizen complaints, but events were working against him. Over 7,000 people were out of work and in no mood to listen to reason. Outside of Boston, companies of "minutemen" were being formed, military supplies were being collected and stored, committees of observation were being appointed to watch the movements of British troops.

At this time, Lord Dartmouth, Secretary of War, urged Gage to arrest and imprison the principal instigators of trouble within the Provincial Congress. Dartmouth did not expect the colonists would or could effectively resist. Gage disagreed, saying that the colonists were good fighters, having observed them during the last French-Indian war, and that it would require a large army to subdue them and would take at least a year or two. He thought Dartmouth's plan to arrest the troublemakers would do little good so he decided to just send an expedition to Concord to confiscate the military stores the Patriots had been depositing there since February, 1775.

On the march to Concord, fighting began at Lexington and continued on at Concord and back to Boston, on 4/19/1775.

K.   2ND CONTINENTAL CONGRESS (5/10/1775)

The 2nd Continental Congress assembled in Philadelphia, as planned, just three weeks after the initial fighting at Lexington and Concord. Most of the original members were present plus some new ones such as, Ben Franklin, John Hancock, James Wilson, and Thomas Jefferson. This time New York sent a larger delegation which had been chosen by the provincial Assembly. One "parish" (county) from Georgia sent a delegate who would soon be followed by a full delegation, which meant that *now all 13 colonies were represented in the Congress.*

John Adams outlined the problems ahead of the Congress, complicated by the slim powers of Congress. Nothing it did was binding on the new makeshift colonial governments. It could request but not order, could not legislate but only recommend, and its power and authority over the people depended entirely on the good will and trust the people granted it.

Some anticipated problems occurred when some individuals took actions not sanctioned by the Congress. For example, seven days after convening, Congress learned that Ethan Allen, Benedict Arnold, and 83 "Green Mountain Boys" captured Fort Ticonderoga on 5/10/1775. The invasion route to Canada was now open. This offensive action posed a problem for the Congress because they were prepared to tell the world that the colonies were fighting a "defensive war", but this action undercut that justification. So, they falsely claimed that England was preparing to invade the colonies from Canada, true later on, but not at that time. The Bay Colony then asked Congress to take over the army then forming in Boston, which they realized was necessary with all of the logistics issues to support an army.

Most of June was devoted to trying to solve these problems. It decided that the Continental Army should be composed of 20,000 troops with every colony responsible for a specified quota. On 6/15/1775, George

Washington was appointed as Commander-in-Chief of the Army. At the end of June, Congress approved 69 articles of war. With these things done, Washington and his staff left for Boston.

On 7/6/1775, the delegates approved a "<u>Declaration of Causes of Taking Up Arms</u>", jointly written by Thomas Jefferson and John Dickinson, but with the most powerful phrases coming from Dickinson. It basically pledged to not seek separation but they were faced with the alternative of choosing an unconditional submission to tyranny or resistance by force, which they have reluctantly chosen.

They made a distinction between the "King's army" and the one they were fighting, the "Ministerial Army" and that King George III was being misled by evil Counselors. *The majority in Congress hoped this appeal to reason and separating the King from evil politicians would cause the House of Commons to vote down Lord North's government and the King would then call to power someone like the Earl of Chatham.*

On 7/8/1775, Congress adopted a 2nd address to England known as the "<u>Olive Branch Petition</u>", offering their final attempt at reconciliation based on the following conditions;

Cease-fire in Boston

Repeal of the Coercive Acts

Immediate negotiations between the colonists and Britain.

The author was John Dickinson and soon it was accepted by Congress. Dickinson, who favored conciliation, realized that if England rejected this petition, then the colonists would be justified in seeking Independence. The petition was sent to England in duplicate to two colonial agents who tried, without success, to persuade Lord Dartmouth to present it to the King. They were informed that "His Majesty" would receive no petition from a *"rebel body"* which is not surprising since England had already learned of the Arnold expedition against Quebec. The petition reached Britain the same day as news of the Battle of Bunker Hill. *On 8/23/1775, the King proclaimed that a general rebellion existed and every effort should be made to suppress the rebellion and bring the traitors to justice.*

Congress then, on 7/13/1775, dealt with Indian issues as they were causing problems on the western frontier. Three departments were created and their commissioners empowered to make treaties. Money was appropriated to purchase rum and other gifts for the Indians plus a draft statement which explained the war as just a family squabble with England which did not concern the Indians.

On 7/18/1775, Congress urged the colonies to adopt *"Committees of Safety"* which would direct and supervise all matters necessary for their defense and safety. They would be appointed by the provincial congress and would be considered the executive power within a colony, with authority to call up the militia, direct military operations within a colony's borders, hunt down loyalists, and enforce the decrees of Congress.

In July, Benjamin Franklin, who had been quiet during the deliberations, admitted that he *now favored Independence. On 7/21/1775, Franklin proposed to Congress his "Articles of Confederation and Perpetual Union".* Those against Confederation were strong enough to prevent even mention of his plan being made in the Congressional journals.

The moderates in Congress who still favored reconciliation defeated a motion on 7/21/1775 to open American ports to the world. *John Dickinson led the moderates.* Other actions were taken by Congress during the remainder of July. *On 7/31/1775, Lord North's "conciliatory proposal" was rejected because it seemed deceptive and not sincere. Congress adjourned on 8/2/1775.*

Through the Fall of 1775, those favoring separation were blocked at every turn by those favoring reconciliation. Also, not a single colony had instructed its delegates to introduce the subject of independence into Congress or given explicit permission to vote for independence if it came up for a decision. *A strong grass-roots sentiment had to develop for independence before any faction in Congress dared push the issue.*

By the end of 1775, each of the four New England colonies had committed itself to independence. On 11/9/1775, Congress learned that the King had refused to receive the "Olive Branch Petition" and England was dispatching a large army to crush the colonies. The ship which carried this news also brought a copy of the *King's proclamation of 8/23/1775 which declared the colonies in open rebellion and called upon all colonists to disclose all known conspiracies and conspirators in rebellion against the British government. In effect, he was declaring the acts of Congress and those who obeyed those acts as treasonable. His proclamation had forced all who had supported the colonial cause to finish what they had started or risk hanging.*

On 11/16/1775, Edmund Burke submitted a proposal for reconciliation to the House of Commons which rejected it by a vote of 2-1. On 12/22/1775, Parliament passed the "<u>Prohibitory Act</u>" which prohibited all trade and commerce with the colonies, declared all colonial ships lawful prize, with their crews subject to impressments into the Royal Navy.

There were still a few supporters of reconciliation in England in addition to Burke and Pitt. Lord Barrington, the Secretary of War, urged that all British troops be withdrawn from America and the colonies allowed independence if they chose, or to state their terms for staying within the Empire. *It is possible that if this policy had been followed, and the worst cause of friction removed, some sort of mutual accommodation could have been negotiated.*

On 12/6/1775, Congress responded to the King's Proclamation rejecting his position. It had just been approved when the Congress learned of the King's speech of 10/26/1775 to Parliament where he accused the colonists of taking actions which were intended to establish an independent empire. Up to this point, the colonists had directed their anger at Parliament and hesitated attacking the King. *But, on 1/9/1776, Thomas Paine's pamphlet, "<u>Common Sense</u>", was published and distributed. Paine attacked the King as a "tyrant" and also the concept of the Monarchy, as well. He also attacked those who believed the liberties of the colonists were derived from the British Constitution, arguing that their rights were of all mankind.*

On 2/27/1776, Congress received a copy of the "Prohibitory Act" which had passed Parliament on 12/22/1775. *This Act gave statutory force to the Ministry's program and made clear that all branches of the British government were united in coercing the colonies into submission. The specific terms were;*

It embargoed all colonial trade

It called for the seizure of all colonial ships

It defined colonial resistance as rebellion and treason

It left a slight opening for reconciliation by empowering the Crown to send commissioners to inquire into colonial grievances and grant pardons

This Act had the impact of causing the moderates to realize that Independence was inevitable. Their attitude was shaped by the rumor that the King planned on hiring German mercenary troops to fight in the colonies. Such a move indicated that the King meant to fight the war without mercy. *News of this Act arrived just after Paine's "Common Sense" was published. These two events caused some of those favoring reconciliation to lose hope and join the Independence Patriots.*

L. MOVEMENT TOWARD INDEPENDENCE

1. **THOMAS PAINE WRITES "COMMON SENSE"**
   He argued that reconciliation was no longer possible and there was no guarantee that, even if it happened, Parliament wouldn't renew its attack on colonial liberties at a later date. He believed that complete independence was the only real guarantee for American liberty and also the only way in which foreign aid could be obtained.

   He referred to King George III as a "brutal tyrant who had violated the compact between him and the people to protect their rights, and so forfeited his right to their loyalty and obedience".[1] *(Morrison pg 219)*

   His arguments persuaded many who were uncertain, including General George Washington who wrote on 1/31/1776 that he was persuaded.

2. **SENTIMENT FOR INDEPENDENCE GROWS**
   Through March, those favoring Independence gained strength in Congress. Toward the end of March, 1776, Congress learned that the British had evacuated Boston. On 4/6/1776, the Patriots persuaded Congress to take its boldest step yet, the opening of all colonial ports to world trade. It seemed obvious now that

a final break with England was unavoidable. ***Almost no one in Congress saw hope for a reconciliation although a strong group of moderates were still hoping.*** Some of those believed that the colonists first had to strengthen themselves and obtain foreign assistance before taking the final step toward independence.

The South was strongly in favor of independence. Even the Georgia delegates appeared with full powers to vote for independence. South Carolina expelled her Royal Governor and voted for independence. North Carolina delegates had full powers.

By the spring of 1776, opposition to Independence was centered in the middle colonies of Pennsylvania, New York, New Jersey, and Maryland. Pennsylvania's objection was crucial. It was believed by those favoring independence that if Pennsylvania could be persuaded to their position, then the other three colonies would also change their vote. The pro-Independence faction looked forward to the Pennsylvania election on May 1, 1776, to elect new assembly members, hoping that enough new members favoring independence would change the instructions to the delegates to support independence. ***Unfortunately for them, those favoring reconciliation won the majority.***

After many efforts to undermine the Pennsylvania government and Congressional delegation, in order to force their support of independence, a "preamble" was passed in Congress 6-4 with three abstentions ***to force Pennsylvania to support independence. This vote was taken 5/15/1776.***

M.   DECLARATION OF INDEPENDENCE

By 5/20/1776, the day the Pennsylvania assembly was to convene, a carefully staged protest of Philadelphia citizens in the state house yard voted to oust the assembly and create a revolutionary government. ***Dickinson and the moderates continued to resist,*** however. ***Then, something happened in Virginia which broke the impasse.*** Virginia Governor Dunmore, helped the Virginians make up their minds for independence by ***telling them to either support the King or be deemed traitors. At the same time he offered*** *freedom to all slaves who left their rebel masters.* His action so infuriated James Madison that he proposed a state constitutional convention to manage the government through the crisis.

On 5/15/1776, the Virginia Convention instructed its delegates to the Continental Congress to declare the colonies free and independent states. It then appointed a committee, presided over by George Mason, to report a "Declaration of Rights" and a plan of government for an independent state. *He subsequently proposed, and the convention adopted, the "Virginia Bill of Rights" on 6/12/1776, which became the "parent" of all American Bills of Rights. On 6/29/1776, the convention adopted a Constitution for an independent Commonwealth of Virginia.*

Meanwhile*, on 6/7/1776, Richard Henry Lee, on orders from the Virginia government, proposed to Congress the following;*

"That these United Colonies are, and of right ought to be, free and independent states, that they are absolved for all allegiance to the British Crown, and that all political connection between them and the state of Great Britain is, and ought to be, totally dissolved".

"That it is expedient forthwith to take the most effectual measures for forming foreign alliances".

"That a plan of Confederation be prepared and transmitted to the respective colonies for their consideration and approbation".[1] *(Morrison pg 221)*

These proposals were discussed on 6/8 and 6/9. *By this time there was no longer a question of "if", regarding Independence, but "when" and under what conditions.* Those who objected to independence now mostly *opposed the timing of the measure,* they wanted to delay in the hope of some reconciliation efforts proving effective. By the end of the second day of discussions, those favoring delay, led by John Dickinson, stated that they were almost ready to support independence and would probably would do so soon. It was agreed to give the middle colonies more time to think about it and agreed to delay for three weeks but, *meanwhile, on 6/11/1776, it was decided to form a committee of five to draft a document justifying their actions to the world.*

The committee chosen to draft the document were Thomas Jefferson of Virginia, Robert R. Livingston of New York, Roger Sherman of Connecticut, Ben Franklin of Pennsylvania, and John Adams of Massachusetts. Jefferson was named the Committee Chairman. His draft didn't really offer anything new. It began with a statement of purpose, to declare the causes of the break from Britain. He then presented a theory of government to justify separation. He argued, as did others like James Wilson, John Adams, and Thomas Paine, that all men were created equal and endowed with certain inalienable rights and that when the colonists immigrated to the New World they lost none of those rights. He also stated that through mutual compacts among themselves and with the King, governments were created. The colonists gave their allegiance to the King, who in return became obligated to protect their natural rights. If the King failed in that obligation , the compacts with the colonists were null and void. Jefferson then listed the various instances where the King had failed in his duty to his colonial subjects.

This Declaration was a godsend to those tender souls among the Patriots who could not get over their duty to honor the King. It explains why the indictment of the Declaration is aimed primarily against King George III.

After the Committee approved his draft, *he presented it to Congress who still needed to persuade the few remaining moderates favoring delay*. During the first two days of July, *Dickinson continued to make his case.* The delegates listened respectfully but *on the afternoon of 7/2/1776, the vote was taken.* Dickinson and two other Pennsylvanians absented themselves from the meeting which left the majority of the Pennsylvania delegation in favor of independence. New York abstained, pleading a lack of instructions. *No negative votes were recorded so that it could be said the Declaration of Independence was passed unanimously.*

The next two days were spent editing Jefferson's draft. Congress made few changes except to eliminate a long passage which blamed slavery in America on the King. *On 7/4/1776, "The Unanimous Declaration of the 13 United States of America" was approved.* On 7/8/1776, it was read from the balcony of Independence Hall and on 7/19/1776, Congress voted to have it signed.

The signing of the Declaration of Independence created a sharp division in the colonies between the *"Whigs" (those favoring Independence)* and the *"Tories" (British Loyalists and sympathizers)*. Approximately 20% of free Americans were Tories with most of their influence in the Middle Colonies and Georgia. Slaves also made up a significant number of Tory loyalists, responding to Britain's promises of freedom for any slave who fought to restore Royal authority. The most prominent Whig strongholds were in New England, Virginia, and South Carolina.

To summarize, the American Revolution was not fought to OBTAIN freedom, but to PRESERVE the liberties that they already had acquired. Independence wasn't the original goal but a reluctant last resort to preserve "life, liberty, and the pursuit of happiness.

N.   SUMMARY OF THE CAUSES OF THE AMERICAN REVOLUTION

The colonists were accustomed to a large degree of self-determination since their original settlements. Many settlers came to America to escape oppressive government in England and elsewhere in Europe. British efforts to tighten their control over the colonies made them wonder why they came to America?

Many British decisions hurt the vital interests of many groups of settlers such as merchants, fur traders, manufacturers, taxpayers, land speculators, and other settlers. These unpopular decisions affecting so many different groups of settlers had the effect of uniting the colonists.

The policy of tighter control over the colonies came in 1763, after the last French–Indian War, when England needed more financial support from the colonies, in their own defense, but also at a time when the colonists were more self-confident in their ability to defend themselves.

There was a legitimate complaint about the absence of "representation" in English decisions affecting the colonists.

As the population of America grew, its' percentage of English-settlers grew smaller, with more settlers having other European roots. That produced a lessening of respect for English traditions and willingness to follow English decisions. Also, as the settlers became more "Americanized", they lost their connection to English customs and laws. By 1763, almost 1/3 of the population were non-English in their origins and they felt no obligation to England.

The possibility of Independence appealed to people spread all over a large, rich, country. They saw no reason to submit to the rule of a smaller country thousands of miles across the Ocean.

The "enlightenment" taught the colonists that society, like nature, was governed by "natural laws". They had learned that a ruler who interfered with their political freedoms would be viewed as a tyrant guilty of violating the laws of nature. Settlers had been raised and taught that it was their duty to oppose "tyrants".

Until 1770, the colonists believed Parliament could regulate their trade but not tax them. *The imposition of the Townshend Acts showed them that commercial legislation could be used for taxation purposes.* The colonists began to believe that they had the right to examine the PURPOSE of each law passed and refuse to obey those which they believed were intended to raise revenues. Parliament, which had repeatedly asserted its right to legislate on all matters, would never allow the colonists such freedom.

There were signs of impending rebellion, such as the "Paxton Boys" in western Pennsylvania in 1763 demanding protection against Indian raids. There was also the "Regulator movement" in North Carolina in 1771 protesting high taxes and corrupt courts.

Misunderstanding due to distance and the time-lag of information moving across the Ocean. The two countries simply did not understand each other, partly due to lack of knowledge but also significantly impacted by the slow-movement of news and information across the Ocean.

> *Uncompromising attitude of the English Government and King George III as evidenced by:*
>
> > The rejection of the "Olive Branch petition" drafted by John Dickinson and approved by Congress 7/8/1775.
> >
> > The Royal denunciation of the colonists as "rebels" in August, 1775.
> >
> > The Parliamentary decree of December, 1775, closing all colonial ports until they accepted British demands. The colonists reasoned that they would have to declare Independence just to have commercial trade with nations other than England.
>
> **On 2/27/1776, Congress received a copy of the English** *"Prohibitory Act" (passed in England 12/22/1775) which gave Parliament the authority to force the colonies into submission.*

O. GROWING COOPERATION AMONG THE COLONISTS AGAINST THE BRITISH

The Stamp Act Congress of 1765 was urged by the Massachusetts Assembly to send delegates from nine colonies to New York to plan united action against the Stamp Act.

The Committees of Correspondence were inaugurated in 1772 by Sam Adams in Massachusetts to create an inter-colonial network of information to be used to develop policies and actions against the British oppression.

Non-Importation and Boycott provisions inaugurated by Massachusetts. The "Sons of Liberty" were created to help in the demonstrations and enforcement of the boycotts.

The First Continental Congress of 1774 was created to oppose the "Intolerable Acts". They created and sent to King George III a "Declaration of Rights and Grievances" requesting a repeal of the Intolerable Acts, voted to impose a boycott on English goods, and began an effort to gather and store military supplies and begin training local militia's. This action was initiated by the Massachusetts "Suffolk Resolves" of 10/8/1774 opposing the Intolerable/Coercive Acts.

On 7/5/1775 the Congress approved the "Olive Branch Petition" begging the King to intercede for the colonies against the Parliament.

On 7/6/1775 the Congress approved the "Declaration of Causes of Taking-Up Arms" written by John Dickinson.

On 7/18/1775 the Congress urged the colonies to create Committees of Safety to direct all matters necessary for their security and defense.

The American Revolution really began in the minds of the colonists when they became convinced that King George III was denying them their God-given rights and privileges.

P.　KEY DATES AND SIGNIFICANT EVENTS

2/10	1763	End of French/Indian War causes England to look for ways to get the colonists to pay their share of the expenses
10/7	1763	King George III Proclamation Line
4/5	1764	Revenue Act/Sugar Act/Plantation Act
9/1	1764	Currency Act
3/22	1765	Stamp Act
3/24	1765	Mutiny Act/Quartering Act
5/30	1765	Virginia Resolves denies Parliament's right to tax the colonists
7/10	1765	King George III removes Grenville from office
10/7	1765	Stamp Act Congress meets in New York city
3/18	1766	Repeal of Stamp Act
3/18	1766	Declaratory Act
June	1766	Rockingham revises Revenue Act of 1764
7/25	1766	Pontiac makes peace with England
6/29	1767	Townshend Act/Revenue Act of 1767
9/4	1767	Townshend dies & replaced by Lord North
12/2	1767	John Dickinson published the first of his 12 "Letters from a Pennsylvania Farmer" opposing Parliament right to tax colonists in any form
2/11	1768	John Adams and James Otis draft and Massachusetts Assembly approves a circular letter to the other colonial assemblies calling their attention to the Townshend Acts
2/27	1768	King names Lord Hillsborough to position of Secretary of State for Colonial Affairs
5/2	1768	Non-Importation movement begins, lasts until 1770

7/1	1768	Massachusetts Legislature refuses to rescind Dickinson letter. Dissolved by Governor Bernard
10/1	1768	1,700 British troops arrive in Boston to maintain order after Townshend Act protests
10/24	1768	England's two Indian superintendents negotiate three Indian treaties with the Iroquois, Cherokee, and Creek Indians
7/1	1769	Massachusetts Assembly repeats its position of "no taxation without representation"
1/28	1770	Duke of Grafton resigns as Prime Minister
1/31	1770	Lord North Ministry
3/5	1770	Boston Massacre
5/10	1773	Tea Act
12/16	1773	Boston Tea Party
3/28	1774	Coercive Acts/Intolerable Acts
3/31	1774	Boston Port Bill
5/20	1774	Massachusetts Government & Administration of Justice Acts
5/24	1774	Virginia House of Burgesses passes Resolution calling for day of fasting and prayer, 6/1/1774
5/26	1774	Because of Virginia Resolution of 5/24, Governor Dunmore dissolves House of Burgesses
6/2	1774	Quartering Act revises earlier Act
6/17	1774	Governor/General Gage dissolves Massachusetts Assembly
6/22	1774	Quebec Act
7/17	1774	Fairfax Resolves states Virginia's position on the coming conflict
9/5	1774	First Continental Congress meets in Philadelphia
9/17	1774	Suffolk County Resolves

9/28	1774	Galloway Plan of Union proposed to First Continental Congress
10/10	1774	Governor Dunmore's War. Chief Cornstalk defeated at "Battle of Point Pleasant"
10/14	1774	Congress approves "Declaration of Rights and Resolves"
10/22	1774	Galloway Plan of Union rejected by 6-5 vote
12/1	1774	"Non-Importation and Non-Consumption Agreement" passed by Congress
1/20	1775	William Pitt, Earl of Chatham, proposes compromise. Defeated by House of Lords 1/23
2/1	1775	Pitt offers same proposal to House of Commons, also defeated
2/20	1775	Lord North "Conciliatory Resolve" offered to colonists, rejected
3/30	1775	Lord North proposes "New England Restraining Act" intended to isolate New England
4/19	1775	War begins at Lexington and Concord, Massachusetts
5/10	1775	2nd Continental Congress meets in Philadelphia
5/10	1775	Green Mountain Boys capture Fort Ticonderoga; Capture Crown Point 5/12
6/15	1775	George Washington appointed as Commander-in-Chief of the Army
7/6	1775	Continental Congress delegates approve "Declaration of Causes of Taking Up Arms" written by Jefferson & Dickinson
7/8	1775	Congress adopts the "Olive Branch Petition"
7/18	1775	Congress urges colonies to adopt "Committees of Safety"

7/21	1775	Benjamin Franklin proposes to Congress "Articles of Confederation & Perpetual Union". It was rejected.
7/31	1775	Lord North "Conciliatory Resolve" rejected by Congress
8/23	1775	King George III declares a "General Rebellion"
10/26	1775	King George III speech accuses colonists of seeking independence
11/9	1775	Congress learns that King George III refused to accept their "Olive Branch Petition"
11/16	1775	Edmund Burke proposes reconciliation to House of Commons which reject it
12/22	1775	Parliament passes "Prohibitory Act"
1/9	1776	Thomas Paine pamphlet "Common Sense" published
1/31	1776	George Washington writes that he supports independence
2/27	1776	Congress receives copy of Prohibitory Act
4/6	1776	Patriots persuade Congress to open all colonial ports to world trade
5/15	1776	Pennsylvania votes to support Independence
5/15	1776	Virginia Convention instructs its delegates to Continental Congress to declare colonies free and independent states
6/7	1776	Richard Henry Lee ordered by Virginia government to propose statement of independence
6/11	1776	Congress decides to form committee to draft document justifying their actions
6/12	1776	Virginia Bill of Rights adopted
6/29	1776	Convention adopts Constitution for an independent Commonwealth of Virginia

| 7/2 | 1776 | Congress votes for Independence |
| 7/4 | 1776 | Declaration of Independence approved |

Footnote 1: THE OXFORD HISTORY OF THE AMERICAN PEOPLE by S.E. MORRISON,
1965 OXFORD UNIVERSITY PRESS, NEW YORK

Q.   REVIEW QUESTIONS

(Multiple Choice)

1. In which year did English policy toward the colonies take a major change?
    a.   1660
    b.   1763
    c.   1770
    d.   1774

2. The Revenue Act of 1764 was also known by what other name(s)?
    a.   Currency Act
    b.   Tea Act
    c.   Stamp Act
    d.   Sugar Act

3. In what year was the Stamp Act passed?
    a.   1763
    b.   1764
    c.   1765
    d.   1766

4. In which order were the following English Laws passed?
    a.   Townshend Duties, Stamp Act, Tea Act, Sugar Act
    b.   Revenue Act, Currency Act, Stamp Act, Townshend Duties
    c.   Sugar Act, Tea Act, Prohibitory Act, Boston Port Bill
    d.   Coercive Acts, Prohibitory Act, Plantations Act, Stamp Act

5. In what years was the "Period of Calm" following the repeal of the Townshend Acts?
    a. 1763-1766
    b. 1767-1770
    c. 1770-1773
    d. 1773-1776

6. Which Treaty ended the French presence in North America?
    a. Treaty of Fort Stanwix
    b. Treaty of Hard Labor
    c. Treaty of Paris 1763
    d. None of the above

7. Who was the author of "Common Sense"?
    a. Thomas Jefferson
    b. John Adams
    c. John Dickinson
    d. Thomas Paine

8. Who was the first colonist to claim, "that these United Colonies are and ought to be free and independent states"?
    a. Richard Henry Lee
    b. John Adams
    c. Thomas Jefferson
    d. George Mason

9. Which state was the last to approve the adoption of the Declaration of Independence?
    a. New York
    b. Pennsylvania
    c. Virginia
    d. None of the above

10. Who was the author of the "Olive Branch Petition"?
    a. Thomas Jefferson
    b. John Adams
    c. Sam Adams
    d. John Dickinson

(True or False)

11. The French/Indian war caused the English to change its policy toward the colonies contributing to its own self-defense.
    a. TRUE
    b. FALSE

12. George Grenville was generally favorable toward the Colonies.
    a. TRUE
    b. FALSE

13. James Otis argued against British "Writs of Assistance" in 1762.
    a. TRUE
    b. FALSE

14. The colonists chief argument against the Sugar Act was because it was designed to raise revenue from the colonists.
    a. TRUE
    b. FALSE

15. The "Suffolk Resolves" were offered against the Coercive Acts/ Intolerable Acts.
    a. TRUE
    b. FALSE

CHAPTER 21 SUMMARY

The Critical 13 Years from 1763 to 1776

1. 1763 was the critical year for England, following the end of the final French and Indian War. It resolved some old problems but also created new ones, such as;

    a. Financial problems. How to pay their debts and generate new sources of revenue.

    b. How to require the colonists to share the financial burden of their own defense

    c. How to deal with settlers moving across the Appalachian Mountains into Indian country and maintain peaceful relations with the Indians.

2. King George III and Prime Minister Grenville passed legislation to generate more revenue from the colonists and more effectively enforce the Navigation Acts;

    a. Revenue Act/Sugar Act/Plantation 1764

    b. Currency Act   1764

    c. Stamp Act   1765 (Repealed 3/18/1766)

    d. Quartering Act   1765

    e. Declaratory Act   1766

    f. Townshend Duties   1767

    g. Tea Act   1773

    h. Coercive Acts/Intolerable Acts   1774

    i. Prohibitory Act   1775

3. Colonial Reactions;

    a. Strongly opposed the Stamp Act which led to its repeal.

    b. React to the Townshend Acts with the Non-Importation Agreements.

    c. The Boston Tea Party was the reaction to the Tea Act

    d. A call for the Continental Congress in reaction to the Coercive/Intolerable Acts.

    e. The Prohibitory Act causes the moderates in Congress to recognize that Independence is inevitable.

4. The colonies move toward Independence;

    a. John Dickinson writes the "Letters from a Pennsylvania Farmer" in December, 1767. He argues against Parliament's right to tax the colonists in any form. There is no mention of independence at this time.

    b. James Otis and John Adams draft a letter to the other colonial assemblies opposing the Townshend Duties in February, 1768.

    c. Colonial Non-Importation movement from 1768-1770.

    d. The Massachusetts Legislature repeats its position of "no taxation without representation" in 7/1769.

    e. Massachusetts forms "Committee's of Correspondence" in 11/1772 and requests the other colonies to do the same. Virginia and most of New England do so by mid-1763.

    f. In response to the "Coercive/Intolerable Acts", Virginia passes a resolution calling for 6/1/1774 as a day of "prayer and fasting". Virginia Governor Dunmore dissolves the House of Burgesses so a group of Virginia political leaders pass the "Fairfax Resolves" outlining their opposition to British policies on 7/17/1774.

    g. Many colonial Committee's of Correspondence call for the Continental Congress to meet in Philadelphia 9/1774. At this time there is still no demand for Independence.

    h. The Massachusetts "Suffolk Resolves" oppose the Coercive/ Intolerable Acts"and suggest preparations to resist English oppression.

i. The First Continental Congress rejects the Galloway Plan of Union which would have maintained the power and authority of the Parliament and Crown.

j. Congress approves "The Declaration of Rights & Resolves" of 10/1774 which maintains that their rights as Englishmen have been violated. The Committee asks John Adams to draft something which will justify their opposition.

k. The Massachusetts Assembly is dissolved by Governor Gage in October, 1774. By the end of the year, ten colonies had Provisional Congresses.

l. The Massachusetts Committee of Safety begins storing arms, ammunition, and training of local militia.

m. War begins at Lexington and Concord on 4/19/1775.

n. The Continental Congress approves the "Declaration of Causes of Taking Up Arms" of 7/1775. It is drafted by Thomas Jefferson and John Dickinson and pledges to NOT seek separation. It is an appeal to King George III to oust the North Ministry which is leading England to war.

o. As a final attempt at reconciliation, Congress passes the "Olive Branch Petition" 7/1775". It is rejected by the King who declares the colonists as "Rebels".

p. In November, 1775, Congress learns that the King refused to accept the "Olive Branch Petition".

q. Upon learning of the English "Prohibitory Act", Thomas Paine publishes "Common Sense" in January, 1776, making the case for Independence.

r. In February, 1776, Congress receives a copy of the "Prohibitory Act" which convinces the moderates that Independence is necessary.

s. In May, 1776, Pennsylvania is the last colony to support the call for Independence.

t. In June, 1676, Richard Henry Lee is asked to draft a statement of Independence and Congress forms a committee to draft the justification for their actions.

u. The draft "Declaration of Independence" is submitted to Congress in July, 1776. John Dickinson is still opposed.

v. The "Declaration of Independence" is officially approved on 7/4/1776.

5. ***CAUSES OF THE AMERICAN REVOLUTION;***

a. The colonists were accustomed to considerable self-determination and resisted greater control by England.

b. The colonists did not believe that they were represented in Parliament, thus they were being taxed without their consent.

c. The arrogance of the British political and military leadership.

d. Many British decisions hurt every aspect of colonial life, thus producing a sense of colonial unity.

e. A growing percentage of the colonial population is no longer of British heritage thus there isn't as much attachment to England as during the early settlement period.

21a

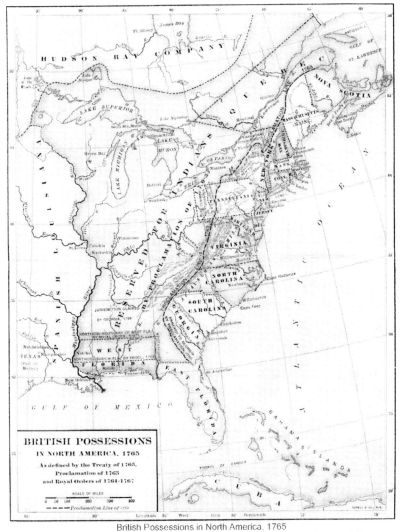

British Possessions in North America, 1765

21b

BRITISH PRIME MINISTERS & SECRETARIES OF STATE					
PRIME MINISTER	DATES	KEY LEGISLATION	DATE PASSED	SECRETARY OF STATE	DATES
NONE	PRIOR TO 1763	WOOL ACT	1689		
		HAT ACT	1732		
		MOLASSES ACT	1733		
		IRON ACT	1760		
		NAVIGATION ACTS	1760'S		
GRENVILLE	1763-1765	ROYAL PROCLAMATION	1763		
		SUGAR ACT(REVENUE)	1764		
		CURRENCY ACT	1764		
		QUARTERING ACT	1765		
		STAMP ACT	1765		
ROCKINGHAM	1765-1766	REPEAL STAMP ACT	1766		
		DECLARATORY ACT	1766		
		REVISED REVENUE ACT	1766		
CHATHAM & GRAFTON	1766-1770	TOWNSHEND ACTS	1767	HILLSBOROUGH LORD	1768-1772
LORD NORTH	1770-1782	REPEAL TOWNSHEND ACTS	1770	EARL OF DARTMOUTH	1772-1775
		TEA ACT	1773		
		COERCIVE ACTS	1774	LORD GEORGE	
		RESTRAINING ACTS	1775	GERMAINE	1775-1782
		PROCLAMATION OF REBELLION	1776		
		PROHIBITORY ACT	1776		

21c

BRITISH ACTIONS & COLONIAL REACTIONS

BRITISH ACTIONS	DATE	COLONIAL REACTION
WRITS OF ASSISTANCE	1760	MASSACHUSETTS CHALLENGE LAW
SUGAR ACT	1764	WEAK PROTEST BY COLONIAL LEGISLATURES
STAMP ACT	1765	BOSTON MOBS, SONS OF LIBERTY VIRGINIA RESOLVES STAMP ACT CONGRESS
TOWNSHEND DUTIES	1767	"LETTERS FROM PENNSYLVANIA FARMER" (J. DICKINSON) BOSTON MASSACRE 1770
TEA ACT	1773	BOSTON TEA PARTY
INTOLERABLE ACTS	1774	FIRST CONTINENTAL CONGRESS

Chapter 22

Revolutionary War Military Campaigns

A.   BACKGROUND

There have been volumes written about the military aspects of the Revolutionary War. My intent in this chapter is to cover those military campaigns which had a significant impact on the Revolution itself. By "significant impact", I mean an event which caused some sort of change in the strategic conduct of the war and/or Revolution.

I chose to focus on the following battles, excluding the beginning and ending campaigns:

EVENT	DATE(S)
The Patriot capture of Fort Ticonderoga	5/10/1775
The Battle of Trenton	12/26/1776
The Saratoga Campaign (Battles of Saratoga, Fort Stanwix, and Oriskany)	8/6/1777– 10/7/1777
The Battles of the Carolina's;	
The Battle of King's Mountain, South Carolina	10/7/1780
The Battle of Cowpens, South Carolina	1/17/1781
The Battle of Guilford Courthouse, North Carolina	3/15/1781

Each of these battles had a political as well as military impact on the Revolution.

B. CHRONOLOGY OF MAJOR BATTLES / DATES (Attachment 22a)

BATTLE/LOCATION	*FROM/TO*
Lexington/Concord, Massachusetts	4/19/1775
Fort Ticonderoga, New York	5/10/1775
Bunker Hill/Breed's Hill, Massachusetts	6/17/1775
Siege of Boston, Massachusetts	Summer 1775 – 3/17/1776
Quebec, Canada	12/31/1775
Long Island (Brooklyn Heights), New York	8/27/1776
Valcour Bay (Lake Champlain)	10/11/1776
Trenton, New Jersey	12/26/1776
Bennington, Vermont	8/16/1777
Brandywine, Pennsylvania	9/11/1777
Saratoga, New York	9/19/1777 – 10/7/1777
Germantown, Pennsylvania	10/4/1777
Monmouth, New Jersey	6/28/1778
Vincennes, Indiana	2/23/1779
Siege of Charleston, South Carolina	2/11/1780 – 5/12/1780
King's Mountain, South Carolina	10/7/1780
Cowpens, South Carolina	1/17/1781
Guilford Courthouse, North Carolina	3/15/1781
Chesapeake Bay, Virginia	9/5/1781
Yorktown, Virginia	9/28/1781 – 10/19/1781

We know that the War began when the British decided to send an armed column to Concord, Massachusetts, to capture the ammunition and supplies being stored there by the Patriots. Paul Revere and others were sent out to warn the countryside on 4/18/1775 that the British were moving out of Boston and headed toward Concord. When the British troops arrived in Lexington, on the road to Concord, they were blocked by a small group of "Minutemen" on the Lexington Green. Someone fired a shot, still unknown today as to which side fired the first shot, and the British soldiers overwhelmed the colonists and continued on to Concord.

By the time the British arrived at Concord, the word had been passed all over the Massachusetts countryside which caused Patriots from all over to move toward Concord to confront the British. There was a brief firefight at the North Bridge and in the town which forced the British to retreat. On their march back to Boston, they were fired on from the sides of the roads and in the woods along the route until the British sent a relief force to escort them back to Boston.

C.   THE CAPTURE OF FORT TICONDEROGA (May 9-10, 1775)

There was no "battle" at Fort Ticonderoga. The Fort was captured from a British "force" of 42 men by Ethan Allen and 83 of his "Green Mountain Boys" plus Benedict Arnold although there was considerable conflict over who was really in command. The significance of Fort Ticonderoga isn't in its capture, but in what happened after the capture.

At the end of the 1775 military campaign, General Washington found himself in a difficult situation. Early attempts to attack the British in Canada had met with defeat and the British Army was firmly entrenched in Boston since their victory at Bunker Hill. Washington knew that he could easily occupy the heights overlooking Boston, which normally would have provided a significant tactical advantage, but he lacked the artillery needed to force the British out of Boston. *Meanwhile, far to the northwest on Lake Champlain, the forts at Crown Point and Ticonderoga contained the very pieces of artillery Washington needed. And these forts, now under American control, were in no immediate threat from the British that winter.*

Washington assigned Henry Knox, a young Boston bookseller, to organize the transport of 59 of these captured artillery pieces from the forts on Lake Champlain to the heights overlooking Boston, where, it was hoped, they would turn the tide against the British in the city below.

To make a long story short, during a period of 49 days from 12/6/1775 to 1/24/1776, Knox and his team moved these cannon *300 miles over rugged terrain, during the height of winter, from Fort*

Ticonderoga in upstate New York, along the Vermont border, and across Massachusetts to Cambridge commons, and then to Dorchester Heights, Massachusetts.

By the middle of March, 1776, just four months before the Declaration of Independence, Washington's army was in position to bombard the British in Boston from Dorchester Heights, using the cannon transported by Knox and his group.

Lord William Howe recognized that only the evacuation of his Army could save it, and on **March, 18th, the victorious American Army marched into the deserted city.**

So, the capture of Fort Ticonderoga indirectly led to the forced retreat of the British Army from Boston. Eventually, Boston would continue as the center of the opposition to British rule in America. It was truly one of the most significant military events of the Revolutionary War and a shot was never fired in the capture. It was a truly significant achievement.

For anyone wanting more detailed information about the Knox campaign and trail, go to the following webpages:

- The Hudson River Valley Institute, Marist College, Poughkeepsie, New York www.hudsonrivervalley.org/themes/knoxtrail

- The New York State Museum describes the markers along the route www.nysm.nysed.gov/services/KnoxTrail

- The Historical Market Database also describes the markers along the route www.hmdb.org/results.asp

  (Attachment 22b represents a picture of Fort Ticonderoga and attachment 22c is a Map of General Knox Cannon Trail)

D.   THE BATTLE OF SARATOGA (9/19/1777-10/7/1777)

The primary significance of this battle was that it provided the final evidence the French needed to now openly support the colonists. Previously, the French had been secretly aiding the colonists but were now willing to join a military and defense alliance with the colonists. The French Foreign Minister, Comte de Vergennes, was fearful of a separate American-English Treaty which would not be in the best interests of the French, so he worked with Ben Franklin on *two Treaties;*

1. Treaty of Amity & Commerce

2. Treaty of Alliance

The key was a promise that neither country would stop fighting until the British recognized American independence. In return, America guaranteed French possession of certain West Indian islands which she currently held. Commerce was to be a on a "most favored nation" basis.

There was also a military significance *in that it prevented the British from completing their plan to isolate New England from the other colonies.* The plan was originally proposed by General John Burgoyne to Lord George Germain, Secretary of State for the Colonies, for the *following three-pronged attack:*

1. A main army of 8,000 troops to move south from Canada down Lake Champlain to capture Fort Ticonderoga and then continue down the Hudson river valley to New York city. This force was to be led by General Burgoyne.

2. General Howe would invade Pennsylvania where he was certain that the Loyalists would rally to the English side. He assumed that he could easily capture Philadelphia and, if the northern expedition needed reinforcements, he could supply them from his Philadelphia garrison. History has proved that General Howe was never ordered to join up with the Burgoyne army moving south from Canada.

3. An auxiliary force, led by Colonel St. Leger, was to move from Fort Oswego eastward along the Mohawk river to Fort Stanwix (Rome, New York) and then join forces with General Burgoyne, coming from the north, and General Howe, coming from the south, at the junction of the Mohawk and Hudson rivers at present-day Albany.

So, the plan was to isolate New England by drawing a "line" down the length of Lake Champlain-Hudson river valley plus dividng north and south New York by the Mohawk river.

The British suffered a major defeat at Saratoga because Burgoyne's northern army was stopped and defeated at Saratoga, St. Leger's army was stopped and forced to retreat at Fort Stanwix (Rome). Just a few miles to the east, there was also a battle at Oriskany which was probably a colonial defeat but it caused the English Indian allies to become discouraged and weakened the British effort at Fort Stanwix. As a result, St. Leger's army decided to retreat from Fort Stanwix and return to Canada.

General Howe was apparently never ordered to attempt to join General Burgoyne at Albany to effect the cut-off of New England. General Clinton did make an attempt to advance north along the Hudson river to attempt a junction with General Burgoyne but retreated back to New York when it became obvious that he would not be able to succeed in time to prevent the surrender of Burgoyne.

So, the major plan by the British to isolate New England from the rest of the colonies with this three-pronged attack failed, *all of which gave the colonists a great victory which enabled the French to openly aid the colonists. Their assistance was the most helpful at the final and victorious battle of Yorktown, Virginia.*

So, Saratoga was a significant victory with a long-term impact for the colonists. For additional information about the Saratoga battles, see the following:

- www.saratoga.com

- www.britishbattles.com

- www.ushistory.org

E.   THE BATTLE OF TRENTON (12/26/1776)

General Washington's victory over the Hessian forces at Trenton, New Jersey, on Christmas night 1776 was very significant for the following reasons;

1. Washington had suffered many defeats in New York and was forced to retreat through New Jersey, and across the Delaware River into Pennsylvania. His troops' enlistments were close to expiring and they were losing faith in him at the same time as the colonists were also losing confidence in the Revolutionary cause. In August, 1776, his army had 20,000 troops but by December, it was reduced to 3,500. He needed a major victory.

2. The victory over the Hessians renewed the troops' faith in Washington and the Patriots in their cause. Since enlistments were due to expire in just a few days or weeks, the victory caused many of his troops to re-enlist, thus saving his Army.

3. It caused the British to reassess their opinion of Washington and the fighting ability of his Army. Three years after the battle, Lord George Germain, Colonial Secretary of State for King George III, told Parliament, "all of our hopes were blasted by that unhappy affair at Trenton".

4. The victory also gave Washington and his Army the confidence to mount another crossing of the Delaware and second attack on Trenton and then follow up with a successful attack at Princeton, New Jersey on 1/3/1777.

F.   BRITISH STRATEGY IN THE CAROLINA'S

The British strategy in the Carolina's was to give support to a large Loyalist population who, the British believed, would help defeat the Patriots if they were protected by British troops. In 1779-1780, the British invaded the south by capturing Savannah, Georgia, and then Charleston and Camden, South Carolina, destroying much of the Southern Continental Army in the process.

Such victories gave the British confidence they would soon control the entire south and that the Loyalists would flock to their cause. Things didn't work out as they planned because the backcountry opposition to the British was so intense. Even though the backcountry had some Loyalist support and there were many battles between Loyalists and Patriots there, the British were never able to maintain a strong foothold in the southern backcountry to use in undermining the Patriot cause in that region.

The Carolina battles are to be viewed within that context, a battle for the support of the backcountry settlers. The British needed that support to help them win the overall Revolutionary War just as much as the Patriots needed the settlers to help defeat the British. This was to be known as "winning the hearts and minds of the populace". The following three battles were as much about building up the confidence of the southern colonists as it was in defeating the British Army

1. **THE BATTLE AT KING'S MOUNTAIN, SOUTH CAROLINA (10/7/1780)**
   By October, 1780, the Revolutionary War had been going on for five years in the Northern colonies. The British now set their sights on the Carolina's. *The defeat of the British Loyalists at King's Mountain began a series of events which would lead to the defeat of General Cornwallis at Yorktown.* This battle was fought entirely by colonial militia against pro-British Loyalist forces with no British or Continental troops involved. More than half of the colonial force were known as "Overmountain men" who were frontier settlers living over the mountains in Tennessee.

   This battle ended the British invasion of North Carolina and forced General Cornwallis to retreat from Charlotte into South Carolina to wait for reinforcements. After the defeats of General Benjamin Lincoln at Charleston, South Carolina, and then the defeat of General Horatio Gates at Camden, South Carolina, General Cornwallis appeared to have a clear path all the way to

Virginia. In September, Cornwallis invaded North Carolina. Major Patrick Ferguson commanded a force of Loyalists/Tories to protect Cornwallis's left flank. A colonial force of 900 men was left to engage the Loyalists at King's Mountain before they could move to Charlotte to support Cornwallis. The colonial militia knew the King's Mountain region and that it would be almost impossible for the Loyalists to defend their positions. The colonials reached King's Mountain on 10/7/1780 and promptly surrounded it and prepared a very slow ascent up the mountain, tightening the noose.

They sent two columns on the outside to flank the Loyalists and two other columns on the inside to engage them. The Loyalists had to expose themselves in order to fire their weapons and, when they did so, they were exposed to the militia sharpshooters skilled in this type of frontier fighting. Major Ferguson was killed and his second in command, Captain Abraham De Pevster, tried to hold on but he was forced to surrender but the Patriots showed no mercy, remembering how British Colonel Tarleton had slaughtered Patriot prisoners at the "Battle of Waxhaws". The battle lasted slightly more than an hour and not a single man of Ferguson's force escaped. When Cornwallis learned of the defeat, he retreated from Charlotte to Winnsborough, South Carolina.

Historians believe the British defeat at King's Mountain was the beginning of the end of the British rule of the colonies. Thomas Jefferson referred to it as the "turn of the tide of success". The battle was the first major Patriot victory to occur after the British invasion of Charleston, South Carolina.

This defeat of the British was significant on its own but the subsequent losses at Cowpens, South Carolina, in January, 1781, and at Guilford Court House, North Carolina, in March, 1781, basically ended the British effort in the Southern colonies.

For additional information about the Battle of King's Mountain, see the following webpages:

- Tennesseans in the Revolutionary War www.tngenweb. org/revwar/kingsmountain

- Sons of the American Revolution www. revolutionarywararchives.org/kingsmtfall05

- National Park Service, U.S. Department of the Interior www.nps.gov/kimo.index

2. **BATTLE OF COWPENS, SOUTH CAROLINA (1/17/1781)**

The Battle of Cowpens was significant in itself, but, as stated above, combined with the battles of King's Mountain and Guilford Court House, *the three battles signaled the end of the British efforts in the Carolina colonies.*

Cowpens, by itself, was a turning point in the re-conquest of South Carolina from the British. On 10/14/1780, Washington named Nathanael Greene to be Commander of the Southern Department of the Continental forces. The Carolina's had been unsuccessful for the colonists, with one defeat after another in 1780, especially the big defeats at Charleston and Camden, South Carolina. Even though the Patriot victory at King's Mountain had bought time and lifted spirits, most of South Carolina was still under British control.

On 12/3/1780, Captain Daniel Morgan was an officer under Greene at Charlotte, North Carolina. Morgan had significant military experience going back to the last French-Indian War. At one time, he had been captured by the British but released in January, 1777, luckily for the Patriots. He and his men played a key role in the victory at Saratoga. Greene realized that his army was too small to withstand the British Army on an open battlefield, so he split his army and gave part of it to Morgan who was to join forces with various militia.

Meanwhile, Cornwallis was planning on returning to North Carolina to conduct the invasion he had postponed after the King's Mountain defeat. Cornwallis ordered Lt. Colonel

Banastre Tarleton to attack Morgan's force which might threaten Cornwallis's force. ***Tarleton was famous among the colonists as the one who had slaughtered Patriot forces after they had surrendered at the Battle of Waxhaws.*** He was also equally as vicious toward civilians. He pursued Morgan throughout North Carolina. Finally, after crossing into South Carolina, Morgan was joined by a force of militia led by Andrew Pickens, at a place called Cowpens, a well-known grazing area for local cattle. Morgan decided he had a large enough force to stand and fight Tarleton. Through clever strategy, Morgan and Pickens defeated Tarleton who escaped. ***The British losses were significant, the Patriots were encouraged, the British discouraged, and the battle served as a turning point in South Carolina.***

Cornwallis, his army greatly weakened, stubbornly decided to pursue Greene's army into North Carolina where they fought a battle at ***Guilford Court House.*** The battle was a technical victory for Cornwallis but ***his army was so weakened that he decided to withdraw toward Yorktown, Virginia, to rest and refit.***

For additional information about the Battle of Cowpens,, see the following webpages:

- www.britishbattles.com

- www.nps.gov/cowp/index

- www.exploresouthernhistory.com/cowpens1

3. **THE BATTLE AT GUILFORD COURTHOUSE, NORTH CAROLINA (3/15/1781)**

This battle was fought when the Patriot General Nathaniel Greene was moving his army north from South Carolina toward Virginia for reinforcements after the Battle of Cowpens. British General Cornwallis pursued him, wanting to destroy Greene's army before he reached Virginia, across the Dan river. The British were technically victorious because Greene's army was forced to retreat, but the British lost over 500 men killed and wounded. ***His army was so weakened that Cornwallis was forced to give up his***

Carolina plan and complete his movement to Yorktown, Virginia, to recover. He was eventually defeated by General Washington there on 10/18/1781 which basically ended the major fighting in the Revolutionary War.

For additional information about the Battle of Guilford Court House, see the following webpages:

- National Park Service, U.S. Department of the Interior

- www.nps.gov/nr/twhp/www/ps/lessons/32guilford

- www.britishbattles.com

- American Revolution, Battle of Guilford Court House

- www.militaryhistory.about.com

In my opinion, these six battles were the most significant of the Revolutionary War because they changed military and political strategy and therefore changed the ultimate course of the War. Certainly, there were other battles which were important, but these stand out in my mind.

22a

22a	CHRONOLOGY OF KEY MILITARY BATTLES
DATES	**EVENT**
4/19 1775	LEXINGTON & CONCORD. FIRST ACTION OF WAR
4/19-4/20	SIEGE OF BOSTON
5/9-5/10	"GREEN MOUNTAIN BOYS" CAPTURE FT. TICONDEROGA
5/15	CONGRESS APPOINTS GEORGE WASHINGTON COMMANDER-IN-CHIEF
	OF CONTINENTAL ARMY
6/17	BATTLE OF BUNKER HILL
8/28-12/31	FAILED COLONIAL INVASION OF CANADA
10/10	SIR WILLIAM HOWE SUCCEEDS GENERAL GAGE AS COMMANDER OF
	BRITISH FORCES IN BOSTON
3/18 1776	BRITISH TROOPS LEAVE BOSTON FOR HALIFAX. PRIMARILY DUE TO
	GENERAL KNOX CANNONS ON DORCHESTER HEIGHTS
6/30	BRITISH ARMY OCCUPIES NEW YORK CITY
8/27	BATTLE OF LONG ISLAND, NEW YORK
10/28	BATTLE OF WHITE PLAINS, NEW YORK
12/25-12/26	GENERAL WASHINGTON CAPTURES TRENTON, NEW JERSEY.
1/3 1777	BATTLE OF PRINCETON, NEW JERSEY
8/6	BATTLE OF ORISKANY, NEW YORK. AMERICA MILITIA SURROUNDED BY
	BRITISH LOYALISTS AND INDIAN ALLIES
8/18	BATTLE OF BENNINGTON, VERMONT. NEW HAMPSHIRE MILITIA DEFEAT
	BRITISH TROOPS & HESSIANS
9/11	BATTLE OF BRANDYWINE, PENNSYLVANIA. BRITISH DEFEAT COLONIALS
9/19-10/7	BATTLE OF SARATOGA. SURRENDER OF BRITISH GENERAL BURGOYNE
10/4	BATTLE OF GERMANTOWN, PENNSYLVANIA. BRITISH DEFEAT COLONIALS
12/19	COLONIAL ARMY WINTER QUARTERS AT VALLEY FORGE, PENNSYLVANIA
3/7-5/8 1778	BRITISH SIR HENRY CLINTON REPLACES GENERAL HOWE AS COMMANDER
6/17	ENGLAND AND FRANCE AT WAR
6/28	BATTLE OF MONMOUTH, NEW JERSEY
2/23-2/25 1779	COLONIAL MILITIA RAID VINCENNES, INDIANA
6/21	SPAIN DECLARES WAR ON ENGLAND
2/11-5/12 1780	BRITISH SEIGE OF CHARLESTON, SOUTH CAROLINA
8/16	COLONIAL MILITIA & ARMY DEFEATED AT CAMDEN, SOUTH CAROLINA
10/7	COLONIAL MILITIA DEFEAT LOYALISTS AT KING'S MOUNTAIN, N.C.
1/17 1781	BATTLE OF COWPENS, SOUTH CAROLINA. DANIEL MORGAN MILITIA & ARMY
	DEFEAT BRITISH COLONEL TARLETON ARMY
3/15	BATTLE OF GUILFORD COURTHOUSE, NORTH CAROLINA
9/5-9/8	FRENCH FLEET DEFEATS ENGLISH FLEET AT BATTLE OF CHESAPEAKE BAY
9/28-10/19	BRITISH GENERAL CORNWALLIS SURRENDERS AT YORKTOWN, VIRGINIA

22b

22c

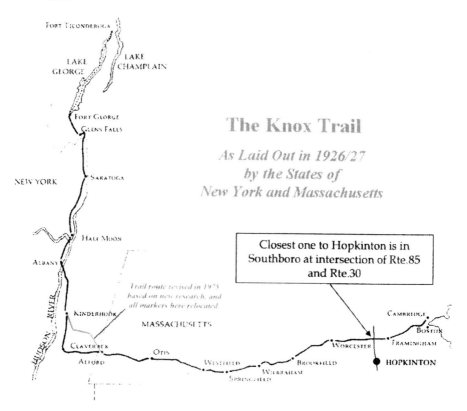

Chapter 23

The War Ends (The Treaty of Paris)

A.   THE TREATY OF PARIS (4/19/1783)

The victory at Yorktown on 10/19/1781 over General Cornwallis ended the major fighting in the War. General Washington did not believe the war would actually end with that battle and still considered the possibility of a sea-borne attack by the French fleet on Charleston South Carolina. The French Admiral, De Grasse refused. Unknown by Washington, once Lord North learned of the Yorktown defeat he began searching for the best way to secure a Peace Treaty. General Sir Guy Carleton was ordered to focus on evacuating British troops back to England, which he accomplished on 11/25/1783.

However, the defeat did not destroy King George's determination to never accept American independence. *With a rising tide of opposition in the House of Commons it became possible that the North Ministry could be overthrown if the war continued.* Lord North then made some last minute attempts to reach separate peace treaties with the Netherlands and/or France. *He offered to Congress a peace without independence which was rejected.*

The King's opponents in Parliament finally combined to *force the resignation of the North Ministry on 3/20/1782* in addition to passing a resolution declaring that anyone who attempts or advocates the continuance of the war would be considered an enemy of the country. This was strongly opposed by the King who saw it as an announcement to the world that England would no longer fight for their colonies. *North*

was replaced by the Marquis of Rockingham who assumed the position for the second time. In 1779, he had proposed that the colonies be granted their independence. Unfortunately, he died on 7/1/1782 just 14 days after assuming the office. **By this time, the King accepted the inevitability of peace and independence. However, he still offered the position to William Petty-Fitzmaurice, the 2nd Earl of Shelburne, a strong opponent to Independence, rather than to someone favoring Independence.**

Formal negotiations began in Paris in April, 1782, between Ben Franklin and Richard Oswald, a liberal Scots merchant. Franklin immediately disregarded his instructions to negotiate only in the presence of French officials. Franklin met Oswald "in secret" because he hoped to persuade England to give up Canada, something he knew France would not accept. Franklin's other negotiators were John Adams, John Jay, Thomas Jefferson, and Henry Laurens, who were all in other parts of the world and unable to be with Franklin at the beginning of negotiations.

When John Jay arrived on 6/23/1782 and learned that Franklin had made the issue of Canada the first discussion point, he objected and threatened to stop the negotiations until the matter of American recognition was first settled. He made his point by insisting that the wording of Oswald's instructions be changed from "to treat with the 13 colonies" to "treat with the United States of America". **Shelburne had hoped to negotiate a peace which would keep America within the Empire, but not as an independent nation.** Jay insisted on Independence and Shelburne finally agreed but refused to give up Canada. **Shelburne now sent Oswald new instructions to treat with the "Commissioners of the 13 United States", thus conceding Independence even before serious negotiations began.** The new instructions were received in September, 1782, and John Adams arrived in Paris in October.

The British territorial concessions were generous, such as;

1. America received all the land west to the Mississippi river, south to Florida, which under a secret treaty was returned by Britain to Spain, and north to the Great Lakes. However, the northern boundary was not finalized until the 1842 Webster-Ashburton Treaty.

2. Britain agreed to evacuate its military posts in what became known as the *"northwest territory"* which was the land west of Pennsylvania, east of the Mississippi river, and north of the Ohio river.

3. America received the right to fish off the coast of Newfoundland. This was important to John Adams to protect the fishing rights of his New England fishermen.

4. The final clause of the Treaty proved to be the most troublesome and would continue well after the Treaty was signed. Shelburne demanded that America promise that the private debts of Americans to British citizens be paid and that all Loyalists be compensated for property lost in the Revolution. The Americans pledged that no obstacles would be placed in the way of collection of British debts in America and it was agreed that the Congress would "recommend" to the states that Loyalists be reimbursed for their losses.

The preliminary Treaty was signed by both sides on 11/30/1782, more than 13 months after the Cornwallis surrender at Yorktown. The Treaty was formalized in Europe on 2/3/1783 between England, France, Spain, and Netherlands. Congress ratified the Treaty on 4/19/1783 exactly 8 years to the day of the first shot fired in the colonies

B.   HOW WAS AMERICA ABLE TO DEFEAT THE WORLD'S GREATEST MILITARY POWER ?

There were four major reasons why America won the war:

1. The people believed in the cause and the troops were more skilled in frontier fighting than the European-trained English troops.

2. French assistance and aid. The French had their own selfish reasons for aiding the colonists and that was to weaken their long-time enemies, the British. The colonists also received assistance from representatives of other European nations, such

as Baron De Kalb and Baron Von Steuben of Germany, Count Pulaski and Thaddeus Kosciusko of Poland.

3. British government arrogance toward the colonists and their overconfidence in their military, which mismanaged the war. Parliament and public opinion eventually opposed the war.

4. The leadership of George Washington.

C. THE ISSUE OF THE "WESTERN LANDS"

The issue of the western lands was one of the most pressing post-war problems to resolve. Congress, as promised, immediately drafted rules for the settlement of the northwest territory. Virginia didn't actually turn over its lands until March, 1784. Jefferson was the primary author of the Ordinance approved by Congress on 4/23/1784 which created 10 equal districts which allowed the settlers within each district to erect their own governments. When a district's population reached 20,000, it could hold a convention, adopt a Constitution, and send a delegate to Congress. When its population matched that of the smallest state, it was to be admitted as an equal state into the Union. Congress made only two changes to Jefferson's plan;

- It dropped his prohibition of slavery in the territory

- It added a provision that forbade the new government to tax or dispose of federal lands within their jurisdictions.

1. **THE LAND ORDINANCE OF 1785 (5/20/1785)**

   It's purpose was to impose a pattern of orderly settlement on the wilderness. Its' terms were;

   a. The Northwest Territory was to be surveyed into ranges 6 miles wide

   b. These were to be divided into townships 6 miles square

   c. The Townships were to be further subdivided into 36 sections, each a square mile (640 acres) in size

   d. Four sections within the township were to be reserved for the United States and one for the support of public schools.

   As the ranges were surveyed, the land would be sold at public auctions in blocks of 640 acres with bidding starting at $1 per acre.

   The sale of public lands reversed one of the oldest American traditions where the colonies, in order to attract settlers, had given away unclaimed public lands or sold them cheaply. By 1787, several ranges had been laid out, including one near Pennsylvania's western border. Before land sales could begin, a group of New England ex-Army officers, calling themselves the "Ohio Company", offered Congress $1 million to disregard the Land Ordinance of 1785 and give their group a large piece of territory, which Congress rejected. But, the company lobbyist and a New York Congressman, made a deal which caused Congress to change its mind and grant 6.5 million acres in the Northwest Territory, a million of which went to the Ohio Company, and the remainder to the New York Congressman and his associates which formed the "Scioto Company". The actual price worked out to be about eight cents per acre. Congress approved this deal because many of its members had been corrupted and because so many settler's ("squatters") had already moved into the area. Naturally, the Indians objected and troops sent to eject the illegal settlers failed, so the Ohio Company was in business. There was so much confusion and disagreement in the area that Congress decided to revise the Jefferson plan of 1784.

2. **THE NORTHWEST ORDINANCE OF 1787 (Passed 7/13/1787)**

This revision was passed while the Constitutional Convention was meeting in Philadelphia. It revoked the promise of immediate self-government and temporarily treated the territory as a "colonial empire". It imposed on the settlers a Governor, Secretary, and three Judges appointed by Congress. These people would control the territory until there were 5,000 adult male settlers at which time a general assembly would assume control of legislative affairs although the Congressionally appointed Governor retained his absolute veto over all legislation. Only those who owned 50 acres of land could vote. No more than five and no less than three states could be created from this territory. When a district population reached 60,000, it could write its own Constitution and apply for admission into the Union.

Congress retained Jefferson's suggestion that the new states be admitted as equals and also his previously discarded provision that slavery be prohibited throughout the territory. *A "Bill of Rights" attached to the Ordinance assured settlers of freedoms they were accustomed to in the original 13 states.*

This Ordinance created a pattern by which virtually every state since has been admitted to the Union. *It represented the ideal type of society America wanted, one that protected civil rights, guaranteed religious liberty, forbade slavery, and promised equal rather than colonial status within the Union.*

Both the 1785 and 1787 statutes did much long-term to shape the settlement and development of the west although the Ohio and Scioto companies failed to achieve very much other than make it more difficult for individuals to settle the area. Disputes happened in all the colonies and in all sections of the country which made it difficult to administer a plan.

By 1790, population in the Vermont area had increased to 85,000 and in 1791 it was admitted as the 14th state of the Union. In 1792, Kentucky had a population of 75,000 and was admitted as the 15th state. An area south of Kentucky, known as the "Watauga region" was settled by two groups of land speculators. The Watauga Association was organized by local settlers in 1772 to govern the region and was eventually absorbed into North Carolina as Washington county in 1776 and remained part of that state until ceded to Congress in 1784. There was some disagreement in the area between those favoring an independent state of Franklin and North Carolina and, for the next four years, the two governments fought over control of the region. The issue was settled in 1788 when the government of Franklin collapsed and North Carolina resumed control for a year, and then gave the land to Congress. *After a short time of managing it, Congress allowed the region to enter the Union in 1796 as the State of Tennessee.*

The Congress of the new Federal Government, not the Articles of Confederation, brought these three states into the Union. Congress deserves credit for its management of this issue. *Britain controlled the west for over a decade prior to the Revolution and failed to provide a settlement plan. Congress did so within three years after it had acquired the land.*

D.   THE POST-WAR ECONOMY

When the war ended, Americans realized that they would now be without the previous economic benefits of England. John Adams, the new Ambassador to England, tried hard to win commercial concessions from England but failed. Why should England help America when they just fought a war to separate from England? The economic problem was that they were now importing more goods from England than they were exporting and that unfavorable balance of trade would eventually hurt the economy. The immediate hopes of redressing the balance of trade were minimal. Tobacco exports from the Chesapeake Bay diminished. The value of South Carolina's exports of indigo and rice diminished as well. New England shipyards were hurt due to a diminished need to build new ships. Bankruptcies increased as merchants were unable to collect on the goods they had sold on easy terms during the war. By mid-1784, America was in a commercial depression which lasted until 1787.

To compensate, America contacted France, Holland, and Sweden to make up the economic difference from lost English business. By 1786, America was beginning to come out of the depression. Tobacco exports increased along with grains and lumber. As merchants became able to grow their business, bank business also picked up, so the post-war era began to look positive again.

E.   HOW THE REVOLUTION CHANGED AMERICAN SOCIETY

Political changes

1. It now became necessary to make political changes with the 13 individual states needing to establish new Constitutions. By early 1777, 11 states had adopted new Constitutions.

2. Some of the most significant changes were the ***adoption of "Bill of Rights"*** which included provisions for the right of jury trial, exemption from unjustifiable search or unreasonable bails and fines, and the prohibition of cruel punishments. Freedom of worship and press were provided.

3. Voting privileges were based on property requirements or some minimal religious test.

4. Annual or frequent election of legislatures were designed to keep them responsive to the popular will.

5. The authority of the Governors were reduced because of the negative experiences with colonial governors. But, the weakening went too far and some powers needed to be restored.

6. The principles of "separation of powers" and "checks and balances" were embraced to prevent one branch of government from dominating another.

Economic and Social Changes

1. The war caused a scarcity of finished goods but home industries were created to meet the needs of consumers. Wages rose but not as much as prices.

2. Manufacturing increased when it was freed from British restrictions but American commerce was excluded from trade with the British West Indies.

3. Large transfers of land were made as the loyalist estates were confiscated and sold.

4. Titles of nobility were abolished along with the laws of "primogeniture and entail" which provided that an entire estate would be inherited intact by the oldest son.

5. The hated "quit-rents" were abolished.

6. Restrictions were removed against the settlement of the western lands.

7. The inconsistency of holding slaves caused all of the states north of Maryland to abolish slavery before 1805 and most of the southern states stopped the importation of slaves.

8. The Episcopal and Presbyterian Churches were reorganized independently of the British Churches. The Methodists, under the leadership of Francis Asbury, established in 1784 the Methodist-Episcopal Church as independent of the British Anglican Church.

9. Roman Catholics made John Carroll the Bishop of Baltimore, the first Catholic Bishop in America.

F.   KEY DATES AND SIGNIFICANT EVENTS

10/17	1781	Colonists victory over Lord Cornwallis of England at Yorktown
3/20	1782	Resignation of Lord North Ministry replaced by Marquis of Rockingham
April	1782	Formal negotiations begin between Ben Franklin and Richard Oswald of England
11/30	1782	Preliminary Treaty signed by both sides
2/23	1783	Treaty formalized in Europe between England, France, Spain, and Netherlands
4/19	1783	Treaty of Paris ratified by Congress
11/25	1783	General Sir Guy Carleton focus on evacuating British troops back to England
March	1784	Virginia turns over its western lands to Congress
4/23	1784	Land Ordinance establishes settlement and government criteria in new lands
5/20	1785	Land Ordinance seeks to impose pattern of orderly settlement in Northwest Territory
7/13	1787	Northwest Ordinance set up a government in the "colonial empire" with a Governor, Secretary, and 3 Judges appointed by Congress. No more than 5 and no less than 3 new states could be created from the territory.

G.   REVIEW QUESTIONS

(Multiple Choice)

1. What was the date of the ratification of Treaty of Paris by the Congress?
    a.   April 1782
    b.   November 1782
    c.   February 1783
    d.   April 1783

2. Which was the final major battle which ended the fighting in the Revolutionary War?
    a.   Saratoga
    b.   Trenton
    c.   Yorktown
    d.   None of the above

3. Which English Ministry was forced to resign after the loss of the Revolutionary War?
    a.   Grenville
    b.   Shelburne
    c.   Rockingham
    d.   North

4. Which British Prime Minister was responsible for the negotiations for the Treaty of Paris?
    a.   Shelburne
    b.   Rockingham
    c.   North
    d.   Greenville

5. Which of the following was NOT a reason for the Colonists victory in the Revolutionary War?
    a. people believed in the cause
    b. larger Army and Navy
    c. British government and military arrogance
    d. French and other foreign aid

6. What was the most important negotiating point for the Americans at the Treaty of Paris?
    a. England gives up Canada
    b. recognition of American independence
    c. territorial concessions
    d. none of the above

7. Who was the first American negotiator at Paris?
    a. John Jay
    b. Ben Franklin
    c. John Adams
    d. Henry Laurens

8. Who was the first British negotiator at Paris?
    a. The Duke of Grafton
    b. General Gage
    c. Lord North
    d. Richard Oswald

(True or False)

9. General Burgoyne was the defeated British General at Yorktown.
    a. TRUE
    b. FALSE

10. The Spanish Navy fleet helped surround the British troops at Yorktown.
    a. TRUE
    b. FALSE

11. The opponents of the King in Parliament forced the resignation of Lord North.
    a. TRUE
    b. FALSE

12. One of the concessions made by England to America at the Treaty of Paris was the cession of Canada.
    a. TRUE
    b. FALSE

13. The immediate economic impact on America of the end of the war with Britain was positive.
    a. TRUE
    b. FALSE

14. The multiple land Ordinances of 1784, 1785, and 1787 were intended to regulate settlement of the northwest territories.
    a. TRUE
    b. FALSE

15. The long-term economic impact of the end of war on America was positive.
    a. TRUE
    b. FALSE

CHAPTER 23 SUMMARY

THE WAR ENDS

1. The Battle of Yorktown ends the military phase of the Revolutionary War on 10/17/1781.

2. King George III was not ready at that time to accept the idea of American Independence. There was growing opposition in the House of Commons to the King and Lord North policies.

3. The Lord North Ministry was forced to resign on 3/20/1782 and replaced by the Marquis of Rockingham, who died 14 weeks later. He was replaced by the Earl of Shelburne, an opponent to Independence.

4. Formal peace negotiations began in Paris in April 1782 between Ben Franklin and Richard Oswald.

5. The other American Peace Negotiators are John Jay, John Adams, Thomas Jefferson, and Henry Laurens.

6. John Jay was the negotiator who caused England to change the instructions to Oswald;

   From: "To treat with the 13 Colonies"
   To: "To treat with the United States of America"

   Jay wanted the issue of American Independence settled before all other issues were discussed. Shelburne wanted a Peace which kept America within the English Empire but not Independent.

Shelburne sends Oswald new instructions to treat with "The Commissioners of the 13 United States". These instructions were received in September, 1782. John Adams arrived in Paris in October, 1782.

7. ***The Peace Treaty terms were;***

   a America receives all of the land west to the Mississippi river, south to Florida, and north to the Great Lakes. (Florida had been returned by England to Spain) The northern boundary with Canada was not settled until 1842.

   b. England agrees to vacate their military posts in the northwest territory and other parts of America.

   c. America receives the right to fish off the coast of Newfoundland. This was important to John Adams to protect the fishing rights of the New England fishermen.

   d. England demands that America pay the private debts of American citizens owed to British citizens and loyalists compensated for their lost property in the War.

8. The preliminary Peace Treaty was signed by England and America on 11/30/1782, more than 13 months after the Battle of Yorktown.

9. ***Primary reasons why America won the War;***

   a. The colonists believed in the cause and the troops were better suited to fight in rural areas.

   b. The military assistance provided by the French and other European nations.

   c. British government and military arrogance and overconfidence.

   d. The leadership of George Washington.

10. ***The immediate post-war problems;***

    a. Land settlement in the northwest territories.

    b. Immediate economic depression due to the loss of English trade. The economy did begin to improve once the government was formed.

Chapter 24

The New Government

A.   THE FOUNDATIONS OF THE NEW GOVERNMENT

The most important challenge of the post-Revolutionary period was that of erecting a stable new Federal government plus 13 state governments. *They struggled with the issue of how central authority could be reconciled with personal liberty.* England's failure to answer that question drove the colonists to rebellion because they feared that their fundamental rights were threatened by the over-emphasis on authority. Now they would be required to seek their own solutions. *For the next six years they experimented with various forms of government, always seeking one strong enough to be effective but also restrained enough to protect their sacred liberties.*

Shortly after Congress resolved on 5/15/1776 that the Crown's authority in all colonies should be ended, Thomas Jefferson told friends that he wished to join the Constitutional Convention because of its' importance in creating a new government for the new nation. He wrote to a member of the Virginia Assembly on 5/16/1776 that "Constitution-making is the whole subject of the present controversy, for should a bad government be instituted for us in the future, it had been as well to have accepted the bad one offered to us from beyond the water, without the risk and expense of the conflict".[1] *(Morrison pg 270)*

1.   PREVIOUS ATTEMPTS AT COLONIAL UNITY

Previous attempts at Colonial Unity were usually focused on some form of self-defense although they were based on concepts of self-government which would eventually surface in the new government principles, laws, and traditions.

a. The New England Confederation of 1643-1648 was designed for protection against the Indians

b. The Albany Plan of Union of 1754 sought protection against the French and Indians

c. The Stamp Act Congress of 1765

d. The Committees of Correspondence of 1772-1773

e. The First and Second Continental Congresses of 1775-1776

The principles of the American Revolution were driven by leaders thinking of preserving and securing the freedom they already enjoyed rather than building something new and different.

The political experience before 1775 set the pattern for the new institutions. State and Federal Constitutions were the work of college-educated men who had studied the political theories of Aristotle, Plato, Cicero, and the other ancient thinkers and writers who had already given deep thought to the problems facing the new nation.

Men such as George Mason, Thomas Jefferson, James Madison, and John Adams knew what they wanted to do and most of them were relatively young. Jefferson was 33, Madison 27, John Adams and John Dickinson were 44. The New York Constitution was drafted by three graduates of King's College (now Columbia), Governeur Morris 24, Robert R. Livingston 30, and John Jay 32. Every one of these men had political experience in colonial assemblies, local conventions, or the Continental Congress. This combination of classical discipline with practical politics accounts for their success at Constitution-making.

Everyone assumed that the new states must have written Constitutions which define and limit the powers of government. They were used to colonial charters and had felt anger at the absence of a written British Constitution defining the respective powers of Parliament and the colonial Assemblies. The objectives of these state constitutions were to establish the rule of law which they believed King George III had violated, to secure life, liberty, and prosperity, and to set up a practical frame of government.

To the Americans of 1776, liberty meant, first, freedom under laws of their own making, and, second, the right to do anything which did not harm another. They felt that the proper way to secure liberty to posterity was to set up a representative government, limited in scope by a statement of natural rights with which no government may change. Therefore, every state Constitution included a Bill of Rights. The first, Virginia's, was drafted by George Mason and adopted by the Virginia Convention of 6/12/1776.

2. **ORIGINS OF THE IDEALS AND PRINCIPLES OF THE DECLARATION OF INDEPENDENCE**
The Virginia Declaration of Rights
The "Virginia Declaration of Rights", of 5/15/1776, is said to be one of the great liberty documents of history. It was *based primarily on the past experiences of free-born Englishmen and subsequent colonial charters.* It began by stating, "that all men are by nature equally free and independent, and have certain inherent rights of which, when they enter into a state of society, they cannot deprive or divest their posterity; namely, the enjoyment of life and liberty, with the means of acquiring and possessing property, and pursuing and obtaining happiness and safety".
The English Magna Carta of 1215
It featured the right to a jury trial and the right to not be deprived of liberty except by the law of the land or the judgment of one's peers.
The Petition of Right of 1628
This was imposed on King Charles I of England and it stated that a man cannot be compelled to give evidence against himself, that standing armies in peace time should be avoided as dangerous to liberty, and that in all cases the military should be under strict subordination to and governed by civil authority.

The English Bill of Rights of 1689

This established the prohibition of excessive bail and of cruel or unusual punishments. It was asserted by the Americans that all of these rights were valid because they were based on the ancient theory of natural law, the key principle of Western Civilization that laws must have divine sanction and subsequently they became the basis of the American Constitutional system.

3. **THE ROLE OF NEW STATE CONSTITUTIONS**

   By the end of 1777, there were ten states which had adopted new Constitutions or modified old ones. Most of those State Constitutions were drafted by legislative bodies and placed in effect without consulting the voters. This approach was opposed by John Adams who did involve the voters in developing his own Massachusetts Constitution in 1780.

   The Massachusetts State Constitution of 1780

   Although there were many different types of state constitutions, *the Massachusetts Constitution followed the most democratic process, utilizing a Constitutional Convention elected by manhood suffrage.* It met in the fall of 1779 to appoint a committee to prepare a draft and then adjourned. The Committee of Three deferred to John Adams whose draft was submitted to the convention in 1780, amended, and then submitted to town-meetings where it was voted on clause by clause. *Objections were noted, revisions made, and eventually the people did ratify the Constitution as a whole on 6/15/1780.*

   It was based on a theory of "mixed government" which meant, "checks and balances", resting on the theory that any "pure" governmental form of government degenerated into something else, for example

   - pure democracy into class tyranny or anarchy

   - pure aristocracy into a selfish oligarchy

   - pure monarchy into absolutism

So, the theory was that to secure the happiness of the people, a government should be a mixture of the following where each branch of the government would keep one another from exceeding their proper limits. ("Checks and balances")

- a strong Chief Executive to represent the principle of authority

- a Senate to represent the property interests

- a Lower House to represent the people

In reality, **the Massachusetts government was composed of;**

- a popularly elected House of Representatives

- an "aristocratic" Senate apportioned according to taxable wealth, not population

- a Governor, re-eligible indefinitely , with a veto over legislation and the power to appoint most state officials. He was chosen by popular vote.

4. **PRINCIPLES OF GOVERNMENT**
It was generally agreed that the old governments had worked well except when the King abused his authority, so the new fundamental laws wouldn't have to do much more than just codify past practice;
a. None of the first Constitutions provided for the legislative, judicial, and executive branches to check one-another.
b. The concept of the "power of the purse" remained part of legislative authority
c. The Governor lost the absolute veto in all states
d. Annual elections for all legislators became part of nine new State Constitutions
e. The "stake of the society" concept which called for a man to own property to vote and even more property to hold office, remained intact in most of the new Constitutions.

f. None of the new Constitutions provided for an amendment process except for Delaware

g. Every state followed the Virginia Constitution and included a Bill of Rights

All of these provisions indicated the moderate spirit of the Constitutions written in 1776-1777. ***None made a sharp break with the political traditions of their states.***

B.   THE ARTICLES OF CONFEDERATION (AOC)

While the framers of State Constitutions struggled with the issue of balancing liberty with authority, ***the Continental Congress struggled with the issue of "federalism", to find a balance between the powers of the Federal government and the rights of the member States.***

Some felt the size of the country required a strong central government. Others identified with their particular state's vested interests, such as;

- North and South differed over the method of assessing a state's contribution to the central government. The South preferred to use population as the basis as long as its large slave population was not counted. The North objected.

- Each of the three major sections of the country, New England, Middle States, and the South, feared that if a simple majority was required to pass legislation, their particular interests could be damaged.

- The "large" and "small" states differed.

- The states whose charters gave them "western lands" differed with those lacking those lands.

- Slave states argued with non-slave states.

At the same time as Thomas Jefferson was assigned to draft the Declaration of Independence, another committee led by John Dickinson was formed to draft a new Constitution (AOC) which they reported to the 2nd Continental Congress in July, 1776. It was approved on 11/15/1777 and submitted to the State Legislatures for ratification.

By February, 1779, all states had ratified except Maryland which finally passed it on 3/1/1781 after opposing it until the seven states with western lands renounced their claims. Maryland had argued on behalf of the six states without western claims that the war had been a common effort and all unsettled western lands should be considered as common property subject to government distribution.

Congress had already declared that the western lands would be disbursed by the government and those lands would be used to form new states which would eventually become members of the Federal Union. Shortly after this announcement, New York and Virginia broke the deadlock and yielded their western lands and then, with Maryland's approval, the Articles of Confederation ("AOC") officially became the Constitution of the United States of America.

The "AOC" became the first central government of America and was a loose union of sovereign and independent states. It consisted of a Congress meeting in Philadelphia to which each of the states sent delegates but each state had only one vote regardless of size or population. The Congress could control foreign affairs, make war or peace, coin and borrow money, raise an army, and settle disputes between the states.

IT'S PRIMARY PROVISIONS WERE;

1. **POWERS OF CONGRESS**
   a. Executive, Legislative, and Judicial functions were vested in a single-house legislature composed of delegates from each state who voted as a unit but with the state having just one vote.
   b. The votes of 2/3 (9 of 13) of the states were required to pass any measure
   c. All powers not delegated to Congress were reserved to the states
   d. Delegated powers to the Congress were;

   • Making war and peace

   • Drafting treaties and alliances

- Controlling Indian affairs

- Maintaining a Postal Service

2. **POWERS OF THE STATES**
   a. Power to tax, which forced Congress to exist by borrowing or requisitioning expenses from the states
   b. Power to regulate commerce which deprived the nation of a uniform commercial policy

3. **STRENGTHS OF THE ARTICLES OF CONFEDERATION**
   a. A national citizenship was created with the citizens assured of the same privileges in all states. This laid the basis for the more workable Union of 1787.

4. **DEFECTS OF THE ARTICLES OF CONFEDERATION**
   a. Provided for no Executive to enforce the laws or a Judiciary to pass on the legality of the laws
   b. Congress consisted of one House and had no power to control commerce, either domestic or foreign
   c. It could raise money only by requisitions upon the states which were generally ignored
   d. A unanimous vote of all 13 states required to amend or change the Articles
   e. Passage of laws required the approval of 9 of the 13 states
   f. Each state, regardless of size or population, had only one vote

5. **ACCOMPLISHMENTS OF THE ARTICLES OF CONFEDERATION (1781-1789)**
   a. Successful completion of the Revolutionary War
   b. Successful negotiation and ratification of the Treaty of Paris of 1783 ending the war
   c. It established and maintained a union of states during a most difficult period of our history
   d. The problem of the northwest territories was settled by the passage of the Northwest Ordinance of 1787.

C.   CONGRESS OF THE CONFEDERATION

The AOC now assumed the duties of the previous "Continental Congress" and added the authority to appoint Executive departments;

- Foreign affairs with Robert R. Livingston as Secretary

- Finance with Robert Morris as Superintendent

- War with General Lincoln as Secretary

- A Board of Admiralty

- A Post-Office department

A committee consisting of one delegate from each state sat between sessions of Congress to exercise all powers except those requiring the consent of nine of the 13 states.

Of the powers that the Articles did not make Federal, the most important was that of Taxation. Congress was not even allowed to tax imports since colonial experience had shown that customs duties could be used against liberty.

The success of the AOC would depend on the "good will" of the states toward the central government. The country had just completed a war against an oppressive central government and many asked, why would we want to replace one oppressive government with another? *One of the early leaders in the campaign to strengthen and improve the AOC was known as the "Continentalist" whose real name was Alexander Hamilton.*

D. POST-WAR PROBLEMS

1. **ECONOMIC ISSUES**

    The transition from war to peace changed the nature but not the number or seriousness of the problems facing the national government but the states worried only about their own welfare. The immediate post-war economic depression negatively impacted the strength of the AOC. *By 1786, less than 1/3 of the states were paying their share of the requisitions required to manage the government, resulting in the Confederation being unable to pay for some necessary services, including protection against foreign actions against America.*

    Congress passed commercial treaties with four European countries but for several years the results were disappointing. The main problem was the double adjustment required of the new country;

    a. from a war to peace economy

    b. from a favored position within the British Empire to an independent status in a competitive world.

    National economic growth was hindered by the right of each state to establish its own customs service which deprived the Confederation of bargaining power with Europe but permitted local protective tariffs. Thomas Jefferson, now the Ambassador to France, wished to strengthen economic relations with France. John Adams now the Ambassador to England, also hoped to revive trade with England although they refused.

    The South recovered prosperity earlier than the North since it produced tobacco, indigo, rice, and naval stores which Britain could buy as cheaply elsewhere. Virginia's prewar exports, in value, were restored by 1786 but in that same year the exports of Massachusetts were only 25% of what it had been in 1774.

2. **INTERNATIONAL ISSUES**

    a. *Problems with Spain*

    Congressional negotiations with Spain showed the weakness of America to protect itself in the post-war era. Spain worried that the growth of the American west, if not slowed, would overrun

Spanish interests in Florida, acquired from England in the Treaty of Paris of 1783, and Louisiana acquired in 1763. In 1784, Spain closed off the Mississippi river to American ship traffic and then sent one of its better diplomats, Don Diego de Gardoqui, to negotiate with John Jay, the Confederation Secretary of Foreign Affairs. In that same year, the Creek, Choctaw, and Cherokee tribes made treaties with Spain for their protection and support of their frontier attacks on settlements along the Cumberland and Tennessee Rivers. Gardoqui offered trading privileges with Spain if America would abandon use of the Mississippi for 25 years. Jay urged Congress to accept the offer. The south opposed it because it threatened their prosperity and the north favored it but Jay finally rejected it because of the significant opposition.

b. ***Problems with England***

In spite of the Peace Treaty of 1783, there were still problems with the British. Congress had recommended that the states should restore Loyalist property, per Treaty terms, but few states complied except for Pennsylvania and Maryland. There were still problems dealing with pre-war debts owed by American citizens to British subjects. Virginia citizens owed the most and insisted that those debts had been cancelled by state legislation during the war and no longer existed. The issue was not finally settled until 1802 when America paid England a lump sum settlement to individual creditors. Another issue was that of the British military posts in America which were required to be evacuated but England failed to do so at some posts on the Canadian border. It was suspected that England failed to act in a timely manner in order to protect its fur-trade. It wasn't until 1796 that this issue was resolved.

E.   EVENTS LEADING TO THE NEW CONSTITUTION

Many leaders of the Revolution, such as, Washington, Hamilton, Robert Morris, John Jay, James Madison, and James Wilson had worked and argued for a stronger union. Their travels, the War, and Congressional experiences made them realize that a central government would need an independent source of income to pay its debts, that new industries could only be protected by national tariffs and local shipping interests only protected by a national navigation law. ***Slowly, even those strong state's rights advocates realized that some local problems could only be solved on a national level.***

In 1782, New York called for a convention to revise the Articles of Confederation in a way which would strengthen the Union. Massachusetts Governor John Hancock in 1783 believed the existence of America required a strong central government. Even Thomas Jefferson admitted the individual states would need to think more "nationally".

1. **MT VERNON CONFERENCE (3/28/1785)**

   In spite of the 1782 call for revision of the Articles by New York, nothing was done until 1785 when four representatives from Virginia, including James Madison and George Mason, met with four commissioners from Maryland to consider problems related to the navigation of the Chesapeake Bay and Potomac River. On 3/28/1785, they moved to Mt. Vernon to include George Washington in the discussions. They quickly agreed on the jurisdiction of the Potomac River and also agreed to draft a proposal to their respective state legislatures for uniform commercial regulations, a uniform currency, and annual conferences on common commercial problems. It was then requested that Pennsylvania also be invited to join to establish water communications between the Chesapeake Bay and Ohio River. The Maryland legislature endorsed this plan on 12/5/1785 but also proposed the addition of Delaware. ***Madison suggested on 1/21/1786 that Virginia invite all of the states to discuss commercial problems at a convention to be held at Annapolis in September, 1786.***

2. **ANNAPOLIS CONVENTION (9/11/1786-9/14/1786)**

   The Virginia invitation was accepted by nine states but four declined. (Georgia, South Carolina, Connecticut, and Maryland). New Hampshire, Rhode Island, and North Carolina failed to reach Annapolis in time to participate. ***Only New York, New Jersey, Delaware, Virginia, and Pennsylvania were represented.***

The meeting opened on 9/11 with John Dickinson, at the time a representative from Delaware, elected Chairman. The small representation of just five states convinced those present that it was useless to proceed with so few delegates. *On 9/13 they decided to appoint a committee to prepare a communication calling upon all of the states to send delegates to a new convention in Philadelphia in early May, 1787, to discuss;*

a. commercial matters such as the current issue between Maryland and Virginia regarding navigation rights on the Chesapeake Bay and Potomac River.

b. *all matters necessary to render the Constitution of the Federal Government adequate to the needs of the Union.*

Congress endorsed the committee draft on 2/21/1787 and announced the purpose of the Philadelphia meeting to be a revision of the Articles of Confederation. Five states had already named delegates to the Philadelphia convention, Virginia, New Jersey Pennsylvania, Delaware, and North Carolina.

3. **SHAYS REBELLION (Aug 1786–Feb 1787)**

Shortly after the invitations were sent, it was learned that Massachusetts had some internal problems of its own. Farmers in western Massachusetts were upset over a recent tax increase which was required to be paid in hard money since they were prevented from issuing paper currency. The protest was first expressed through county conventions but it soon grew with mobs marching on courthouses to block foreclosures. The protesters were mostly small farmers who felt they were dominated by an eastern-dominated legislature .Daniel Shays, a former Army Captain, found himself to be the leader of the uprising which lasted from August 1786 to February 1787 when 4,000 Massachusetts militia crushed the rebellion. *The significance of this event was that it revealed the need for fixing the national government.* Massachusetts had requested assistance but Congress was unable to do so and that opened the eyes of many of the delegates that something needed to be done to strengthen the government.

F.   THE CONSTITUTIONAL CONVENTION (5/25/1787 - 9/17/1787)

55 of the 74 delegates and 12 of the 13 states (Rhode Island refused to attend) met in Philadelphia on 5/25/1787 for what became known as the *"Constitutional Convention"*. Some of the great Revolutionary leaders were absent, such as, John Hancock, currently Governor of Massachusetts, John Adams, Ambassador to England, Thomas Jefferson, Ambassador to France, Sam Adams, Richard Henry Lee, and Patrick Henry who was invited but refused to attend. However, many of the original leaders did attend, such as, Washington, Roger Sherman, Ben Franklin, George Wythe, James Wilson, John Dickinson, George Mason, William Livingston, and Robert Morris. The average age of the delegates was 42 with only four in their 60's. More than half of them had served at one time or another in their local government and had been elected by their state legislatures. *A decade of experience with the Articles of Confederation had caused many of them to revise their thinking about the role of the central government but it would require 16 weeks of hard discussion and compromise on what revisions were required.*

They remained in constant week-day sessions from 5/25 to 9/17 and agreed at the beginning that all sessions would be secret in order to promote the free expression of ideas without pressure from outsiders or reprisals from the public. Disagreements were expected between various interests, such as, large and small states, agrarian and commercial interests, nationalists and confederationalists, pro and anti-slavery interests, etc. *There was also much which united them, such as;*

- the need to revise the Confederation

- a new government with a single executive, judiciary, and a 2-house legislature based on a written Constitution

- a new government had to have an independent source of income

- some form of proportional representation

- control over foreign affairs and commerce

Bottom-line, their task was to create a central government weak enough to please the states but strong enough to deal with national matters.

1. **THE VIRGINIA PLAN**

   The Convention opened with a presentation by Edmund Randolph on 5/29/1787 proposing;

   a. 2 Houses with members apportioned per population with the Upper House to be elected by the lower

   b. A National Executive and Judiciary to be appointed by the Congress

   c. Provision for Amendment

   d. Provision for binding members of state governments by oath to support the new Constitution.

   It did <u>not</u> include two features which would become a central part of the new government;

   a. the ideas of ***"separation of powers"*** and ***"checks and balances"*** among the 3 branches of government

   b. the concept of ***"dual sovereignty"*** which would allow the states and central government to act within their own spheres of power directly upon the people

   The convention formed a committee to debate the plan. Some delegates opposed direct, popular elections, probably remembering the recent Shay's rebellion and fearing the "excesses of democracy". George Mason, James Madison, and James Wilson supported creating the broadest possible electoral mandate. After considerable debate, popular election was approved by a vote of six states to two with two divided.

   The Convention then debated whether the Executive should be vested in one man or several, then the method of election and apportionment of the Senate. Madison favored the Senate being elected by the people but Elbridge Gerry and George Mason argued that the commercial and monied interest would be more secure in the hands of the state legislatures. The Convention agreed.

2. **THE NEW JERSEY PLAN**

The delegates debated the Virginia Plan for 2 weeks until a new plan, (***"New Jersey Plan"***) was offered by William Patterson on 6/15/1787. ***It proposed;***

a. One state……..one vote.

b. Additional powers to Congress such as the right to levy taxes and regulate commerce.

c. A multiple executive and provided for a limited judiciary.

d. It maintained the AOC unicameral legislature and voting by states.

This plan was not much more than an amended Articles of Confederation and appealed primarily to the smaller states. Pennsylvania, Massachusetts, and Connecticut plus the two Carolina's defeated the plan on 6/19/1787. But, everyone realized there must be a concession to "states rights" if they wanted to get something passed.

3. **THE GREAT COMPROMISE (The Connecticut Compromise)**

The deadlock was broken on 7/16/1787 when the Convention adopted the "Great Compromise" suggested by Roger Sherman. It provided for;

a. House of Representatives would be popularly elected and apportioned according to population

b. Senate would consist of two members from each state, elected by the state legislatures

c. Money Bills would originate in the House of Representatives

The compromise settled the basic differences between the large and small states, such as;

a. The southern states, which contained many negro slaves, proposed slaves to be counted as part of the population for purposes of representation, thus increasing the number of southerners in the House of Representatives. But, slaves were not to be counted as part of the population for purposes of direct taxation, thus decreasing the southern tax burden.

The northern states opposed. The issue was settled by the "3/5 Compromise" by which five slaves were to be counted as three free persons for both representation and direct taxation.

b. Finally, the Convention voted Congress the power to admit new states into the Union.

These compromises settled the differences between north and south. The Framers left it to the state to determine who should vote for members of the legislature. In effect, this excluded many from voting as property qualifications restricted the electorate in most states.

G.   THE POWERS OF CONGRESS

1. **POWERS DELEGATED TO CONGRESS**
   a. Collect taxes, duties, and excises
   b. Regulate foreign and interstate commerce although, to please the south, it was forbidden to levy export duties or stop the importation of slaves before 1808
   c. Coin or borrow money
   d. Declare War
   e. Maintain an Army
   f. Establish post roads

2. **POWERS WITHDRAWN FROM THE STATES**
   a. Coin money or make anything but gold and silver legal tender
   b. Levy customs duties
   c. Pass "ex post facto laws" or laws impairing the obligation of contract
   d. These were powers abused by the states during the Confederation period

3. **COMPROMISE REGARDING COMMERCIAL REGULATION**
   Both the north and south agreed that Congress should regulate foreign and interstate commerce but the south feared that New

England, combined with the middle states, could regularly outvote the south in the legislature, and asked for certain protections.

The southern states opposed giving the central government the power to levy tariffs. Since the south was primarily agricultural, they feared that Congress would pass a tariff on their exports of indigo, rice, and tobacco. The northern states were more commercial and wanted the central government to have the power to establish uniform regulations on commerce with foreign nations. *The issue was settled by granting Congress the power to control foreign commerce and to levy tariffs on imports but not on exports.*

Concerns of the south;

a. They insisted on a 2/3 majority vote to enact all commercial regulations. This would give the south a veto over any navigation act designed to protect northern shipping and manufacturing.

b. They wanted assurance that Congress would never levy an export tax which would limit the ability of its tobacco, rice, and other staples to compete in the world market.

c. It demanded protection against a sudden cut-off of its slave trade by Congress.

This compromise agreed that a majority vote in Congress would be necessary to pass Acts regulating commerce, a point the north had advocated. The south, in return for this concession, received a clause in the Constitution which prohibited export taxes, another which guaranteed the slave trade for 20 years, and a third which required all states to return fugitive slaves, and finally, a provision requiring a 2/3 majority in the Senate for the ratification of all treaties, a number of which were expected to deal with commercial matters

4. **SECTIONAL CONFLICTS ON OTHER ISSUES**
Sectional differences surfaced in the debates over three issues which were loosely connected;
a. *The African Slave trade*
George Mason opposed continuing the slave trade but was opposed by General Charles Cotesworth Pinckney and John Rutledge who defended the practice as vital to the economic

interests of the south. In fact, Rutledge threatened that the three states of the lower south would secede unless permitted to continue this practice.

b. ***Export Taxes***

The southern states main profits came from exporting agricultural products and insisted that export taxes be outlawed. They wanted free competition in freight rates having little shipping of their own.

c. ***The power to pass a Navigation Act***

The southern states demanded the requirement of a 2/3 majority in Congress for passing a Navigation Act which restricted shipping to the American flag.

These 3 issues were then discussed and compromised, as follows;

a. There would be no Federal interference in the slave trade for 20 years

b. A Navigation Act could be passed like any other law by a simple majority

c. Federal Taxes on exports were forbidden

The above agreements were then included in "23 Resolutions" and submitted to a committee chaired by Governeur Morris, including;

a. Article VI on sanctions, traced to the New Jersey Plan. Patterson had proposed that if any state ignored or failed to enforce an Act of Congress, the Executive should have the power to call forth the power of the States to enforce and compel obedience. Madison and Hamilton objected that it would hurt the smaller states. This principle is contained in two key clauses of the Constitution. In Article VI, section 2, we find, "This Constitution, and the laws of the United States, which shall be made in pursuance thereof, and all treaties made, or which shall be made, under the authority of the United States, shall be the Supreme Law of the Land, and the judges in every State shall be bound thereby, or laws of any State to the contrary notwithstanding".[1] *(Morrison pg 310)*

b. Article III, section 2, gives Federal Judges jurisdiction over "all cases", in law and equity, arising under this Constitution, United States, and treaties made under their authority".[1] *(Morrison pg 310)*

These clauses gave the Constitution a different character from that of earlier Federal Governments. State Officials would now be bound to enforce Acts of Congress. The Federal Judiciary may declare null and void any law in violation of the Constitution established by the people.

This marked a turning point in the Convention._The Confederalists, whose support were in the small states, agreed to not leave the convention and conceded that the Articles of Confederation would be discarded, not just revised. The Nationalists, whose support were in the larger states, agreed to give up the idea of equal representation, (every state having an equal vote). Alexander Hamilton was totally opposed to this compromise as was James Madison, who continued to work for the success of the convention but Hamilton lost interest in the proceedings.

5. **COMPROMISE ON THE PRINCIPLE OF FEDERALISM**

    The Federal Constitution gave new meaning to the term "federal" by establishing a "union of sovereign states". It established that the Federal government is supreme and sovereign within its sphere, but that sphere is defined and limited by the Constitution. This seems to be identified in the latter part of the Constitution, which declares, "powers not delegated to the United States by the Constitution, nor prohibited by it to the states, are reserved to the States respectively or to the people".[1] *(Morrison pg 312)*

H. DISCUSSIONS ABOUT THE OFFICE OF THE PRESIDENT

This subject produced the sharpest conflict of the Convention . In the early discussions, the delegates could only agree that the Executive should be an agent of the legislature with authority to execute the national laws and to appoint to offices in cases not already delegated. Gradually, as the debate continued, the nationalists won the argument over those favoring a weak Executive. ***The Office of the President, as it took shape during the final days of the Convention, became the strong Executive position advocated by Hamilton and Madison. <u>The delegates agreed to give the President significant powers because they had found a way to check his authority</u>.*** He could veto legislation but a 2/3 majority of the legislature could override his veto. He needed the advice and consent of the Senate to make appointments. He could negotiate treaties but they became operative only after 2/3 of the Senate approved. He was to become Commander-in-Chief of the Armed Forces but only Congress could declare war and appropriate money to fight the war.

The method of electing the President was also a difficult decision. The Virginia Plan called for the President to be chosen by Congress for a single seven year term although discussions ranged from three years to life. The Nationalists, led by James Wilson, favored direct election by the people. They argued that the House of Representatives would reflect local interests and the Senate would reflect the interests of the states themselves. The President alone would represent the nation and his choice by the people would help anchor their attachment to the Union.

The issues were settled by authorizing a four year term and establishing the *"Electoral College"* which meant the people would only indirectly elect the President, through elected delegates, or "electoral voters".

1. **THE POWERS OF THE PRESIDENCY;**
   a. Make treaties with the "advice and consent" of 2/3 of the Senate
   b. Serve as Commander-in-Chief of the Army and Navy
   c. Name diplomatic agents with the consent of the Senate

d. Execute the laws passed by Congress

e. Veto Acts of Congress which could be overridden by a 2/3 vote.

2. **THE ELECTORAL COLLEGE COMPROMISE**

   It was finally agreed that each state would choose/elect "electors" equal to the combined number of their Senators and Representatives. *The Presidential candidate which received the majority of the votes cast by the electors would become President.* If no one received a majority, then the House of Representatives, voting by states, would select the President from the top five candidates. *The runner-up would become the Vice-President.* The Electoral College was a device by which it was intended to keep the election in the hands of the politicians without seeming to do so. The delegates assumed that subsequent elections would end up in the House of Representatives because there might not be clear winners and there needed to be a process for a "tie-breaker".

3. **INFLUENCING FACTORS**

   The delegates did have some colonial precedents upon which to copy. For example, the duties and powers of the President were almost completely copied from the 1777 Constitution of the State of New York. The bicameral legislature was standard in all states except Pennsylvania. Money bills continued to originate in the House of Representatives, just as in colonial days, but now the House was allowed to amend. The 3/5 clause regarding the counting of the South's negroes was one of the suggested amendments to the Articles of Confederation which failed to receive unanimous support and become law. The easier amendment process and insistence on ratification by the people were refinements taken from the Massachusetts Constitution of 1780.

I. THE JUDICIAL BRANCH

A Federal Court system was established.

1. Congress was authorized to create a Supreme Court and such inferior courts as were deemed necessary with judges named for life by the President. *The Federal Courts were granted jurisdiction over;*
    a. Cases arising under the Constitution, laws, and treaties
    b. Cases affecting relations with other powers
    c. Cases in which the United States was a party
    d. Controversies between 2 or more states or between citizens of 2 or more states

2. *The Doctrine of Judicial Review (See "Glossary")*
    The Supreme Court was **NOT** given specific power to declare void Acts of Congress or the State Legislatures which conflicted with the Constitution. The following points indicate the Framers intended the Court to have this power;
    a. The fact that all were familiar with the doctrine through practices of state courts
    b. The inclusion of the "supreme law of the land clause" which made the Constitution, Federal Laws, and Federal treaties supreme over State laws in cases of conflict.

J.   AMENDING THE CONSTITUTION

Congress was given power to propose Amendments or they could be drafted by a convention called on demand of 2/3 of the States. They were to become effective when ratified by 3/4 of the states acting through their legislatures or special conventions.

K.   THE DIVISION OF SOVEREIGNTY

The Framers realized that the national government could never enforce its laws unless given some sovereignty but were aware that the states would object to surrendering any of their sovereign powers. They solved this problem by dividing sovereignty between the two governments, using three approaches;

1. ***"Principle of Delegated Powers"***
    Certain powers were specifically delegated to the national government and all others reserved for the states. So, the National government can do only those things the Constitution allows but the States can do all things not specifically forbidden in the Constitution.

2. ***"The Supreme Law of the Land Clause"***
    In cases of conflicts between the national and state governments, the Framers ruled that the Federal Constitution, laws, and treaties were to be the "Supreme Law of the Land", taking precedence over state laws. The judges in each state were to determine when such a conflict existed and to declare the state laws void.

3. **"The Principle of Dual Citizenship"**
    To give the national government a workable compulsive power, all people were made citizens of both the state in which they lived and the United States. This allowed the national government to compel each citizen to pay taxes and obey its laws. This was the most important principle used to create an effective Federal Government.

L.   RATIFICATION OF THE CONSTITUTION

On 9/17/1787, the Convention sent the draft Constitution to the Continental Congress for transmission to the State Legislatures. One of the early criticisms of the document was that it lacked a ***"Bill of Rights"***. Opponents of that view pointed out that there were protections against "ex post facto laws" and "bills of attainder". There were also clauses which guaranteed "habeas corpus" and jury trials in all criminal cases.

Even before Political Parties were formalized, "politics" played a role in how the Constitution was to be discussed and ratified. Those discussions did lead to political and philosophical differences which eventually formed the basis of our political parties, as we will see.

<u>*The struggle for ratification came down to those who supported, called "Federalists" and those who opposed, "Anti-Federalists".*</u>

1. **FEDERALISTS**

   The "Federalists" were those who favored the Constitution, such as Washington and Franklin. Only 39 of the 55 delegates signed the Constitution. They believed that the new nation needed more national power, that the immediate peril was not tyranny but possible dissolution. In general, they represented the business and property interests and those who considered the country more important than their state. They claimed that the Constitution would provide a stable government, maintain law and order, further economic prosperity, and command respect abroad.

2. **ANTI-FEDERALISTS**

   The "Anti-Federalists" were those who agreed with Thomas Paine's sentiment that the government is best which governs the least. In general they were farmers, city workers, and others who gave their loyalties to their states or local communities, *were suspicious that the new Constitution served the propertied interests, threatened the powers of the states, and left the people unprotected against federal encroachment upon their civil liberties. Out of respect for that last point, the Federalists pledged to add a Bill of Rights to the Constitution.* They also included westerners who feared the new government would barter away their right to navigate the Mississippi river and liberals who had learned from history that strong governments tended toward tyranny.

3. **RATIFICATION DEBATE**

Supporters of the Constitution began a campaign of education through pamphlets and newspaper articles. The most famous and effective were the essays which appeared in a New York newspaper, written by Madison, Hamilton, and John Jay, later published as *"The Federalist Papers"*.

The struggle for ratification was tough although in some of the smaller states they ratified almost immediately because they were so pleased with the "Great Compromise". *But, once the draft reached the states for discussion, opposition began to increase.* Local leaders feared that a stronger central government would come at the expense of state and local government authority. George Clinton, former Governor of New York for ten years, was one of the strongest critics. He also made the argument that the Articles of Confederation were now beginning to improve and maybe now wasn't the time to launch a new government. Some complained that the draft was the work of men of "property" who did not understand or respect the views or situation of the "plain people". Even Patrick Henry was concerned that the new government had some elements of Monarchy and it wouldn't take much effort for a President to abuse and expand his power. He was also suspicious of the "power to tax", viewing it as the power to destroy.

In a month's time, five states gave strong approval, Delaware on 12/7/1787, Pennsylvania on 12/12/1787, New Jersey on 12/18/1787, Georgia 1/2/1788 and Connecticut on 1/9/1788, in their popularly chosen conventions.

In response to earlier concerns about the lack of protections for individual rights, *Massachusetts Federalists proposed a "Bill of Rights" as a supplement to the Constitution.* This had not been originally provided by the Federal Convention partly because the Constitution set forth limited and specific powers for which no Bill of Rights was considered to be necessary. The lack of a Bill of Rights was a strong anti-Federalist argument so the

Massachusetts Federalists agreed to support a set of amendments to be recommended to the states, to be presented by John Hancock as a "Bill of Rights".

At that point, both Hancock and Sam Adams changed their votes to support the Constitution and it was ratified by Massachusetts on 2/6/1788 by a vote of 187–168.

After Massachusetts ratified, Maryland easily passed it on 4/28/1788, South Carolina on 5/23/1788, and *New Hampshire* by a slim margin on 6/21/1788 after two conventions. *It became the 9th state to ratify and the last required to make it the supreme law of the land.* But, 4 states with 40% of the population were still undecided. Those states were Virginia, New York, North Carolina, and Rhode Island.

4. **REMAINING OPPOSITION**

Virginia

The Virginia Federalists were Washington, Madison, John Marshall, Edmund Pendleton, and Edmund Randolph. The Virginia Anti-Federalists were George Mason, Richard Henry Lee, and Patrick Henry.

The Virginia debate was the longest and most profound. Mason and Henry led the fight for the Anti-Federalists and it seemed for awhile that they would defeat ratification *until Edmund Randolph, an original opponent, suddenly supported it. He was persuaded by Washington and Madison that a "Bill of Rights" would subsequently be added. Virginia then ratified by a vote of 89–79 on 6/25/1788.* Once he knew that his cause had been lost, Patrick Henry became a solid supporter. His example of loyalty set an effective example for others who also eventually pledged their support.

New York

We know that the New York Federalists were led by Hamilton and John Jay. The opponents were led by Governor Clinton and the large landowners who feared heavier taxation if the state lost its right to levy customs duties. ***The Federalists didn't have the necessary votes for ratification until news of Virginia's ratification reached the convention. It was eventually approved on 7/26/1788 by a narrow vote of 30-27.***

Other

Less than eight months after Delaware approved, all but two states had approved. North Carolina held off until 11/21/1789 and Rhode Island on 5/29/1790.

5. **RATIFICATION SUMMARY** *(Attachment 24a summarizes State Ratification dates.)*

   The relatively swift success of ratification (12/7/1787 to 5/29/1790, a period of roughly 29 months) was due to a number of factors;

   a. Aggressive information campaign by the Federalists

   b. Public apathy generally due to the difficult nature of reading the document

   c. Many people were swayed by the influential Federalists, like George Washington and Benjamin Franklin in particular.

   d. Attractions built into the final Constitution to please a diversity of interests made it difficult to achieve a broad range of opposition, such as; The addition of a Bill of Rights and a promise to protect Slavery for 20 years.

   Congress then declared the new Constitution ratified and arranged for the first Presidential and Congressional elections announcing 3/4/1789 as the beginning of the first Presidential term. The new House of Representatives, which had no quorum until 4/1/1789, counted the electoral ballots on 4/6/1789. It took another week for Washington to learn officially that he had been selected as President. The old Congress then selected New York as the first capital of the new government.

(Attachment 24b summarizes the differences between the Articles of Confederation and the new Federal Constitution.)

M.   WHAT WAS TO BE THE IMPACT OF THE NEW CONSTITUTION ?

The Government which formed under the new Constitution was solidly anchored in the past with many of the new leaders having served during the Revolutionary period. ***The "Bill of Rights" sent to the states for approval came primarily from similar bills previously enacted by the states.*** The first Tariff Laws were modeled after that of Pennsylvania. America in 1789 drew heavily on the past to guide it through the present and future.

The Constitution provided the means for unity but not unity itself. Even President Washington wasn't able to overcome the various sectional and local differences which prevented the development of a strong sense of unity.

After 1789, American began to change. The door to the west had been slightly opened and with it new immigrants arrived with a different set of beliefs and experiences. Irish Catholics and southern and eastern Europeans began to arrive and all of these immigrants worked to alter the old English-dominated Protestant nature of the colonies. Many later policies had their roots in colonial experiences but they became shaped to fit new circumstances.

American greatness owes a deep debt to luck. Its people had the luck to be given a rich continent to explore and exploit. ***They had more than 100 years of experience with various forms and degrees of self-government before they ventured out on their own in 1776.***

N.   THE CONSTITUTION OF 1787 AND TODAY

Although a liberal document for the 18th century, the Constitution as adopted contained few of its democratic features of today, such as;

1.   **SYSTEM OF CHECKS AND BALANCES**
   a. The Courts could check the Legislature and President. The President could use his veto power to negate the popular will
   b. Congress could frustrate the President by refusing to ratify treaties or appointments

c. Although designed partially to prevent any branch of the government from developing tyrannical powers, the system also frustrated the popular will.

2. **DENIAL OF POPULAR RULE**

    a. Despite the fact that property qualifications kept many from voting, the Framers allowed the people to choose only the House of Representatives

    b. The Senate was removed two steps from the people, they chose members of a state legislature who, in turn, selected the Senators.

    c. The President was removed 3 steps from the people because members of the Electoral College were chosen by State Legislatures.

    d. The Judges were removed 4 steps from the people because they were appointed by the President, for life

3. **THE REPRESENTATIVE PRINCIPLE**

    a. *The Constitution did not create a Democracy, but a Representative government.*

    b. Once the people chose their Representatives, those Representatives made and executed laws based on the popular will.

    c. The Framers probably realized that Congressmen would be more conservative than the people who elected them.

4. **THE TRANSFORMATION THROUGH AMENDMENTS**

    a. Few changes have been made in the Constitution. Of the 22 Amendments, the first 10 (Bill of Rights) were part of the original document while the 18th and 21st Amendments cancel each other.

0.   GLOSSARY

1. **Ex post facto laws**   Article 1 of the U.S. Constitution specifically prohibits a law made retroactive to punish an action that wasn't illegal at the time it was committed.

2. **Bills of attainder**   Article 1, Section 9, Paragraph 3, of the U.S. Constitution specifically prohibits a Legislative Act which singles out an individual or group for punishment without a trial.

3. **Habeas Corpus**   The right of every person to challenge the terms of his/her incarceration in court before a Judge.

4. **Doctrine of Judicial Review**   Was not included in the original Constitution but was established by the Court Case of "Marbury vs Madison" in 1803 which permits the Supreme Court of the United States to overturn Legislative Acts of Congress which violate the Constitution. Such decisions are final and not subject to further appeal.

5. **Enumerated powers** Those specific powers given to the National Government "enumerated" in the U.S. Constitution. All powers not specified as belonging to the Federal Government, belong to the State Governments.

P.   Attachments

Q. KEY DATES AND SIGNIFICANT EVENTS

	1648	New England Confederation designed to protect against the Indians
7/10	1754	Albany Plan of Union designed to protect against French & Indians
10/19	1765	Stamp Act Congress
	1773	Committees of Correspondence created in multiple states
	1776	First & Second Continental Congresses
5/15	1776	Congress resolves that Crown's authority in all colonies should be ended
6/12	1776	Virginia adopts its' State Constitution
Feb	1779	All States ratify the new Articles of Confederation except Maryland
6/15	1780	Massachusetts ratifies State Constitution
3/1	1781	Articles of Confederation ratified by all states
	1782	New York calls for Convention to revise the Articles of Confederation
4/19	1783	Treaty of Paris ends Revolutionary War
1787		Shays' Rebellion
5/25	1787	Constitutional Convention meets in Philadelphia
5/29	1787	Edmund Randolph proposes the Virginia Plan
6/15	1787	William Patterson proposes the New Jersey Plan
6/19	1787	New Jersey Plan defeated
7/16	1787	Convention adopts the "Great Compromise" (Connecticut Compromise) proposed by Roger Sherman
9/17	1787	Constitutional Convention sends draft Constitution for transmission to the State Legislatures

| 7/2 | 1788 | Federal Constitution ratified by 9 state minimum |
| 5/29 | 1790 | Rhode Island final state to ratify Constitution |

R.   REVIEW QUESTIONS

(Multiple Choice)

1. Which of the following organizations was NOT intended as an attempt at Colonial Unity?
    a. New England Confederation
    b. Albany Plan of Union
    c. Stamp Act Congress
    d. None of the above

2. Which of the following political documents and underlying principles show up in the Federal Constitution?
    a. English Magna Carta 1215
    b. Petition of Right 1628
    c. English Bill of Rights 1689
    d. All of the above

3. The Articles of Confederation needed to be revised because of what defect?
    a. weak Executive
    b. no judiciary
    c. required unanimous vote to amend or change the Articles
    d. All of the above

4. In what year were the Articles of Confederation passed?
    a. 1776
    b. 1779
    c. 1781
    d. 1783

5. For how many years were the Articles of Confederation in effect?
   a. 5
   b. 6
   c. 7
   d. 8

6. Which of the following representation plans had the most influence on the final Constitution?
   a. Virginia Plan
   b New Jersey Plan
   c. Connecticut Plan
   d. None of the above

7. Who was the author of the "Great Compromise"?
   a. Thomas Jefferson
   b. Roger Sherman
   c. Edmund Randolph
   d. George Mason

8. Which was the 9th and deciding state to ratify the Federal Constitution?
   a. Massachusetts
   b. South Carolina
   c. New Hampshire
   d. Virginia

9. Which was the final state to ratify the Federal Constitution?
   a. North Carolina
   b. New York
   c. Rhode Island
   d. None of the above

(True or False)

10. The primary challenge of the post-Revolutionary period was that of creating a stable Federal Government plus 13 State Governments.
    a. TRUE
    b. FALSE

11. On 5/15/1776, Congress resolved that the Crown's authority in all colonies should be ended.
    a. TRUE
    b. FALSE

12. The post-Revolutionary War leaders were primarily interested in building a new and different government rather than preserve and secure the freedoms they always had.
    a. TRUE
    b. FALSE

13. The "Virginia Declaration of Rights" contained the phrase "all men are by nature free and independent" etc.
    a. TRUE
    b. FALSE

14. The "Mt. Vernon and Annapolis Conventions" led to the formation of a new Constitution.
    a. TRUE
    b. FALSE

15. The "Virginia Plan" was the key element in the final Federal Constitution.
    a. TRUE
    b. FALSE

CHAPTER 24 SUMMARY

THE NEW GOVERNMENT

1. ***The key issue of the post-war period was the issue of how to reconcile central authority with personal liberty.***

2. Previous attempts at Colonial unity were the;
   a. New England Confederation   1643 - 1648
   b. Albany Plan of Union   1754
   c. Stamp Act Congress   1765
   d. Committees of Correspondence   1772-1773
   d. First & Second Continental Congresses   1774 - 1775

3. Political documents shaping the Federal Constitution;
   a. British Magna-Carta   1215
   b. British Petition of Right   1628
   c. British Bill of Rights   1689
   d. Virginia Declaration of Rights   1776

4. The Massachusetts Constitution is the 1st to reflect the theory of "Checks & Balances" in 1780.

5. The Articles of Confederation (AOC) are ratified on 3/1/1781.

6. Events which lead to the Constitutional Convention;
   a. The New York convention calls for a revision to the AOC.
   b. Mt. Vernon and Annapolis Conventions lead to a call for a Constitutional Convention.

7. The Constitutional Convention;

a. Meet in Philadelphia 5/25/1787.

b. 55 of 74 delegates and 12 of the 13 States attend. The average age of the delegates is 42.

c. There are major disagreements between;

- North and South

- Large states and small states.

- Agrarian and commercial interests.

- Nationalists and States-rights.

- Pro-slavery and anti-slavery.

d Issues of Unity;

- Agree on the need to revise the AOC.

- Need for a strong Executive, Judiciary, 2-House Legislature, and a written Constitution.

- The government must have an independent source of revenue.

- Some form of proportional representation.

- Governmental control over foreign affairs and commerce.

e. ***The key challenge was to balance a strong central government with respect for State's rights.***

8. The "Great Compromise" (The Connecticut Plan) was proposed by Roger Sherman.

a. Balances the Virginia and New Jersey plans

b. Provisions;

- The House of Representatives are popularly elected apportioned by population.

- The Senate will consist of two members from each State, elected by the State Legislatures.

- c. Compromise on slavery;

- The South wanted slaves counted as part of the population for the purpose of representation which would increase the number of southerners in the House of Representatives.

- The North is granted a 3/5 compromise by which 5 slaves are to be counted as 3 free persons.

- This compromise finally settles the differences between north and south on this issue.

9. Powers of Congress;
   a. Collect taxes and duties.
   b. Regulate foreign and interstate commerce.
   c. Coin or borrow money.
   d. Declare War.
   e. Maintain an Army.

10. Office of the Presidency;
    a. One 4-year term.
    b. Establish the Electoral College.
    c. Make treaties with the advice and consent of 2/3 of the Senate.
    d. Commander-in-Chief of the Military.
    e. Appoint diplomatic agents with the consent of the Senate.
    f. Execute the laws passed by Congress with the power of Veto subject to 2/3 Congress over-ride vote.

11. Judicial Branch;
    a. Establish the Federal Court system comprised of the Supreme Court and Lower Courts.
    b. Doctrine of Judicial Review was not included in the Constitution but was implied.

12. Division of Sovereignty;
    a. Principle of delegated powers, specific to the National government and State governments.

b. The Supreme Law of the Land clause. National laws take precedence over State laws.

c. Principle of Dual citizenship. All people are made citizens of both the state and national government.

13. Ratification of the Constitution

a. Delaware is the first State, 12/7/1787, and Rhode Island is the last State, 5/29/1790.

b. Federalists against the Anti-Federalists

- ***Federalists support Ratification*** led by Washington, Franklin, Madison, Hamilton

- ***Anti-Federalists oppose Ratification*** led by Patrick Henry, Richard Henry Lee, George Mason. Patrick Henry changes his vote after it is approved, as a show of national loyalty.

24a

#	S T A T E	MO	DATE	YR
1.	DELAWARE	12	7	1787
2.	PENNSYLVANIA	12	12	1787
3.	NEW JERSEY	12	18	1787
4.	GEORGIA	1	2	1788
5.	CONNECTICUT	1	9	1788
6.	MASSACHUSETTS	2	6	1788
7.	MARYLAND	4	28	1788
8.	SOUTH CAROLINA	5	23	1788
9.	NEW HAMPSHIRE	6	21	1788
10.	VIRGINIA	6	25	1788
11.	NEW YORK	7	26	1788
12.	NORTH CAROLINA	11	21	1789
13.	RHODE ISLAND	5	29	1790

RATIFICATION STATES AND DATES

24b

ARTICLES OF CONFEDERATION	CATEGORY	FEDERAL CONSTITUTION
EACH STATE HAS 1 VOTE IN CONGRESS REGARDLESS OF SIZE OR POPULATION	REPRESENTATION	REPRESENTATION IN HOUSE OF REPS BASED ON POPULATION. REPRESENTATION IN SENATE BASED ON EQUALITY
CONGRESS HAS NO POWER TO TAX	TAXES	CONGRESS HAS AUTHORITY TO LEVY AND COLLECT TAXES
CONGRESS HAS NO POWER TO REGULATE FOREIGN OR INTERSTATE COMMERCE	COMMERCE	CONGRESS HAS AUTHORITY TO REGULATE FOREIGN AND INTERSTATE COMMERCE
NO CHIEF EXECUTIVE TO ENFORCE LAWS	EXECUTIVE	PROVIDES FOR A PRESIDENT AND ADVISERS TO ENFORCE LAWS
NO PROVISION FOR A NATIONAL SYSTEM OF COURTS	JUDICIARY	PROVIDES FOR A NATIONAL SYSTEM OF COURTS HEADED BY THE U.S. SUPREME COURT
REQUIRES 9 VOTES OF THE 13 STATES TO PASS A LAW	LEGISLATION	A MAJORITY VOTE IN THE 2 HOUSES OF CONGRESS TO PASS A LAW
UNANIMOUS VOTE OF ALL STATES REQUIRED TO AMEND THE ARTICLES OF CONFEDERATION	AMENDMENT PROCESS	AMENDMENTS MAY BE PROPOSED BY A 2/3 VOTE OF EACH HOUSE OF CONGRESS, OR A CONVENTION CALLED BY 2/3 OF THE STATES AND RATIFIED BY THE LEGISLATURES OF 3/4 OF THE STATES OR CONVENTIONS
EACH STATE RETAINS ITS SOVEREIGNTY AND INDEPENDENCE	STATE AND FEDERAL SOVEREIGNTY	CONSTITUTION PROVIDES FOR A FEDERAL SYSTEM OF GOVERNMENT, WITH THE U.S. CONSTITUTION AS THE SUPREME LAW OF THE LAND

24c

"Federal System of Government"

FEDERAL GOV POWERS	CONCURRENT POWERS	STATE GOV POWERS
LEVY & COLLECT TAXES	LEVY & COLLECT TAXES	REGULATE MARRIAGE & DIVORCE
COIN & BORROW MONEY	BORROW MONEY	CONTROL EDUCATION
REGULATE FOREIGN & INTERSTATE COMMERCE	BUILD HIGHWAYS	REGULATE INTRA-STATE COMMERCE
PROVIDE FOR NATURALIZATION	CHARTER BANKS & CORPORATIONS	DETERMINE VOTING QUALIFICATIONS
DECLARE WAR		EXERCISE POLICE POWERS SUCH AS;
RAISE & SUPPORT ARMY & NAVY		HEALTH
ESTABLISH FEDERAL COURTS		SAFETY
"ELASTIC CLAUSE" (IMPLIED POWERS)		MORALS
POWERS DENIED TO FED GOV		POWERS DENIED TO STATE GOV
ARTICLE 1, SECTION 9, AMENDMENTS 1-10		ARTICLE 1, SECTION 10, AMENDMENT 14

24d

U. S. CONGRESS

HOUSE OF REPRESENTATIVES	CATEGORY	SENATE
REPRESENTATION BASED ON POPULATION	NUMBER OF MEMBERS	TWO FROM EACH STATE
25 YEARS OF AGE, CITIZEN OF U.S. FOR AT LEAST 7 YEARS AND RESIDENT OF THE STATE FROM WHICH ELECTED	QUALIFICATIONS	30 YEARS OF AGE, CITIZEN OF U.S. FOR AT LEAST 9 YEARS AND RESIDENT OF THE STATE FROM WHICH ELECTED
DIRECTLY BY VOTERS OF THE DISTRICT COMMERCE	HOW ELECTED	DIRECTLY BY THE VOTERS OF THE STATE SINCE THE 17TH AMENDMENT
2 YEARS	LENGTH OF TERM	6 YEARS
SPEAKER OF HOUSE OF REPRESENTATIVES	PRESIDING OFFICER	VICE PRESIDENT OF U.S.
	SPECIAL OR EXCLUSIVE POWERS	
IMPEACHMENT OF PRESIDENT & OTHER FEDERAL OFFICIALS	IMPEACHMENT	TRY IMPEACHMENT CASES BROUGHT BY HOUSE OF REPRESENTATIVES
INTRODUCE REVENUE BILLS	REVENUE BILLS	
ELECT PRESIDENT WHEN NO CANDIDATE RECEIVES MAJORITY VOTE IN ELECTORAL COLLEGE	SPECIAL ELECTIONS	ELECT VICE-PRESIDENT IF NO CANDIDATE RECEIVES MAJORITY VOTE IN ELECTORAL COLLEGE
	RATIFY TREATIES	RATIFY TREATIES BY REQUIRED 2/3 VOTE
	APPOINTMENTS	CONFIRM APPOINTMENTS MADE BY PRES.

24e

POWERS OF THE PRESIDENCY

EXECUTIVE POWERS	LEGISLATIVE POWERS	JUDICIAL POWERS
ENFORCE THE CONSTITUTION AND LAWS OF THE U.S.	RECOMMEND TO CONGRESS SPECIFIC LEGISLATION IN MESSAGE TO CONGRESS	MAY GRANT PARDONS AND REPRIEVES IN CASES INVOLVING OFFENSES AGAINST THE U.S. EXCEPT CASES OF IMPEACHMENT
APPOINT GOVERNMENT OFFICIALS SUCH AS; CABINET MEMBERS JUDGES AMBASSADORS POSTMASTERS	MAY SIGN OR VETO BILLS PASSED BY CONGRESS	APPOINTS MEMBERS OF THE FEDERAL COURTS WITH CONSENT OF SENATE
COMMANDER-IN-CHIEF OF ARMED FORCES	MAY CALL SPECIAL SESSIONS OF CONGRESS	
RESPONSIBLE FOR DETERMINATION & CONDUCT OF FOREIGN POLICY	MAY INFLUENCE VOTE OF CONGRESSMEN BY VIRTUE OF HIS POSITION AS HEAD OF HIS POLITICAL PARTY AND AS THE GRANTOR OF POLITICAL FAVORS (PATRONAGE)	
AUTHORITY TO MAKE TREATIES WITH FOREIGN COUNTRIES SUBJECT TO APPROVAL BY 2/3 VOTE OF THE SENATE	MAY INFLUENCE LEGISLATION AND THE NECESSARY PUBLIC OPINION BY MEANS OF RADIO/TV SPEECHES AND MEETINGS WITH THE PRESS	
AUTHORITY TO APPOINT AMBASSADORS, MINISTERS, AND CONSULS TO FOREIGN COUNTRIES, SUBJECT TO APPROVAL BY SENATE		

24f

FEDERAL SYSTEM OF CHECKS AND BALANCES

EXECUTIVE BRANCH	LEGISLATIVE BRANCH	JUDICIAL BRANCH
HOW EXECUTIVE BRANCH CHECKS LEGISLATIVE BRANCH	HOW CONGRESS CHECKS EXECUTIVE BRANCH	HOW JUDICIAL BRANCH CHECKS CONGRESS & EXEC BRANCH
PRESIDENT MAY VETO BILLS PASSED BY BOTH HOUSES OF CONGRESS	CONGRESS MAY OVERRIDE PRESIDENTIAL VETO OF A BILL BY 2/3 VOTE	BY DECLARING LAWS UNCONSTITUTIONAL
PRESIDENT MAY CALL SPECIAL SESSIONS OF CONGRESS	CONGRESS MAY REMOVE PRESIDENT THROUGH IMPEACHMENT BY HOUSE OF REPS & TRIAL BY SENATE	
PRESIDENT MAY RECOMMEND LEGISLATION TO CONGRESS	ALL TREATIES & APPOINTMENTS MADE BY PRESIDENT MUST BE RATIFIED BY THE SENATE	
HOW EXECUTIVE CHECKS POWER OF JUDICIAL BRANCH	HOW CONGRESS CHECKS POWER OF JUDICIAL BRANCH	
PRESIDENT APPOINTS JUDGES	SENATE MUST APPROVE ALL APPOINTMENTS OF FEDERAL JUDGES	
PRESIDENT MAY GRANT PARDONS & REPRIEVES	BY PASSING A NEW LAW IN PLACE OF ONE DECLARED UNCONSTITUTIONAL BY THE SUPREME COURT	
	BY EITHER INCREASING OR DECREASING THE NUMBER OF JUDGES ON THE SUPREME COURT	

Chapter 25

The Federalist Era

A.   WASHINGTON'S FIRST ADMINISTRATION (1789-1793)

George Washington inherited the first Presidency of a new nation without much precedent and many serious problems facing him immediately upon taking office;

- Create a new government

- Financial and commercial problems

- Weakened Army and Navy

- No Federal Judiciary to enforce the laws

- Pass a "Bill of Rights" as amendments to the new Constitution.

1. **FIRST ACTS OF THE NEW GOVERNMENT**
   a. Formation of the First Cabinet
   b. Passage of a "Bill of Rights" as Amendments to the new Constitution
   c. Hamilton Financial Plan
   d. Judiciary Act of 1789

2. **FORMATION OF THE FIRST CABINET**
   Although the Continental Congress performed somewhat as a "government" while conducting the Revolutionary War, the challenge to the new President was to identify the necessary

positions for managing a government, craft their roles, and then recruit the best possible candidates to fill those positions.

Heads of departments had to be appointed by the President with the consent of the Senate.

Congress made the Secretaries of State and War directly responsible to the President and he could remove them without Congressional approval.

a. The **Secretary of State** position required someone with diplomatic experience;

- Franklin was too old and feeble

- John Adams had been elected Vice-President

- John Jay had made enemies by negotiating an unpopular treaty with Spain

So, Washington selected Thomas Jefferson who, as Minister to France, had shown himself to be an excellent diplomatic.

b. The **Secretary of the Treasury position;**

- The Treasury Department was created by Congress in its **"Treasury Organic Act" of 9/2/1789**. It required the Secretary of the Treasury to prepare plans for the management of the revenues, support of public credit, prepare estimates for the revenues, report expenditures, and, in general, oversee the Federal Finances.

- Robert Morris declined but suggested Alexander Hamilton who fit Washington's desired profile.

c. The **Secretary of War position;**

- General Knox, who had been General Washington's Chief of Artillery, continued in the position he held during the War and Confederation period.

d. The **Attorney General position;**

- Edmund Randolph appointed after his term as Governor of Virginia had expired.

The Federal Constitution created the ***Office of the Vice President*** in order to provide an acting Chief Magistrate in the event of the death or disability of the President. In order to give him something to do, he was made President of the Senate with a tie-breaking vote.

3. **INCLUSION OF "A BILL OF RIGHTS" IN THE NEW CONSTITUTION**

As we saw in the previous chapter, the anti-Federalists who refused to ratify the new Constitution were the most concerned at the lack of a "Bill of Rights" to protect individual liberties against a possible tyrannical government.

In his Inaugural Address, President Washington hinted that Congress should promptly add a Bill of Rights to the Constitution to appease the Anti-Federalists. James Madison took the lead in the effort and Jefferson supported the idea as a legal check to be placed in the hands of the judiciary.

After the new government began to function, Congress proposed a Bill of Rights. A list of 12 changes were sent to the states and, a few years later on 12/15/1791, 10 of those changes were accepted by enough states to be added to the Constitution. ***Those Ten Amendments are referred to as the "Bill of Rights". (Attachment 25a.)***

Although several leading Anti-Federalists continued calling for a new Federal Convention and weren't persuaded by the additional amendments, most of the opponents were eventually persuaded.

Once Massachusetts added a "Bill of Rights" and ratified the Constitution, then Virginia did the same, followed by New York upon the news that Virginia had ratified.

4. **HAMILTON FINANCIAL PROGRAM**
   a. **Payment of Debts**

The new government would assume responsibility for all debts contracted by the central government during the Revolutionary War and Confederation periods.

- Calls for full payment of the domestic debt, government bonds, and certificates held by Americans.

- Calls for full payment of foreign debt, loans extended by our war allies, France, Spain, and Holland.

- Calls for the "assumption" of $21.5 million of state debts by the Federal government. James Madison opposed and then proposed to discriminate between the original holders and subsequent purchasers. His proposal was defeated in the House of Representatives. The New England states favored "assumption" since they had the largest unpaid debt. The southern states, however, had mostly paid their debts or made arrangements to pay it, and feared that an increase in the national debt would then require their citizens to be taxed to pay for it. *They also feared that Federal "assumption" would increase federal power at the expense of the states. Virginia, led by James Madison, led the opposition to the "assumption plan" which was defeated in the House on 4/12/1790.*

On 6/20/1790, however, Alexander Hamilton worked a "deal" to get "Assumption" passed. He obtained enough southern votes to pass it in return for moving the National Capital from Philadelphia (north) to Washington, D.C. (south). *The Assumption plan was adopted by the House on 7/26/1790.*

In spite of the *"compromise"* the southern states were still uneasy about the deal as evidenced by the *"Virginia Resolutions" drafted by Patrick Henry on 12/16/1790 believing that there was nothing in the Constitution which authorized Congress to assume state debts.*

Such repayments, according to Hamilton, would firmly establish the credit of America at home and abroad.

b. Excise Tax – To raise funds, an excise tax was imposed on various commodities such as distilled liquors.

c. **Protective Tariff** - Congress had already passed a tariff on imports. Hamilton urged tariffs on manufactured goods to discourage the import of such goods and encourage manufacturing in America. Congress rejected Hamilton's proposal for a protective tariff, it raised rates slightly for revenue purposes.

d. **Money Management** - Plans to charter a National Bank.

5. **THE JUDICIARY ACT OF 9/24/1789**

A Supreme Court was created consisting of a Chief Justice and five Associates for 13 District Courts and three Circuit Courts.

The 25th section of this Act dealt with a provision intended to prevent state judiciaries from putting its own interpretation on the Federal Constitution and then acting in violation of it.

John Jay was appointed the first Chief Justice and the first session opened in New York city on 2/2/1790. The first significant case was in early 1791 involving British debts. One of the circuit courts declared as invalid a Connecticut law which infringed on Article VI of the Treaty of Peace. In 1792, a Rhode Island state law was declared unconstitutional.

6. **INDIAN RELATIONS**

Washington's Indian policy was based on the following principles:

a. Indian lands should be guaranteed to them by treaties and land purchases were prohibited except by the Federal government.

b. The Federal government should regulate and control Indian trade.

c. White citizens would be punished for abusing Indians and they for attacking whites.

d. Indians living on their own lands would not be taxed or considered citizens of America. They were to govern themselves by tribal law. They should be welcomed as citizens if they chose to settle among white people.

Few of these principles were enforced in practice due to the weakness of the Federal government.

7. **WASHINGTON'S FOREIGN POLICY**
The immediate goals of Washington's foreign policy were to;
a. Secure the navigation of the Mississippi river because support of the commercial class would be lost if their commerce was not protected.
b. Secure the British surrender of the northwest posts otherwise there would be a demand for another war with England.
The Federal government had to satisfy all parts of the country that their essential interests were being protected. To achieve these goals peacefully would require years of patient and skillful diplomacy. *War already seemed likely in Europe and to become involved would hamper Washington's efforts to build a new government and strengthen the nation.*
Hamilton and Jefferson initially agreed on the goals but differed on the methods;
c. Jefferson wanted commercial and diplomatic ties with France. He hated England and believed that Hamilton wanted to make America like England.
d. Hamilton believed the interests of England and America were complementary, not competitive. He saw England as having achieved the perfect balance between liberty and order. He believed it would be good for American commerce to retain its ties to England. As it was, 75% of America's foreign commerce was with England and 90% of American imports came from England. Hamilton planned to finance his new fiscal system with customs duties which was the only large source of revenue then available to the Federal government. It would not have been in the commercial interests of America to engage in a trade war with England.
At Hamilton's suggestion, the First Tariff Act of 1789 levied higher duties on foreign than on American vessels but placed English and French vessels in the same class. That pleased

England but angered France, especially after their support to America during the Revolutionary War.

Washington ended his first term in the shadow of a pending European war which kept alive a political debate between the Federalists, led by Hamilton, who tended to support England, and the Anti-Federalists, led by Jefferson, who supported France at least until the French Revolution turned radical and the "Citizen Genet" affair caused even Thomas Jefferson to urge neutrality.

B.   WASHINGTON'S SECOND ADMINISTRATION (1793-1797)

His first administration dealt more with domestic issues because of the need to create a new government and get it functioning as soon as possible. The second administration, by necessity, took on a more international flavor because of the pending conflict between England and France with the resulting impact on American politics.

Some of the more important and time-consuming events of the 2nd Administration were;

- The French Revolution, Citizen Genet, and American Politics

- Barbary Pirates

- Jay's Treaty

- Pinckney's Treaty

- Problems with France

There were also a few major domestic issues such as;

- The Whiskey Rebellion

- Further Indian problems

- Growing Political disagreements and the gradual formation of political parties

1. **FRENCH REVOLUTION AND AMERICAN POLITICS**

The French Revolution, beginning with the capture of the Bastille (prison) on 7/14/1789, was followed in America with considerable interest. Many Americans supported the democratic tendencies of the French Revolution, such as abolishing titles of nobility and the adoption of a somewhat similar "Bill of Rights" to the American model. *In the early stages of the Revolution, the French intended to replace the "rule of law" by the "rule of reason", which eventually became extreme and caused many Americans to reconsider their support.*

Meanwhile, in April 1793, Americans learned that France had declared war on England and Spain, King Louis XVI executed, and replaced by the Girondin Party. *Immediately, domestic politics surfaced.*

Hamilton, anti-France, proposed terminating the 1778 French-American Alliance, by which France aided our Revolution, because of the changed French government but also because that Alliance required us to help protect French interests in the Caribbean. *Jefferson, although pro-France, wished to keep America neutral as did President Washington who announced on 4/22/1793 his "Neutrality Proclamation", followed by Congress passing a "Neutrality Act" in the next session.*

Meanwhile, the new French government sent their Minister to America, *"Citizen Genet"*, who immediately began to *undermine President Washington's Neutrality policy*. Finally, after Genet caused a lot of trouble in America, the President finally requested the new French government to recall him, which they did. The new Minister arrived in 1794 with an order to send Genet home under arrest. Genet refused, stayed in the country, married the daughter of Governor Clinton of New York, and settled down to live in the Hudson river valley.

2. THE BEGINNINGS OF POLITICAL PARTIES

In 1792, the conflict between the ideas and economic interests personified by Hamilton and Jefferson began to crystallize in the form of political parties. Hamilton's strong influence on President Washington also aroused determined opposition by Jefferson and his supporters.

The personal feud between Jefferson and Hamilton became philosophical and political as well. *The year 1794 saw the beginnings of political parties evolving from different approaches to the issues of:*

a. Monarchy vs Republicanism

b. Oppression vs Liberty

c. Anarchy vs Order

d. Atheism vs Religion

e. Poverty vs Prosperity

Americans began falling into the groupings known as "Federalists" and "Anti-Federalists". Jefferson referred to his supporters in 1791 as "Republicans" in order to imply that all others were "Monarchists". Hamilton retained the name "Federalist" to imply that his opponents were "Anti-Federal". (Attachment 25b summarizes the Political Party differences.)

There was no clear-cut economic/social explanation as most loyalties were local in nature. There was some ideology involved but that doesn't totally explain how the parties were distinguished. *Thus, there was no clean distinction between the two parties created by Hamilton and Jefferson, as such; Jefferson favored:*

a. Democratic agrarian order based on the individual freeholder

b. Broad diffusion of wealth

c. Relative freedom from industrialism, urbanism, and organized finance

d. Sympathy for debtor interests

e. Distrust of centralized government

f. Belief in the perfectibility of man

g. Confidence in the view that people, acting through representative institutions, could be left to govern themselves

h. Believed that a Republic must be based on an agrarian democracy

i. *Favored a "strict" interpretation of the Constitution*

j. Opposed to the Hamilton "assumption plan" of state debts and creation of the National Bank

Hamilton favored:

a. A balanced and diversified economic order

b. An active government encouragement of finance, industry, commerce, and shipping

c. Sympathy for the creditor interests

d. Advocacy of a strong national government under executive leadership

e. Distrust of the ability of the people to govern themselves

f. Belief that the best government was controlled by the elite.

g. Believed that Republican government could only succeed if directed by a governing elite

h. *Believed in a "loose or broad" interpretation of the Constitution*

i. Favored the Hamilton assumption of state debts and establishment of the National Bank

Events which shaped the development of political parties:

a. The Jeffersonians became known as "Democratic-Republicans", or just as "Republicans"

b. The Hamiltonians remained known as "Federalists" for their support of the new Constitution

c. Political parties served as spokespersons for different interests and made them more effective as participants in government. They also helped overcome the checks and balances between the three branches of government and coordinate them into an effective system

d. Antagonism between two sectional interests:

- Planting, slaveholding interest primarily in the rural south

- Mercantile/shipping/financial interest of the seaport cities

e. *American political history until 1865 is largely the story of these rival interests, capitalist and agrarian, northern and southern, contending for the control of the Federal government.*

f. Dissatisfied with the Washington administration fiscal policies, Jefferson and Madison toured New England and New York to learn of the people's attitudes towards the Federalists.

g. *Public attitudes were also affected by competing Newspapers such as:*

- National Gazette, anti-administration, led by Phillip Freneau

- Gazette of the United States, Federalist, edited by John Fenno, began 4/15/1789

Letters written to the Newspapers by both Jefferson and Hamilton showed their dislike and distrust of one another. President Washington attempted the role of "peacemaker" but was unable to bring them together.

h. *Jefferson's attitude toward Hamilton became more negative over the issue of the "National Bank" which Hamilton proposed on 12/13/1790. Madison joined Jefferson in opposition on the grounds that the chartering of the bank was beyond the powers of Congress and Jefferson's position was that it was not necessary.*

i. There was no provision in the Constitution for political parties and President Washington hoped to govern without them but realized that he didn't know what to do when organized opposition appeared, which happened in 1791. It became clearer in 1792 when the anti-Federalists won control of the House of Representatives.

j. *Upon becoming President, John Adams management of the "French Crisis" split the Federalist party into the Hamilton and Adams factions.*

3. **THE CRUCIAL YEAR OF 1794**

There were a number of *significant events which helped shape the nation during 1794;*

- Defeat of the Whiskey Rebellion

- Barbary Pirates

- Continuing problems with England on the high seas, in the northwest territories, and the subsequent Jay's Treaty.

- Problems with Spain over the right of transit at New Orleans

- President Washington's Cabinet problems

a. *The Whiskey Rebellion*

The new Federal government succeeded in defeating an insurrection of western frontiersmen, known as "moonshiners", in their rebellion against Federal "revenooers". In 1791, Congress passed an Act levying a moderate excise tax on distilleries.

This Act seemed as unjust to the Appalachian frontiersmen as did the Stamp Act to the Bostonians. Throughout this region, distilling was an effective way of using surplus corn. The opposition to the Act centered in Washington County, Pennsylvania, led by a frontier lawyer named David Bradford who organized the resistance to the law. People signed "covenants" to never pay the tax, law-abiding distillers were terrorized, federal marshals threatened, committees of safety organized, and the people were urged to fight for their liberties. Washington county almost seceded from Pennsylvania and the Union if it had not been for the moderating influence of Hugh Brackenridge and Albert Gallatin.

Pennsylvania Governor Mifflin, a Jeffersonian Republican, refused to enforce the act due to fear of damaging his popularity. ***President Washington and Hamilton viewed the issue as a test of the Federal government's ability to enforce the laws without the assistance of the states.*** Congress had the authority to call out the militia to enforce the laws of the Union. On 8/7/1794, Congress authorized the President to call up 15,000 militia from four states. When confronted by the militia, the protesters fled or quit with two of the leaders caught and convicted of treason, although later pardoned by the President.

b. *The Barbary Pirates*

Congress voted to re-establish the Navy after the continuing capture and imprisonment of 126 American sailors in Algiers, Tunisia. The President signed the law authorizing the building of six warships and recruitment of 2,000+ men. Three new ships, Frigates, were built, *the U.S.S. Constitution, Constellation, and United States* were under construction but not enough money was appropriated for their completion in time to be used against the Pirates so the President was forced to pay a "ransom" of nearly $1 million for their return. *This embarrassing outcome led many in Congress to call for a stronger central government and military to prevent something like this from happening again.*

c. *Trouble with England, again*

In England's war against France, their ships at sea raided and captured American ships that were violating President Washington's Neutrality Act by trading with both warring countries, making themselves "fair game" for both the French and English Navy to capture them and their cargoes. News of these captures caused outrage to the American trading community which was the backbone of the Federalist party. Congress began war preparations and then, subsequently, learned of a speech by Lord Dorchester to the native Indians encouraging them to drive the Americans back across the Ohio River once and for all time.

Congressional opponents of England demanded commercial retaliation which certainly would have led to a war for which America was not well prepared just a few years after the Revolutionary War. Tensions cooled when the British Foreign Minister revoked the order allowing for the capture of foreign ships.

In April, 1794, after this news reached Philadelphia, the President nominated Chief Justice Jay as an "Envoy Extraordinary to England" to try to prevent another war between America and England.

The main object of Jay's mission, however, was to obtain British evacuation of the northwest posts. In 1792, the Governor of Canada proposed that the entire area between the Great

Lakes and the Ohio river with some land from New York and Vermont be erected into a satellite Indian state. Meanwhile, the British government informed America that it would retain the northwest posts, regardless of American actions. Meanwhile, Governor Simcoe of Upper Canada set up a new garrison 100 miles southwest of Detroit.

d. **Indian Troubles**

Major General "Mad Anthony" Wayne was placed in command of a military force which eventually defeated an Indian force at the "Battle of Fallen Timbers", 8/20/1794, followed by a Peace Conference on 6/16/1795 at Greenville, Ohio. 1,130 Indian delegates from tribes between the Great Lakes, Mississippi, and Ohio rivers attended. The Conference lasted for six weeks and, finally, on *8/3/1795, the "Treaty of Greenville",* signed between the Assembled tribes and the "fifteen fires" of the States. The Indians ceded the southeastern corner of the Northwest Territories plus the sites of Vincennes, Detroit, and Chicago. *This ended almost 20 years of Indian fighting and the last phase of the War of Independence.*

e. *Jay's Treaty (6/25/1795)*

This Treaty obtained the prime objects of his mission;

- British promise to evacuate the Northwest Posts by 1796.

- A limited right of American vessels to trade with the British West Indies.

It preserved the peace, secured America's territorial integrity, and established a basis for western expansion. Other unsettled questions were referred to commissions to discuss and settle;

- Maine and New Brunswick boundary dispute

- Payment by America of pre-war debts to England and/ or loyalists and citizens

- Payment by Britain to America for illegal captures of American ships.

The Treaty wasn't well received at first primarily by pro-French citizens seeking a war with England. ***The Senate passed the Treaty with a bare 2/3 majority and the President approved it on 6/25/1795.***

f. ***Treaty of San Lorenzo (10/27/1795) (Pinckney's Treaty) Allowed the United States the right of transit at New Orleans.*** Baron de Carondelet, Spanish Governor of Louisiana, attempted to establish an Indian satellite state in the southwest, built a Fort at Chickasaw Bluffs (present-day Memphis, Tennessee) and persuaded the Creek and Cherokee Indians to denounce their earlier Treaties with America. Thomas Pinckney was sent to Madrid, Spain, by President Washington to discuss the issue.

Spain was receptive because it suspected that Jay's Treaty included a secret Anglo-American alliance and feared losing their Louisiana interests to America. ***The Treaty gave America the right to navigate the lower Mississippi River, and the transit rights at New Orleans. Spain then evacuated her posts on the east bank of the Mississippi River.***

g. ***Cabinet Problems***

Edmund Randolph replaced Thomas Jefferson as Secretary of State upon Jefferson's retirement. It was later proved that Randolph was secretly working against the President's policies. It caused the President to give up his attempt to govern with a bi-partisan cabinet. Thomas Pickering, a New England Federalist, now became the Secretary of State. Hamilton had already resigned after the Whiskey Rebellion and was replaced by the first Auditor of the Treasury, Oliver Wolcott, and James Mc Henry became Secretary of War. All three were Hamilton supporters.

C.   THE ELECTION OF 1796

By refusing to stand for a third term, Washington established the two-term tradition in American politics, ***which became Constitutional in 1951 by virtue of the 22nd Amendment.***

The Republicans nominated Jefferson and Aaron Burr while the Federalists countered with John Adams and Thomas Pinckney. *The central issue was Jay's Treaty.* The election resulted in a narrow Federalist victory with Adams receiving 71 votes in the Electoral college and Jefferson the Republican receiving 68 electoral votes to become Vice-President, *so the process produced two leaders of different political parties. This problem was fixed by the 12th Amendment in 1804.*

1. **WASHINGTON'S FAREWELL ADDRESS (9/17/1796)**
   Some of the key points in his Address were;
   a. Plea for Union
   b. Fear of political parties and politicians
   c. Observe good faith and justice toward all nations, cultivate peace and harmony with all
   d. Doctrine of international isolation from the problems of Europe because they have different interests. *Participate only in temporary alliances.*

D. PRESIDENT JOHN ADAMS ADMINISTRATION (1797-1801)

John Adams was viewed as extremely experienced in politics and political science but did not have a suitable temperament for the Presidency. He did not have a good reputation as an Executive, did not generate personal loyalties, and had few close friends in the political world. He also appeared to be *politically naïve as he retained Washington's Cabinet unaware that they were plotting against him with Hamilton.* Three key members, Pickering, Wolcott, and Mc Henry were devoted to Hamilton and would refer every major issue to him, act on his advice, and then persuade the President to approve. *Hamilton, who Adams detested, actually ran the Adams administration until 1799 when Adams discovered their betrayal and fired them.* On 5/6/1800 he requested the resignation of Mc Henry, effective 5/31/1800. On 5/10 he requested the resignation of Pickering who was then dismissed from office on 5/12. Pickering was succeeded by John Marshall on 5/13/1800.

Adams faced a more difficult foreign situation in 1797 than did Washington in his first administration. Those issues were;

1. **RELATIONS WITH FRANCE**

    France's reaction to Jay's Treaty was aggressive against American shipping. By June, 1797, more than 300 American vessels had been captured by France. The French government, the "Directory", refused to accept the new American Minister to France, and the official government language toward America became very threatening. Adams announced that he would follow Washington's policy of neutrality but that he would not allow any "indignities". He sent a three- man mission to Paris, consisting of Elbridge Gerry, a Jeffersonian, plus two strong Federalists, John Marshall and Charles Cotesworth Pinckney.

    In the first year of the Adams administration there was no news about the success of the mission. Meanwhile, war was on the horizon in Europe. By late 1797, just Britain, America, and Russia were still neutral. The three-man mission arrived in Paris in October, 1797 during the height of the Directory's successes.

    a. *The "XYZ Affair"*

    Relations with France were further damaged when Talleyrand, the French Foreign Minister, sent three representatives to demand a bribe of the American envoys before they would agree to meet with them. The envoys were insulted and refused the offers. The American envoys sent dispatches back home where they arrived in early 1798 and were sent to Congress by President Adams. *The reaction against France was devastating, including those who were pro-French.*

    Adams and the Federalists adopted a policy of armed neutrality, developed a separate Navy department, and strengthened the military. The American Navy teamed up with the English Navy to defeat French privateers at sea.

    b. *Resolution of the French Problem*

    Adams purpose was to protect American commerce and force the French Republic to respect our sovereignty. He was willing

to accept war if declared by France but hoped to avoid it.
Most Federalists agreed with him but not Hamilton and his
strongest supporters. Meanwhile, Jefferson assured Talleyrand
that peace was in their best interests and that President Adams
was serious about wanting to avoid a war but would fight, if
necessary. Talleyrand then informed Jefferson that any new
American Minister to France would be welcomed, they lifted
their embargo on American shipping, and promised to respect
American shipping.

The Hamilton Federalists did not believe the apparent change
in French attitude and was prepared to declare War on France
as soon as Congress convened. Hamilton had plans to not only
fight the French, but also the Spanish, as French allies, and he
planned to capture New Orleans and Florida.

Adams stopped the Hamilton plan by nominating a new
Minister to France on 3/18/1799. The Republicans asked
for a commission of three which the President accepted but
Secretary Pickering delayed its departure. President Adams,
out of town, learned of the delay, and quickly returned to
Philadelphia to send the mission to Paris. They reached Paris
in time to deal with Napoleon Bonaparte who had replaced
the Directory and became the "First Consul". For seven
months the negotiations dragged on because he would not
admit any French liability unless America reinstated the
Alliance of 1778 which Congress had renounced during the
height of anti-French feeling in America. The American
missionaries signed a "Commercial Convention" on
9/30/1800 which required captured warships to be returned
but not captured privateers. This was known as the "Treaty
of Morfontaine".

Substantial gains to America from this quasi-war were the
protection of American commerce and the rebirth of the
American Navy.

2. **FEDERALIST INTOLERANCE AND THE ELECTION OF 1800**

Since the Federalists made some modest gains in the Congressional elections of 1798, they were feeling very confident of their position within the government, especially since they had lost the House of Representatives in 1792.

a. *Alien & Sedition Acts of 1798*
This was the first application of the Federalists new-found strength in the Congress. Its primary purpose was to weaken the Democratic-Republican party (Jefferson) and its platform was;

- A Naturalization Act which increased from 5-14 years the time required for immigrants to become American citizens. *The Federalists wanted to lengthen the naturalization process since most immigrants upon becoming American citizens tended to vote for the Democratic-Republican candidates.*

- An Alien Act which empowered the President to deport any alien whom he considered dangerous to the country.

- Alien-Enemies Act which authorized the detention of enemy aliens in time of war. Although not used by Adams, these laws caused some aliens to leave the country and frightened others to refrain from speaking out against the Federalists.

- Sedition Act which provided fines and imprisonment for any person who uttered or wrote "false, scandalous, and malicious" things about the President. *Even Hamilton disapproved of this law and many considered it a violation of the 1st Amendment.* The Sedition Act remained in effect and was used to bring to trial and convict 10 Democratic-Republican printers and editors

b. *The Virginia & Kentucky Resolutions (1798-1799)*
Instead of weakening their political opponents, the Federalist passage of the Alien & Sedition Acts actually strengthened their opponents. Many citizens felt that the Federalist party threatened their civil liberties and the Democrat-Republican party used that negative reaction against the Acts to pass these Resolutions.

At the urging of Madison and Jefferson, the State Legislatures of Virginia and Kentucky *passed Resolutions condemning these Acts as unconstitutional.* The Resolutions presented the *States Rights doctrine claiming that;*

- The Federal government was created by the States to serve as their agent

- State Legislatures could declare laws of Congress unconstitutional and null and void. *This was known as "nullification" which would become a major issue leading to the American Civil War some 75 years later.*

The "compact" or "States rights" theory embodied in the Resolves is significant because Kentucky declared that whenever Congress transcended its powers each state had the right to judge for itself the mode and measure of redress.

Both State Legislatures were preparing for the coming Presidential election to rally their followers. The principle of the Resolves of 1798-1799 became an issue in the battle over State rights vs the Central government authority.

The "Federalist Reign of Terror" as the Republicans called the 2nd half of the Adams administration alarmed the nation fearing for its personal liberties.

E.   THE ELECTION OF 1800

Presidential candidates were selected by party caucuses in Congress. The Republicans nominated Jefferson and Burr again. The Federalists again nominated John Adams with Charles Cotesworth Pinckney.

Neither in this nor in any Presidential election prior to the Jacksonian era did candidates make speeches or issue statements. Electioneering was done by newspapers, pamphlets and occasional public meetings.

It was a close election with 73 Republican and 65 Federalist electors chosen. *Jefferson and Burr tied for first place requiring the House of Representatives to cast the final votes with each state having one vote and requiring a majority of one vote for election.*

The Federalists saw an opportunity for making trouble and some voted for Burr, fearing Jefferson. Burr refused to go along with their plan. It took 35 ballots and, by 2/17/1801, they were still deadlocked. There was talk of a civil war but finally , three Federalists swung the election to Jefferson by a majority of two states.

The Presidential election cannot fairly be called a popular verdict since over half the electors were chosen by state legislatures. In the Congressional elections, the Republicans obtained a significant majority and most of the newly elected Senators were Republicans which meant that the Federalists lost every branch of government except the Judiciary which Jefferson soon attempted to purge by impeachment.

So, the Federalists became the minority party even though it contained more talent and virtue but less political common sense. *It had been their task to get the new government started and they succeeded to a large degree. However, they didn't have the political vision to see the changing nature of the electorate nor the judgment to resist the temptation to press their Congressional advantage to pursue unwise and threatening policies, such as the Alien & Sedition Acts which frightened enough voters to cause them to lose their entire power.*

F.   SUMMARY OF THE FEDERALIST ERA (Attachment 25c)

Although the Federalists lost the Executive and Legislative branches of government, Federalist judges, appointed for life, for many years dominated the Supreme Court. Never again did they win a national election and slowly disappeared from American political life.

Accomplishments of the Federalist Party;

1. Used the Constitution to develop a workable system of government

2. Stabilized government and expanded Federal power at the expense of the States

3. Endowed the new Republic with a firm financial system

4. Established the national credit and fostered economic prosperity

5. Placed an emphasis on a diversified economy and prepared the way for the industrial civilization of the 19th century

6. Created a Court system

7. Demonstrated the ability of the government to enforce its laws

8. Admitted three new States into the Union

9. Kept the nation from War and instituted a foreign policy of isolation

Reasons for the downfall of the Federalist Party;

1. The spread of democratic ideals throughout the nation, especially in the west

2. The growing realization that the Federalist party did not trust the common people

3. Widespread opposition to the Federalist economic measures

4. Considerable opposition to the Federalist's pro-English policies

5. Bitter intra-party rivalry between Adams and Hamilton

6. Opposition of the people to the Alien & Sedition Acts

The people were wise when they elected Federalists at a time when order and efficiency were needed to place the new nation on its feet. They were equally wise when they repudiated the party as soon as the Republic was established. Hamilton and his followers belonged to the Aristocratic past_rather than the democratic future. Their defeat demonstrated that any party, to enjoy success in America, must be concerned with the welfare of the many rather than the few.

G.   MISCELLANEOUS INFORMATION

THE ECONOMIC AND SOCIAL CONDITIONS IN 1789

The population as of 1790 was slightly less than four million with approximately 600,000 slaves. Most people still lived along the coastline with about 100,000 living in the frontier regions. No more than five cities had a population in excess of 10,000; Philadelphia, New York, Boston, Charleston, and Baltimore. More than 90% of the people were engaged in farming- related activities.

WHAT WAS FIRST BANK OF U.S.?

It was a private Bank which held all United States Funds and issued Notes which were to serve as money. Its' charter expired in 1811.

WHAT WAS THE CHIEF PROBLEM OF OUR FOREIGN RELATIONS DURING THE FEDERALIST ERA?

France was involved in a general European War with England which had always been a serious rival. Despite our 1778 Alliance with France, President Washington declared our Neutrality which President Adams continued in spite of considerable pressure to end. *To preserve this Neutrality while dealing with significant domestic challenges was a great challenge of American diplomacy at a time when the new nation was militarily and economically weakened.*

WHY DID PRESIDENT WASHINGTON CHOOSE NEUTRALITY?

America was open to attack by the English in Canada, Spanish in Florida, and the Indians in the west. The country had not yet recovered from the effects of the Revolutionary War and *another conflict would have crippled our economy at a time when we needed peace to organize the government and stabilize the financial situation.*

WHY WAS IT SO HARD FOR AMERICA TO REMAIN NEUTRAL?

France resented our neutrality especially since they had helped us during our time of need. France continued to try to involve us, through the efforts of Citizen Genet and the attacks on our shipping. England refused to give up their fur-trading posts in the Northwest territories, interfered with our commerce, and denied us the privilege of their West Indian trade plus they insisted on the right to stop and search American ships.

HOW DID PRESIDENT WASHINGTON TRY TO SETTLE THE DIFFICULTIES WITH ENGLAND?

Sent John Jay to England to negotiate a treaty (Jay's Treaty of 1795) which achieved the following;

- England would withdraw its troops from the Northwest

- Arbitration commissions were created to settle outstanding financial claims

- Limited rights were won to trade with the British West Indies

The Treaty was ratified in 1795 but had to overcome significant opposition because;

- There was no provision protecting our freedom of the seas

- There was no mention of England having violated our Neutrality rights such as the seizure of our ships and the impressments of American sailors

- It only granted a limited right to trade with the British West Indies

Although not totally supported, the Treaty did keep us out of war and helped maintain the peace at a time of great need.

WHAT EFFORTS WERE MADE TO SETTLE OUR DIFFICULTIES WITH FRANCE?

President Adams sent three commissioners to Paris for negotiations but they were insulted and the matter became worse. This was known as the *"XYZ affair"*. In response, he ordered Naval warfare against France which lasted until Napoleon Bonaparte came to power. With Napoleon, we made a peace which was further strengthened eventually with the Louisiana Purchase in 1803.

WHAT DIFFICULTIES DID AMERICA FACE WITH SPAIN?

The right to navigate the Mississippi river was a significant problem with Spain which controlled the region. The issue of the "right of deposit" (goods) at the port of New Orleans was also significant since Spain controlled the port. The problem of settling the southern boundary of the United States.

WHAT EFFORTS WERE MADE TO SETTLE THE DIFFICULTIES WITH SPAIN?

The Pinckney Treaty of 1795 ("Treaty of San Lorenzo") was signed which provided for;

- Spain accepted the 31st degree parallel as southern boundary of the United States

- Granted America "right of deposit" at the port of New Orleans free of any duties

- Guaranteed Americans the right of free navigation of the Mississippi river

- Promised to curb Indian attacks on the American frontier settlements in the southwest

WHAT DIFFICULTIES DID THE NEW NATION FACE WITH THE INDIANS?

- Continued Indian attacks against frontier settlements in the Northwest territories

- The danger of Indian attacks on the southeastern border settlements

- These dangers hindered the advance of settlers into the frontier areas

WHAT EFFORTS WERE MADE TO SOLVE THE INDIAN PROBLEMS?

An expedition led by General "Mad Anthony" Wayne defeated the Indians at the "Battle of Fallen Timbers" in 1794. The resulting "Treaty of Greenville" of 1795 provided for;

- The Indians surrendered their rights to southern and eastern Ohio and promised to maintain peaceful relations with the settlers.

- The Creeks and Cherokees yielded their lands in the southeastern part of the United States.

  These agreements plus the Jay and Pinckney Treaties stimulated our westward expansion and helped prove that the new nation was national-minded, by looking after the interests of the west as well as the older East-coast.

WHY WAS THE ELECTION OF THOMAS JEFFERSON IN 1800 REFERRED TO AS THE "REVOLUTION OF 1800"?

It brought the new Democratic-Republican Party into the country's political life. It ended the Federalist Party control of the Legislative and Executive branches of the government and *represented the triumph of;*

- democracy and individual freedom over conservatism

- the common man over the so-called aristocracy of wealth and social position

- Jeffersonian simplicity over Federalist grandeur and excessive pride

- the doctrine of "strict interpretation" of the Constitution as opposed to a "broad interpretation" of the Constitution which had the effect of enlarging the Federal Government at the expense of State Governments.

WHAT WERE SOME OF THE MAJOR IDEAS AND PRINCIPLES WHICH GUIDED THOMAS JEFFERSON'S CAREER?

Faith in the common man, mostly the small farmer and landowner, whom he regarded as the foundation of the Republic. Belief in popular education, religious freedom and faith in human reason. Belief in the rights of the states as opposed to the all-powerful central government. Belief in the supremacy of civil over military authority. Belief in simplicity in government as opposed to pomp and ceremony of an aristocracy. Urged peace, commerce, and honest friendship with all nations and entangling alliances with none.

WHAT CHANGES IN GOVERNMENT POLICY DID PRESIDENT JEFFERSON INITIATE?

He allowed most of the major features of the Hamilton financial program plus supported;

- Repeal of the unpopular Whiskey Tax

- Repeal of sections of the Alien and Sedition Acts which were still in effect and the pardoning of those men who had been imprisoned under the Sedition Law

- Reduction in the size of the Army and Navy

- Reduction of the Federal debt under Sec Treas Albert Gallatin

H.   KEY DATES AND SIGNIFICANT EVENTS

4/6	1789	George Washington with 69 votes unanimously elected President , John Adams with 34 votes chosen as Vice-President
4/8	1789	House of Representatives first session
4/15	1789	Establishment of Federalist newspaper, "Gazette of the United States", edited by John Fenno
4/30	1789	Washington inaugurated as first President in New York city
7/4	1789	First Tariff Act levied higher duties on foreign vessels than American and placed English and French vessels in the same class.
7/27	1789	Department of State first Executive department created with Thomas Jefferson appointed as Secretary of State
8/7	1789	War Department created
9/2	1789	Treasury Organic Act established the Treasury Department. Still in effect today
9/9	1789	Discussion of a "Bill of Rights"
9/11	1789	Alexander Hamilton appointed as Secretary of Treasury
9/12	1789	Henry Knox appointed as Secretary of War
9/24	1789	Federal Judiciary Act passed
9/25	1789	Amendments submitted to the states for ratification; 10 ratified by the states and ***become the Bill of Rights***
9/26	1798	Thomas Jefferson appointed as Secretary of State.
9/26	1789	John Jay becomes Chief Justice of the Supreme Court
9/26	1789	Edmund Randolph becomes Attorney General
11/20	1789	New Jersey first state to ratify Bill of Rights

12/19	1789	Maryland second state to ratify Bill of Rights
12/22	1789	North Carolina third state to ratify Bill of Rights.
Jan	1790	The first issue of Washington's first term was the ***fiscal program developed by Alexander Hamilton*** and submitted to the House of Representatives in a series of reports on the national and state debt, an excise tax, and a national bank. ***Controversy over these proposals led to the Party split between Federalists and Republicans.***
1/14	1790	First report on the public credit dealt with the debt inherited from the Articles of Confederation.
2/22	1790	James Madison proposal to discriminate between original holders and subsequent purchasers rejected by the House 3-1 vote.
4/12	1790	Assumption proposal rejected by House of Representatives, led by James Madison and Virginia, vote of 31-29.
7/10	1790	North-South compromise on Assumption plan…Washington, D.C. becomes National Capital, Philadelphia temporary capital by vote of 32-29.
7/26	1790	2nd part of the compromise, Assumption plan approved by House vote of 34-28.
8/4	1790	Funding provision of Assumption plan becomes law
12/13	1790	Hamilton submits to House his report on a National Bank
12/16	1790	Virginia still opposed to Assumption plan, passes "Virginia Resolves", drafted by Patrick Henry. ***Basis of opposition is that they find no authorization in the Constitution for Congress assuming state debts.***

2/15	1791	Jefferson opinion that the National Bank was unconstitutional was based on a "strict construction" of the Constitution. ***Argues that creation of the national bank was not among the powers specifically delegated to Congress.***
2/23	1791	***Hamilton opinion argues doctrine of "implied powers" ("loose construction") that the proposed bank was related to Congressional power to collect taxes and regulate trade. In his view, a delegated power implied the employment of such means as were proper for its execution.*** It was not until 1819 that Chief Justice John Marshall's opinion in ***the case of "Mc Culloch vs Maryland" that the doctrine of "implied powers" became part of the Constitution.*** Washington not convinced of wisdom of either side's argument but he favors the Hamilton theory because he thinks he should defer to the Cabinet officer closest to the issue.
2/25	1791	U.S. Bank chartered but President Washington asks members of his Cabinet to submit written opinions on the constitutionality of the measure.
3/3	1791	Hamilton 2nd report on public credit recommended excise tax on manufacture of distilled liquors as means of supplementing revenue yielded by the tariff. This levy imposed a heavy burden on backwoods farmers for whom distilling was a means of disposing of surplus grain. It was strongly opposed.
3/4	1791	Vermont added as 14th state
12/15	1791	***Bill of Rights ratified by the states and becomes part of the Constitution;*** Bank of the United States chartered by Congress

2/21	1792	**Presidential Succession Act passed the House after passing the Senate 27-24 provided that in case of the removal, death, resignation, or disability of both the President and Vice-President, the succession hierarchy would be;**

President pro-tempore of the Senate
Speaker of the House
Sec of State (Jefferson proposed, first defeated by Federalists but eventually approved by Act of 1886)

6/1	1792	Kentucky admitted as 15th state
Jul–Oct	1792	Jefferson & Hamilton feud
9/29	1792	President Washington issues Proclamation warning that the excise tax would be enforced.
12/5	1792	Presidential Election…Washington 132 Electoral votes, John Adams 77 Electoral votes. Anti-Federalist George Clinton 50 votes for Vice President.
1/21	1793	King Louis XVI executed in France
2/1	1793	France declares War on England, Spain, and Holland.
4/8	1793	Citizen Genet affair
4/22	1793	Washington Neutrality Act
6/5	1793	Jefferson informs Genet that he overstepped his authority. Genet promises to comply but he breaks his promise to Jefferson to cease his activities.
7/31	1793	Jefferson offers his resignation as President Washington begins to lean toward Hamilton policies. Resignation effective 12/31/1793. Replaced by Edmund Randolph 11/2/1794.
8/2	1793	Cabinet recommends Genet recall

3/5	1794	11th Amendment proposed by Georgia and other states against Supreme Court decision in "Chisholm vs Georgia" case of 1793 providing that a state was not sue-able by a citizen of another state. Ratified 1/8/1798.
April	1794	President Washington nominates Chief Justice John Jay as a special envoy to England to try to prevent war.
4/19	1794	Senate confirms Jay nomination as special envoy to England.
6/5	1794	Neutrality Act passed
Jul-Nov	1794	The Whiskey Rebellion was the result of discontent over the enforcement of an excise tax in Western Pennsylvania.
8/20	1794	General Mad Anthony Wayne defeats Indians at the Battle of Fallen Timbers.
11/19	1794	Jay's Treaty
1/2	1795	Timothy Pickering named as Secretary of War.
1/29	1795	Naturalization Act requires a five year residency.
1/31	1795	Hamilton resigns as Secretary of the Treasury and is succeeded by Oliver Wolcott Jr., but he continues as an unofficial adviser on major policy decisions.
May	1795	Whiskey Rebellion insurgents tried for treason with two convicted but pardoned by President Washington. "Mad Anthony" Wayne won the Battle of Fallen Timbers. Congress defines rights of Neutrals at sea
6/25	1795	Senate ratifies Jay Treaty. House Republicans attempt to block treaty by denying appropriations to enforce provisions.

7/22	1795	Hamilton supports Jay Treaty terms in papers authored as "Camillus".
8/3	1795	The Treaty of Greenville requires the Indians to cede the southeast corner of the Northwest Territory plus Vincennes, Detroit, and Chicago.
8/19	1795	Edmund Randolph resigns as Secretary of State due to suspicion of corruption which was never tried in court. Washington believed Randolph had conspired with French Minister Fauchet to block ratification of Jay's Treaty.
10/27	1795	Pinckney's Treaty (Treaty of San Lorenzo). Signed at Madrid, Spain. Necessary because of the failure of the Jay-Gardoqui negotiations
1/27	1796	Randolph is succeeded by Timothy Pickering as Secretary of State. James McHenry becomes Secretary of War.
3/24	1796	The House of Representatives request background documents on the Jay Treaty but it is refused by President Washington, asserting Executive authority.
4/30	1796	Appropriation approved for Jay Treaty enforcement
6/1	1796	Tennessee admitted 16th state
9/17	1796	President Washington farewell address
Dec	1796	Charles Cotesworth Pinckney named Minister to France but they refuse to receive him.
12/7	1796	Presidential Election of John Adams
5/31	1797	Relations with France turn bad
10/4	1797	Commissioners arrive in Paris
10/8	1797	Commissioners unofficially received by French Foreign Minister Talleyrand who finds pretext for delaying meetings.

10/18	1797	XYZ Affair
10/18	1797	John Adams inaugurated as 2nd President
1/17	1798	Commissioner John Marshall gives firm negative response to XYZ demands
3/19	1798	President Adams reports to Congress on the failure of negotiations. Elbridge Gerry remains in Paris after being told by Talleyrand that if he departed, France would declare war on America.
4/3	1798	President Adams submitted to Congress the" XYZ affair" correspondence which aroused public opinion regardless of political party.
	1798–1800	Undeclared naval war with France. Federalists are pro-war against France and are led by Pickering who wants an immediate declaration of war. President Adams favors a peaceful resolution while strengthening national defense.
6/18	1798	The Naturalization Act is changed from a five year to a 14 year period of residence required for full citizenship. It is repealed in 1802.
6/25	1798	The Alien Act authorizes the President to order out of America all aliens regarded as dangerous to public peace and safety, or suspected of treasonable or secret inclinations. Expired in 1802.
7/6	1798	The Alien Enemies Act authorizes the President, in time of declared war, to arrest, imprison, or banish aliens subject to an enemy power.
11/16	1798	Congress repeals Treaties with France, terminating the alliance
11/20	1798	The Kentucky Resolutions are passed by the State legislature in two stages; drafted by Thomas Jefferson.

12/24	1798	The Virginia Resolutions are authored by James Madison and passed by the State legislature.
3/5	1799	An undeclared Naval begins with the French capture of a U.S. ship and continues until a 2/1/1800 battle between the Constellation and a French ship.
Oct	1799	Congress passed Amendment XI to the Constitution, which the States ratified. It prohibited the Federal Judiciary to entertain any suit brought against a State by a citizen of another State or Nation. Thus, the States recovered a traditional Royal prerogative, to be sued only with their consent.
5/6	1800	President Adams sends a Peace Commission to Paris. They arrive in Paris in time to deal with Bonaparte who had replaced the Directorate. President Adams realized he was the victim of a Cabinet conspiracy by Pickering and Mc Henry who are working with Hamilton to defeat him in 1800. President Adams requests the resignation of Mc Henry, effective 5/31.
5/10	1800	President Adams requests the resignation of Pickering who is dismissed from office.
5/13	1800	John Marshall succeeds Pickering as Secretary of State
12/3	1800	***The major campaign issues of the Presidential Election are;***

> Alien & Sedition Acts
> Increase by the Federalists of direct taxes occasioned by heavy defense needs
> Reduction of trade with France
> Growth of anti-English sentiment over impressment of American sailors

2/11	1801	***Results of the Election are;***

> Thomas Jefferson & Aaron Burr
> > 73 Electoral votes each
>
> John Adams
> > 65 Electoral votes
>
> Thomas Pinckney
> > 64 Electoral votes
>
> John Jay
> > 1 Electoral vote

The Election is thrown into the House of Representatives where it is still deadlocked. The Federalist caucus supports Burr; Hamilton uses his influence to support Thomas Jefferson break the deadlock.

2/17	1801	On the 36th ballot Jefferson is chosen as President by 10 States and Burr is selected as Vice President.
12/9	1803	To prevent a similar situation in the future, the 12th Amendment is proposed by Congress
9/25	1804	The 12th Amendment is ratified which provides for separate balloting for President and Vice President.

I.   REVIEW QUESTIONS

(Multiple Choice)

1. What were some of the first problems faced by President Washington?
    a. Dealing with Indian problems resulting from westward expansion
    b. Creating a new government
    c. Passing a "Bill of Rights"
    d. All of the above
    e. None of the above

2. Who was the first Secretary of State of the first Washington administration?
    a. Ben Franklin
    b. John Adams
    c. John Jay
    d. Thomas Jefferson

3. Who was the first to be offered the position of Secretary of Treasury?
    a. Alexander Hamilton
    b. Robert Morris
    c. John Jay
    d. None of the above

4. Which state was the first to Ratify a State Bill of Rights?
    a. Virginia
    b. Massachusetts
    c. New York
    d. None of the above

5. What issues did the Hamilton Financial plan attempt to resolve?
    a. Payment of foreign debts
    b. Create a National Bank
    c. Assume State debts
    d. All of the above

6. Who was appointed the first Chief Justice of the Supreme Court?
    a. Ben Franklin
    b. John Jay
    c. John Marshall
    d. Timothy Pickering

7. Which country failed to live up to its promises to vacate the Northwest Territory military outposts?
    a. England
    b. France
    c. Spain
    d. None of the above

(True or False)

8. The Federalists supported the principles of the French Revolution.
    a. TRUE
    b. FALSE

9. The Jeffersonian Anti-Federalists believed in limited government and strict interpretation of the Constitution.
    a. TRUE
    b. FALSE

10. The Federalist Party opposed the creation of the National Bank.
    a. TRUE
    b. FALSE

11. The year 1794 was referred to as "The Crucial Year" of the Washington Presidency.
    a. TRUE
    b. FALSE

12. The Jay Treaty was passed and approved by the President on 6/25/1794.
    a. TRUE
    b. FALSE

13. The key issue in the Election of 1796 was the Jay's Treaty.
    a. TRUE
    b. FALSE

14. President John Adams was an Anti-Federalist.
    a. TRUE
    b. FALSE

15. The Virginia and Kentucky Resolutions of 1798-1799 were opposed to the Alien & Sedition Acts.
    a. TRUE
    b. FALSE

CHAPTER 25 SUMMARY

THE FEDERALIST ERA

A. **PRESIDENT WASHINGTON'S FIRST ADMINISTRATION** (1789-1793)

1. *Issues confronting the new President;*
    a. Create a new government.
    b. Financial and commercial problems.
    c. A weakened Army and Navy.
    d. Create a Federal Judiciary and Court system.
    e. Pass a "Bill of Rights" to complete the Ratification of the Constitution.

2. *Actions taken;*
    a. Appoint Cabinet members.
    b. Pass the "Judiciary Act" of 1789 which creates a Supreme Court and a lower Court system.
    c. Alexander Hamilton develops and proposes a Financial plan to fix the national financial and commercial problems.
    d. A *"Bill of Rights"* is developed and proposed to Congress and eventually ratified by all 13 States, thus completing the new Constitution.
    e. The development of an Indian policy.
    f. The development of a Foreign policy

3. *The beginnings of Political Parties;*
    a. *Result from personal and policy differences between Jefferson and Hamilton.*

b. *"Federalists" and "Anti-Federalists" evolve from their position for or against ratification of the new Constitution. They eventually evolve into political factions and then become formal political parties with Congressonal candidates.*

B. **PRESIDENT WASHINGTON'S SECOND ADMINISTRATION (1793-1797)**

1. *Foreign issues dominate;*
   a. The French Revolution and the Citizen Genet affair.
   b. Problems with the English and the resulting Jay's Treaty.
   c. Problems with Spain resulting in Pinckney's Treaty.
   d. The Barbary Pirates.

2. *Domestic issues;*
   a. Whiskey Rebellion.
   b. Indian problems on the new frontier.
   c. Growing political unrest furthers the development of political factions and parties.
   d. Washington's Neutrality Policy.

3. Washington's Farewell Address.

C. **PRESIDENT ADAM'S ADMINISTRATION** (1797-1801)

1. *Problems with France;*
   a. French reaction to Jay's Treaty and the "XYZ Affair".
   b. Adams retains Washington's Neutrality policy.

2. *Adams Cabinet betrays him.*

3. *The "Federalist Party" passes the "Alien & Sedition Acts".*
   a. The "Virginia" and "Kentucky Resolves" are passed as a reaction to the "Alien & Sedition Acts".

4. *The Election of Thomas Jefferson in 1800 ends the "Federalist Era".*
   a. A Constitutional Issue arises.
   b.. The beginnings of formal Political Parties.

25a

BILL OF RIGHTS

1. FREEDOM OF SPEECH, PRESS, RELIGION, AND PETITION

Congress shall make no law respecting the establishment of religion or prohibiting the free exercise thereof, or abridging the freedom of speech, or of the press, or the right of the people to peaceably to assemble, and to petition the government for a redress of grievances.

2. RIGHT TO KEEP AND BEAR ARMS

A well-regulated militia, being necessary to the security of a free state, the right of the people to keep and bear arms, shall not be infringed.

3. CONDITIONS FOR QUARTERS OF SOLDIERS

No soldier shall, in time of peace, be quartered in any house, without the consent of the owner, nor in time of war, but in a manner to be prescribed by law.

4. RIGHT OF SEARCH AND SEIZURE REGULATED

The right of the people to be secure in their persons, houses, papers, and effects, against unreasonable searches and seizures, shall not be violated, and no warrants shall issue, but upon probable cause, supported by oath or affirmation, and particularly describing the place to be searched, and the persons or things to be seized.

5. PROVISIONS CONCERNING PROSECUTION

No person shall be held to answer for a capital, or otherwise infamous crime, unless on a presentment or indictment of a Grand Jury. Nor shall any person be subject for the same offense to be twice put in jeopardy of life or limb. Nor shall anyone be compelled in any criminal case to be a witness against himself or be deprived of life, liberty, or property, without due process of law. Nor shall private property be taken for public use without just compensation.

6. RIGHT TO A SPEEDY TRIAL AND WITNESSES

In all criminal prosecutions, the accused shall enjoy the right to a speedy and public trial by an impartial jury of the state and district wherein the crime shall have been committed. The accused shall be informed of the nature and cause of the accusation, to be confronted with witnesses against him, and to have a compulsory process for obtaining witnesses in his favor, and to have the assistance of counsel for his defense.

7. RIGHT TO A TRIAL BY JURY

In suits at common law, where the value in controversy shall exceed $20, the right of trial by jury shall be preserved and no fact tried by a jury shall be otherwise re-examined in any court of the United States.

8. EXCESSIVE BAIL, CRUEL AND UNJUST PUNISHMENT

Excessive bail shall not be required, nor excessive fines imposed, nor cruel and unusual punishment inflicted.

9. RULE OF CONSTRUCTION OF THE CONSTITUTION

The enumeration in the Constitution, of certain rights, shall not be construed to deny or disparage others retained by the people.

10. RIGHTS OF THE STATES UNDER THE CONSTITUTION

The powers not delegated to the United States by the Constitution, nor prohibited by it to the State, are reserved to the States, respectively, or to the people.

25b
P O L I T I C A L   P A R T Y   D I F F E R E N C E S

FEDERALIST PARTY	CATEGORY	DEMOCRAT-REPUBLICAN PARTY
ALEXANDER HAMILTON & JOHN ADAMS	LEADERS	THOMAS JEFFERSON, JAMES MADISON, EDMUND RANDOLPH
FAVORS "LOOSE" INTERPRETATION OF CONSTITUTION BASED ON DOCTRINE OF "IMPLIED POWERS"	VIEWS OF THE CONSTITUTION	FAVORS "STRICT" INTERPRETATION OF CONSTITUTION LIMITING POWERS OF CONGRESS TO THOSE SPECIFICALLY DELEGATED BY THE CONSTITUTION
FAVORS STRONG CENTRAL GOVERNMENT USING BOTH DELEGATED AND IMPLIED POWERS. DISTRUSTED "COMMON PEOPLE". AND FEARED "EXCESSES OF DEMOCRACY".	VIEWS OF GOVERNMENT	FAVORS STRONG STATE GOVERNMENT WITH A LIMITED CENTRAL GOVERNMENT AND POWERS. GOVERNMENT SHOULD WORK FOR THE COMMON PEOPLE AND ADVOCATE DEMOCRATIC PRINCIPLES.
SUPPORT FINANCIAL PLAN AS BENEFICIAL TO NATIONAL ECONOMIC INTERESTS	VIEWS OF HAMILTON FINANCIAL PLAN	OPPOSED FINANCIAL PLAN AS HARMFUL TO STATE INTERESTS
FAVORS NATIONAL BANK TO STABILIZE CURRENCY AND CREDIT STRUCTURE OF THE COUNTRY	VIEWS OF PROPOSED NATIONAL BANK	OPPOSES BASED ON BELIEF THAT ACTION IS UNCONSTITUTIONAL AND FAVORS "MONEYED INTERESTS"
FAVORS NATIONAL PROTECTIVE TARIFF	VIEWS OF TARIFF ISSUE	OPPOSED TO NATIONAL PROTECTIVE TARIFF
BELIEVES IN GOVERNMENT BY THE "WELL-BORN, ELITE, EDUCATED, AND RICH, KNOWN AS "ARISTOCRACY"	VIEWS OF DEMOCRACY	BELIEVES IN GOVERNMENT BASED ON THE PRINCIPLE OF "THE EQUALITY OF MAN", DEMOCRACY.
COMMERCIAL, MANUFACTURING CLASSES. BANKERS, CREDITORS. STRONG IN THE NORTH AND NEW ENGLAND.	SUPPORTING GROUPS	SMALL FARMERS, SHOP-KEEPERS, LABORERS AND FRONTIERSMEN. STRONG IN SOUTH AND WEST.
FAVORS ENGLAND AGAINST FRANCE AND NAPOLEON	FOREIGN POLICY	FAVORS FRANCE AGAINST ENGLAND

25c

THE ERA OF "FEDERALISM" (1789-1798)

A.   WHAT WAS IT?

1.   THE ERA OF FEDERALISM WAS THAT PERIOD OF
TIME WHEN THOSE FAVORING THE RATIFICATION
OF THE NEW FEDERAL CONSTITUTION CONTROLLED
THE NEW GOVERNMENT. THEY WERE KNOWN AS
"FEDERALISTS".

2.   WHO WERE THE LEADERS?

a. ALEXANDER HAMILTON

b. JAMES MADISON

c. JOHN JAY

3.   WHAT WERE THEIR GOVERNMENT BELIEFS?

a. STRONG CENTRAL GOVERNMENT AND CHIEF
EXECUTIVE WITH LIMITED STATE GOVERNMENT
AUTHORITY.

b. STRONG GOVERNMENT SUPPORT OF FINANCIAL,
COMMERCIAL, AND ECONOMIC POLICIES.

c. BALANCED AND DIVERSIFIED ECONOMIC ORDER.

d. DISTRUST OF "PURE" DEMOCRACY.

e. FAVOR "BROAD/LOOSE" INTERPREPETATION OF
THE NEW FEDERAL CONSTITUTION.

f. FAVOR HAMILTON FINANCIAL PLAN.

g. OPPOSE EXCESSES OF THE FRENCH REVOLUTION
AND SUPPORT CLOSE TIES WITH ENGLAND.

h. SUPPORT HAMILTON AND OPPOSE JEFFERSON.

B.   WHO WERE THEIR OPPONENTS?

1. THOSE WHO WERE OPPOSED TO RATIFICATION OF THE
NEW FEDERAL CONSTITUTION WERE KNOWN AS THE
"ANTI-FEDERALISTS".

2. WHO WERE THE LEADERS?

a. THOMAS JEFFERSON

b. PATRICK HENRY

c. GEORGE MASON

3. WHAT WERE THEIR GOVERNMENT BELIEFS?

    a. FAVOR STRONG STATE GOVERNMENTS
    WITH A LIMITED FEDERAL GOVERNMENT.

    b. FAVOR "STRICT/NARROW" INTERPRETATION OF
    THE NEW FEDERAL CONSTITUTION.

    c. OPPOSE THE HAMILTON FINANCIAL PLAN.

    d. FAVOR AN AGRICULTURAL/AGRARIAN
    DEMOCRACY OVER THE INTERESTS OF THE
    WEALTHY AND PROPERTIED CLASSES.

    e. FAVOR A GOVERNMENT OF THE PEOPLE
    ACTING THROUGH THEIR ELECTED
    REPRESENTATIVES.

    f. SUPPORT THE INITIAL GOALS OF THE
    FRENCH REVOLUTION.

    g. OPPOSE CLOSE TIES WITH ENGLAND.

    h. FAVOR A BROAD DIFFUSION OF WEALTH.

    i. SUPPORT JEFFERSON AND OPPOSE HAMILTON.

C.   ACHIEVEMENTS OF THE FEDERALIST POLITICAL PARTY;

1. USED THE NEW FEDERAL CONSTITUTION TO CREATE
A WORKABLE SYSTEM OF GOVERNMENT.

2. CREATED FINANCIAL & JUDICIARY/COURT SYSTEMS.

3. ADMITTED 3 NEW STATES INTO THE FEDERAL UNION.

4. KEPT THE NATION OUT OF THE EUROPEAN WAR
BETWEEN ENGLAND & FRANCE.

5. SOLVED THE REMAINING PROBLEMS WITH ENGLAND
RESULTING FROM THE REVOLUTIONARY WAR.

D.   REASONS FOR THE FAILURE OF THE FEDERALIST
POLITICAL PARTY;

1. PASSAGE OF THE "ALIEN & SEDITION ACTS" WHICH
CAUSED A NEGATIVE REACTION AGAINST THE PARTY.

2. GROWING SPIRIT OF DEMOCRATIC IDEALS, ESPECIALLY
IN THE WEST, WHICH OPPOSED THE PRINCIPLE OF
GOVERNMENT OF THE WEALTHY & ELITE.

3. OPPOSITION TO ITS' PRO-ENGLISH POLICIES.

4. PERSONAL FEUD BETWEEN HAMILTON & JOHN ADAMS
WHICH SPLIT THE FEDERALIST POLITICAL PARTY.

5. GROWING PERCEPTION OF THE CITIZENS THAT THE
FEDERALISTS DID NOT TRUST THE COMMON PEOPLE TO
GOVERN THEMSELVES.

Appendix 1

APPDX 1		CHAPTER REVIEW ANSWERS																					
CHAPT	#	1	2	3	4	5	6	7	8	9	10	11	12	13	14	15	16	17	19	21	23	24	25
Q	1	B	D	D	C	C	D	C	A	C	C	C	C	C	C	A	D	D	E	B	D	D	D
U	2	D	A	A	B	C	D	A	B	D	A	B	D	C	D	C	A	D	B	D	C	D	D
E	3	C	C	C	D	A	B	B	C	C	C	D	B	B	B	C	B	D	C	C	D	D	B
S	4	B	A	A	C	A	A	C	B	B	A	B	C	D	C	B	C	D	A	B	A	C	B
T	5	B	A	C	A	B	A	A	C	C	D	C	C	B	B	B	C	B	B	C	B	D	D
I	6	A	B	D	C	D	B	A	C	D	D	D	C	A	B	B	B	D	B	C	B	C	B
O	7		C	B	C	C	B			B	B	B	B	B	C	A	B	B	C	C	D	B	A
N	8		B	A	A	B				B	B	B	B	B	B	B	C	C	D	C	A	D	B
	9		C	B	D	A				A	A	A	A	B	A	A	A	B	A	B	B	C	A
	10		A	A	D	B				A	A	A	A	A	B	A	B	A	B	A	D	B	B
	11		A	B	A	A				B	A	A	A	A	A	A	B	A	B	A	A	A	A
	12		A	A	B					B	B	B	B	B	A	A	A	A	B	B	B	B	B
	13		A	B	A					A	B	A	A	A	B	B	A	A	B	B	A		A
N	14		B	A	B					B	B	B	B	B	A	A	B	B	A	A	A		B
U	15		A	B	A					A		A		B	A	A	A	B	A	A	B		A
M	16			A	A										A								
B	17			B	B																		
E	18				A																		
R	19				B																		
S	20				A																		

Appendix 2

Biographies of Key Individuals in American Colonial History

JOHN ADAMS (1735-1826)

Lawyer, Ambassador to England, and the 2nd American President 1796

Graduated from Harvard 1755 and admitted to the Bar 1758

First came into prominence 1765 when he drafted the instructions to the Representative Assembly against the Stamp Act

Defended John Hancock against a charge of smuggling brought by the Massachusetts Governor

Most famous case 1770 when he defended the British troops involved in the "Boston Massacre".

Elected to the Legislature 1771

Elected to the Continental Congress 1774

June, 1776, he seconded the motion by Richard Henry Lee to move toward Independence

Served on the committee to draft the Declaration of Independence

June, 1779, elected to the Massachusetts Constitutional Convention

Participated in the negotiations of the Treaty of Paris which ended the Revolutionary War

Appointed as Minister to Holland 1780

Appointed as Minister to England 1785

Elected as Vice President 1788

Courageously withstood calls for War against France and maintained President Washington's Neutrality Policy and avoided war when the country was too weak for another war.

He and Hamilton had a personal rivalry which fractured the Federalist Party and led to its defeat in the Election of Thomas Jefferson, a Republican, 1800.

After leaving the Presidency he retired to his home in Quincy, Massachusetts, and lived a quiet life in retirement.

He and Jefferson eventually reconciled their differences and both died on the same day, hours apart.

SAM ADAMS (1722-1803)

Born in Boston of a prominent family and second cousin to John Adams.

Graduated from Harvard 1740 and studied law.

His life from 1740-1756 was unsuccessful with many financial problems due to his incompetence.

Failed as a Boston Tax Collector 1756-1764, leaving him greatly in debt.

The Stamp Act of 1764 provided the opportunity for him to achieve power and influence.

1765 elected to the Massachusetts General Court

Became the primary agitator against the English attempts to enforce discipline on Boston.

Was an early advocate of Independence long before most citizens considered the possibility.

Responsible for the formation of Boston's Committee of Correspondence 1772 and its spread throughout the colony.

Primarily responsible for the Declaration of Rights published by the Committee

Considered as the leader of the "Boston Tea Party"

Active in passage of the "Suffolk Resolves"

Attended the First and Second Continental Congresses

Slowly faded from the scene after the Declaration of Independence

Continued as a member of Congress until 1781

Retired from public life 1796

ETHAN ALLEN (1738-1789)

Born in Litchfield, Connecticut, of a modest family.

Education hindered by death of father at age 17 in 1755. Assumed financial responsibility for family.

Served in French-Indian War 1757

Acquired large land holdings in an area known as the "New Hampshire Grants", disputed territory by both New Hampshire and New York

Formed the "Green Mountain Boys", a group which harassed New Yorkers in the area

Intended to petition the King to confer a separate status on the area, now known as Vermont, but the idea was put on hold by the battles at Lexington and Concord.

Instructed by the Connecticut Assembly to capture Fort Ticonderoga which he accomplished with the assistance of Benedict Arnold.

Attempted to capture Montreal but was captured and imprisoned by the British for 3 years

Released 1778 and returned to Vermont but continued to advocate separate status for Vermont

WILLIAM BRADFORD (1590-1657)

Born in Yorkshire, England. Began at age 12 to read the Bible and joined a Separatist sect.

Migrated with the Puritans to Holland 1609 and lived there in Leyden until 1620.

Sailed on the Mayflower in 1620 and became the first Governor of the Plymouth colony 1621.

Elected Governor over 30 of the next 35 years and was primarily responsible for the colony's moderate success.

Authored the "History of the Plymouth Plantation from 1620-1647" which was not published until 200 years after his death.

AARON BURR (1756-1836)

Born in Newark, New Jersey, of distinguished family. Parents died during his infancy. Raised by uncle.

Graduated from the College of New Jersey (Princeton) 1772

Studied Law 1774

Enlisted in the Revolutionary Army 1775, serving under Benedict Arnold and as an Aide to General Washington with whom he didn't get along very well.

Resigned from the Army 1779 and resumed a Legal career 1782.

Moved to New York 1783 and began 20 year rivalry with Alexander Hamilton

Elected to the State Assembly 1784 and appointed State Attorney General 1789.

Elected to the U.S. Senate 1790, defeated for re-election 1796 and returned to the Assembly.

Nominated for Vice President 1800 and tied in Electoral Votes with Jefferson for President. After 35 ballots, Hamilton persuaded enough Federalists to vote for Jefferson who becomes President with Burr as Vice President.

Hamilton again influences Burr's defeat for Governor of New York 1804.

Burr fatally wounds Hamilton in a duel, indicted in both New York and New Jersey, flees to Philadelphia and then to the south.

Involved himself in a series of intrigues against the Government, eventually arrested in Alabama 1807. Tried for treason but acquitted.

Leaves for Paris and then returns to New York 1812, resumes Law practice. Dies 1836.

JOHN DICKINSON (1732-1808)

Born in Maryland and moved with his family to Delaware.

Educated by private tutors until he studied Law in Philadelphia and London

Returned from London 1757 to begin Law practice in Philadelphia and entered politics

Was a strong advocate of reconciliation with England until Independence was the obvious choice.

Appointed by the Pennsylvania Legislature to the Stamp Act

Congress 1765

Published his "Letters From a Farmer in Pennsylvania" 1767-1768 regarding the proposed Non-Importation and Non-Exportation proposals of the colonists

Drafted many conciliatory petitions to the King for the 1st and 2nd Continental Congresses

Though still opposed to Independence, he drafted the "Declaration....Setting Forth the Causes and Necessity of Taking Up Arms" 1775.

1776 assisted in drafting the Articles of Confederation but voted against the Declaration of Independence

Served in the Militia during the Revolutionary War

Represented Delaware in Congress 1779

Member of the Constitutional Convention and supported Ratification

BENJAMIN FRANKLIN (1706-1790)

Printer, author, philanthropist, inventor, scientist, diplomat, statesman

Born in Boston, received a minimal education. At age 12 he served as an apprentice printer

Learned through self-instruction and discipline

Went to Philadelphia 1726, becomes owner of "Pennsylvania Gazette" 1730.

Didn't become involved in politics until 1754

Represents Pennsylvania in London 1757

Worked for reconciliation in London until 1775

Appointed to 2nd Continental Congress 1776

Participated 1781 in negotiations leading to the Treaty of Paris ending the Revolutionary War

Member of the Constitutional Convention 1787

Good reputation as a mediator and compromiser

ALEXANDER HAMILTON (1755-1804)

Born on a Caribbean Island, deserted by his father and his mother died when he was 13.

Attended Kings College (Columbia University) until he became involved in debates on the Revolutionary War

Served in New York and New Jersey militia during the War

1777 appointed as Aide to General Washington

Moved to Albany 1781 to study Law

1786 delegate to the Annapolis Convention and introduced the resolution leading to the Constitutional Convention.

Strong advocate in New York for Ratification of the Constitution. Key participant in the "Federalist Papers"

Appointed by President Washington as Secretary of Treasury. Authorized vigorous Financial plan to rebuild a war-torn country. Washington's most influential advisor.

Became the leader of the Federalist political party but eventually caused its downfall by under-cutting President Adams and splintering the party

Personal feud with Thomas Jefferson

Killed in a duel with Aaron Burr.

JOHN HANCOCK (1737-1793)

Born in Braintree (now Quincy), Massachusetts. Raised by a wealthy Uncle.

Graduated from Harvard 1754 and entered his Uncle's mercantile business which he eventually inherited plus a large estate.

Elected to the General Court 1769-1774

Elected as President of the 1st and 2nd Provincial Congresses of 1774-1775

Served as a delegate to the Continental Congress 1775-1780

First to sign the Declaration of Independence

1780 elected Governor of Massachusetts until 1785 and then served in Congress. Returned to Governorship 1787

Was serving in his 9th term as Governor when he died 1793.

PATRICK HENRY (1736-1799)

Skilled orator and political leader

Early failures as a farmer and storekeeper and deeply in debt by 1759.

Admitted to Virginia Bar as Lawyer 1760.

Enters House of Burgesses 1765 and becomes a leader against the aristocratic faction

Early opponent against the Stamp Act

Member of Virginia's 1st Committee of Correspondence

Delegate to the 1st & 2nd Continental Congresses

Makes key speech favoring Independence in House of Burgesses

1776 helped draft the State Constitution and then elected Governor

Returned to Legislature 1780-1784 and then Governor again 1784-1786

Opposed the Constitutional Convention 1787 and refused to be a delegate to it

Opposed Ratification of the new Constitution because of the absence of a Bill of Rights

1788 retired to his legal practice and private life

THOMAS JEFFERSON (1743-1826)

Born on father's plantation, "Shadwell", in Albemarle County, Virginia.

Graduated from William & Mary College 1762, admitted to Bar Association 1767

Elected to the House of Burgesses from 1769-1775.

Member of the Committee of Correspondence and delegate to Continental Congress

Chosen to draft the Declaration of Independence

October, 1775, returned to Virginia Legislature, the House of Delegates. Worked on proposals for the abolition of slavery which were finally accepted within 10 years.

Elected Governor 1779 and then returned to Congress 1783

Succeeded Ben Franklin as Minister to France

Favored the new Constitution but preferred inclusion of a Bill of Rights.

Becomes Secretary of State under President Washington 1790.

Strong critic of Alexander Hamilton's National Bank proposal as an unconstitutional expansion of the Federal government authority

Resigned from the Washington Cabinet 1793 but remained the leader of the new Democratic-Republican Party

Finished behind President Adams in election 1796 and became Vice President

Strongly opposed the Federalist's Alien & Sedition Acts

Chosen as President by the House of Representatives 1800. Was first President to be inaugurated in Washington, D.C.

Responsible for the Louisiana Purchase

Re-elected as President 1804 and found it difficult to maintain neutrality in War between England and France

Retired permanently 1809 to his home at Monticello, Virginia.

Responsible for the chartering and design of the University of Virginia

Reconciled with John Adams 1813. Both men died on the same day, July 4, 1826, 50th Anniversary of the Declaration of Independence

RICHARD HENRY LEE (1732-1794)

Born of a wealthy family at "Stratford" estate in Westmoreland County, Virginia.

Educated by private tutoring and in England

Returned to Virginia 1752 and became a Justice of the Peace 1757

Entered House of Burgesses 1758 for 17 years of continuous service.

1766 organized a local non-importation association in opposition to the English Stamp Act and Townshend Duties

Close friends with Jefferson and Patrick Henry

1773 proposed a system of inter-colonial correspondence committees to coordinate the opposition activities of several colonies against the British

1774 chosen as one of Virginia's delegates to the 1st Continental Congress

June 1776 introduced the resolution which directly led to the Declaration of Independence.

Retired from Congress 1779 because of ill health but elected to the Virginia Legislature and then returned to Congress 1784 until 1787

Opposed Ratification of the Constitution because of strong central government and lack of Bill of Rights

Chosen as one of the first Senators from Virginia

Ill health forced his resignation from the Senate in 1792

JAMES MADISON (1751-1836)

4th American President born in Port Conway, King George County, Virginia, of a moderately wealthy family of Virginia planters.

Educated at the College of New Jersey (Princeton), graduated 1771.

Begins political career 1774 and chosen as member of his county's committee on public safety

1776 elected to the Virginia Constitutional Convention and because of significant contributions he was placed on the Governor's Council 1778

Elected to Congress for single term, 1779-1783, and favored revision of the Articles of Confederation

Member of Virginia House of Delegates 1784-1786 and advocated religious freedom

1785 proposed series of interstate conferences which led to

the Annapolis Convention of 1786 and the Constitutional Convention in 1787.

Dominant figure at the Constitutional Convention, played key role in developing the "Virginia Plan" which was a very significant portion of the final Constitution

Joined with Hamilton and John Jay writing as the "Federalists" in support of Ratification. He wrote 29 of the 85 essays under the name of "Publius".

Played key role in getting the Bill of Rights added to the Constitution

Opposed Hamilton's Financial plan during President Washington's first Administration

Favored close ties to France, opposed the Federalists ties to England and President Washington's Neutrality Proclamation of 1793 as well as Jay's Treaty 1795.

Remained in Congress until 1797 and then spoke out against the Federalist Alien & Sedition Acts in 1798, writing with Jefferson the Virginia and Kentucky Resolutions in opposition.

Became Secretary of State in President Jefferson's administrations.

Elected President 1808 and continued the policies of the Jefferson administration

Retired to his home at "Montpelier" Virginia in 1817 until his death in 1836.

GEORGE MASON (1725-1792)

Planter and public official born in Fairfax County, Virginia. Received minimal formal education. Self-educated.

Large landowner became involved in local politics.

1759 elected to Virginia House of Burgesses but returned to private life after a single term.

1775 became member of State Convention and Committee of Safety.

Drafted Virginia's first Constitution in May, 1776, which included a "Declaration of Rights" which was used by Jefferson in his draft of the Declaration of Independence.

Member of the Virginia House of Delegates from 1776-1788 and was delegate to Constitutional Convention 1787.

Lifelong opponent of slavery and opposed the compromise which allowed the continuation of the slave trade until 1808

Favored revision of the Articles of Confederation but believed the new Constitution provided for too much centralized government. Left the convention, returned home to oppose Ratification.

His opposition helped the movement to add the Bill of Rights

ROBERT MORRIS (1734-1806)

Merchant and financier born in Liverpool, England. Came to America 1747 joining his father in Maryland.

Minimal formal education but joined a large mercantile business in Philadelphia and at age 20 became a key member of the firm

Slow to accept the possibility of Independence.

Served as Vice President of the Pennsylvania Committee of Safety 1775-1776.

Served as delegate to the Continental Congress 1775-1778

Opposed Declaration of Independence and delayed signing it until after it had been adopted.

Left Congress and was elected to the Pennsylvania Assembly until 1779.

Supervised the financial policy during the Revolutionary War

Delegate to the Constitutional Convention 1787.

Elected as one of Pennsylvania's first Senators serving 1789-1795 as Federalist supporter of Hamilton

Went bankrupt and from 1798-1801 was in debtor prison and died in Philadelphia

JAMES OTIS (1725-1783)

Born in West Barnstable, Massachusetts.

Graduated from Harvard 1743 and admitted to the Massachusetts Bar Association 1748.

Settled in Boston. 1761 he opposed the British "Writs of Assistance" based on the doctrine of natural law underlying the rights of citizens. He lost the case but was elected to the Massachusetts General Court.

Opposed the Royal Governor and until 1769 was the major political leader against the British

1764 wrote "The Rights of the British Colonies Asserted and Proved". Joined Stamp Act Congress 1765.

Strong opponent of the British oppression of colonial rights but reluctant to support Independence, at first.

September, 1769, struck in the head by a Crown official and was mentally unstable afterwards

He was struck and killed by lightning on 5/23/1783.

THOMAS PAINE (1737-1809)

Born in Thetford, England and received minimal formal education and spent the first 37 years of his life in poverty, failing at a number of jobs.

A meeting with Ben Franklin encouraged him to seek his fortune in America and in 1774 he arrived in Philadelphia.

For awhile, he worked for the "Pennsylvania Magazine"

1776 he published his famous pamphlet "Common Sense" calling for Independence from England

Then joined the Army as an aide to General Nathaniel Greene

April, 1777, appointed as Secretary of the Congressional Committee on Foreign Affairs

November, 1779, became the Clerk of the Pennsylvania Assembly

Continued his vocal support of the Independence movement

Lived quietly and without controversy until 1787 when he left for England and then to France where he favored the French Revolution.

Imprisoned in France 1793-1794

Returned to New York 1802 and not welcomed. He lived with a poor reputation until his death 1809.

TIMOTHY PICKERING (1745-1829)

Soldier, public official, and political leader.

Born in Salem, Massachusetts, graduated from Harvard 1763 and returned to Salem. Admitted to the Massachusetts Bar Association while in Salem 1768.

Member of the Militia from 1766.

Appointed Adjutant General to General Washington 1777. Became Quartermaster General 1780-1785.

Helped found the town of Wilkes-Barre and elected to both the Constitutional Ratifying Convention and Pennsylvania Constitutional Convention 1788-1789.

Became Secretary of War 1795 under President Washington and then Secretary of State under President Adams 1796

Was a Hamiltonian Federalist who worked against President Adams, behind his back, and dismissed by President Adams 1800.

Returned to Massachusetts as influential Federalist leader in the Senate 1803-1811.

Served in the House of Representatives. From 1813-1817 opposed the policies of Presidents Jefferson and Madison

After 1817 he focused on farming and died in Salem 1829.

PAUL REVERE (1735-1818)

Silversmith and Patriot.

Born in Boston as the son of a silversmith. Attended local schools and followed his father's trade.

1756 joined a military expedition against Crown Point, a French fort, during the French-Indian War

Active in local politics and a leader in the Boston Tea Party

Principal express rider for the Boston Committee of Safety, warning Hancock and Sam Adams of the approaching British 4/18/1775.

Engraved the first Continental money and official seal of the colonies

After the Revolution, he returned to his silversmith occupation

ROGER SHERMAN (1721-1793)

Born in Newton, Massachusetts but grew up in Stoughton. Minimal formal education but a self-educated man.

Moved to New Milford, Connecticut 1743 to open a cobbler shop

Appointed as county surveyor 1745

Served in a succession of local offices while developing a mercantile business

Admitted to the Connecticut Bar Association 1754 and served in many legal and political positions.

Elected to the 1st Continental Congress 1774 as a strong Patriot in favor of the colonial non-importation movements.

Remained in Congress until 1781 and then served again 1783-1784.

Signed the Declaration of Independence

Helped draft the Articles of Confederation

Through the Revolutionary War he was a member of the Connecticut Council of Safety

Became a delegate to the Constitutional Convention 1787 and introduced the "Connecticut Compromise" which broke the deadlock and paved the way for an agreement on Ratification. It provided for "dual representation" which pleased both the large and small states.

By signing the Constitution, he became the only person to sign the Articles of Confederation, Declaration of Independence, and the Constitution.

He was known for impeccable honesty and integrity

He served in the House of Representatives 1789-1791 and the Senate 1791-1793, at the time of his death in New Haven, Connecticut.

JAMES WILSON (1742-1798)

Born in Scotland and studied at various Scottish Universities until his father's death interrupted his education.

Emigrated to Philadelphia 1765 where he entered the University of Pennsylvania

Admitted to the Pennsylvania Bar Association 1768 and settled in Carlisle 1770 and developed a reputation as the best lawyer in Pennsylvania.

1774 wrote "Considerations on the Nature and Extent of the Legislative Authority of the British Parliament" which concluded that Parliament had no power over the colonies.

Elected to the 2nd Continental Congress 1775-1777 and signed the Declaration of Independence.

Supported the struggle for currency reform after 1781.

Played key role in the Constitutional Convention correctly stating the key problem as that of a strong central government which still respected the rights of the States.

Primarily responsible for achieving Ratification in the State of Pennsylvania and writing the State Constitution 1790.

Appointed by President Washington as an Associate Justice to the first Supreme Court 1789.

Became a Constitutional Law expert and participated in all of the key decisions of the Court

Due to a poor decision involving land speculation during the 1790's he experienced financial ruin and damaged his health. He died in Edenton, North Carolina, 1798.

THOMAS HUTCHINSON (1711-1780)

Born in Boston, died in England

Graduated from Harvard 1727

Elected to Massachusetts House of Representatives 1737-1749, Speaker 1746-1748.

Supported Ben Franklin's proposed Albany Plan of Union which failed to be approved

Became Lt. Governor 1758 and Chief Justice 1760

Supported enforcement of the Sugar and Stamp Acts

His house sacked and personal papers scattered in response for his support of the British Acts

Served as Royal Governor 1770-1774 and argued for the supremacy of Parliament over the colonies

His letters to England calling for tougher position against the colonists becomes known and caused him to become even more unpopular

After the Boston Tea Party 1773 he becomes more conciliatory toward the colonists while living in exile in England

COLONIAL POPULATION 1625-1790

YEAR	U.S. POP
1625	1,980
1641	50,000
1650	52,000
1688	200,000
1700	294,258
1715	435,000
1749	1,000,000
1754	1,500,000
1760	1,700,000
1765	2,200,000
1775	2,400,000
1790	4,000,000

COLONIAL POPULATION AS OF 1700

NEW ENGLAND COLONIES:		_130,000_
MASSACHUSETTS BAY	80,000	
CONNECTICUT	30,000	
NEW HAMPSHIRE	10,000	
RHODE ISLAND	10,000	
CHESAPEAKE COLONIES:		_87,258_
VIRGINIA	55,000	
MARYLAND	32,258	
MIDDLE COLONIES:		_65,000_
NEW YORK	30,000	
PENNSYLVANIA/DELAWARE	20,000	
NEW JERSEY	15,000	
CAROLINA COLONIES:		_12,000_
SOUTH CAROLINA	7,000	
NORTH CAROLINA	5,000	
GEORGIA NOT FOUNDED YET		
TOTAL POPULATION		294,258

BRITAIN	8 MILLION
13 COLONIES	2.4 MILLION
BRITISH CANADA	300,000

POPULATION OF EUROPEAN DESCENT	2.4 MILLION
NATIVE AMERICANS	50,000 - 100,000
FREE BLACKS	30,000
ENSLAVED BLACKS	510,000

POPULATION BY COLONY

COLONY	WHITE	ENSLAVED	%
CONNECTICUT	195,000	6,000	3.1
DELAWARE	40,000	4,000	10.0
GEORGIA	40,000	10,000	25.0
MARYLAND	225,000	65,000	28.9
MASSACHUSETTS	255,000	5,000	2.0
NEW HAMPSHIRE	75,000	1,000	1.3
NEW JERSEY	125,000	10,000	8.0
NEW YORK	195,000	25,000	12.8
NORTH CAROLINA	245,000	75,000	30.6
PENNSYLVANIA	290,000	6,000	2.1
RHODE ISLAND	55,000	4,000	7.3
SOUTH CAROLINA	155,000	100,000	64.5
VIRGINIA	500,000	200,000	40.0
TOTAL	2,395,000	511,000	21.3

PHILADELPHIA	40,000
NEW YORK (MANHATTAN)	25,000
BOSTON	16,000

675

ETHNIC POPULATION DISTRIBUTION % AS OF 1775	
ETHNIC GROUP	PERCENTAGE
ENGLISH	48.7
AFRICAN	20.0
SCOTCH-IRISH	7.8
GERMAN	6.9
SCOTTISH	6.6
OTHER	5.3
DUTCH	2.7
FRENCH	1.4
SWEDISH	0.6

Index

Q

CPSIA information can be obtained at www.ICGtesting.com
Printed in the USA
LVOW08*0346051214

417283LV00002B/3/P